ECONOMIC AND SOCIAL COMMISSION FOR ASIA AND THE PACIFIC
BANGKOK, THAILAND

WATER RESOURCES DEVELOPMENT IN ASIA AND THE PACIFIC SOME ISSUES AND CONCERNS

WATER RESOURCES SERIES
No. 62

UNITED NATIONS
New York 1987

ST/ESCAP/SER.F/62

UNITED NATIONS PUBLICATION

Sales No. E.87.II.F.15

ISBN 92-1-119443-1

ISSN 0082-8130

Price $US 21.00

FOREWORD

This issue of the Water Resources Series — a routine serial publication of ESCAP Natural Resources Division — addresses itself to a number of concerns of water resources development in various countries in the region. These papers were presented as background documents for review and discussion at the thirteenth session of the ESCAP Committee on Natural Resources, held during 14-20 October 1986. The report of the session with the conclusions and recommendations of the Committee is included in part five of this volume.

A number of government representatives provided the Committee with additional information in the form of country papers. These are included, without formal editing by the United Nations. The views expressed by individual authors and/or respective government agencies which prepared these country papers are their own and do not necessarily reflect the views of the United Nations. Similarly the issue papers prepared by the ESCAP secretariat for discussion at the thirteenth session of the Committee on Natural Resources and reproduced here, are based on materials and information received from various government and other agencies in their respective countries. Therefore their accuracies and applicabilities are subject to verification and confirmation by these agencies.

In the presentation of data in tables in the text, the use of a dash (—) indicates nil or a negligible amount and the use of leaders (. . .) indicates that no data were available at the time of preparation of the tables.

National currency equivalents for countries included in the publication

Country	Currency and abbreviation	Unit of currency per United States dollar (period average)			
		1979	1980	1983	1987
China	RMB	–	–	1.99	3.70
Indonesia	Rupiah (Rp)	623.05	627.07	987.0	1 027.00
Philippines	Peso (P)	7.378	7.492	13.97	22.00
Thailand	Baht	20.419	20.439	22.96	25.50
USSR	Roubles (Rou)	–	–	0.75	–

Note: Conversion given shows market rate/par or central rate taken as monthly average in the market of the country.

CONTENTS

Page

PART ONE

I. PROGRESS IN THE IMPLEMENTATION OF THE MAR DEL PLATA ACTION PLAN (SUMMARY OF GOVERNMENT RESPONSES) 3

II. WATER RESOURCES DEVELOPMENT IN CHINA: A REVIEW OF IMPLEMENTATION OF THE MAR DEL PLATA ACTION PLAN 39

III. MAR DEL PLATA ACTION PLAN IMPLEMENTATION IN THE PHILIPPINES 41

IV. WATER RESOURCES DEVELOPMENT IN INDONESIA 44

    A. Policies, plans, programmes 44
    B. Irrigation 56
    C. Water supply 66
    D. Flood control 70
    E. Hydropower 72
    F. Water quality and pollution control 77

V. PROGRESS IN THE IMPLEMENTATION OF THE MAR DEL PLATA ACTION PLAN IN THAILAND 81

VI. USSR EXPERIENCE IN THE EXECUTION OF THE MAR DEL PLATA ACTION PLAN ON WATER RESOURCES 89

PART TWO: GROUNDWATER

VII. GROUNDWATER RESOURCES DEVELOPMENT IN THE ESCAP REGION 95

VIII. GROUNDWATER EXPLORATION AND DEVELOPMENT IN CHINA 112

IX. GROUNDWATER RESOURCES DEVELOPMENT IN THE PHILIPPINES 114

X. GROUNDWATER DEVELOPMENT IN INDONESIA 117

XI. INTEGRATED GROUND AND SURFACE WATER MANAGEMENT IN ARID ZONES 125

PART THREE: ENVIRONMENTAL ISSUES

XII. ENVIRONMENTAL ISSUES OF WATER RESOURCES DEVELOPMENT IN THE ESCAP REGION 131

XIII. APPLICATION OF ENVIRONMENTAL IMPACT ASSESSMENT TO WATER RESOURCES DEVELOPMENT PROJECTS 144

XIV. ENVIRONMENTAL ISSUES OF WATER RESOURCES DEVELOPMENT IN INDONESIA 157

XV. PROBLEMS OF RIVER WATER QUALITY CONTROL UNDER CONDITIONS OF INTENSIVE IRRIGATION DEVELOPMENT IN ARID ZONES 160

CONTENTS *(Continued)*

Page

PART FOUR: SMALL DAMS AND MINI-HYDRO

XVI. POTENTIAL FOR SMALL DAMS AND MINI-HYDROPOWER GENERATION IN THE LEAST DEVELOPED COUNTRIES AND DEVELOPING ISLAND COUNTRIES OF ESCAP REGION 167

PART FIVE: ESCAP COMMITTEE ON NATURAL RESOURCES THIRTEENTH SESSION, 14-20 OCTOBER 1986

XVII. REPORT OF THE ESCAP COMMITTEE ON NATURAL RESOURCES ON ITS THIRTEENTH SESSION, 14-20 OCTOBER 1986 181

XVIII. LIST OF DOCUMENTS PRESENTED TO THE THIRTEENTH SESSION OF THE COMMITTEE ON NATURAL RESOURCES 195

XIX. LIST OF PARTICIPANTS AT THE THIRTEENTH SESSION OF THE COMMITTEE ON NATURAL RESOURCES 198

Part One

I. PROGRESS IN THE IMPLEMENTATION OF THE MAR DEL PLATA ACTION PLAN (SUMMARY OF GOVERNMENT RESPONSES)*

INTRODUCTION

Within the framework of United Nations General Assembly resolutions 34/191 of 18 December 1979 on the follow-up to and implementation of the Mar del Plata Action Plan of the United Nations Water Conference and 35/18 of 10 November 1980 on proclaiming the International Drinking Water Supply and Sanitation Decade, the Economic and Social Council, in its resolution 1981/80 of 24 July 1981 on water resources development, called upon the Committee on Natural Resources of the Economic and Social Council at its ninth session in 1985 to review further the overall progress made in the implementation of the Mar del Plata Action Plan by Governments and by the United Nations system. The review would take place at the same time as and would include the mid-period review of the International Drinking Water Supply and Sanitation Decade. The global review would be preceded by regional analysis and review as appropriate.

In order to enable implementation of these mandates, the Secretary-General, in consultation with the concerned organizations of the United Nations system, through the Intersecretariat Group for Water Resources of the Administrative Committee on Co-ordination, formulated a questionnaire as a means of gathering the necessary information from Member States for the purpose of comparison. On 1 December 1983, copies of this questionnaire, "Progress in the implementation of the Mar del Plata Action Plan: present status of and prospects for water resources development at the national level", were circulated by the ESCAP secretariat to 39 member and associate member countries in the region. As of 15 January 1985, completed questionnaires were received from 22 countries and areas: Afghanistan, Australia, China, Fiji, Guam, Hong Kong, India, Indonesia, Japan, Malaysia, New Zealand, Niue, Pakistan, Papua New Guinea, Philippines, Republic of Korea, Singa-

pore, Sri Lanka, Tonga, Trust Territory of the Pacific Islands, Vanuatu and Viet Nam.

A. POLICY, PLANNING, LEGISLATION AND INSTITUTIONAL ARRANGEMENTS

1. National water policy and planning

Recognizing the need for the formulation of a national water policy within the concept of and consistent with national economic and social policies, the Mar del Plata Action Plan recommended that each country should formulate and keep under review a general statement of policy in relation to the use, management and conservation of water, as a framework for planning and implementing specific programmes and measures for efficient operation of schemes.

In this context, the response to the questionnaire has been analyzed in table 1. Out of the 22 countries and areas which responded to the questionnaire, 16 have a national water policy statement; 7 have indicated that revision has taken place in their policy statements, and 8 have indicated that revision is under study. In three cases the policy statement has been shown to have undergone a revision and further revision is under study. A shift in priorities in water resources development has been made by 7 countries in their revision of the policy or plan. Australia's new policy places greater emphasis on economic efficiency; Guam has indicated a change in priority at the local level based on economic factors, total system effect and resource availability; Papua New Guinea has reduced emphasis on water supply and sewerage in urban areas but has continued it in rural areas; the Philippines has given top priority to the acceleration of indigenous energy programmes; the Republic of Korea has given top priority in its national economic development programme to stabilizing water supply in quantity and quality in view of urbanization and industrialization activities; and the Trust Territory of the Pacific Islands has modified priorities from expansion of the lagoon water system to ground-water development and individual water systems for rural areas.

---

* Originally issued as E/ESCAP/NR.13/4-5.

Table 1. National water policy

Country or area	Availability of water policy statement		Revision of water policy — Has taken place		Revision of water policy — Under study		Revision of water policy — Includes shift in priorities		Water policy established by — Decree		Water policy established by — Cabinet decision		Water policy established by — Legislature	
	Yes	No	Yes	No	Yes	No	Yes	No	Yes	No	Yes	No	Yes	No
Afghanistan	x		x		x		x						x	
Australia	x				x		x			x	x		x	
China	x				x		x							
Fiji	x		x		x			x		x	x		x	
Guam	x		x								x		x	
Hong Kong	x		x		x					x		x	x	
India		x	x										x	
Indonesia	x		x		x		x					x		
Japan		x							x		x		x	
Malaysia		x					x			x	x			x
New Zealand	x		x				x			x		x	x	
Niue	x		x				x				x			
Pakistan	x				x		x				x			
Papua New Guinea	x		x		x		x				x			
Philippines	x		x				x		x					
Republic of Korea	x				x		x		x					
Singapore	x		x		x						x			x
Sri Lanka		x									x			x
Tonga	x		x		x		x			x	x		x	
Trust Territory of the Pacific Islands		x					x		x					
Vanuatu		x									x			
Viet Nam	x				x		x				x			

The water policy has been established solely by decree of the Head of State in three cases; by Cabinet decision in six; by Legislature in four; and by Cabinet decision and Legislature in seven. In the case of Japan, water policy has been established by all three methods.

Table 2 covers national planning. Twelve countries and areas have a comprehensive master plan for water resources development. Afghanistan has master plans for some river basins and is making efforts to prepare plans for all of them. A national perspective for water resources development has been formulated by India. Though New Zealand does not have a national master plan, it has regional policies and functional policies covering an energy plan, a land development policy, and a wild and scenic rivers policy. Tonga has indicated existence of a master plan and its indication of formulating one probably means revision of the existing plan. Seven countries are making efforts to formulate their master plans.

Concerning the usefulness of international assistance comprising an interdisciplinary mission to advise on the formulation of a master plan, 11 countries and areas have shown interest, including 6 which have master plans. Nine are willing to consider using financial resources from their IPF (indicative planning figure) within their UNDP country programmes for such interdisciplinary missions.

Eleven countries and areas have experienced problems in renovating major project structures and 18 anticipate such problems in the future. Measures to be taken differ and relate to the problems experienced or anticipated by the respective countries. Afghanistan undertakes detailed inspection, repairs and, where necessary, reconstruction. Australia plans application of appropriate policies of maintenance and financing to minimize future problems. India plans to provide for modernization of existing irrigation systems and replacement of works as required. Japan has pointed out that complete renovation of the many old

Table 2. National planning

Country or area	Availability of comprehensive master plan		Efforts to formulate master plan		Would international assistance be useful?		Willingness to finance assistance from indicative planning figure		Problems in renovation of major project structures			
									Experienced		Anticipated	
	Yes	No	Yes	No	Yes	No	Yes	No	Yes	No	Yes	No
Afghanistan	X		X		X		X			X	X	
Australia		X	X			X		X		X	X	
China	X											
Fiji		X		X	X			X		X		
Guam	X				X		X		X		X	
Hong Kong	X								X		X	
India		X				X		X	X		X	
Indonesia		X	X		X		X			X	X	
Japan		X							X		X	
Malaysia	X									X	X	
New Zealand		X				X		X		X	X	
Niue		X	X		X						X	
Pakistan	X					X	X		X		X	
Papua New Guinea		X	X		X		X		X		X	
Philippines	X				X		X		X		X	
Republic of Korea	X									X		X
Singapore	X							X		X		X
Sri Lanka	X				X			X	X		X	
Tonga	X		X		X		X		X		X	
Trust Territory of the Pacific Islands		X		X					X		X	
Vanuatu		X	X		X		X			X	X	
Viet Nam	X				X		X		X		X	

barrages which have passed the end of their useful life requires about 600 billion yen; shortage of finances may become a constraint. New Zealand anticipates problems in the future in respect of dams, canals and water supply pipelines; in the case of pipelines, local authorities shall be required to adopt leak prevention measures before subsidies for new works are approved. Niue plans to replace old water mains with PVC pressure pipes and old tower tanks with pressure boosters at ground level. Pakistan has programmes for canal and tube-well rehabilitation, irrigation water management, and watershed management for improving storage. The Philippines plans for improvement and rehabilitation of existing projects, and construction of new ones. Sri Lanka indicates its intention to renovate, rehabilitate and repair on a project scale; to use a different maintenance basis; and to improve management, operation and maintenance. Tonga foresees replacement of asbestos

pipes and renovation with finances mobilized through community and government contribution and aid programmes. The Trust Territory of the Pacific Islands plans to use funds from the United States of America to finance replacement of defective pipes. Vanuatu collects a head tax in the rural areas, part of which could be used for rebuilding water supplies. Viet Nam foresees an increase in national investment and international assistance.

The extent to which prices or charges are used to recover fixed and recurrent costs from direct beneficiaries of projects is reflected in table 3. Generally the incidence of recovery of recurrent costs is higher than that of fixed costs. For urban water use, 15 countries and areas recover fixed costs and 19 recover recurrent costs either fully or partly. For industrial water use, 14 countries recover fixed costs while 17 recover recurrent costs, and for rural water

Table 3. Recovery of water charges

Country or area	Recovery of fixed costs (original investment)										Recovery of recurrent costs (operation and maintenance)									
	Urban water use — Commercial		Urban water use — Domestic		Industrial water use		Rural water use		Irrigation water use		Urban water use — Commercial		Urban water use — Domestic		Industrial water use		Rural water use		Irrigation water use	
	F	P	F	P	F	P	F	P	F	P	F	P	F	P	F	P	F	P	F	P
Afghanistan	X		X								X		X							
Australia	X		X		X		X		X		X		X		X			X		X
China											X		X		X		X			X
Fiji	X		X		X		X				X		X		X					X
Guam											X		X				X			X
Hong Kong	X		X		X		X				X		X		X		X			
India	X		X		X		X		X		X		X		X		X			X
Indonesia	X		X		X		X		X		X	X	X		X		X			
Japan	X			X	X			X			X	X	X		X		X		X	
Malaysia	X		X		X		X		X		X		X		X		X			X
New Zealand	X		X		X				X		X	X	X		X		X			
Niue																				
Pakistan									X											X
Papua New Guinea	X		X		X						X		X		X					
Philippines	X			X	X			X	X		X		X		X			X		
Republic of Korea	X		X		X		X		X		X		X		X		X		X	
Singapore	X			X	X			X			X		X		X		X			
Sri Lanka	X		X		X			X			X		X		X		X			X
Tonga	X		X		X		X		X		X		X		X		X			X
Trust Territory of the Pacific Islands											X		X							
Vanuatu											X		X		X		X			
Viet Nam																				

F = fully   P = partly

use 13 recover fixed costs and 14 recover recurrent costs. Similarly, in the case of irrigation water use, 10 countries recover fixed costs and 14 recover recurrent costs. It may be noted that for irrigation water use, fixed costs are recovered only partly. The capacity to pay charges for irrigation water use depends on the economic worth of the agricultural produce from land. Generally the capital cost of supplies from built storage or through pumping systems has to be subsidized.

The structure of charges levied for water use appears in table 4. Water supplies for households, industry and commercial use in major urban centres are metered fully in 10 countries or areas, and partly in the remaining 12. One levies charges for urban water supply solely on a flat-rate basis; 10 base their recovery solely on a volumetric (block) rate; 5 apply both bases and 3 have indicated the use of other bases. It appears that generally the volumetric (block) rate method of levying urban water use charges is preferred. There is an indication that the structure of charges based on area irrigated is preferred in the case of irrigation water use. Five countries and areas relate charges solely to the volume of water used for irrigation, 7 to the area irrigated and 3 to crop harvested. One country, however, levies charges on the basis of both area irrigated and crop harvested. Peak demand pricing or drought pricing as an instrument of policy to ration water for households and industries during periods of shortages or excessive demand is generally not practised. Only 3 countries have indicated the use of such a pricing method to induce voluntary rationing.

Table 4. Structure of water charges

Country or area	Extent to which major urban supplies are metered			Structure of the charges levied							Peak demand/ drought pricing used	
				Urban supply			Irrigation water use charges relate to					
	F	P	Not at all	Flat rate	Volume (Block) rate	Other	Volume of water	Area irrigated	Crop harvest	Other	Yes	No
Afghanistan		x		x	x							x
Australia		x		x	x		x					x
China		x			x		x	x				
Fiji	x				x			x				x
Guam	x				x		x					x
Hong Kong	x					x						x
India		x		x	x			x	x			x
Indonesia		x			x			x				x
Japan	x				x			x				x
Malaysia	x			x	x			x				x
New Zealand		x				x	x			x	x	
Niue		x										
Pakistan		x							x			x
Papua New Guinea		x			x						x	
Philippines	x			x	x				x			x
Republic of Korea	x				x			x				x
Singapore	x				x							x
Sri Lanka		x			x			x				x
Tonga	x					x	x				x	
Trust Territory of the Pacific Islands		x		x							x	
Vanuatu	x				x							x
Viet Nam		x										x

F = fully　　P = partly

2. National water legislation

The Mar del Plata Action Plan called upon each country to examine and keep under review existing legislative and administrative structures concerning water management and, in the light of shared experience, to enact, where appropriate, comprehensive legislation, for a co-ordinated approach to water planning. It was stated that it might be desirable for provisions concerning water resources management, conservation and protection against pollution to be combined in a unitary legal instrument, if the constitutional framework of the country permitted. It was expressed that legislation should define the rules of public ownership of water and should be flexible enough to accommodate future changes in priorities and perspectives. In pursuance

of the above, table 5 covers the aspects regulated and adequacy of the existing national water legislation. Among the 22 countries and areas which responded to the questionnaire, legislation regulates the ownership of surface water in 15 countries and areas and of ground water in 10. Right to use water is regulated by 16 countries for surface and by 10 countries for ground water. Protection of water quality is regulated through legislation by 19 countries and areas for surface water and by 14 for ground water. It shows that the majority of respondents have legislation which regulates the ownership, right to use and protection of the quality of water.

Eleven countries and areas consider their current national water legislation sufficient and compatible with the

Table 5. National water legislation

Country or area	Aspects regulated by existing legislation												Adequacy of existing legislation									
	Ownership of water				Right to use water				Protection of water quality				Whether sufficient and compatible with development plans		Are amendments or revisions being formulated?		Extent of centralized co-ordination provided		Do local levels of Government hold water resources administrative responsibilities?		If revision needed could international assistance be of help?	
	Surface		Ground water		Surface		Ground water		Surface		Ground water		Yes	No	Yes	No	All	Some	Yes	No	Yes	No
	Yes	No	Yes	No	Yes	No	Yes	No	Yes	No	Yes	No										
Afghanistan	x		x		x		x		x		x		x			x	x		x		x	
Australia	x		x		x		x		x		x		x					x	x			x
China		x				x			x									x	x			x
Fiji	x			x	x			x	x			x		x	x			x		x		x
Guam		x		x		x		x	x		x		x				x			x	x	
Hong Kong	x		x		x		x		x		x		x			x		x	x		x	
India	x			x	x			x	x		x			x	x			x	x			x
Indonesia	x		x		x		x		x		x		x				x		x			x
Japan		x	x		x		x		x		x		x				x		x			x
Malaysia	x			x	x			x	x		x		x		x			x	x		x	
New Zealand		x		x	x		x		x			x		x	x			x	x		x	
Niue			x					x	x		x			x	x		x				x	
Pakistan	x			x	x		x		x		x			x			x		x			x
Papua New Guinea	x		x		x		x		x		x		x			x			x			x
Philippines	x		x		x		x		x		x		x				x		x		x	
Republic of Korea	x			x	x		x		x		x		x			x	x		x			x
Singapore	x		x		x		x		x		x		x			x		x				x
Sri Lanka	x			x	x			x	x		x			x	x			x		x	x	
Tonga	x		x		x		x		x		x			x	x		x		x		x	
Trust Territory of the Pacific Islands	x								x		x		x				x		x			
Vanuatu		x		x		x		x		x		x		x						x	x	
Viet Nam		x		x		x		x		x		x										

objectives of their national long-term economic and social development plans. In the case of seven countries, amendments or revisions are being formulated. Some States in Australia are revising floodplain management legislations and improving water quality control regulations. Fiji thinks its legislation needs a total review; Malaysia requires amendment in its existing legislation in areas of management principles, water right administration, water source protection and floodplain management; and New Zealand is considering revision of legislation for water quality management and statutory provision for water allocation plans. Niue is drafting new legislation. Pakistan is considering revision of water rates for irrigation and recovery of fixed costs of the development projects. Sri Lanka has indicated revision to provide for allocation of water resources among users according to purpose and to facilitate the development of institutional capability. Tonga is considering amendments in respect of water quality and standards and community water supplies in villages. Viet Nam is drafting water use regulations.

Legislation in nine countries and areas provides for centralized co-ordination of all the water-related responsibilities of central government departments and agencies and in another 10 countries such co-ordination is provided for to some extent. Regional and local levels of government hold responsibilities in the administration of water resources in 13 countries and areas. Afghanistan has entrusted the regional and local-level authorities with the responsibility of providing and maintaining irrigation systems. State Governments in Australia have legislative responsibility for water management and local government is responsible for provision and maintenance of services. In India, water and its development is a state subject; however, the Union Government co-ordinates the sharing of water of the interstate rivers and any dispute arising is settled under the Interstate Water Dispute Act 1956. Malaysia has delegated responsibilities at regional and local levels for issuance of licences for water use, pollution control and silt control. In New Zealand, regional water boards are responsible for promoting the protection of water supplies and for conservation and the most beneficial use of water. Projects are maintained and operated by provincial agencies in Pakistan except for some inter-provincial works. In Papua New Guinea, operation, maintenance, billing and collection are carried out at the local level for urban water supply and the provinces are responsible for rural water schemes. Local agencies in the Philippines are deputed specific functions. Within the Trust Territory of the Pacific Islands, local governments are responsible for the operation of the systems and quality monitoring. Eight countries have indicated that international co-operation in the form of consultancy missions or financing could be of help in the formulation of new, or revision of existing, legislation.

3. Institutional arrangements

Thirteen countries and areas out of the 22 which responded have established a central mechanism or a body involving ministries and other organizations which deal with water, for co-ordinating all water interests at the national level. The co-ordinating body has the responsibility for preparation, implementation and evaluation of plans and policies for the development and management of water resources within the framework of national development planning (see table 6). The mechanisms for co-ordination provided by the countries and areas are of various types, such as principal ministry, department, authority, council, board and committee. In Afghanistan, co-ordination is provided by the Ministry of Irrigation. Australia has established the Australian Water Resources Council for the purpose. India has set up the National Water Resources Council for the purpose. In New Zealand, the National Water and Soil Conservation Authority looks after this function. In Pakistan, the Central Ministry of Water and Power and the Water and Power Development Authority provide co-ordination functions. Papua New Guinea has the National Water Supply and Sewerage Board, Water Resources Board and Department of Health for the purpose. Water activities are co-ordinated in the Philippines by the National Water Resources Council. The Republic of Korea co-ordinates its activities through a Central River Management Committee. In Tonga, activities are co-ordinated by the Tonga Water Board and in the Trust Territory of the Pacific Islands, by the Trust Territory Environmental Protection Board.

Six countries have plans to establish in the future institutional structures for central co-ordination at the national level. For co-ordinating water-related interests and developing comprehensive inter-disciplinary policy for water resources development, 10 countries and areas have identified the need for modifying the institutional structures and 12 for strengthening the existing mechanisms.

In order to overcome constraints, such as the shortage of qualified manpower and financing through multilateral or bilateral co-operation, Afghanistan requires manpower training and technical and financial assistance. Fiji requires manpower training in all fields. India has indicated the need for sophisticated equipment and training of professionals in advanced technology. Malaysia has indicated the need for technical and financial assistance. Pakistan has listed the need for consultancy services in special areas of advanced technology, transfer of technology through foreign training and financial aid. Papua New Guinea has mentioned that funding, training and development could help its efforts to overcome these constraints. The Philippines has indicated provision of technical assistance and extension of loans. Sri Lanka has recorded the need for long-

Table 6. Institutional arrangements

Country or area	Existence of a central mechanism for co-ordinating all water interests at the national level		Does the mechanism have responsibility for preparation, implementation and evaluation of plans and policies for water development and management?		If no co-ordinating mechanism exists, does the government have plans to establish an institutional structure?		Relative to present structure for co-ordinating interdisciplinary water policy has any need been identified?			
							To modify institutional structure		To strengthen existing structure	
	Yes	No	Yes	No	Yes	No	Yes	No	Yes	No
Afghanistan	X		X					X	X	
Australia	X		X				X		X	
China		X					X		X	
Fiji		X				X	X			X
Guam		X		X	X				X	
Hong Kong	X		X					X		X
India	X							X	X	
Indonesia		X		X	X			X	X	
Japan										
Malaysia		X			X		X		X	
New Zealand	X		X				X			
Niue	X		X		X		X		X	
Pakistan	X		X				X			
Papua New Guinea	X		X					X		X
Philippines	X		X				X		X	
Republic of Korea	X		X						X	
Singapore		X				X	X			X
Sri Lanka		X			X		X		X	
Tonga	X		X					X	X	
Trust Territory of the Pacific Islands	X		X				X			X
Vanuatu		X			X					
Viet Nam	X		X					X		X

term consultancy services with the aim of setting up an institutional infrastructure. Multilateral or bilateral co-operation could help Tonga in training manpower, and in the supply of equipment and materials. Provision of training for water-system operation and for water resources development, and financial assistance for rural water supply has been mentioned by the Trust Territory of the Pacific Islands. Vanuatu has listed the need for finances and assistance in the form of qualified manpower. Need for expatriate expertise and technical equipment is mentioned by Viet Nam. Generally, the need for training manpower and financial aid has been identified by 12 countries and areas.

B. SHARED WATER RESOURCES DEVELOPMENT

Under regional co-operation, the Mar del Plata Action Plan recommended that countries sharing water resources, with appropriate assistance from international agencies and other supporting bodies, on the request of the countries concerned, should review existing and available techniques for managing shared water resources and co-operate in the establishment of programmes, machinery and institutions necessary for the co-ordinated development of such resources. It further recommended under international co-operation that in relation to the use, management and development of shared water resources, national policies should take into consideration the right of each State sharing the resources to equitably utilize such resources as the means to promote bonds of solidarity and co-operation and that a concerted and sustained effort was required to strengthen international water law as a means of placing co-operation among States on a firmer basis.

Among the 22 respondents, 7 countries or areas have bilateral or multilateral agreements for the development of shared water resources (table 7). Afghanistan has two

Table 7. Shared water resources development

Country or area	Existence of multilateral/bilateral agreement(s) for development of shared water resources		Whether the agreement provides for establishing joint institutional mechanisms		Are bilateral/multilateral negotiations under way?		Have the guidelines prepared by UNEP been drawn upon?			
							in concluding recent agreements		in the present negotiations	
	Yes	No	Yes	No	Yes	No	Yes	No	Yes	No
Afghanistan	x			x	x			x	x	
Australia										
China	x		x			x				
Fiji										
Guam		x				x	x			x
Hong Kong	x			x		x	x			x
India	x		x		x					
Indonesia		x				x	x			x
Japan										
Malaysia	x		x		x			x		
New Zealand										
Niue										
Pakistan	x		x							
Papua New Guinea										
Philippines										
Republic of Korea										
Singapore										
Sri Lanka										
Tonga										
Trust Territory of the Pacific Islands										
Vanuatu										
Viet Nam	x		x		x		x			

agreements, one with the USSR on the Amu River basin and the other with the Islamic Republic of Iran on the Helmand River basin; China has an agreement with the Democratic People's Republic of Korea on the Yalu River; India has a treaty with Pakistan related to the Indus basin. Malaysia indicates that it has an agreement with Thailand covering the Golok River basin. Viet Nam has a multilateral agreement on the Lower Mekong basin. Except for Afghanistan, the agreements entered into, provide for the setting up of joint institutional mechanisms. Afghanistan, Malaysia and Viet Nam have bilateral/multilateral negotiations under way as well. Viet Nam had drawn upon the guidelines prepared by UNEP in concluding its agreement.

C. ASSESSMENT OF WATER RESOURCES

1. Observation networks and data collection

The observation networks for collecting time-dependent data are generally inadequate, especially in respect of ground water, as shown in table 8. Taking into account the five types of time-dependent data, overall only about 40 per cent of the respondent countries and areas have adequate observation networks. Such a situation calls for concerted efforts for improvement. However, it is noted that even though a network is classified as inadequate by many countries it has sufficient reliability. There is a general awareness of the need to plan for expanding the networks. In general, the emphasis is on ground water and water quality. Sixteen countries and areas have plans to expand their networks on ground water and 16 plan to expand those for water quality.

Information concerning networks for collecting time-independent data is given in table 9. Fifty per cent of the countries and areas have adequate and reliable networks in respect of physiographical and geological data. For other categories of time-independent data the networks are inadequate. Only two countries or areas, Guam and Tonga, have adequate networks for well logs. Not many countries have plans to expand their networks for physiographical

Table 8. Observation network and data collection
(Time – dependent data)

Country or area	Precipitation Adequacy Suff	Adequacy Insuf	Reliability Suff	Reliability Insuf	Plans Yes	Plans No	Evaporation Adequacy Suff	Adequacy Insuf	Reliability Suff	Reliability Insuf	Plans Yes	Plans No	Surface water Adequacy Suff	Adequacy Insuf	Reliability Suff	Reliability Insuf	Plans Yes	Plans No	Ground water Adequacy Suff	Adequacy Insuf	Reliability Suff	Reliability Insuf	Plans Yes	Plans No	Water quality Adequacy Suff	Adequacy Insuf	Reliability Suff	Reliability Insuf	Plans Yes	Plans No
Afghanistan	x		x		x			x		x		x		x		x	x			x		x	x			x		x	x	
Australia	x		x		x		x		x		x		x		x		x		x		x		x			x	x		x	
China		x												x												x		x		
Fiji	x			x	x			x		x	x			x		x	x			x		x	x			x		x	x	
Guam	x		x			x	x		x			x		x			x		x		x		x		x		x			
Hong Kong	x		x			x		x		x		x	x		x			x		x		x		x	x		x			x
India	x		x					x		x	x		x		x		x			x			x							
Indonesia		x		x	x			x		x	x			x	x		x			x		x	x			x	x		x	
Japan	x		x		x			x		x	x		x		x					x	x		x		x		x		x	
Malaysia	x		x			x	x		x			x	x			x		x		x	x		x			x		x	x	
New Zealand	x		x		x		x		x		x		x		x		x			x	x		x			x	x		x	
Niue		x		x		x	x			x		x		x		x	x			x		x		x		x		x		x
Pakistan	x		x					x	x				x		x		x		x		x					x	x		x	
Papua New Guinea	x		x				x		x		x		x		x		x		x		x					x	x		x	
Philippines		x	x		x		x		x		x		x		x		x			x	x		x			x	x		x	
Republic of Korea	x		x		x			x	x		x			x	x		x			x	x			x		x	x		x	
Singapore	x		x			x	x		x			x	x		x		x			x	x			x	x		x			x
Sri Lanka	x		x		x		x		x		x		x			x	x			x	x		x			x	x		x	
Tonga		x		x		x		x		x		x	x			x		x		x	x		x			x	x		x	
Trust Territory of the Pacific Islands	x		x			x								x	x		x			x	x		x			x		x	x	
Vanuatu		x	x		x			x	x			x		x	x			x		x	x		x			x	x		x	
Viet Nam	x							x						x						x		x				x				x

Table 9. Observation network and data collection
(Time — independent data)

Country or area	Physiographical						Geological						Hydrogeological						Boring description						Well logs					
	Adequacy		Reliability		Plans to expand network		Adequacy		Reliability		Plans to expand network		Adequacy		Reliability		Plans to expand network		Adequacy		Reliability		Plans to expand network		Adequacy		Reliability		Plans to expand network	
	Suff	Insuf	Suff	Insuf	Yes	No	Suff	Insuf	Suff	Insuf	Yes	No	Suff	Insuf	Suff	Insuf	Yes	No	Suff	Insuf	Suff	Insuf	Yes	No	Suff	Insuf	Suff	Insuf	Yes	No
Afghanistan	x		x		x		x		x		x			x	x		x			x		x	x			x		x	x	
Australia		x	x			x		x	x			x		x	x			x		x	x			x		x	x			x
China			x			x		x	x			x		x	x		x			x	x		x			x	x		x	
Fiji	x		x		x		x		x		x			x	x		x			x	x		x			x	x		x	
Guam	x												x						x		x				x			x	x	
Hong Kong		x		x		x	x		x			x		x	x		x			x	x			x		x	x			x
India	x		x					x	x					x		x	x			x	x		x			x	x		x	
Indonesia		x		x	x		x		x		x			x	x		x		x		x		x			x	x		x	
Japan	x		x				x												x											
Malaysia		x	x			x	x		x			x		x	x		x			x	x		x			x	x		x	
New Zealand		x	x					x		x			x		x		x			x		x			x		x		x	
Niue																														
Pakistan	x		x				x		x					x	x					x	x					x	x		x	
Papua New Guinea	x					x	x		x			x		x			x			x	x			x		x	x			x
Philippines			x		x				x		x				x		x			x	x		x			x	x		x	
Republic of Korea	x		x					x	x							x				x		x			x		x		x	
Singapore	x		x				x		x																					
Sri Lanka	x		x			x	x		x						x		x			x	x		x			x	x		x	
Tonga	x		x		x		x		x		x			x	x		x			x	x		x			x	x		x	
Trust, Territory of the Pacific Islands	x		x		x		x		x		x		x		x		x		x		x		x			x	x		x	
Vanuatu	x		x		x		x		x		x						x			x	x		x			x	x		x	
Viet Nam	x						x						x						x							x				

and geological data. About 41 per cent of the respondent countries or areas have plans to expand their networks for the collection of hydrogeological data, boring descriptions and well logs information.

Table 10 shows that 15 countries and areas are taking initiatives to remedy the situation regarding the inadequacy and reliability of their networks for data collection. Concerning the application of modern methods, among the 22 respondents 11 are using remote sensing, 8 are using isotope techniques and 17 are using geophysical methods for prospecting and measurement.

2. Data processing and dissemination

The use of computers for processing, storage, retrieval and dissemination of hydrological and other related data has been introduced fully by two countries for precipitation, by four for surface water and by 1 for ground water.

Fifteen countries and areas are processing precipitation and surface water data and 13 are using computers for ground water. In some Pacific island countries data processing has not been started (see table 11).

In 18 countries and areas a mechanism exists for dissemination of precipitation, in 17 for surface-water data and in 11 for ground-water data. Adequacy of their dissemination systems is expressed by 12 countries and areas for precipitation and surface water. Sixteen countries are planning to improve and modernize processing of precipitation and surface-water data and 14 are considering making improvements in respect of ground water.

3. Areal assessment of water resources

For the overall assessment of the water resources of a country, adequate and reliable hydrological and meteorological data covering the whole territory are required. In

Table 10. Observation network and data collection: use of modern methods

Country or area	If adequacy/reliability of data collection is insufficient, are initiatives taken to remedy the situation?		Are the modern methods of prospecting and measurement used in the country?					
			Remote sensing		Isotope techniques		Geophysical methods for ground-water prospecting	
	Yes	No	Yes	No	Yes	No	Yes	No
Afghanistan	X			X	X		X	
Australia	X		X		X		X	
China	X		X					
Fiji	X		X			X	X	
Guam				X		X	X	
Hong Kong		X	X			X		X
India	X			X	X			
Indonesia	X		X		X		X	
Japan		X	X		X		X	
Malaysia	X			X		X	X	
New Zealand	X		X		X		X	
Niue		X					X	
Pakistan	X		X				X	
Papua New Guinea				X		X		X
Philippines	X		X		X		X	
Republic of Korea	X			X		X		X
Singapore		X		X		X	X	
Sri Lanka	X		X		X		X	
Tonga		X		X		X	X	
Trust Territory of the Pacific Islands	X			X		X	X	
Vanuatu	X			X		X		X
Viet Nam	X		X		X		X	

Table 11. Data processing and dissemination

Extent of automation (use of computers) introduced in processing, storage, retrieval and dissemination of data

Country or area	Precipitation						Surface water						Ground water					
	F	P	Not at all	to users	adequacy	improvement plans	F	P	Not at all	to users	adequacy	improvement plans	F	P	Not at all	to users	adequacy	improvement plans
Afghanistan			x	x		x			x	x	x	x			x	x		x
Australia		x		x	x	x		x		x	x	x		x		x	x	x
China		x																
Fiji		x		x		x		x				x		x				x
Guam		x		x				x		x		x		x		x		
Hong Kong		x		x	x	x	x			x	x	x		x		x		x
India		x		x	x	x		x		x	x	x		x		x	x	x
Indonesia		x		x	x	x		x		x		x		x				x
Japan	x			x				x		x	x	x			x	x		
Malaysia	x			x	x	x		x		x	x	x			x			x
New Zealand		x		x	x	x	x			x	x	x		x		x	x	x
Niue			x	x					x						x			
Pakistan		x		x	x	x		x		x	x	x		x		x	x	x
Papua New Guinea		x				x	x			x	x	x		x				x
Philippines		x		x	x	x		x		x	x	x		x				x
Republic of Korea		x		x	x	x		x		x	x	x		x				
Singapore		x		x	x	x		x		x	x	x						
Sri Lanka			x	x	x	x			x	x		x			x	x	x	x
Tonga															x	x	x	x
Trust Territory of the Pacific Islands		x						x		x	x	x		x		x	x	x
Vanuatu			x	x		x		x		x					x	x		x
Viet Nam		x		x	x	x		x		x	x	x		x		x	x	x

F = fully　**P** = partly

this respect the present state of investigation programmes followed by nine countries for surface water have sufficient adequacy and reliability. Only four countries have adequate ground-water investigation programmes whereas seven have programmes of sufficient reliability, as listed in table 12. In the other countries efforts are needed to improve or adopt investigation programmes. Sixteen countries have plans to extend investigation programmes up to the period 1990-2000.

Regarding external assistance required to prepare adequate areal assessment of water resources up to the period 1990-2000, Afghanistan and Fiji have mentioned their requirements in all aspects of surface water and in most of the aspects of ground water, including training, fellowship, expertise and equipment input. In respect of surface water India has indicated the need for assistance to assess surface water yield and regional flood frequency. Concerning ground water it has mentioned hydrogeological maps, aquifer modelling and artificial recharge. Indonesia has indicated its requirements with respect to surface water to prepare hydrological maps and to assess components of the water balance. It also needs training and fellowship facilities, expert advice in methodologies, and equipment. Malaysia's requirements are for training, fellowships and expert advice. Niue has indicated the need with respect to surface water for the assessment of components of the water balance and with respect to ground water for topographical, geological and hydrogeological maps, and hydrogeological and geophysical studies. Its external assistance needs include training within the country, provision of fellowships abroad and provision of equipment. Pakistan

Table 12. Areal assessment of water resources and co-ordination

Country or area	Present state of investigation programmes for overall assessment of water resources								Existence of a government investigation programme up to the period 1990-2000		Problem of co-ordinating experience in respect of use of data by others			Establishment of a new body with comprehensive responsibility for water assessment		Strengthening existing body for comprehensive responsibility for water assessment	
	Surface water				Ground water												
	Adequacy		Reliability		Adequacy		Reliability										
	Suff	Insuf	Suff	Insuf	Suff	Insuf	Suff	Insuf	Yes	No	To a large degree	To some degree	Extent not known	Yes	No	Yes	No
Afghanistan		x	x		x		x		x			x		x		x	
Australia	x	x			x	x			x			x			x	x	
China	x		x						x		x				x	x	
Fiji	x		x		x		x			x	x						x
Guam	x		x		x		x		x			x		x		x	
Hong Kong	x		x		x		x		x			x					x
India	x	x			x		x		x			x			x	x	
Indonesia	x		x		x		x		x			x			x	x	
Japan	x		x		x	x			x				x				
Malaysia	x		x		x		x		x			x			x		x
New Zealand	x		x		x		x		x					x		x	
Niue					x		x			x		x		x			
Pakistan	x		x		x		x		x				x				
Papua New Guinea	x	x							x		x	x		x		x	
Philippines		x		x	x		x		x		x				x	x	
Republic of Korea	x	x			x		x		x			x			x	x	
Singapore	x		x						x								
Sri Lanka		x		x	x		x		x		x				x	x	
Tonga			x				x		x			x		x			x
Trust Territory of the Pacific Islands	x		x		x		x		x			x			x	x	
Vanuatu	x		x		x		x		x		x			x			
Viet Nam		x			x				x			x		x			x

has mentioned the need for external assistance in fellowships abroad and equipment only. Similarly, no specific requirements for external assistance for the areal assessment of surface and ground-water resources are indicated by Papua New Guinea. However, it has expressed the need for assistance in training, fellowship, expert or consultant advice in methodologies and equipment. The Philippines has indicated a requirement for assistance in preparing topographical maps, areal surveys and hydrological maps for assessment of surface water, and geological and hydrogeological maps in connection with ground water. Need for assistance in training, in fellowships, expert advice and equipment is also included. External assistance required by Sri Lanka and Viet Nam is indicated for hydrological maps and assessment of components of the water balance in respect of surface water and for geological and hydrogeological maps, and for geological, hydrogeological and geophysical studies, including aquifer modelling in the case of ground water. Furthermore, assistance is required to include training, fellowships, expert or consultant advice and equipment. Tonga has indicated a requirement for training, fellowship, expert advice and equipment. No indication of specific assistance required for the areal assessment of surface and ground water is made. The assistance needs of Vanuatu are mentioned for hydrological maps and surface water yield; and concerning ground water for hydrogeological maps, hydrogeological and geophysical studies, including aquifer modelling. Requirements also include assistance in training, fellowships, expert advice and equipment.

4. Institutional aspects

Most of the countries have experienced problems of co-ordination in respect of data collected by one entity of the government for use by the others. Table 12 shows that 19 countries and areas, out of 22 respondents, have experienced such a problem to a varying degree. To overcome this co-ordination problem, 5 countries plan to establish a new body with comprehensive responsibilities for water resources assessment, and 13 are considering strengthening the existing body and assigning to it the responsibility for comprehensive water resources assessment, including collection, analyses and dissemination of data.

D. FLOOD LOSS MITIGATION

Information on flood loss mitigation carried out by the respondent countries and areas is reflected in tables 13 A and B. Fourteen have floods as a major concern and 13 have the necessary policy framework and institutional

arrangements for flood control. In relation to non-structural measures, 4 respondents, Australia, India, Japan, and Singapore have adequate and reliable flood forecasting and warning systems and 2 have floodplain zoning and flood-risk mapping. There are 10 countries which have flood forecasting and warning systems but consider their systems inadequate. Though inadequate, New Zealand, Pakistan and the Philippines have sufficient reliability in their flood forecasting and warning systems. Management of catchment areas for flood prevention is taken up adequately by 3 countries. Structural measures in the form of dykes, retention reservoirs and river channel improvement are provided adequately by 6 countries and 9 have provided sufficient reliability in such structures. All the countries which face flood problems foresee intensification of efforts to improve or expand the structural and non-structural measures for flood control.

Disaster preparedness programmes with the necessary organizational structure for emergency operations, including flood-fighting and rescue operations, exist in 16 countries and areas. Australia, China, New Zealand, the Philippines and Tonga have preparedness programmes at both the regional and community levels, while others have them at the regional level only. Twelve countries have provisions for systematic collection of data on damage caused by floods. The degree of severity of the constraints experienced by the countries in the flood loss mitigation efforts varies. Lack of qualified manpower and institutional structure is, for most respondents a moderate constraint. Ten countries or areas indicate that the shortage of financial resources is a severe or very severe constraint; 8 indicate a similar degree of severity for lack of equipment. To overcome the constraints, 12 countries have indicated that external assistance in the form of technical advisory and consultancy missions, training of personnel and provision of equipment would help.

E. INTERNATIONAL DRINKING WATER SUPPLY AND SANITATION DECADE

1. Policy and planning

Since the launching of the International Drinking Water Supply and Sanitation Decade by the General Assembly in 1980, 14 countries and areas among the 22 which responded to the questionnaire have pronounced national goals and objectives of the Decade as part of the national development policy (table 14). Fifteen countries and areas are planning for the Decade within the broader framework of national development plans. The portion of the national budget allocated for Decade activities as a percentage of the development budget within the current plan

Table 13(A). Flood loss mitigation

Country or area	Are floods a major concern?		Existence of policy framework and institutional arrangement		Flood forecasting and warning system — Adequacy		Flood forecasting and warning system — Reliability		Floodplain zoning and flood-risk mapping — Adequacy		Floodplain zoning and flood-risk mapping — Reliability		Management of catchment areas — Adequacy		Management of catchment areas — Reliability		Provision of structural measures — Adequacy		Provision of structural measures — Reliability		Efforts to improve structural and non-structural measures	
	Yes	No	Yes	No	Suff	Insuf	Suff	Insuf	Suff	Insuf	Suff	Insuf	Suff	Insuf	Suff	Insuf	Suff	Insuf	Suff	Insuf	Yes	No
Afghanistan	x			x																	x	
Australia	x		x		x		x			x	x			x	x			x	x		x	
China	x		x			x				x				x				x			x	
Fiji	x			x																	x	
Guam		x																				
Hong Kong																						
India	x		x		x		x			x							x		x		x	
Indonesia	x		x			x		x		x		x		x		x		x		x	x	
Japan	x		x		x		x		x		x		x			x	x				x	
Malaysia	x		x			x		x		x		x		x		x		x	x		x	
New Zealand	x		x			x	x			x	x			x		x					x	
Niue																						
Pakistan	x		x			x	x											x	x		x	
Papua New Guinea		x		x																	x	
Philippines	x		x			x	x			x		x		x		x	x		x		x	
Republic of Korea	x		x			x		x		x		x	x		x		x		x		x	
Singapore		x	x		x		x		x		x		x		x		x		x		x	
Sri Lanka	x		x			x		x		x		x		x		x		x	x		x	
Tonga		x		x		x		x		x		x		x		x		x		x		x
Trust Territory of the Pacific Islands		x		x																		x
Vanuatu		x		x																		x
Viet Nam	x		x			x		x		x		x		x		x		x			x	

Insuf = Insufficient   Suff = Sufficient

Table 13(B). Flood loss mitigation

Country or area	Existence of disaster preparedness programmes		Level of preparedness programmes		Provisions for collecting damage data		Lack of qualified manpower			Shortage of financial resources			Institutional deficiencies			Lack of equipment			Would external co-operation help?	
	Yes	No	Reg	CL	Yes	No	M	S	VS	M	S	VS	M	S	VS	M	S	VS	Yes	No
Afghanistan		x				x	x			x			x			x			x	
Australia	x		x	x			x			x			x			x				x
China	x		x	x	x						x						x		x	
Fiji	x		x		x			x				x	x				x		x	
Guam																				
Hong Kong																				
India	x		x		x						x		x			x			x	
Indonesia	x		x		x			x				x	x				x		x	
Japan	x			x	x		x			x			x			x				
Malaysia	x		x			x	x				x		x			x			x	
New Zealand	x		x	x	x		x				x		x					x		x
Niue																				
Pakistan	x				x					x										
Papua New Guinea		x				x			x			x			x			x	x	
Philippines	x		x	x		x	x				x		x				x		x	
Republic of Korea	x		x		x		x			x			x				x		x	
Singapore	x		x		x															x
Sri Lanka	x		x			x	x					x	x				x		x	
Tonga	x		x	x	x		x			x			x			x			x	
Trust Territory of the Pacific Islands	x		x			x														
Vanuatu		x				x														
Viet Nam	x		x		x		x				x		x				x		x	

Reg = Regional   M = Moderate   VS = Very Severe   CL = Community level   S = Severe

Table 14. International Drinking Water Supply and Sanitation Decade

Country or area	Pronouncement of national goals and objectives of the Decade as part of development policy		Is planning for the Decade carried out within the framework of national development plan?		Proportion of the budget for the decade as a percentage of national development budget within current plan				Relative to previous plan period, this percentage represents			Establishment of a national action committee		Does the committee have responsibility to co-ordinate activities of all national bodies?	
	Yes	No	Yes	No	below 4%	4% to 5%	7% to 10%	over 10%	substantial increase	modest increase	about the same level	Yes	No	Yes	No
Afghanistan	x		x		x						x	x		x	
Australia	x		x		x						x		x		
China	x		x		x					x		x		x	
Fiji		x		x				x	x				x		
Guam				x											
Hong Kong		x		x									x		x
India	x		x			x			x			x		x	
Indonesia	x		x		x				x			x		x	
Japan															
Malaysia	x		x		x				x			x		x	
New Zealand		x		x	x								x		
Niue	x		x									x		x	
Pakistan															
Papua New Guinea		x	x					x			x		x		
Philippines	x		x					x	x			x		x	
Republic of Korea	x		x		x					x			x		
Singapore	x		x		x					x			x		
Sri Lanka	x		x			x			x			x		x	
Tonga	x		x		x						x	x		x	
Trust Territory of the Pacific Islands		x	x				x			x			x		
Vanuatu	x			x					x				x		
Viet Nam	x		x							x		x		x	

varies with the countries and areas. Ten have indicated allocations below 4 per cent. Seven have mentioned substantial increases and 5 indicate modest increases in the allocation relative to the previous plan period. Instead of filling the various parts of the questionnaire, Pakistan has recorded a footnote on policy and planning. Its Government aims at increasing the access to potable water from 38 per cent of the population in 1982-1983 to 60 per cent in 1987-1988, and at increasing sanitation facilities availability to people from 16 to 26 per cent. In the sixth plan, the share of the public sector social development programme has been substantially increased and falls in the category of over 10 per cent as delineated in the questionnaire.

2. Institutional aspects

Among the 22 respondent countries and areas, 10 have established national action committees or similar bodies with representation from various concerned ministries/departments to promote Decade activities.[1] The committees are entrusted with the responsibilities of co-ordinating the activities of all national bodies in the field of water supply and sanitation. In Afghanistan, the National Action Committee is composed of the Prime Minister and five ministers. Four ministries constitute the National Action Committee in China. In Indonesia, the Committee is composed of two ministries, the Central Bureau of Statistics and the Directorates of Geology and Energy. Malaysia has two ministries and the Departments of Environment and Chemistry represented on its Committee. The National Action Committee of Niue is composed of representatives of six agencies, the agriculture, public works, health, education and justice departments and the development planning office. The development planning office of Niue co-ordinates the activities of the action committee with the central co-ordinating mechanism responsible for all water interests. In the Philippines, the National Action Committee for all water activities is represented by six ministries and nine other related organizations. The National Water Resources Council is the central mechanism for co-ordinating these interests, and is also designated as the National Action Committee for the International Drinking Water Supply and Sanitation Decade in the Philippines. The National Action Committee in Sri Lanka is composed of representatives of five ministries and the National Water Supply and Drainage Board. In Tonga, the Action Committee is represented by two ministries, the Central Planning Department and the Tonga Water Board. The representative of the Ministry of Health in Tonga is the chairman of the Village Water Committee. The National Action Committee in Viet Nam is represented by four ministries; two state

committees, one for science and technology and the other for planning; the Institute for Sciences; the Department of Geology; and the Department of Meteorology and Hydrology. The Ministry of Water Hydraulics and the National Action Committee co-ordinate all the activities. Composition of the National Action Committee (Apex Committee) in India includes representatives of five ministries (Urban Development, Water Resources, Welfare, Industries, Health and Family Welfare), five Departments (Rural Development, Steel, Expenditure, Economic Affairs and Environment) and the Planning Commission. The Ministry of Works and Housing has been redesignated as Ministry of Urban Development and the Secretary of this Ministry acts as its Chairman.

F. WATER RESOURCES DEVELOPMENT AND USE FOR AGRICULTURE

1. Irrigation plans and targets

In the context of current national development plans, the development of new and improved irrigation is expected to contribute to less than 25 per cent of the projected increase in crop production in 9 countries and areas. China, Malaysia and Pakistan expect it to contribute to 50 to 75 per cent of the increase, and Afghanistan, Indonesia and the Philippines place it at 25 to 50 per cent of the increase. The reason for Pakistan's attaching a high level of importance to new and improved irrigation is due to the impact of increased water supply availability after the construction of Tarbela Dam and of reclamation programmes. Fifteen countries have targets for agricultural water development relative to development of new irrigation during their current and future plan periods. For agricultural water development relative to the other areas of activity, the number of countries which have indicated targets is as follows: for rehabilitation of existing irrigation — 13 in the current plan period, 15 in the future; for flood protection — 14 in the current period, 12 in the future; for drainage and reclamation — 14 in the current period, 12 in the future; for the introduction of aquaculture — 11 in the current period, 10 in the future (table 15A).

During the current plan period, 9 countries have indicated their targets for new irrigation areas. Fiji plans to add 250 ha, Hong Kong 160 ha and India 13,740,000 ha, Japan 250,000 ha, Malaysia 11,200 ha, New Zealand 11,500 ha, the Philippines 305,000 ha, the Republic of Korea 261,000 ha, Sri Lanka 82,000 ha. Figures for rehabilitation of existing irrigation by the respondent countries are: Australia 4,000 ha, Fiji 50 ha, Hong Kong 360 ha, Japan 810,000 ha, Malaysia 198,000 ha, New Zealand 800 ha, the Philippines 131,000 ha, the Republic of Korea 16,000 ha and Sri Lanka 44,000 ha. Fiji and the Republic

---

[1] National action committees have also been set up in Bangladesh, Bhutan, Burma, Maldives, Mongolia, Nepal and Thailand, which have not replied.

Table 15(A). Irrigation plans and targets

Country or area	Importance attached to development of irrigation in terms of its contribution to crop production increase			Targets for agricultural water development during the current plan period (1980-1985)										Targets for agricultural water development during future plan period (1985-1990)									
				New irrigation		Rehabilitation of existing irrigation		Flood protection		Drainage and reclamation		Introduction of aquaculture		New irrigation		Rehabilitation of existing irrigation		Flood protection		Drainage and reclamation		Introduction of aquaculture	
	Less than 25%	25 to 50%	50 to 75%	Yes	No	Yes	No	Yes	No	Yes	No	Yes	No	Yes	No	Yes	No	Yes	No	Yes	No	Yes	No
Afghanistan		x		x		x		x		x			x	x		x		x		x			x
Australia	x			x		x		x		x			x	x			x	x		x			x
China			x	x		x		x		x		x		x		x		x		x		x	
Fiji	x			x		x		x		x		x		x		x		x		x		x	
Guam				x								x		x									
Hong Kong				x		x			x	x			x	x		x			x	x			x
India		x		x		x		x		x		x		x		x		x		x		x	
Indonesia		x		x		x		x		x		x		x		x		x		x		x	
Japan	x			x		x		x		x			x										
Malaysia			x	x		x		x		x		x		x		x		x		x		x	
New Zealand	x			x		x				x			x	x		x							
Niue	x				x		x		x		x		x										
Pakistan			x	x		x		x		x				x		x		x		x			
Papua New Guinea																							
Philippines		x		x		x		x		x		x		x		x		x		x		x	
Republic of Korea	x			x		x		x		x			x	x		x		x		x			x
Singapore																							
Sri Lanka	x			x		x		x			x	x		x		x		x			x	x	
Tonga					x		x		x		x	x			x		x		x		x		x
Trust Territory of the Pacific Islands	x																						
Vanuatu	x				x		x		x		x	x			x		x		x		x	x	
Viet Nam				x		x		x		x		x		x		x		x		x		x	

Table 15(B). Irrigation plans and targets
(Thousands of hectares)

Country or area	Extent of target area and annual percentage increase for current plan period (1980-85)										Extent of target area and annual percentage increase for future plan period (1985-90)										In absence of targets, are there plans to make projections for 1990?									
	New irrigation		Rehabilitation of existing irrigation		Flood protection		Drainage and reclamation		Introduction of aquaculture		New irrigation		Rehabilitation of existing irrigation		Flood protection		Drainage and reclamation		Introduction of aquaculture		New irrigation		Rehabilitation of existing irrigation		Flood protection		Drainage and reclamation		Introduction of aquaculture	
	Area ha	Inc %	Area ha	Inc %	Area ha	Inc %	Area ha	Inc %	Area ha	Inc %	Area ha	Inc %	Area ha	Inc %	Area ha	Inc %	Area ha	Inc %	Area ha	Inc %	Yes	No	Yes	No	Yes	No	Yes	No	Yes	No
Afghanistan																														
Australia			4				0.25				40		1				0.25				x		x		x		x			x
China													0.20		10		22					x		x		x	x			x
Fiji	0.25	3	0.05				16		0.01		1								0.03											
Guam									0.03																					
Hong Kong	0.16		0.36				0.03				0.30	17.5	0.40	2.2			0.05	13.3							x					x
India	13 740	5			2 000						15 000				3 000															
Indonesia	250		810				1 530				600	3	360		670		460		220											
Japan																														
Malaysia	11.2		198		21.6		189				4.4		72.5		25		150													x
New Zealand	11.5	6.9	0.8								8.3	3.7	3								x		x							
Niue																														
Pakistan							997				1 312						1 263					x		x		x	x			x
Papua New Guinea																														
Philippines	305	5	131		66				191		163	2	236																	
Republic of Korea	261	4	16				12				229	6	9				13													
Singapore																														
Sri Lanka	82		44		11		2		1		93		81		4		4		2											
Tonga																														
Trust Territory of the Pacific Islands																						x			x		x			x
Vanuatu																					x			x	x		x			x
Viet Nam																					x			x	x			x		x

Inc = Increase

Note:

Plan periods:	Current	Future
Pakistan	1978-83	1983-88
The Philippines	1984-88	1989-93
Sri Lanka	1980-84	1984-88
Japan	1983-92	

of Korea have targets of 16,000 ha and 12,000 ha respectively for drainage and reclamation. Japan, Malaysia and Pakistan have larger programmes for drainage and reclamation of 1,530,000 ha, 189,000 ha and 997,000 ha respectively during their current plan periods. Japan has a longer current plan period, 1983-1992, and therefore has not indicated its targets for the future plan. Countries whose plan periods differ from the years specified in the questionnaire are shown as a note to table 15B. Protection of agricultural lands against floods is contemplated by: Malaysia 21,600 ha, the Philippines 66,000 ha, Sri Lanka 11,000 ha and India 2,000,000 ha.

Targets for new irrigation during the future plan period are: Australia 40,000 ha, Fiji 1,000 ha, Indonesia 600,000 ha, Hong Kong 300 ha, India 15,000,000 ha, Malaysia 4,400 ha, New Zealand 8,300 ha, Pakistan 1,312,000 ha, the Philippines 163,000 ha, the Republic of Korea 229,000 ha and Sri Lanka 93,000 ha. Nine countries have plans for rehabilitation of existing irrigation in the future: Australia 1,000 ha, Fiji 200 ha, Indonesia 360,000 ha, Malaysia 72,500 ha, New Zealand 3,000 ha, the Philippines 236,000 ha, the Republic of Korea 9,000 ha and Sri Lanka 81,000 ha. Future plans for drainage and reclamation are: Australia 250 ha, Fiji 22,000 ha, Hong Kong 500 ha, Indonesia 460,000 ha, Malaysia 150,000 ha, Pakistan 1,263,000 ha, the Republic of Korea 13,000 ha and Sri Lanka 4,000 ha. Five countries have planned flood protection: Fiji 10,000 ha, India 3,000,000 ha, Indonesia 670,000 ha, Malaysia 25,000 ha and Sri Lanka 4,000 ha.

In the case of introduction of aquaculture, the Philippines is the only country which has indicated a substantial area, 191,000 ha, in the current plan period. Indonesia has a sizeable target of 220,000 ha in the future plan period. Sri Lanka has mentioned 1,000 ha and 2,000 ha for the current and future plans respectively. Fiji plans for 10 ha in the current period and 30 ha in the future; Guam indicates 30 ha in the current plan period.

It may be noted that 6 island countries and areas in the Pacific do not have any targets for the development of agricultural water and correspondingly no irrigation, rehabilitation and reclamation area targets are mentioned. Singapore falls in the same category. To these countries the development of irrigation is not relevant.

Regarding projections for 1990, Afghanistan and New Zealand have plans for new irrigation and rehabilitation of the existing ones, and the Republic of Korea is considering the introduction of aquaculture.

2. Manpower development for irrigation and related activities

Fifteen countries and areas reported irrigation to be a relevant subject. In 12 countries and areas, institutional

facilities for the training of manpower in relation to agricultural water resources development and management exist at postgraduate level and in 13 at college graduate level. Thirteen have facilities for training of extension workers and 14 for training of technicians (see table 16A). Six countries have surveyed the needs for manpower for agricultural water development. The Republic of Korea has given the number of trainees required at various levels to meet the manpower needs for the two plan periods. In the current and future plan periods, it needs 450 and 500 postgraduates, 3,200 and 5,000 college graduates, 1,000 and 2,000 extension workers, and 18,000 and 25,000 technicians respectively. Afghanistan needs 15 and 25 postgraduates, 250 and 400 college graduates, 500 and 750 extension workers and 600 and 1,000 technicians respectively. Figures recorded by the Philippines are for the current plan only. It needs 5 postgraduates, 195 college graduates, 250 extension workers and 1,000 technicians. Other countries have not mentioned any figures for the trainees needed. National training institutions can meet fully the needs for postgraduates in 5 countries and partly in 3, for college graduates fully in 7 countries and partly in 3 and, for extension workers fully in 8 countries and for technicians in 9.

Eleven countries and areas have problems of attracting and retaining qualified manpower within the agricultural sector. To overcome this problem they are taking various measures, like setting competitive salary scales, improving living conditions, creating working conditions conducive to professional satisfaction and improving career development prospects through training as shown in table 16B. Ten countries and areas are operating courses with special emphasis on irrigation water use and management; seven have these courses open to students from other countries. Ten countries have shown interest in sending students for external training under exchange programmes within the framework of technical co-operation among developing countries or any other arrangement.

Most of the countries and areas have in-service/on-the-job training programmes; 11 are considering expansion of existing programmes and 8 are considering developing additional ones.

3. National advisory services

Thirteen countries and areas have a policy to encourage the establishment of advisory services in the public sector, 7 have such policy for setting up the services in the quasi-public sector and 5 in the private sector (see table 16B). Afghanistan has established the Water and Power Engineering Company in the public sector. Australia receives advisory services from government departments, semi-government authorities and private consulting firms. In Guam,

Table 16(A). Manpower development for irrigation and related activities

Country or area	Inst. Post-graduate Yes	No	Inst. College graduate Yes	No	Inst. Extension worker Yes	No	Inst. Technicians Yes	No	Survey Yes	No	1980–1985 PG	CG	EW	T	1985–1990 PG	CG	EW	T	Extent PG F	P	LE	Extent CG F	P	LE	Extent EW F	P	LE	Extent T F	P	LE
Afghanistan	x		x		x		x		x		15	250	500	600	25	400	750	1 000	x			x			x					x
Australia	x		x		x		x			x									x			x			x			x		
China	x		x		x		x		x																					
Fiji		x	x		x		x			x												x			x			x		
Guam		x		x						x																				
Hong Kong	x		x			x		x		x									x			x					x			x
India	x		x		x		x													x			x			x			x	
Indonesia	x		x		x		x			x													x			x			x	
Japan	x		x		x		x			x									x			x			x			x		
Malaysia	x		x		x		x			x																				
New Zealand	x		x			x		x		x									x			x			x			x		
Niue		x		x		x		x																						
Pakistan	x		x		x		x		x										x			x						x		
Papua New Guinea																														
Philippines	x		x		x		x		x		5	195	250	1 000					x			x			x			x		
Republic of Korea	x		x		x		x				450	3 200	1 000	18 000	500	5 000	2 000	25 000	x			x			x			x		
Singapore																			x											
Sri Lanka	x		x		x		x			x									x			x			x			x		x
Tonga		x		x		x		x	x																					
Trust Territory of the Pacific Islands																										x				
Vanuatu		x	x		x			x		x															x			x		
Viet Nam	x		x		x		x		x										x			x			x			x		

PG = Postgraduate   EW = Extension worker
F = Fully   LE = Limited extent
CG = College graduate   T = Technician
P = Partly

Table 16(B). Manpower development for irrigation and advisory services

Country or area	Problem of attracting manpower		Measures taken to overcome problems of attracting manpower								Are courses on irrigation operated?		Are courses open to other countries?		Interest in sending trainees under TCDC or other arrangement		Existence of in-service/on-the-job training programmes						Existence of policy to establish national advisory services					
			Competitive salary		Improving living conditions		Working condition conductives to satisfaction		Improving career development								New exist		Being expanded		Additional being developed		Public		Quasipublic		Private	
	Yes	No	Yes	No	Yes	No	Yes	No	Yes	No	Yes	No	Yes	No	Yes	No	Yes	No	Yes	No	Yes	No	Yes	No	Yes	No	Yes	No
Afghanistan	x			x	x		x		x			x		x	x			x	x		x		x		x		x	
Australia		x									x		x				x		x		x		x		x		x	
China												x			x									x				x
Fiji	x			x		x		x		x		x		x	x		x		x		x			x				x
Guam		x										x			x								x					x
Hong Kong	x		x		x			x	x			x			x		x			x	x		x		x			x
India		x									x						x		x		x		x					
Indonesia		x									x			x	x		x		x		x		x		x			x
Japan		x										x		x		x	x						x					x
Malaysia	x		x						x		x		x				x		x					x	x			x
New Zealand		x									x		x				x		x					x	x			
Niue									x							x	x		x					x			x	
Pakistan	x		x		x		x		x		x		x		x		x		x		x		x		x		x	
Papua New Guinea																												
Philippines	x		x		x		x		x		x		x				x		x		x		x				x	
Republic of Korea	x		x		x		x		x		x		x		x		x		x		x		x		x		x	
Singapore																												
Sri Lanka	x			x	x		x		x		x			x			x		x		x		x					x
Tonga																												
Trust Territory of the Pacific Islands	x		x		x		x		x			x			x		x		x		x			x	x			x
Vanuatu	x			x	x		x		x			x			x		x		x		x			x				x
Viet Nam	x		x		x		x		x		x				x		x		x		x		x					x

the Green Revolution Commission provides advisory services. India has plans to set up a national irrigation management institute. The Central Water Commission and the National Water Development Agency in the Government of India provide advisory services in the water sector. New Zealand draws advice from government organizations, universities and private consultants. In Pakistan, advisory services are provided by government organizations, semi-autonomous bodies, water-users associations and private consultants. In the Philippines, advisory services are provided by the Farm Systems Development Corporation, National Irrigation Administration, MERALCO Corporate Farm and San Miguel Corporation. The Republic of Korea has established the Agricultural Development Corporation, Farmland Improvement Association and Farmers Irrigation Fraternity. Public Advisory Services are planned under the new water act in Sri Lanka.

4. Constraints

In terms of degree of severity of the constraints in the formulation and implementation of national programmes for agricultural water development, generally the countries and areas have indicated moderate constraints of lack of qualified manpower, of institutional deficiencies and of lack of equipment. Shortage of financial resources is classified as severe and very severe by most of the countries, as shown in table 17.

Twelve countries and areas have indicated that multilateral or bilateral co-operation in the form of advisory and consultancy missions, and upgrading and building up of institutions could assist in overcoming the constraints; 13 have indicated that scholarships for studies abroad and training of personnel within the country would assist in overcoming them; 11 have mentioned the need for external assistance in the form of equipment; and 14 have expressed the need for financing.

G. EDUCATION, TRAINING AND PUBLIC INFORMATION

1. Education and training

Australia, Papua New Guinea, the Republic of Korea, Tonga and Viet Nam have carried out a comprehensive survey of manpower needs in the field of water resources development during the last five years. Australia, Papua New Guinea, the Republic of Korea and Viet Nam covered in their survey the subject areas of water resources assessment; community water supply and sanitation; hydropower and industrial water supply; water resources planning and

administration. Papua New Guinea, the Republic of Korea and Viet Nam also covered agriculture and fisheries. Tonga in its survey of manpower needs considered the areas of community water supply and sanitation and water resources planning and administration to be very important.

The manpower situation in terms of availability and adequacy during the last five years is reflected in table 18A. In Afghanistan, Papua New Guinea, the Trust Territory of the Pacific Islands and Vanuatu, the manpower situation concerning skilled workers, technicians and higher technicians is stated as critical, whereas the situation concerning engineers and university-educated specialists is critical in Afghanistan, Fiji, the Trust Territory of the Pacific Islands and Vanuatu. Fiji faces a critical situation with respect to higher technicians and research scientists as well. Afghanistan and Vanuatu have a critical situation with regards to administrators, policy makers, planners and lawyers. The situation has improved in 6 countries and areas in respect of skilled workers, in 5 for administrators, policy makers, planners and lawyers, and in 7 concerning technicians, higher technicians, engineers, university-educated specialists, and research scientists. However, it has deteriorated in 2 countries for some categories of manpower. A greater number of countries have experienced no significant change in the availability and adequacy of manpower.

Critical or deteriorating situations of manpower are caused to a varying extent by the transfer of staff from water resources to other fields, by migration to other countries, by lack of suitable candidates and by lack of funds to employ water resources manpower, as shown in table 18B. Twelve countries and areas have taken action to establish new or enlarge existing institutions for training and education in the field of water resources during the last five years. The new and enlarged institutions will alleviate shortages of skilled workers in 8, of technicians in 10, of engineers and university-educated specialists in 7 and of research scientists and administrators in 4 countries and areas.

The categories of constraints encountered in respect of increasing education and training activities fall under lack of trainers, teachers and professors; lack of equipment and teaching aids; limitations in educational infrastructure; lack of students with suitable background; and lack of proper programmes and curricula. The extent of these constraints for technical training, undergraduate education and postgraduate education varies from country to country and within the country and areas, depending on the level of training or education. Most countries and areas feel that external co-operation would help in alleviating some of the problems mentioned above (table 18C). Assistance in the form of fellowships for training abroad is considered suitable by 13 countries and areas. Need for technical advice

Table 17. Constraints in the implementation of agricultural water development programme

Country or area	Degree of severity of constraints in the implementation of national programme				Would multilateral or bilateral co-operation assist in overcoming constraints?											
	Lack of qualified manpower	Shortage of financial resources	Institutional deficiencies	Lack of equipment	Advisory and consultancy missions		Scholarships for studies abroad		Training within the country		Upgrading/ building up institutions		Provision of equipment		Financing	
	M / S / VS	M / S / VS	M / S / VS	M / S / VS	Yes	No	Yes	No	Yes	No	Yes	No	Yes	No	Yes	No
Afghanistan	S	S	S	S	x		x		x		x		x		x	
Australia	M	S	M			x		x		x		x		x		x
China	M	S	M	S												
Fiji	VS	VS	S	S	x		x		x		x		x		x	
Hong Kong	VS	S	S		x		x		x			x		x	x	
India	M	M	M	M	x		x		x		x		x		x	
Guam		S		M	x						x		x		x	
Indonesia	S	S	VS	S	x		x		x		x		x		x	
Japan	M	S	M	M		x		x		x		x		x		x
Malaysia																
New Zealand	M															
Niue	M	S	M	M	x		x		x			x	x		x	
Pakistan	S	VS	M / S		x		x		x		x		x		x	
Papua New Guinea																
Philippines	M	S	M	S	x		x		x		x		x		x	
Republic of Korea	M	S	M	M	x		x		x		x		x		x	x
Singapore																
Sri Lanka	S	VS	M	M	x		x		x		x		x		x	
Tonga																
Trust Territory of the Pacific Islands	M	S	M	M	x		x		x		x		x		x	
Vanuatu	VS	VS	M	S	x		x		x		x		x		x	
Viet Nam	M	VS	M	VS	x		x		x		x		x		x	

M = Moderate   S = Severe   VS = Very severe

Table 18(A). Education and training

Country or area	Survey of manpower needs in last 5 yrs — Yes	— No	Particular subject areas covered by the survey — WRA	AF	CWSS	HIWS	WRPA	Skilled workers C	I	D	NC	Technicians C	I	D	NC	Higher technicians C	I	D	NC	Engineers and university educated specialists C	I	D	NC	Research scientists C	I	D	NC	Administrators, policy makers, planners, lawyers C	I	D	NC
Afghanistan		x						x				x				x				x				x				x			
Australia	x		x	x	x	x	x				x				x				x				x				x				x
China		x																													
Fiji		x							x				x			x				x				x							x
Guam		x									x				x				x		x				x						x
Hong Kong		x									x				x				x		x					x					x
India		x							x				x				x				x				x				x		
Indonesia		x								x			x				x				x					x			x		
Japan																															
Malaysia																															
New Zealand		x									x				x				x				x	x							x
Niue																															
Pakistan																															
Papua New Guinea	x		x	x	x	x	x	x				x				x			x	x					x						x
Philippines		x							x				x					x		x					x						x
Republic of Korea	x		x	x	x	x	x		x				x				x				x				x				x		
Singapore		x									x				x				x				x				x				x
Sri Lanka		x								x				x				x				x			x						x
Tonga	x				x		x				x			x					x				x			x			x		
Trust Territory of the Pacific Islands		x																													
Vanuatu		x						x			x	x			x	x							x			x				x	
Viet Nam	x		x	x	x	x	x	x				x				x				x				x					x		

WRA = Water resources assessment
AF = Agriculture and fisheries
CWSS = Community water supply and sanitation
HIWS = Hydropower and industrial water supply
WRPA = Water resources planning and administration

C = Critical
I = Improved
D = Deteriorated
NC = No significant change

Table 18(B). Education and training

Country or area	To what extent deterioration of manpower situation was caused by?												Establishment of new or enlargement of existing institutions				Are the new or enlarged institution designed to alleviate shortages of?									
	Transfer from water resources to other fields			Movement to other countries			Lack of suitable candidates			Lack of funds to employ manpower			Action taken		Action planned		Skilled workers		Technicians		Engineers and university educated specialists		Research scientists		Administrators, policy makers, planners, lawyers	
	Large extent	Some extent	Small extent	Large extent	Some extent	Small extent	Large extent	Some extent	Small extent	Large extent	Some extent	Small extent	Yes	No	Yes	No	Yes	No	Yes	No	Yes	No	Yes	No	Yes	No
Afghanistan					x			x			x			x		x										
Australia													x		x			x	x		x		x		x	
China													x													
Fiji			x			x		x		x			x			x										
Guam			x			x			x	x			x			x										
Hong Kong													x		x		x		x		x		x		x	
India																										
Indonesia													x		x		x		x		x		x		x	
Japan																										
Malaysia																										
New Zealand													x			x										
Niue																										
Pakistan																										
Papua New Guinea	x	x					x						x		x		x		x		x		x			
Philippines	x				x			x			x		x		x		x		x		x		x			x
Republic of Korea													x				x		x							
Singapore													x				x		x		x			x		x
Sri Lanka			x	x				x				x	x				x		x		x			x		x
Tonga			x		x			x			x		x				x		x		x	x		x		x
Trust Territory of the Pacific Islands																										
Vanuatu		x			x		x			x			x				x		x		x		x			x
Viet Nam													x				x		x		x		x		x	

Table 18(C). Education and training

Country or area	Extent of constraints encountered in respect of increasing education and training activities																				Would external co-operation help?		Kind of assistance most suitable							
	Lack of trainers, teachers and professors			Lack of equipment and teaching aid			Limitations in educational infrastructure			Lack of students with suitable background			Lack of proper programmes and curricula									Technical advice on strategies		Institution building		Foreign teaching staff		Fellowships for training abroad	
	TT	UE	PE	TT	UE	PE	TT	UE	PE	TT	UE	PE	TT	UE	PE						Yes	No	Yes	No	Yes	No	Yes	No	Yes	No
Afghanistan	VS	VS	VS	VS	VS	VS	VS	VS	VS												x		x		x		x		x	
Australia																									x		x		x	
China																						x								
Fiji	S	VS	VS	S	VS	VS	M	M	VS	M	M	VS	M	M	VS						x		x		x		x		x	
Guam	S	S	VS	VS						VS	VS	VS	S	S	S						x			x					x	
Hong Kong																														
India	M			M			M	M					M	M	M						x		x		x		x		x	
Indonesia	S	S	S	S	S	S	S	S	S	VS	VS	VS	VS	VS	VS						x		x		x		x		x	
Japan																														
Malaysia																														
New Zealand																						x								
Niue																														
Pakistan																														
Papua New Guinea	S	S		M	M		VS	M		VS	VS	VS	M	M							x		x		x		x		x	
Philippines	M	M		S	S		M	M		M	M		M	M							x		x		x		x		x	
Republic of Korea			M																		x		x							
Singapore			M																		x								x	
Sri Lanka	M	S	VS	M	M	M	M	M	M	M	M	M	M	M	S						x		x		x		x		x	
Tonga	M	M	M	S	S	S	M	M	M	S	S	S	M	M	M						x			x		x	x		x	
Trust Territory of the Pacific Islands	M	S	S	M	M	S	VS	S	VS	M	M	S	M	M	M						x		x		x			x		
Vanuatu	VS	VS	VS	VS	VS	VS	VS	VS	VS	VS	VS	VS	VS	VS	VS						x		x		x		x		x	
Viet Nam				M	M	S	M														x		x		x		x		x	

TT = Technician Training   PE = Postgraduate education
S = Severe   UE = Undergraduate education
M = Moderate   VS = Very severe

on strategies and appropriate teaching programmes; institution-building; and provision of foreign teaching staff is also reflected by several respondents.

2. Public information and participation

The Mar del Plata Action Plan recommended that countries should accord priority to conducting programmes for national information campaigns directed to all people concerning the proper utilization, protection and conservation of water. In this context, 15 countries and areas have taken action to facilitate public understanding of problems related to water resources use and management and to promote community participation in the solution of these problems.

H. RESEARCH AND DEVELOPMENT

Table 19A shows that 16 countries and areas have research institutes or centres dealing with hydrology and assessment of water resources and with hydraulics; 15 with hydrobiology and hydrochemistry, and with irrigation and drainage; 13 with water supply and waste treatment, and with water resources planning and management. Only 10 have research facilities in the field of structural and geotechnical engineering relating to water projects. Action to strengthen water resources research has been taken by 9 countries and areas and is planned in 7. In 11 countries and areas, research programmes include study of the use of local materials for construction, and in 9 they include the use of labour-intensive methods of construction. In 8 countries and areas the possibility of interchangeability in and servicing of spare parts for installed facilities of different origins is studied and in 10 standardization of equipment is considered.

Guam is executing between 50 and 75 per cent of its research programmes according to the demand of the various economic sectors which depend on water resources; 3 are utilizing between 25 to 50 per cent and 10 less than 25 per cent. The impact of research programmes on the practical activities in the field of water resources planning, development and management is varied among the countries. Likewise the extent of constraints encountered in the areas of research has been variable; such constraints include lack of financial resources and of equipment, shortage of qualified manpower, and institutional problems. Generally the lack of financial resources is considered severe and very severe, and shortage of qualified manpower as moderate (table 19B). Concerning multilateral and bilateral co-operation to overcome the constraints, the general stress is on assistance for fellowships for training abroad and on the supply of equipment.

I. TECHNICAL CO-OPERATION AMONG DEVELOPING COUNTRIES IN WATER RESOURCES DEVELOPMENT

At present, 16 countries and areas among 22 respondents have an arrangement for technical co-operation with other developing countries in the field of water resources. Australia, through its South Australian Department of Agriculture and Water Research Institute, is co-operating with Indonesia, Israel, Saudi Arabia, Sri Lanka, Sudan and Thailand, for education and training, research and development, and exchange of consultants and information. Afghanistan is co-operating with Bulgaria, Czechoslovakia, the German Democratic Republic, Hungary, India and the USSR for education and training, research and development, exchange of consultants and information exchange; China provides co-operation to Asian countries for education and training, exchange of consultants and information. Japan provides such co-operation through the Japan International Co-operation Agency for expert services and training. The Department of Irrigation and Drainage and Meteorological Service of Malaysia co-operates with Thailand for exchange of consultants and information. New Zealand, through its Ministry of Foreign Affairs, co-operates in the fields of weir and storage tank construction in ferro-cement concrete, hydrogeology, geophysical survey, drilling, bore testing, supply evaluation and water chemistry and is co-operating with the Cook Islands, Niue, Samoa, Thailand and Tonga for education and training, research and development, joint manufacturing ventures, exchanges of consultants and information. The Philippines is co-operating with Yugoslavia for education and training, research and development and for information exchange. In the Republic of Korea, the Agricultural Development Corporation is involved in technical co-operation for irrigation, drainage and water management, and is co-operating with Ethiopia, Ghana, India, Indonesia, Jordan, Kenya, Senegal, Sudan and Thailand. Singapore is co-operating with Malaysia for the same activities. Tonga, through its Water Board, is co-operating with Fiji, New Zealand, Samoa and Tuvalu for information exchange concerning ground-water study and desalination. It also has plans to initiate arrangements for TCDC in water resources development. Viet Nam co-operates with the Lao People's Democratic Republic through its National Lower Mekong Committee and the Department of Geology for education and training, research and development, and exchange of information on consultants. It co-operates with the USSR in all the activities listed.

As shown in table 20, generally the countries are willing to participate in the future in establishing joint regional/subregional organizations or institutions for the promotion of TCDC covering various activities, such as education and training, research and development, standardiza-

Table 19(A). Research and development

Country or area	Existence of research institutes or centres dealing with														Strengthening of water resources research				Research programmes conducted in areas of water resources technologies							
	Hydrology and assessment		Hydrobiology and hydro-chemistry		Irrigation and drainage		Water supply waste treatment		Hydraulics		Structural and geotechnical engineering		Planning and management		Action taken		Action planned		Local material for construction		Labour intensive methods		Interchangeability of spare parts		Standardization of equipment	
	Yes	No	Yes	No	Yes	No	Yes	No	Yes	No	Yes	No	Yes	No	Yes	No	Yes	No	Yes	No	Yes	No	Yes	No	Yes	No
Afghanistan	x		x		x			x	x		x		x			x		x		x		x		x		x
Australia	x		x		x		x		x		x		x		x		x		x			x	x		x	
China	x		x		x		x		x		x		x		x		x		x							
Fiji		x		x		x		x		x		x		x	x			x		x		x		x		x
Guam	x		x		x		x		x			x		x	x			x					x		x	
Hong Kong	x		x		x		x		x		x		x		x			x		x		x		x		x
India	x		x		x		x		x		x		x			x	x		x		x		x		x	
Indonesia	x		x		x		x		x		x			x		x	x		x		x		x		x	
Japan	x		x				x		x				x				x			x		x	x		x	
Malaysia	x		x		x				x						x				x			x				
New Zealand	x		x		x			x	x		x		x		x		x		x			x		x	x	
Niue																										
Pakistan	x		x		x		x		x		x		x		x											
Papua New Guinea	x		x		x	x	x						x						x		x			x		x
Philippines	x			x	x		x		x			x	x		x			x	x		x			x		x
Republic of Korea	x		x		x		x		x		x		x		x		x		x		x		x		x	
Singapore	x		x		x		x		x		x		x		x		x		x					x		x
Sri Lanka		x		x		x		x	x			x		x	x			x	x		x			x	x	
Tonga		x		x		x	x		x			x		x	x		x		x		x		x		x	
Trust Territory of the Pacific Islands		x		x				x				x		x	x		x		x		x					
Vanuatu		x		x		x		x		x		x		x	x		x			x	x			x		x
Viet Nam	x		x		x		x		x		x		x		x			x	x		x		x		x	

Table 19(B). Research and development

Country or area	Proportion of research programme executed on demand of various economic section				Impact of research on practical activities			Extent of constraints encountered in the area of research												Would multilateral and bilateral co-operation help?							
	Less than 25%	15 to 50%	50 to 75%	More than 45%	Max	Mod	Min	Lack of financial resources			Lack of research equipment			Shortage of qualified manpower			Institutional problems			Technical advisory missions		Training within country		Fellowship abroad		Supply of equipment	
								Mod	S	VS	Mod	S	VS	Mod	S	VS	Mod	S	VS	Yes	No	Yes	No	Yes	No	Yes	No
Afghanistan	x								x			x			x			x		x		x		x		x	
Australia					x			x			x			x			x				x		x		x		x
China																											
Fiji	x						x			x			x			x			x	x		x		x		x	
Guam			x		x					x			x	x				x								x	
Hong Kong	x					x																					
India	x					x		x			x			x			x			x		x		x		x	
Indonesia	x				x			x				x		x				x		x		x		x		x	
Japan						x		x			x			x			x				x		x		x		x
Malaysia						x		x			x			x				x		x		x		x			x
New Zealand		x			x									x				x		x		x		x			x
Niue																											
Pakistan										x							x										
Papua New Guinea					x				x				x	x			x			x		x		x		x	
Philippines		x			x				x			x		x			x			x		x		x		x	
Republic of Korea	x				x			x				x		x			x				x			x		x	
Singapore	x						x							x				x			x		x				x
Sri Lanka	x						x		x			x			x			x		x		x		x		x	
Tonga		x				x			x			x			x			x			x	x				x	
Trust Territory of the Pacific Islands	x				x				x			x		x				x		x		x		x		x	
Vanuatu	x						x			x			x			x		x		x		x		x		x	
Viet Nam						x			x				x	x				x		x		x		x		x	

Max – Maximum, Mod – Moderate, Min – Minimum

S – Severe, VS – Very Severe

Table 20. Technical co-operation among developing countries

Country or area	Existence of arrangement for technical co-operation with other developing countries		Does government have plans to initiate arrangements for TCDC?		Willingness to participate in establishing joint regional/subregional organizations or institutions												Willingness to support a pilot project to assess needs and resources for TCDC		Awareness of existence of TCDC Directory		Use of the TCDC Directory for obtaining services		Would water authorities be interested in?			
					Education and training		Research and development		Standardization of services, equipment		Joint manufacturing		Exchange of consultants/experts		Information exchange								Receiving TCDC information		Registering services offered	
	Yes	No	Yes	No	Yes	No	Yes	No	Yes	No	Yes	No	Yes	No	Yes	No	Yes	No	Yes	No	Yes	No	Yes	No	Yes	No
Afghanistan	x				x		x		x		x		x		x		x			x			x		x	
Australia	x				x		x		x		x		x		x		x		x			x	x		x	
China	x				x		x		x				x		x					x		x	x		x	
Fiji	x				x		x						x				x				x		x		x	
Guam		x		x								x	x		x				x			x	x			x
Hong Kong					x		x			x		x	x		x		x			x			x			
India	x				x		x		x		x		x		x		x		x				x			
Indonesia	x				x		x		x		x		x				x									
Japan	x					x		x		x		x	x			x		x	x		x					
Malaysia	x				x			x	x			x	x		x		x			x			x		x	
New Zealand	x				x		x		x				x		x		x			x		x	x		x	
Niue													x									x				
Pakistan					x		x		x		x		x		x		x									
Papua New Guinea																										
Philippines	x				x		x		x		x		x		x		x			x			x		x	
Republic of Korea	x				x				x				x		x		x			x			x		x	
Singapore	x			x		x	x			x	x			x		x		x		x			x			x
Sri Lanka		x		x	x		x			x	x		x		x		x		x			x	x		x	
Tonga	x		x		x			x		x	x		x		x		x		x				x		x	
Trust Territory of the Pacific Islands		x			x		x		x		x		x		x		x		x				x		x	
Vanuatu	x				x		x		x		x		x		x		x		x				x		x	
Viet Nam	x				x		x		x		x		x		x		x		x				x		x	

-tion of engineering services and equipment, joint manu-facturing ventures for the production of machinery, equip-ment and tools, exchange of consultants/experts and infor-mation exchange. Ten countries and areas are willing to support the development of a pilot project, on a cost-shar-ing basis, involving travel through these countries by a group of experts from the region/subregion to take stock of needs and resources and to formulate specific project proposals for the joint promotion of TCDC in the field of water resources development.

Only 6 countries have shown their awareness of the existence of the Directory of Services for Technical Co-operation among Developing Countries and only 1 country had occasion to use the Directory. Sixteen countries and areas have indicated their interest in receiving TCDC-related information and 14 are interested in registering water-related services in TCDC.

J. CONCLUSIONS AND RECOMMENDATIONS

The response to the questionnaire has not been en-couraging. It was circulated to 39 member and associate member countries and areas of the region on 1 December 1983. The date of return of the completed question-naire was indicated as 30 April 1984. Up to 15 January 1985, only 22 countries and areas had responded. This note prepared by the secretariat is based on these 22 returns and can be considered to reflect an indicative study only. A better response would have given a more representative picture.

The questionnaire was devised to serve as a means of securing the necessary information to review the overall progress made in the implementation of the Mar del Plata Action Plan. It was envisaged that the analysis of the in-formation would help to identify specific measures to im-prove the effectiveness of the support provided by the United Nations system and to promote exchange of infor-mation and views among Member States and the interna-tional organizations concerned.

The study reflects that most of the respondents have a national water policy statement specifying their priorities of water resources development within the context of na-tional development planning. In line with the recommen-dations of the Action Plan to keep the water policy under review, some have revised their policy and others have it under review. The water policy is established in most cases by Cabinet decision.

Half of the respondents have a comprehensive master plan for water resources development and some are making efforts to formulate one. Most have shown interest in inter-national assistance and nine have indicated their willing-

ness to finance the assistance from their IPF (indicative planning figure).

The respondents which do not have a national policy statement and those which have not formulated a national master plan for water resources development may wish to give serious consideration to the formulation of these instruments.

Most of the respondents have either experienced, or are anticipating in the future, problems with the major project structures which are approaching the end of their useful life. Huge public investments are required to reno-vate those. To remedy the situation, countries and areas may wish to make efforts to mobilize resources from within and through multilateral and bilateral arrangements. De-veloped countries may be called upon to co-operate further in this respect.

Most of the respondents levy water charges on the direct project beneficiaries to recover fixed and recurrent costs either fully or partly. The incidence of recovery of recurrent costs is more than that of fixed cost. Though the situation seems to have improved since the Water Con-ference, the countries and areas may wish to make further efforts to reduce government subsidies and to generate funds for efficient maintenance and operation of the pro-jects.

Urban water supplies are mostly metered and the struc-ture of the charges preferred for it is on a volumetric (block) rate basis. For irrigation water use charges, a grea-ter number of countries recovers charges on the basis of area irrigated. A few countries and areas practise peak demand pricing or drought-pricing as an instrument of pol-icy to ration water during periods of shortage.

The analysis reflects that most of the respondents have national water legislation which regulates the owner-ship, right to use and protection of the quality of water. Fifty per cent consider their current legislation sufficient and compatible with the objectives of long-term national economic and social development plans. Their legislation provides for centralized co-ordination to a variable extent. Countries and areas lacking water legislation may wish to consider framing such a legal instrument.

More than half of the respondents have established a central mechanism or a body for co-ordinating all water in-terests at the national level with responsibilities for pre-paration, implementation and evaluation of plans and policies. The types of mechanism of co-ordination provid-ed by the countries vary and include principal ministry, department, authority, council, board and committee. Half of the countries and areas have indicated modifying the institutional structure or strengthening the existing mechanism. Others which do not have such a mechanism may wish to consider establishing one for an interdisciplinary approach to the integrated and co-ordinated development of water resources.

There are five countries and areas among the respondents which currently have a bilateral agreement[2] that provides for the setting up of a joint institutional mechanism concerning the shared water resources, and two have bilateral agreements only. All countries and areas sharing water resources may wish to make concerted and sustained efforts for reviewing existing techniques for managing shared water resources and for co-operating in the establishment of programmes, machinery and institutions necessary for the co-ordinated development of such resources.

There are five categories of time-dependent data: precipitation, evaporation, surface water, ground water and water quality. The observation networks for collecting time-dependent data are generally inadequate, especially in respect of ground water. Such a situation calls for improvement. The importance of all categories of data for the planning of water resources development and management cannot be over-emphasized. Confidence in the data depends on the reliability of the network and its usefulness depends on the extent of its adequacy.

Categories of time-independent data are physiographical, geological, hydrogeological, bore descriptions and well logs. In general, 50 per cent of the networks for collecting physiographical and geological data have sufficient adequacy and reliability. For other categories of time-independent data, the networks are inadequate. Countries and areas may wish to consider improving the situation in this aspect of data collection.

It is noted that 70 per cent of the respondents are taking initiatives to remedy the situation regarding insufficient adequacy and reliability of data collection. Concerning the application of modern methods, the majority of the respondents are using geophysical methods for prospecting and measurement. Countries and areas may wish to consider the need for introducing remote sensing and isotope techniques.

More than half of the countries and areas which responded are processing data, but a majority of those are doing it only partly. In some of the Pacific island countries, data processing has not been started. Generally the mechanism for dissemination of the data to the users exists and improvements in this respect are planned. The countries and areas may wish to consider the introduction of mini-computers for processing storage and easy retrieval of water resources data.

_____

[2] There are similar agreements between some other countries which did not respond to the questionnaire.

For the areal assessment of water resources, less than half of the countries and areas have adequate and reliable investigation programmes for surface water, whereas for ground water only a few have adequate programmes. In other countries efforts are needed to improve or adopt investigation programmes. The need for external assistance for the assessment of water resources has been expressed by most of the countries. The requirements include training, fellowships, expertise and equipment inputs.

In most of the countries and areas problems of co-ordination in respect of data collected by one entity of the government for use by the others have been experienced. A few plan to establish a new body with comprehensive responsibility, and more than half plan to strengthen the existing ones. However, more effort is required to streamline collection, analyses and dissemination of data.

Sixty-four per cent of the countries and areas have floods as a major concern and have the necessary policy framework and institutional arrangements for flood control. However, there is a need for improvement of various non-structural measures in various countries. Less than half of the countries which face flood problems consider provision of structural measures adequate. All the countries foresee intensification of efforts for flood control. Disaster preparedness programmmes exist in most of the countries and areas but lack of finances and equipment is a severe constraint.

Sixty-five per cent of the countries and areas have pronounced national goals and objectives for the International Drinking Water Supply and Sanitation Decade as part of their national development policy and have increased budget allocations relative to the previous plan period. Forty-five per cent have established national action committees or similar bodies to co-ordinate activities of all national bodies.

Generally the development of new and improved irrigation is expected to contribute to less than 25 per cent of the projected increase in crop production. Sixty-eight per cent of the countries and areas have targets for development of agricultural water for the two plan periods. About 30 per cent of the respondents have substantial programmes for bringing new areas under irrigation, for rehabilitation of the existing irrigation systems and for drainage and reclamation of waterlogged and saline lands. Only two countries are considering introduction of aquaculture on a large scale.

Irrigation is a relevant subject to 68 per cent of the countries and areas. In all of these, institutional facilities for training in relation to agricultural water resources development and management exist for various levels. For irrigation, a few countries and areas have surveyed the needs for manpower. The countries and areas face the problem of attracting and retaining qualified manpower. To overcome this problem they have considered appropriate measures and given incentives. Among those dealing with irrigation, the majority operate courses in this field and have those courses open to other countries and areas. Most of the countries and areas have in-service training programmes, and have a policy to encourage the establishment of advisory services in the public sector.

In addition to other constraints in the formulation of programmes for agricultural water development, the shortage of financial resources is classified as severe; multilateral or bilateral assistance is necessary to overcome this constraint.

A comprehensive survey of manpower needs in the last five years has been carried out by a few countries and areas. The manpower situation for various levels in terms of availability and adequacy is critical in some of them. Generally there is no significant change in the manpower situation. In a few countries and areas the situation has improved. Countries and areas may wish to make further efforts to improve the manpower situation.

A critical or deteriorating situation of manpower is caused to a varying extent by the transfer of staff to other fields, by migration to other countries and areas, by lack of suitable candidates and by lack of funds. Half of the respondents have taken action to establish new, or enlarge existing, training institutions. Most feel that external co-operation would help in alleviating some of the problems. Assistance in the form of fellowships for training abroad and availability of qualified trainers, teachers, lecturers and professors is stressed.

More than half of the countries and areas have research institutes or centres dealing with various disciplines in the field of water resources. Some have taken action and some have planned action to strengthen water resources research. Research programmes for various aspects of construction are conducted by less than half of the respondents. The impact of research programmes has been felt to a variable extent. Apart from other constraints, the lack of financial resources is considered a very severe constraint. To overcome the constraints in the research field, the general stress is on provision of fellowships and on the supply of equipment. It is recommended that efforts should be made to mobilize national and external resources.

Many among the respondent countries and areas have, at present, an arrangement of technical co-operation with other developing countries and are generally willing to participate in the future in establishing joint regional/sub-regional organizations or institutions for the promotion of

TCDC covering various water activities. Nine are willing to support the development of a pilot project, on a cost-sharing basis, involving travel through these countries by a group of experts from the region in order to assess their needs and formulate specific project proposals. A few countries and areas are aware of the existence of the TCDC Directory and only one had the occasion to use it. Generally the countries and areas are interested in receiving TCDC-related information and in registering water-related services in TCDC. Promotion of TCDC may be hampered owing to lack of financing among the co-operating countries and areas. Avenues should be investigated for providing such support. To promote TCDC, ESCAP, on its part, has published a register of regional water specialists available for TCDC, presenting information on some 200 regional water specialists who had indicated their willingness and availability to provide their services. Subsequently, a supplement containing information on 150 additional such specialists was also published. The member countries may consider increased use of TCDC services in their water resources development efforts.

It appears that the most significant avenue of regional co-operation in the area of water resources development would be in the field of human resources development. In realization of the importance of the role of adequate manpower in any development activity, the establishment of a regional network for training in water resources development was approved at the intergovernmental meeting of the member countries held at Bangkok from 27 to 31 May 1986. It is expected that the activities of the regional network will be strongly supported by the member countries in order to achieve the goals of providing adequate training to an increased number of personnel in the field of water resources development.

Finally, taking an overall view, the countries have achieved significant progress in implementing the recommendations of the United Nations Water Conference. However their performance would improve considerably if the constraints highlighted could be overcome. In this context and in line with the ESCAP medium-term plan for the period 1984-1989, the regional activities in the field of human resources development; water resources assessment, development and management; mitigation of damage caused by water-related natural disasters and other water development activities need to be promoted further to accelerate the implementation of the recommendations. Shortage of financial resources is a serious obstacle in the way of developing and least developed countries in achieving high development rates. The developed countries are urged to assist others by bilateral and/or multilateral arrangements in financing water resources development projects.

II. WATER RESOURCES DEVELOPMENT IN CHINA:
A REVIEW OF IMPLEMENTATION OF THE MAR DEL PLATA ACTION PLAN*

Great progress in water resources development has been made in the past 37 years since the founding of the People's Republic of China. The capabilities against flood, drought and water-logging have been enhanced; farmland irrigation areas have been enlarged; industrial and urban water supply systems have been developed; navigation waterways have been improved and the protection of natural environment has been emphasized. By end of 1985, 177,000 km of embankments were constructed, embracing 10 per cent of the total country land; More than 80,000 reservoirs, big, medium and small, were built with a total storage capacity of 430 billion cubic metres; the mechanical and electrical power for irrigation and drainage reached to 80 million horsepower. Over 5,000 irrigation systems, big and medium, were completed. Now the irrigated areas, which make up half of the total cultivated land, supply two thirds of the food grain for the whole country. Three quarters of low-lying land, two thirds of saline land in the north and one half of low-yielding land in the south have been improved. In 1985, the total water supply for industry and agriculture topped 480 billion cubic metres, out of which 117.6 billion cubic metres were for industrial and urban use. The drinking water resources for 84 million people living in the mountains and islands have been solved. The soil erosion on 460,000 km^2 has been controlled.

Water resources development efforts in the past three years were evident in the following aspects. The flood control capabilities of the main rivers were improved by reinforcement of embankments; The head-to-tail canal systems in the existing irrigated areas were completed and perfected; Water resources development in the arid mountainous areas, in the low-lying land or plains liable to water-logging was encouraged and diverting water into the water deficient cities was emphasized.

Thirteen big reservoirs, as Panjiakou, Daheiding, Biliuhe and Tingxia, and 90 medium reservoirs were built, with an increase of 16 billion cubic metres of water in storage. Almost 200 big and medium sluice gates were set up. Three main drainage canals were completed in the Sanjiang Plain. In addition, the north part of the project diverting the Luanhe River has provided the municipality of Tienjing with 1.14 billion cubic metres of water. Water from Biliuhe Reservoir has started flowing into Dalian city

and the Yellow River will enter into Qingdao city in the near future.

The objectives of water resources development in the seventh Five-Year Plan (1986-1990) are as follows:

1.   To continue the reinforcement of embankments along the main rivers, particularly on important river sections for raising flood control capacity.

2.   To conduct overall balance and rational utilization of water resources in water deficient cities and areas. Projects of inter-basin water transfer in the North China Plain are given priorities;

3.   To improve and perfect the existing water project for irrigation, drainage and storage;

4.   To provide safe drinking water in rural areas and pastures;

5.   To practise multi-purpose utilization and comprehensive benefits of water resources development;

6.   To work on soil conservation, protection of water resources and environmental ecology.

In the 1980s the Chinese Government has made fruitful efforts in the evaluation of national water resources.

The total annual average precipitation is 6,190 billion m^3, equal to 648 mm in depth. This figure is 20 per cent less than the annual average precipitation depth of the global land surface. Of the total precipitation, 56 per cent evaporated and 44 per cent became runoff of rivers and streams. The total annual average amount of stream runoff is about 2,700 billion m^3, and the ground water resources is over 800 billion m^3. Deducting the duplication, the total amount of annual average water resources (surface and ground water) are about 2,800 billion m^3, which places China at number six in the world. But the water amount per capita is only one quarter and the water amount per unit of cultivated land is only one half of those in the world. So water resources in China are not abundant.

The distribution area of water resources is extremely uneven in the country. In general, it is decreased from 1,800 mm in the southeast to 200 mm in the northwest. The area south of the Yangtze River takes up 36 per cent of the whole country, but receiving 83 per cent of the runoff, i.e. 650 mm in depth. On the contrary, the large area north of the Huaihe River which takes 64 per cent of

---

*Country paper prepared for the thirteenth session of the ESCAP Committee on Natural Resources. This paper has been reproduced without formal editing. The views expressed in it are those of the author and do not necessarily reflect those of the United Nations.

Water resources development in 1984 and 1985

Item	Unit	1984	1985
1. Irrigated area	ha	49 865 000	49 443 000
– Effective irrigated farmland	ha	48 400 000	47 933 000
Area actually irrigated	ha	39 933 000	38 671 000
%		83	81
– Irrigated forestry	ha	824 000	848 000
– Irrigated grassland	ha	641 000	662 000
2. Farmland from flood and drought	ha	33 038 000	32 870 000
3. Area by tube-well irrigation	ha	11 281 000	11 132 000
4. Area irrigated and drained by mechanical and electrical power	ha	30 914 000	30 534 000
– Area irrigated by M & E power	ha	26 182 000	26 298 000
5. Area liable to water-logging	ha	24 235 000	24 206 000
Area free from water-logging	ha	18 399 000	18 584 000
%		76	76.8
6. Saline and alkaline land	ha	7 331 000	7 692 000
Reclamation of saline alkali soil	ha	4 474 000	4 569 000
%		61	59
7. Soil eroded area	ha	120 mil.	129 mil.
Soil conservation area	ha	44.6 mil	46.6 mil.
%		37	36
8. Irrigated area larger than 667 ha	No	5 319	5 281
– Irrigated area larger than 20,000 ha	No	140	137
9. Reservoir	No	84 998	83 219
Storage capacity	mil m^3	429 800	430 100
– Big reservoir	No	338	340
Storage capacity	mil m^3	306 800	307 600
– Medium reservoir	No	2 387	2 401
Storage capacity	mil m^3	65 800	66 100
– Small reservoir	No	82 273	80 478
Storage capacity	mil m^3	56 600	56 400
10. Length of embankment	km		177 048
Farmland protected	ha		31 060 000
11. Sluice gates	No	25 862	24 816
– Big	No	290	284
– Medium	No	1 941	1 967
– Small	No	22 631	22 565
12. Tube-well available for farmland irrigation	No	2 400 000	2 370 000
13. Guaranteed horse-power for irrigation and drainage	ha	81 mil.	80.78 mil.
14. Stationary irrigation and drainage station	No	478 000	462 000
15. Water turbine pump station	No	27 621	23 724
16. Drinking water provided			
– Human being	No	76 730 000	84 670 000
– Stock	head	43 190 000	46 100 000
17. Total water supplied by water projects	mil m^3	429 000	481 900
18. Area affected by flood and drought	ha	26 451 000	37 186 000
Area damaged by flood and drought	ha	12 409 000	19 012 000
– Area affected by flood	ha	10 632 000	14 197 000
– Area damaged by flood	ha	5 395 000	8 949 000
– Area affected by drought	ha	15 819 000	22 989 000
– Area damaged by drought	ha	7 015 000	10 063 000

the whole land only receives 17 per cent of the total annual runoff, i.e. 74 mm in depth. As the great amount of runoff flows in the small areas in the south and the small amount of runoff flows in the great areas in the north, the distribution of water and land resources is unbalanced.

Another character is that the distribution duration of precipitation and stream runoff is concentrated in a few months of the year and varies greatly from year to year. But there is not much change in the ground water distribution. Precipitation in the four concentrated months is 60-70 per cent of the annual figure in the southeast China and 70-80 per cent in other places of the country. The proportion of max. precipitation to the min. is 1:2 or 1:3 in the south and 1:3 to 1:5 in the north. The proportion of max. runoff to the min. is 1:2 or 1:3 in the Yangtze, the Pearl and Songhua rivers, 1:4 in the Yellow River, 1:15 in the Huaihe River and 1:20 in the Haihe River.

The other problem is river sedimentation. The Yellow River has the highest silt content in the world. It's annual average silt discharge topps 1.6 billion tons, out of which 1/4 of the silt is deposited in the river channel, raising the river bed up to a suspended river. The silt discharge of the Yangtze River is also high, next to the Yellow.

The economic hydro potential in China is 676 Gw and the exploitable potential is 378 Gw.

The inland waterway totals 108,000 km long, but the navigable waterway in which ships, 1,000 tons and over can go, is only 2,700 km, taking 2.5 per cent of the waterway's length in China.

III. MAR DEL PLATA ACTION PLAN IMPLEMENTATION IN THE PHILIPPINES*

A. REPORT ON MAR DEL PLATA ACTION PLAN IMPLEMENTATION IN THE PHILIPPINES.

1. Water supply and rural sanitation

Following the formulation of an Integrated Water Supply Program for 1980-2000 in July 1980, a more detailed master plan encompassing water supply as well as sanitation services for the rural sector has been drawn up jointly by the Ministry of Public Works and Highways (MPWH), Ministry of Health (MOH), Ministry of Local Government-Barangay Water Program (MLG-BWP), Rural Waterworks Development Corporation (RWDC), Local Water Utilities Administration (LWUA), Metropolitan Waterworks and Sewerage Systems (MWSS) and the National Water Resources Council (NWRC). Envisioned to evaluate the provision of water supply and sanitation services to the majority of the rural households in the shortest practicable time and in the most cost-effective manner, the Master Plan provides the framework for co-ordinated development activities of all entities concerned within the sector.

At the forefront of water supply development are the MWSS for Metro Manila and the suburb areas with a present population of about 7.9 million; the LWUA which cater to the needs of the provincial urban areas accounting for about 14.75 million population; and the Ministry of Local Government-Barangay Water Program (MLG-BWP), RWDC and MPWH for the rural areas accounting for about 33.3 million population. About 66 per cent of the country's 56 million population is now served by the public water systems, with service average of 92 per cent in Metro Manila, 54 per cent in other urban areas and 53 per cent in rural areas. The rest of the population rely mainly on open wells, rainwater cisterns, rivers and streams, many of which are of doubtful quality which may cause water borne and related diseases.

About 66 per cent of the total Filipino household have sanitation facilities which vary, depending on geographical locations and the socio-economic and cultural traits of the people. Some 137 trainors or supervisors have undergone National Sanitation Training Programs and have been sent to their respective assigned areas to conduct Regional Training Program for about 3,000 rural sanitary inspectors.

2. Irrigation development

Spearheaded by the National Irrigation Administration (NIA) and the Farm System Development Corporation (FSDC), about 491,590 hectares were newly irrigated and about 495,560 hectares were rehabilitated/improved as of 1985. Corollary to this was the organization of 2,779 Integrated Service Associations (ISAs) which aims to provide the necessary institutional support services to farmers. To

* Country paper prepared for the thirteenth session of the ESCAP Committee on Natural Resources This paper has been reproduced without formal editing. The views expressed in it are those of the author and do not necessarily reflect those of the United Nations.

date, about 126,000 farmers are members of ISAs. As of 1985, total service area of operating irrigation systems was about 1,537,360 hectares which is roughly 50 per cent of the total potential irrigable areas. Of this total service area, 607,546 hectares are under the national systems, 703,775 hectares are under the communal systems and 226,039 hectares are serviced by individual pump systems.

3. Flood control

In support of the thrust of the government towards food self-sufficiency, extensive flood control works were undertaken in the major river basins focusing on the Agno and Pampanga River Basins, the rice bowls of the country. Almost simultaneous with the aforestated Central Luzon activities, was the implementation of the Manila and Suburbs Flood Control and Drainage Program which involved the installation of drainage mains, outfalls, river walls, pumping stations and related facilities. This was followed by the construction of the Napindan Hydraulic Control and Structure Project and the still on-going Mangahan Floodway Project. Also undertaken were flood control projects in the Bicol River Basins. Construction of shore protection works or seawalls was likewise pursued to protect coastal communities from destructive wave action. To complement the downstream control works, multipurpose Small Water Impounding Management (SWIM) Projects and debris (Sabo) dams and erosion control works were also initiated.

4. Water use regulation

To rationalize the utilization, development, conservation and protection of the nation's water resources, regulation of water use is pursued within the context of the Water Code of the Philippines. This is essentially effected thru the issuance of water permits to all water appropriators for whatever purpose except single family domestic use. Corollary to this measure is the monitoring of water uses by maintaining an updated water rights registry.

5. Framework planning

River Basins framework plans have been formulated which are intended to establish a sufficient analytical framework on which to base concrete recommendations for the development of the river basins including, where necessary, measures to improve the data base for subsequent planning efforts for water resources development.

6. Assessment of water resources

In the pursuant of the Philippine Government's concern for an effective water resources management and development, the National Water Resources Council (NWRC) has been undertaking the collection/gathering of water data nationwide. This activity involves the establishment, operation and maintenance of 298 national stream gauging observation network in various river basins nationwide and also includes the establishment of station network for groundwater, rainfall, water quality and sediment data.

In support of the above-mentioned activities and to systematize the planning, development and management of the country's water resources, the NWRC is continuing with the operation and maintenance of a computer based system for the storage, retrieval and analysis of water data. This system features package programme for statistical analysis of hydrologic data.

7. Training programme

The expansion of water resources development activities in the country intensifies the continuing need for highly skilled manpower to staff the various agencies engaged in water resources development and management. In order to provide a steady source of qualified personnel, the NWRC has initiated the development of a continuing training programme in water resources. A number of scholars from various agencies have enrolled in the diploma and masters degree study programmes in Water Resources Engineering including Hydrogeology at the University of the Philippines.

To keep abreast with current trends in water resources development and to ensure efficiency in operation, the water resources agencies develop and upgrade their own staff capabilities through participation in training programmes in various fields of water utilization. A number of water resources personnel have attended local and foreign training programmes consisting of seminars, workshops as well as academic courses.

B. INFORMATION AND PHILIPPINE EXPERIENCE ON MEASURES TAKEN SPECIFICALLY IN RESPONSE TO THE MAR DEL PLATA ACTION PLAN AND THE PROBLEMS ENCOUNTERED IN CARRYING OUT THE RECOMMENDATIONS OF THE UNITED NATIONS WATER CONFERENCE.

1. Although hydrologic data are sufficient in some areas, lack of information in others adversely affect the develop-

ment of water resources. The institutionalization of a national water resources data system network under NWRC is an important undertaking in this direction. The NWRC with the various water resources agencies, has fully embarked on a nationwide water resources data collection programme with particular emphasis on the improvement and expansion of the stream gauging and groundwater observation station networks.

2. Rapid decline of groundwater level and saltwater intrusion have been observed in some highly developed areas like Metro Manila due to overpumping. A remedial measure instituted is by regulating well-spacing and groundwater withdrawals in accordance with the Philippine Water Code. Tapping alternative surface water supply sources constitutes a long-term solution.

3. Due to the archipelagic nature of the country, transporting water samples collected from existing water supply facilities to laboratories poses a problem in terms of time requirements for the qualitative analysis of water samples. Establishment of more laboratory facilities to adequately cover the country is being undertaken.

4. In view of the Philippines' geographical and prevailing rainfall conditions, floods and drainage problems have been a major concern particularly in Metropolitan Manila and in the major river basins of the country. The implementation of flood control and drainage projects have been a continuing pre-occupation of the government.

5. Soil erosion mainly caused by deforestation is an environmental problem being encountered in the Philippines. Considering the rapid denudation of forest lands, forest protection has become one of the major concerns of the Ministry of Natural Resources. The intention is to conserve the remaining forest resources of the country, most specifically the timber stands, and protect these resources from illegal and unwise utilization.

6. River and its tributaries have been seriously degraded by organic and inorganic pollutants from industrial waste discharges and they are the main cause of water pollution. The National Environmental Protection Council (NEPC) is responsible for making an inventory and likewise monitoring toxic and hazardous substances especially those being used in Metro Manila. The National Pollution Control Commission monitors water quality and their concern on the regulation of water pollution has been extended to in-

clude the monitoring and classification of various rivers in the Philippines experiencing varying degrees of degradation.

7. Retaining qualified and experienced personnel in water resources is another problem being encountered in the Philippines. Development of a continuing training programme in the field of water resources has been initiated to provide a steady source of supply of trained personnel and in order to give incentives to the qualified staff.

C. INFORMATION ON OPPORTUNITIES FOR MUTUAL SUPPORT IN IMPLEMENTING THE MAR DEL PLATA ACTION PLAN.

The launching of the International Drinking Water Supply and Sanitation Decade (IDWSSD) (1981-1990) is probably the most significant global project that has fostered intensive co-operation and co-ordination among nations involved in water supply development. The Philippine Government has since committed itself to an extension programme designed to install safe and dependable water supply and sanitray facilities within easy reach of all Filipino households, both in the urban and rural communities.

The preparation of the Philippine Rural Water Supply and Sanitation Master Plan exemplified the high degree of co-operation and co-ordination among local agencies and international institutions as well as the participation of the private sector. International institutions like the World Bank, World Health Organization, United Nations Development Programme and local agencies such as the Ministry of Public Works and Highways, Ministry of Health, Rural Waterworks Development Corporation, Local Water Utilities Administration, National Water Resources Council, Ministry of Local Government and Metropolitan Waterworks and Sewerage System as well as private construction and consulting groups participated in the exercise. This master plan is now being updated.

Other water resources development projects being supported by international lending institutions, bilateral technical assistance programmes, grants-in-aid thru the United Nations agency assistance programme are being implemented with the same degree of co-operation and co-ordination among government agencies, private sector and international institutions.

IV. WATER RESOURCES DEVELOPMENT IN INDONESIA*

A. POLICIES, PLANS, PROGRAMMES

1. Synopsis

As a renewable natural resource, water, in Indonesia is considered as the favour of God. This view is reflected in the state philosophy the Pancasila, the Indonesian Constitution (1945) and the Overall Strategy for National Development.

Since the ancient time water resources development has improved progressively. In the first, second and third five year development plans starting from 1969-1970 up to 1983-1984 water resources development in Indonesia played an important role in giving support to other development sectors.

The general management of water resources development has been designed to meet the requirements of the two approaches of the National Development i.e. the Sectoral and Regional approaches.

On sectoral approach, water resources development should provide infrastructure to support other strategic development sectors, while on regional approach water resources development has to be spread over in most of the provinces. There are 27 provinces in Indonesia occupying 1,904,569 km^2 area with more than 13,000 islands and 147,490,298 population according to the 1980 sensus (1985 estimation, Indonesian population are 165,000,000).

The condition mentioned above requires a careful planning for water resources development and their management. In this case water resources development will evolve into a decision making process in multi-complex nature of water resources development with conflicting interest and effect many other development sectors within the National Development Plan.

The experience and conceptual approach for overall water resources development management in Indonesia is discussed in this paper.

2. Introduction

The 1945 Constitution of the Republic of Indonesia, stipulated that: "land, water and natural resources are

---

* Country paper prepared for the thirteenth session of the ESCAP Committee on Natural Resources. This paper has been reproduced without formal editing. The views expressed in it are those of the author and do not necessarily reflect those of the United Nations.

some of the gifts of Almighty God, and shall be controlled by the state and utilized for the optimal welfare of the people in a just and equitable manner"

This principle is the basis for implementing the water resources management which was elaborated in the Republic of Indonesia Law No. 11-1974, dealing with water resources; the Republic of Indonesia Regulation No. 22-1982 dealing with water management; and the Republic of Indonesia Regulation No. 23-1982 dealing with irrigation.

As guideline for implementing the national development, every five year the People's Consultative Assembly sets out an overall strategy of national development or guidelines of States Policy. Based on this guidelines the Government of the Republic of Indonesia issues a five year — development plan document for implementation. Water resources development management, is implemented by the Directorate General of Water Resources Development, Ministry of Public Works, except for goundwater which is developed by the Ministry of Minning and Energy.

3. The national development plan in Indonesia

The objectives, priorities and policy direction for The National Development Plan in Indonesia are set out in the Five Year Development Plan. This is an indicative plan and to a larger extent encompasses development programmes in the public sector. It provides directions of the intended development process and expresses scale of priority but does not specify in detail the blue prints for execution of the programmes and projects.

For the public sector, such details are spelled out in the Government Annual Budget which in effect represents major portion of the annual plan. This procedure allows for an annual review of the development activities, resources flexibility into the plan facilitating adjustments and improvements in the plan whenever changing situations demand, while at the same time maintaining the broad priority. The objectives, priorities and policies specified in the Plan apply to both public and private sector and within this framework the private sector is free to formulate and execute its own plans.

The overall strategy of national development or guidelines of state policy covers the basic blue print of national development, the general blue print of the long range development (25 to 30 years) and the general blue print of the five year development.

In the basic blue print of national development it is stated that the objective of the national development is to establish a prospereus and welfare population based on Pancasila; furthermore the basic national development is the development of the Indonesian citizens as a whole and the development of the Indonesian people. Beside that aspect of national development, the main capital and dominant factors are also stated clearly.

4. Water resources development strategy and policy

Among the 18 national development sectors in Indonesia as stated in the five year development plan, water resources development belongs to the agriculture and water resources sector. As water resources aspects have a social function, the use of water should reach all the requirements of other important development sectors within the national development in a well balanced manner. To achieve this, a good and carefull water resources development planning and implementation is a prerequisite. In this connection as a more detailed elaboration on what has been stated in the overall strategy of national development and the fourth five years development plan, (Plan IV) the following guidelines within the Directorate General for Water Resources Development have been formulated:

4.1. *Water resources development strategy*

In order to achieve the development targets set out in Plan IV and to ensure the overall success of the plan, the infrastructure support on water resources provided by the Directorate General for Water Resources Development, Ministry of Public Works to the following strategic sectors is of great importance:

4.1.1. Agricultural development; particularly food production and export crops.

4.1.2. Industrial development.

4.1.3. Transmigration programme.

4.1.4. The increase of energy supplies.

4.1.5. Communication development.

4.1.6. The raising of public health standards.

4.1.7. The increase of community welfare.

4.1.8. Tourism development.

4.1.9. The increase of work opportunities.

4.1.10. Development of co-operatives.

4.1.11. Improvement of human settlements and the environment.

4.2. *Water resources development policy*

The following development approach has been adopted:

4.2.1. To continue and accelerate water resources development for the benefit of the people, while ensuring that the resources are not over exploited.

4.2.2. Rehabilitation and upgrading of irrigation systems to support the agricultural intensification programmes.

4.2.3. Development of small to medium size irrigation schemes which are quick yielding and where the land owners are agriculturally motivated and are responsive to this form of development.

4.2.4. The development of tidal and non tidal swamps is to be continued using simple techniques. These techniques will be gradually improved.

4.2.5. Phased development in irrigation and reclamation planning so that immediate benefits can be obtained by the farmers at the end of each phase.

4.2.6. Accelerated river improvement and flood protection and surface drainage works programme.

4.2.7. Rehabilitation, upgrading and new construction of surface water reservoirs.

4.2.8. Develop and improve water law and regulation.

5. Planning and programming

Guidelines of state policy and the five years development plan reflected in the sectoral and regional development strategy and policy further translated into water resources development strategy and policy are finally formulated into programmes and projects for implementation.

In water resources development there are 9 programmes consisting of 202 projects.

Programmes and projects may be grouped into two: physical projects and non physical projects or software projects:

The nine programmes in water resources development are:

5.1. Rehabilitation, operation and maintenance for irrigation.

5.2. Development of new irrigation system.

5.3. Swamp reclamation.

5.4. Research on agricultural and water resources development.

5.5. Improvement and efficiency of government apparatus.

5.6. Improvement of the government physical infrastructure.

5.7. Conservation of land, forest, and water.

5.8. Management of natural resources and environment.

5.9. Education on agricultural and water resources aspects.

Programmes no. 5.1, 5.2, 5.3 and 5.7 are physical programmes while programmes no. 5.4, 5.5, 5.6, 5.8 and 5.9 are non physical or software programmes.

From the view point of water resources development programme, physical programmes may also be catagorised as the main programme while the software programmes as the supporting programmes.

For implementation in the fields or region, these 9 programmes are divided into 202 projects. The number of projects may be increased or decreased according to the necessity of annual implementation. In the Central Government, programmes, projects are managed and supervised by the Director General directly or through the Directorate and/or the regional extension office of the Ministry of Public Works concerned.

6. Implementation

The sequences of annual implementation of water resources development projects go through the process of state budget, physical implementation of programmes and projects and supervision of construction.

6.1. *Progress of implementation*

The progress of implementation on water resources development since 1983 are reported in the following supporting papers attached to this Country Paper:

IV.B.   Irrigation

Lowland development (not reproduced in this volume)

X   Ground water development in Indonesia

IV.C.   Water supply

IV.D.   Flood control

IV.E   Hydropower

IV.F.   Water quality and pollution control

XIV   Environmental issues of water resources development in Indonesia

Cartography and remote sensing (not reproduced in this volume)

Training (not reproduced in this volume)

7. Water resources development Project-Monitoring and Evaluation (PME)

7.1. For monitoring of all water resources development projects, in all management level, a monitoring system has been introduced within the Directorate General of Water Resources Development.

There are five levels of monitoring and evaluation: level A (physical and financial progress), level B (operation and maintenance — water management), level C (irrigated crop production), level D (farm — income generation and management) and level E (socio economic impact). Monitoring systems for levels A and B are already in place while levels C, D and E are being developed.

The objectives of PME are to supply accurate, reliable, relevant, timely and action-oriented data for:

(a)   The planning of water resources project including irrigation, river works, swamp development and power prior to implementation;

(b)   Supplying operational information to managers responsible for implementation, operation and maintenance and crop production of projects; and

(c)   Evaluating the degree of success of the implemented project, comparing performance with targets and objectives set at the time of project appraisal and improving planning of similar projects.

7.2. *Conceptual framework for PME*

7.2.1. *Basic consideration*

(a)   Instutional aspects.

The introduction of a full Project Monitoring and Evaluation system (PME) may require some organizational adjustments within the executing agencies and increased co-ordination and co-operation between different government agencies.

It is therefore improtant to understand the working relationship between DGWRD and government agencies responsible for meeting national development targets. Furthermore, with the DG's emphasis on PME's functions as a management tool, it is necessary to increase understanding and improve capabilities of the management.

(b)   Current monitoring and evaluation.

Level A

A monitoring system for level A (physical and financial progress) is already in place in DGWRD using a format.

These formats are submitted by project officers to DGWRD on a quarterly basis. Information from them is passed to the Ministry of Finance, and to DPP. The system covers PME level A. It will remain as a separate but related system outside the establishment of the system for levels C, D and E monitoring and evaluation. When finance is available for the project, the monitoring and evaluation on progress of construction and expenditure is initiated.

This will continue up to the completion of the project.

At the project level the technical divisions are responsible for assembling the data required while the Administrative divisions complete the forms and transmit them to DGWRD.

Level B.

Monitoring and evaluation of operation and maintenance are the responsibility of DGWRD. Improvements are required in these aspects for example regarding water availability and use, and maintenance of irrigation systems.

Level C and D

Primary data collection at levels C and D is the responsibility of agencies other than DGWRD, usually at the provincial levels.

For example for agriculture at kabupaten level production statistics are co-ordinated by the Bureau of Statistics assisted by Ministry of Agriculture officers who collect most of their data from the Ministry's extension service. The data includes both historical data and forecasts. The kabupaten data is forwarded to the Governor's office monthly to be cleared by all levels of authority. At present this monitoring is carried out to conform with administrative boundaries and is not project specific.

This data is used by DGWRD for project preparation and appraisal and for Project Completion Reports (PCR).

It appears that very little continuous monitoring has been carried out on a systematic basis that would be useful to project management at levels B, C and D and experience with the PCR's produced by DPP has shown clearly that the data available for evaluation purposes is not satisfactory, mainly because the data is not project specific. One of the main criteria used in designing the conceptual framework is the requirement that data should meet the test of supplying information useful to management.

Level E.

Several benchmark surveys have been carried out incorporating level E indicators in combined levels C, B and E surveys by DGWRD.

The information from these surveys is useful for planning purpose but has limited applicability as an aid to project management.

7.2.2.   *Primary or secondary data for levels C and D*

It has been decided that in designing a PME framework for levels C & D, the primary or secondary data should depend on the quality and quantity of secondary data available.

Field testing has shown that secondary data can be obtained on most of the indicators at level C and D. In table below secondary data sources servicing the main information requirements at these levels are shown.

Table: Level C and D (PME) – Secondary Data Sources

Information Required	Data Source	Time Scale
1. *Services*		
Water Users Associations	DPU (P) Agriculture/Local Government:	Seasonal
Extension	Agriculture Programmes	Seasonal
Marketing Facilities	Agriculture Co-operatives	
Research	Agriculture	Seasonal
2. *Production Inputs*		
Credit	Peoples Bank	Seasonal
Labour	Agriculture	
Seed	Agriculture Co-operatives	Seasonal
Fertilizer	Agriculture Co-operatives	Seasonal
Chemicals	Agriculture Co-operatives	Seasonal
Packing Materials	Agriculture Co-operatives	Seasonal
Transport	Farmers/Private Traders	Seasonal
Taxes	Local Government	Seasonal
Capital Costs	Farmers	Seasonal
3. *Outputs*		
Area Planted	Agriculture	Seasonal
Area Harvested	Agriculture	Seasonal
Yields	Agriculture	
Production	Agriculture	
Prices	Bulog; Co-operatives Private Enterprise	Seasonal
Income	Surveys	Seasonal

The main advantages of using secondary data are:

(a) Indonesia has a well developed data collection system in the agricultural sector, which can supply information of reasonable quality for most level C and D indicators, particularly for planning purposes, at low cost.

(b) The resources required to establish a secondary data system are far less than those required for a primary data system.

The disadvantages of secondary data are:

(a) Data is collected and processed too late for immediate management information needs.

(b) Since data is generally collected for estimates of quantities on an administrative boundary basis it is not always of suitable quality and has to be adjusted to service the needs of project and/or technical irrigation boundaries.

The advantages of using secondary data cannot be ignored and with the co-operation of the agencies responsible for collecting the primary data, improvements for project specific monitoring should be possible.

For example, it might be possible to persuade the agency concerned to increase its sampling density for yield estimation in project areas.

The advantages of using primary data are greater accuracy and timeliness of the data for management information purposes. The main disavantage is cost. Nonetheless because of the emphasis on PME as a management information system supplying data for decision makers in the short, medium and long term, emphasis has to be placed on primary data collection. In the initial stages of the PME programme for DGWRD it is sensible to use both primary and secondary data sources. Field testing of models in the near future is recommended for improving the system and refining design. In future years the emphasis placed on secondary or primary data collection can be adjusted as dictated by experience.

7.2.3.   *Co-operation between DGWRD with other agencies*

The requirements of the various agencies may be different. For instance DGWRD requires data on an irrigation boundary and project specific basis, where as the Ministry of Agriculture requires and collects data in conformity with administrative boundaries. DGWRD has the responsibility (through the Directorate of Planning and Programming) for project preparation and appraisal and Project Completion Reports incorporating all aspects of project design and evaluation and, therefore, requires project specific monitoring data. One of the main features of data

collection and analysis requiring considerable attention is the monitoring of the effects of irrigation development on crop production and farm incomes. In this regard levels B, C and D are inseparable and the monitoring system requires careful treatment of this issue.

7.3.   *The example of irrigation*

Continuous monitoring and evaluation of irrigated crop production is a relatively new subject. However the irrigation operations and farming practices are fairly advanced, so a balance has to be struck between simplicity and sophistication.

7.3.1.   *Level B: Operation and maintenance*

The method of operating the physical system depends to a large extent on the way the facilities are designed. Frequencies, and scale of maintenance necessary, are also important. However, within the limits of the technical design, the responsibility for operation and maintenance does allow substantial scope for increasing system efficiency, supply reliability, area benefitted and for devising operation schedules that serve the beneficiaries more effectively. Information feedback on results of operations decisions (for instance in the case of irrigation information on cropping patterns, field applications, water discipline, and farmer co-operation) may help to improve technical, performance. A design for monitoring and evaluation facilities should assist management decision-makers at level C in supplying them with information on the beneficiaries and with feedback on the seasonal performance.

7.3.2.   *Level C: Physical benefits*

Physical benefits of water resources projects may include: increased crop production due to irrigation, flood control or swampy area development; or hydro power; or domestic, municipal and industrial supplies, etc. Using an irrigation project as an example, a basic objective is the provision of water in a controlled manner to provide a basis to improve crop yields over the maximum area allowed by the available water resources.

The cropping index is an efficient indicator for level B, the performance of O & M management, but optimum crop yields require also inputs such as seeds, fertilizers, agrochemicals, as well as extension and credit services. The attainment of the production goals of the project demands that irrigation water, input supplies, and farm services are made available to the beneficiaries in a timely and co-ordinated manner.

The monitoring system should provide, sufficient data on only a few selected key indicators that will reflect the condition of the main factors affecting irrigated crop production.

The tendency to generate data and attempts to pursue ultimate levels of accuracy in its measurement, must be resisted, particularly in the formative years of the system; due regard must be given to the ability of management to absorb the data, and to use it. The inexperience of those responsible for carrying out the work, must also be taken into account. The result of PME have to meet the demands of agencies other than DGWRD, therefore, co-ordination is required.

7.4. *Resources*

PME requires:

(a) A suitably staffed and equipped central PME unit in DGWRD.

(b) Project PME units, (including survey teams for selected primary data projects).

(c) Consultants with PME skills, and knowledge.

(d) Finance.

7.5. *The ideal PME programme*

DGWRD has defined the following levels of PME to assist in proposing a system and a programme for implementation.

7.5.1. *Level A: Construction of physical facilities*

At this level, information requirements may include the application of financial, labour, staff, equipment and other material resources and as inputs produced through appropriate management actions, the physical facilities according to design, staying within budget estimates and completing the work on time. The information system for this engineering and cost accounting aspect is generally already in place in DGWRD.

Information is required at critical times during each and every cropping season in view of the ever changing environmental and economic factors. Seasonal reviews, in the form of short-term on-going evaluation are necessary. The farmer would promote co-ordination among various management entities in charge of specific areas of responsibilities; the latter is helpful to preparing integrated agricultural development plans for the following crop season. In many instances, these constitute the major role of a

monitoring and evaluation facility for an irrigation project. These aspects are similar for any project that produces agricultural benefits.

7.5.2. *Level D: Management and income generation*

The interest of beneficiaries for which substantial public investments have been made, can be maintained if their efforts are rewarded with increased net income. This vital goal depends naturally on the appropriate and efficient use of the purchased inputs, as well as adequate marketing channels and favourable terms of trade between inputs and products. Unfavourable marketing and economic situations may result in shortfalls in the various project targets. Information on management and profit margins would be useful for devising ways and means for assisting beneficiaries in maintaining their enterprises for sustaining the economic justifications of the investment, even under adverse situations.

7.5.3. *Level E: Attainment of socio-economic development goals*

Increase in physical benefits, and rise in income have an impact beyond the direct beneficiaries of the irrigation project. Such impact may include: positive improvement in land values creating the necessary environment for spontaneous development; developing agricultural land for those most in need, improvement in employment opportunities for the landless as hired labourers in intensified agricultural practices; changing income distribution among members of the society.

These developments guide policy formulation at the regional and national level. The intended and unanticipated effects and impact of development effort should, therefore, be carefully monitored and analyzed.

Apart from these five levels of management information requirements, there is, in addition, the need for examining other manifestations of project results: equity in benefit distribution, participation of beneficiaries in decisions affecting them, dynamic technological change and a host of sociological considerations. To the extent that these may affect project, these issues should also be addressed by the monitoring and evaluation system.

A comprehensive monitoring and evaluation programme would include PME activities for all projects at all the various stages of a project as depicted in the following Table:

Table: Levels of PME at the successive stages of a project.

Stages of project		Activities
1. Pre-implementation period (survey and design, feasibility report, appraisal report stage).	A, B, C, D, E.	Benchamark data collection and analysis. Note Benchamark, survey for levels C, D, E should be completed before the appraisal report is written.
2. Implementation period (construction of infrastructure and start of operation and maintenance)	A, B, C, D, E.	Continuous data collection and analysis each season and every year.
3. Project Completion (Completion of construction of physical works).	A, B, C, D, E.	Ex-post evaluation (project completion report)
4. Project completion to full development.	A, B, C, D	Continuous data collection and analysis
5. Full development	A, B, C, D, E.	Ex-post evaluation (full development report)

7.6. *PME Programme*

7.6.1. *General approach*

In summary, in designing the conceptual frame work for PME, the following points have to be taken into account.

(a) The objectives of PME (see introduction and section 7.1) and the managerial, planning and evaluation requirements of DGWRD.

(b) The fact that level A monitoring is already in place and that level B monitoring is the responsibility of the project and provincial irrigation serivices O & M Divisions. Therefore the PME system under consideration is confined to levels C, D and E.

(c) It is desirable, in the initial stages of the PME program that both primary and secondary data are collected, utilising the advantages of both.

(d) DGWRD requires its own monitoring system for data collection for project preparation, appraisal, and management information on effects of water resources development and for evaluation (in particular for Project Completion Reports).

(e) DGWRD has resource constraints of manpower and finance. Therefore a compromise has to be struck between cost, scale and accuracy.

Taking this factors into consideration the PME program requires two classes of projects:

(1) A PME secondary data program which would be relatively inexpensive and could be applied to a fairly large number of projects.

(2) Primary data project with the emphasis on monitoring as an aid to management. Primary data projects would have two categories:

2.1. Level C and D surveys carried out on selected projects.

2.2. Level E socio-economic surveys carried out on a few selected projects.

7.6.2. *Secondary Data Program Levels C & D*

A simple PME system based on secondary data has been developed for application on a wide range of projects, with particular reference to agriculture. It should be clearly understood that although the system is simple it will require considerable diligence and effort to apply as it involves the collection of a large amount of data. It requires additional field testing which could lead to changes in its design.

Data on the following key indicators should be collected every season: data sheets have been designed and include the following:

C1 Series: Basic PME information sheet and project inventory.

C2 Series Level C agriculture production inputs:

C2.1. Water
C2.2. Labour
C2.3. Credit
C2.4. Seed
C2.5. Chemicals (Pesticides)
C2.6. Chemicals (Rodenticides)
C2.7. Fertilizers (Ammonium Nitrate or Urea)
C2.8. Fertilizers (TSP)

C3. Series Level C agricultural production outputs:

C3.1. Area planted
C3.2. Area harvested
C3.3. Yield
C3.4. Production

D1 Series Level D farmers incomes:

D1.1. Farm prices
D1.2. Farm production income

D2 Series Level D project agricultural production: Support services:

– Number of co-operatives
– Number of rice mills
– Number of extension workers
– Number P3AS
– Land tenure

Actual quantities are compared with targets set at the beginning of each season.

7.6.3. *Primary data project Levels C, D and E*

Where surveys are considered necessary and are included in the PME, such projects are referred to as "primary data projects" using primary data as the data base. Surveys may be conducted to obtain Levels C and D data or Level E data. At Level C and D the same indicators would be used as for the secondary data programme with additional detail on some aspects. A greater level of accuracy and the timely production of data for management purposes would be expected.

For other water resources projects a similar system would be used, with appropriate indicators.

7.6.4. *Main users of PME information*

The main users of PME information would be:
– Those working in projects, whose task is to operate the monitoring and/or evaluation system.

– Those responsible for management of the project.

– Those responsible for the post-project operation and maintenance of project facilities.

– Local organisation supplying inputs to projects or those with executive responsibility for project inputs e.g. production committees.

– Those with responsibility within DPP in the Directorate General of Water Resources Development whose task is to monitoring and evaluate projects.

– Other GOI agencies and the Ministry of Agriculture.

– Aid agencies if any.

7.7. *Procedures*

Level A PME is already in place in DGWRD. Level B (Water management) is a separate exercise providing information which is relevant for PME at Levels C and D. Procedures for levels C, D and E are described in this section.

7.7.1.   *Secondary data programme (Levels C and D)*

The following sequence of events is necessary to operate a simple PME system based on secondary data:

1. Terms of reference for PME for each proejct are written by the central unit.

2. PME field units are established.

3. PME field units receive training.

4. Each season the central PME unit sends forms to the field units.

5. The field units record targets for each key indicator as set by the respective agencies.

6. Each season the field units fill in the secondary data forms.

7. Copies of the data and written summaries are sent to the central PME unit, and other agencies concerned.

8. Production staff, the central PME unit and the agencies concerned take action on each season's data and written summaries.

9. Forms for the next season are sent out to each field unit by the central PME unit and the cycle begins again.

10. The results are used for project planning and evaluation.

7.7.2. *Primary data programme (Levels C and D)*

The following sequence of events is necessary to operate PME primary data programme at Levels C and D.

1. Terms of reference and, if necessary, invitation document for consultancy services for PME are set specifically for each project.

2. The field unit or consultant prepares a proposal for PME.

3. The proposal is considered by the central PME unit of DGWRD.

4. If the proposal is approved, financial negotiations between the field unit or consultant, and DGWRD takes place.

5. If financial agreement is reached the field unit or consultant appoints the necessary staff.

6. The field unit staff receive training.

7. Surveys are carried out each season as required.

8. Data and report are presented to the central PME unit and the agencies concerned for reaction and follow up.

9. The results are used for project planning evaluation and to improve project management and implementation.

7.7.3. *Primary data project (Level E)*

The following sequence of events is necessary PME for primary data programme at Level E:

1. Invitation documents for consultancy services for Level E PME are drawn up for each project by the central PME unit.

2. The consultants produce proposals.

3. These proposals are considered by the central PME unit.

4. After negotiation the consultants are selected to undertake the study.

5. The study is undertaken.

6. The results of the study are considered by the project, the central PME unit of DPP and the agencies concerned.

7. The results of the study are used in the planning and evaluation of the project.

7.8. *Methodology*

7.8.1. *Secondary data programme (Levels C and D)*

All data for the programme is collected from the various secondary data sources.

The central PME unit of DPP has compiled a standard set of forms to be filled in each season by the field unit.

Actual data for each key indicator are compared to targets set before the start of each season, for each key indicator.

7.8.2. *Primary data projects (Levels C and D)*

Data are collected from primary source, normally by direct farmer interviews. The methodology is described in the following subsections.

7.8.3. *Level C programme*

(a) Information required.

In figure 1 below the information required at Level C, possible data sources for the information and users of the data are shown in summary form.

The central PME unit has the responsibility to draw up a standard questionnaire for use on water resources projects. The number of questions asked for any particular study will depend on the resources available including money and skills.

(b) Institutional requirements

Institutional capability at two levels is required.

Staff Member	Activity
1. Central M & E Unit	
Head of PME Unit	Administrative and Management.
Irrigation Agronomist	Technical direction of Level C programme.
Agricultural Economist	Technical direction of Levels D & E Programme and overall technical direction.
Data Processor	Technical direction and supervision of data processing and analysis.
Secretaries Data clerks	

2. Seksi * M & E cells (each)

Head of field cell	Management of cell and maintaining data ledger.
Supervisor	Supervision of enumerators.
Enumerators	Enumeration: field processing of Level C data.

The surveys would be carried out by survey teams attached to the Seksi, supervised by the central M & E unit.

*DGWRD irrigation sections covering roughly the same area as a Kabupaten (local government administrative district)

8. Training, research and development

To improve the capability of the DGWRD staff in conducting water resources development, various training has been facilitated as the following:

8.1. CGSC (Construction Guidance Service Centre)

8.1.1. *Objective:* Supporting the development of agriculture infrastructure in increasing food production and upgrading of irrigation construction technology in Indonesia.

8.1.2. *Main activities:*
(1) Monitoring of irrigation project construction.
(2) Technical information services.
(3) Standardization (quality test, cost analysis, procedure).
(4) Computer services, in supporting data supervision and analysis.
(5) Laboratory test:
 – Soil test, concrete, asphalt, material and and quality.
 – Hydraulic laboratory management.
(6) Training especially "know-how" of construction supervisors.

8.1.3. *Information services (within the frame work of exchange of information):*

– facilities: data storage with "micro-filming" system (using micro photo facilities), storage, library using computer index.

– form of information:
Technical information brochure (general, standing procedure, technical criteria).
regular magazine/periodical (irrigation & drainage, and advance technology in water resources development).

– Methods of spreading up the technology/information:
periodic training and through project execution (i.e. manual, standard and regulation).

– Standard manual model, still being prepared:
 – material specification and construction work.
 – construction methods.
 – construction monitoring.
 – supervisory procedures.
 – operation and maintenance procedures of equipment and machines.
 – heavy equipment manual.

8.1.4. *Research and development:*
– research, laboratory test, model test, computer application studies, etc.

8.1.5. *Training facilities:*
– training in construction of irrigation structure.
– form of activities, discussion, workshop, seminar, symposium and exercises.
– supporting facilities: dormitory, library, audio visual equipment, and others.

8.1.6. *Others:*
– training is also organized for Asian countries and includes seminars and field trips.

8.2. VSTC (Volcanic Sabo Technical Centre)

8.2.1. *Objective:*
– development of sabo techniques in Indonesia.
– transfer of technology, spread the information and training.

8.2.2. *Main activities:*
– research and development, especially in the flood control techniques, lava and volcanic activities.
– spreading information and technology through training and exercise.

8.2.3. *Training:*
Sabo engineering (survey, planning, hydraulic model test), Sabo project management, volcanic monitoring system (through programmes: general course, intensive course and comprehensive course).

8.2.4. *Supporting facilities:*
– concrete laboratory.
– soil laboratory.
– geotechnical laboratory.
– hydraulic laboratory.

8.3. *Hydraulic laboratory in solo*

8.3.1.   *Objective:*
To upgrade knowledge in the field of hydraulic structure models, structure model test, reporting system, evaluation and interpretation of model test.

8.3.2.   *Main activities:*
— Hydraulic scale model, sediment transport, energy dissipator, undersluice and sediment trap.
— Laboratory exercises.
— Field exercises.
— Hydraulic laboratory test.

8.3.3.   *Information services (within the frame work of exchange of information):*
— periodical information.
— training & exercises, project execution (manual, existing standard regulation).

8.3.4.   *Research and development:*
— Laboratory test, model test, interpretation of model test.

8.3.5.   *Training facilities:*
— Accomodation, transport, library, exercise equipment.
— Laboratory facilities including field laboratory.

8.3.6.   *Others:*
seminars, field trips.

8.4. *Water resources research development*

8.4.1.   *Objectives:*
— to increase the ability in water resources development.
— transfer of technology.
— to increase the ability in water resources research and development.
— to execute seminars, workshop, conference, study tour, etc.

8.4.2.   *Exercise programme/short term non formal education:*

(1) Computer application in water resources development.
(2) Hydraulic model test for hydraulic structures.
(3) Course on water quality monitoring.
(4) Engineering geology explorations for hydraulic structure design.
(5) Theory and training of laboratory and field investigation of soils.

(6) Optimization techniques in water resources development.
(7) Measurement and calculation of discharge and reservoir sedimentation.
(8) Dam inspection in Java.

8.4.3.   *Information services (within the frame work of exchange of information):*

— Facilities:
storage data using computer system (complete system), library, storage, using "micro-filming" system.
— Form of information:
 — publication/bulletin information techniques (general, procedure standard, technical criteria).
 — publication periodical/bulletin in hydrology, groundwater, water quality and flood control.
— Spreading technology/information methods:
 — periodical training and through project execution (i.e. manual, regulation and standard).
 — standard manual model or regulation.

8.4.4.   *Research and development:*
— Laboratory test research, model test investigation and application; computer studies, etc.

8.4.5.   *Training facilities:*

(1) Training on computer application of water resources development.

(a) Objectives:
to increase knowledge and ability in computer application in water resources development.

(b) Form of training:
— Lectures and workshops, introduction to computer and fortran language.
— Application of programme in hydrology, hydraulics, mathematics, statistics and computer graphics.
— Development of computer programmes in water resources development.

(c) Facilities:
— Mini computer Honeywell, Bull Mini 6 (includes plotter and digitizer).
— Micro Computer Apple IIe and Superbrain.
— Programmes for water resources development, statistics mathematics and computer graphics.
— Lecture rooms.
— Library.

(2) Training "Hydraulic Model Test for Hydraulic Structures".

(a) Objectives:

To increase ability in hydraulic structure models, structure model test, reporting system, evaluation and structure model test interpretation.

(b) Form of training:
- Lectures in Hydraulic Scale Model, Sediment transport. Energy Dissipator, Underslice and Sediment trap.
- Laboratory practices.
- Field practices.

(c) Facilities:
- laboratory facilities.
- lecture rooms.
- library.

(3) Training on "water Quality Monitoring".

(a) Objectives:

to increase ability in water quality management and water quality monitoring.

(b) Form of training:
- Lectures:
- water quality management.
- water quality monitoring for natural water and industrial waste.
- water quality analysis.
- Field practice:
- water quality sampling.
- field measurement and analysis
- water sample transportation.

- Laboratory practice:
- water quality analysis with atomic absorption spectrophotometer.
- water quality analysis with U – Vis Spectrophotometer.
- Miscellaneous analysis.

(4) Training on engineering geology explorations for hydraulic structures design.

(a) Objectives: to increase ability:
- Base knowledge in geology and technical geology especially in relation to structure designing/hydraulic.
- Field practice, includes core driling, field permeability test, standard penetration test, sampling, grouting test.
- Laboratory of technical geology and me--chanical rock.
- Data analysis and technical report writing.

(b) Form of training:
- Lectures on introduction to geology, technical geology, field test, laboratory test, data analysis and technical report writing.
- Field practice.
- Laboratory practice.
- Workshop.

(c) Facilities:
- Lecture rooms.
- Laboratory.
- Field test equipment.
- Library.

(5) Theory and training of laboratory and field investiation of Soil Mechanics.

(a) Objectives:

to increase the ability in the field of laboratory trial methods and soil mechanic test in the field.

(b) Form of training:
- Lectures on soil mechanics, trials in laboratory and field test.
- Field practice (sounding, boring, quality control instrumentation).
- Laboratory practice: Direct shear, triareal, consolidation, compaction, grain size analysis, permeability.

(c) Facilities:
- Lecture rooms.
- Soil mechanics laboratory.
- Field test equipment.
- Library.

(6) Training optimization technique on water resources development.

(a) Objective: to increase the knowledge on:
- optimization on planning and operating authorities.
- optimization of the irrigation water use, drinking water and others.
- water resources development planning.

(b) Form of training:
- Lecture on optimization technique for resources management and lectures on planning and analysis of water resources system.
- Discussion.
- Workshop.
- Field trip.

(c) Facilities:
  – Lecture rooms.
  – Library.

(7) Training measurement and calculation of discharge and reservoir sedimentation.

  (a) Objectives:
    Introduction to measurement methods, analysis, discharge data, and sediment, reservoirs soundings in office and in the field.

  (b) For of training:
    – Lecture on theory of measurement and discharge calculation and reservoir sedimentation.
    – Field practice.

  (c) Facilities:
    – Lecture rooms.
    – measurement equipment.
    – library.

(8) Training/short visit/dam inspection in Java.

  (a) Objectives:
    – transfer of knowledge in weirs/dam techniques.
    – co-operation in weirs/dam techniques among the developing countries.

  (b) Form of training:
    – Studies and discussion on dam and weirs.
    – Visit to weirs and dams in Java.

  (c) Facilities:
    – vehicles.
    – discussion rooms.
    – library.

(9) Others.
    Water resources research development carried out training, seminars, and field trip for ASEAN countries.

8.5. *PLAV (Audio Visual Training Project)*

8.5.1. *Main activities:*
  (1) operation and maintenance training at "juru" (gate operator) level.

  (2) O & M training at chief of "juru" level.

  (3) O & M training at groundwater development.

  (4) training on the use of irrigation water at the farm level for water association (P3A).

  (5) training for observer.

8.5.2. *Information services:*

  – Form of information.

    – programme arrangement on O & M problems, guideline and manual for O & M staff, training to be used in Regional Training Centres and Provincial Public Works.

Some information on specific TCDC capacities are provided in table at next page.

B. IRRIGATION

1. Objectives

(1) Irrigation is artificial supplying of water to ensure the optimum growth of plants or crops. Rice is a staple food in Indonesia. Paddy/Rice is the most water demanding crop compared to the other food crops. Experiences proved that the best cultivated method for rice in order to get optimum yield is to grow on impounding water field. To consider the above mentioned, the main purpose or objective of irrigation development in Indonesia is focused to irrigate the rice farm field to support rice production for staple food.

(2) Irrigation development is part of water resources development in which the objectives are not only to support rice production but also to support other sectors, to provide raw water for drinking water supply, industrial water, domestic use, towns and cities, sanitation, fishery (fresh and brackish) and mini hydropower.

2. Irrigation method

(1) Most irrigation methods for rice cultivation are by flooding or impounding on a continous basis and to some extent it is also done by intermittent system especially during the shortage of water usually in dry season.

(2) The crop pattern is arranged double cropping pattern yearly but in several irrigation area it does not fulfill the pattern due to shortage of water. In such case the crop pattern is arranged in the monsoon season fully for rice crop and in dry season partly for rice and other upland crops (cassava, soyabean, green bean, onion, sweet potato, potato, vegetable, tomato, others food crops, tobacco and cotton).

(3) Irrigation method for upland crops usually used is intermittent flooding method or manual showering method.

Information on the specific capacities of TCDC activities in the fields of water resources development

No.	Specification	Aspect Of Water Resources Development					Remarks
		Hydrology	Groundwater Dev. & Hydrogeology	Water Quality Management	Flood Control	Equipment, Tools and Machinery	
1	2	3	4	5	6	7	8
1.	Expert Services	available in some institutions and agencies	limited (in ground water dev. project, water resources research and development centre)	limited (just available in water resources research & development center)	relatively available (in some project of river basin development)	limited	
2.	Equipment & Machinary	available for measuring, monitoring and data collecting of hydrometeorology aspects	survey equipment for the activities of investigation, exploration and exploitation of ground water and development	survey & laboratory analysis equipment in the aspect of water quality	equipment & machinary in the stages of survey, design and project implementation	heavy equipment to support the activities in WRD. Project. (Irrigation, Swamp development, flood control project, etc).	
3.	Exchange of information, research publication	research publication of the National network of hydrometeorology, project report, etc.	− project report − manual	− water quality monitoring report − manual, standard and guidelines of water quality − water pollution monitoring	− project report, standard and guidelines	− manual, guidelines and standard in heavy equipment O&M	

Some training, research and development centres which deal in improving the staff capabilities under the guidance of the water resources research and development centre in Bandung such as:

   − CGSC (construction Guidance Survice Centre) − Jakarta.
   − VSTC (Volcanic Sabo Technical Centre) − Yogya.
   − Hydraulic laboratory − S a l a
   − Hydraulic model test − Bandung
   − Audio visual training centre − Surabaya.
   − Water Resources Research and Development Centre − Bandung.

with aspects of:
   − Computer application
   − Water quality monitoring
   − Geology exploration
   − Soil mechanics
   − Optimation techniques of water resources development.
   − Discharge and reservoir sedimentation.

3. Irrigation water resources system

There are three major water resources for irrigation development. These are surface water, swampy areas and ground water.

(1) Surface Irrigation System gets water supply from the rivers, lakes and reservoirs.

(2) Swampy Area Irrigation System gets irrigation water supply from swampy lands.

(3) Ground Water Irrigation System uses ground water.

4. Irrigation supply system

There are three types of irrigation supply systems.

(1) Gravity irrigation system; Pumped or Lifted Irrigation System, Tidal Irrigation System .

5. Technical classification system

(1) The technical system, where water delivery can be measured and controlled, is the most complete system with measuring devices and gates on every required point. It has separate irrigation and drainage network and a tertiary

system developed with all the related facilities. The delivery and distribution efficiency ranges between 50 per cent to 60 per cent.

(2) The semi-technical system, where water delivery can be controlled but measured only at the headworks, does not always have some appurtenant structures (side spillway, desilting basin, etc.), even though these are usually necessary; can be called semi-complete system. Drainage networks are not separated from irrigation networks, or frequently not developed at all in this system. Although the semi-technical system has a tertiary system, it does not meet design criteria of technical systems for canal and structure density. Its efficiency therefore is lower, ranging from 40 per cent to 50 per cent. The command area of a semi-technical system can usually reach about 2,000 ha.

(3) Simple Irrigation System. Water delivery of a simple irrigation system can not be controlled and measured although most of the systems have a gate constructed at the head works to prevent flooding into canals.

The headworks is a non-permanent structure made from the cheapest local materials. The aim of this type is to bring water from its nearest source to the farm field by the simplest means and the lowest cost. Typically this type of system does not cover more than 500 ha.

6. Irrigation development programme in I, II, III Five Year Development Plan

(1) In general, growth in rice production can be attributed to increases in harvested areas facililated by higher cropping intensities through irrigation activities, and to introduction of high yielding varieties (HYVS) and other agricultural inputs. The exact inputs of each factor is difficult to identify.

(2) Activities in irrigation development can be divided by two main programmes.

— Extensification is to extend new irrigation areas

— Intensification is to upgrade existing irrigation system.

(3) Irrigation inventory in September 1982 which was about the end of third year of Third Five Year Development Plan shows the position of irrigation system managed by Government as listed in table 1 and can be summarized as follows.

— Total irrigation area   4,659,743 ha
— Total potential irrigated area consist of
    o   Technical system   2,095,850 ha
    o   Semi-technical system   1,123,088 ha
    o   Simple irrigation system   976,359 ha
        Total   4,195,297 ha
— Total unpotential area   464,446 ha
— Total number of irrigation areas are   5,780 nos
    and average irrigation area size is   806 ha

(4) 2,680,495 ha (64 per cent) out of 4,195,297 ha potential irrigation area was in Java, 844,853 ha (20 per cent) was in Sumatra, 332,717 ha (8 per cent) was in Sulawesi, and the rest (8 per cent) in other islands.

(5) 1,728,962 ha (82 per cent) out of Technical irrigation system was in Java.

Table 1. Government Recapitulation, Irrigation Inventory September 1982

| Province | Commanded Area | Potential | | | | Unpotential Area | Number of Scheme | Average Commanded Area/Irr. Scheme |
		Area	Technical	Semi Technical	Simple			
1	2	3	4	5	6	7	8	9
D.K.I. Jaya	25 108	20 202	0	5 716	14 486	4 906	28	897
Java Barat	921 335	888 391	618 582	138 752	131 057	32 944	787	1 171
Java Tengah	813 234	756 278	456 691	100 322	199 865	56 956	746	1 030
D.I. Yogyakarta	67 733	65 377	0	41 498	23 879	2 356	96	705
Java Timur	959 547	950 247	654 289	131 196	164 762	9 300	779	1 232
Total Java	2 786 957	2 680 495	1 728 962	417 484	534 049	106 462	2 436	1 144
D.I. Aceh	193 817	154 233	0	75 432	78 801	39 584	241	804
Sumatera Utara	282 486	205 210	70 816	102 925	31 469	77 276	547	516
Sumatera Barat	230 521	205 892	9 948	84 200	111 744	24 629	907	254
Lampung	166 686	139 686	119 216	19 882	0	27 588	81	2 058
Sumatera Lainnya	164 982	140 420	34 929	70 746	34 745	24 562	452	365
Total Sumatera	1 038 492	844 853	234 909	253 185	256 759	193 639	2 228	466
Sulawesi Selatan	276 637	210 079	38 966	117 809	53 304	66 558	179	1 545
Sulawesi Lainnya	127 811	122 638	25 800	62 044	34 794	5 173	218	586
Total Sulawesi	404 448	332 717	64 766	179 853	89 098	71 731	397	1 019
Nusa Tenggara Barat	159 942	141 901	50 408	82 571	8 922	18 041	245	653
Other Province	269 904	195 331	16 805	89 995	88 531	74 573	474	563
Total	4 659 743	4 195 297	2 095 297	1 123 083	976 359	464 446	5 780	806

Table 2: Rice Field Full & Not Full Development

Inventory September 1982

| Province | Potential Area (Ha) | Rice Field Full Devt. (Ha) | Rice Field Undeveloped Yet | | | All of PTSD |
			PISD (Ha)	PTBD (Ha)	Jumlah	
DKI Jaya	20 202	8 483	0	11 719	11 719	0
Java Barat	888 391	794 321	13 190	80 889	94 079	446 232
Java Tengah	756 278	704 465	549	51 264	51 813	125 608
D.I. Yogyakarta	65 317	59 143	333	5 901	6 234	13 216
Java Timur	950 247	933 288	1 153	15 806	16 959	191 018
Total Java	2 680 495	2 499 691	15 225	165 579	180 804	776 074
Dista Aceh	154 233	131 731	67	22 435	22 502	8 573
Sumatera Utara	205 210	163 167	849	41 194	42 043	18 600
Sumatera Barat	205 892	155 721	9 500	40 671	50 171	51 122
Lampung	139 098	75 435	15 504	48 159	63 663	45 215
Sumatera Lainnya	140 420	85 495	9 433	45 492	54 925	41 984
Total Sumatera	844 353	611 549	35 353	197 951	233 304	165 494
Sulawesi Selatan	210 079	176 260	13 159	20 660	33 819	77 283
Sulawesi Lainnya	122 638	71 959	17 413	33 266	50 679	48 156
Total Sulawesi	332 717	248 219	30 572	53 926	84 498	125 439
N.T.B.	141 901	125 266	1 025	15 610	16 635	17 377
Other Province	195 331	113 723	11 289	70 319	81 608	67 490
Total	4 195 297	3 598 448	93 464	563 385	596 849	1 151 874

(6) Based on the inventory, 596,849 ha (14 per cent) out of irrigation potential area was not coverted yet to wet rice field. (table 2).

(7) Positions of Government irrigation system before First Five Year Development Plan based on inventory done in 1968 are listed on table 3 and is about 3,390,297 ha consisting of

—	Technical irrigation system	1,451,349 ha
—	Semi technical irrigation system	1,298,337 ha
—	Simple irrigation system	640,611 ha
	Total =	3,390,297 ha

Table 3. Government irrigation area, 1968, 1981 & 1982

Irrigation network	Year 1968 (ha)	Year 1981 (ha)	Year 1982 (ha)	Increasing (82-68) (ha)
Technical	1 451 349	1 968 663	2 095 850	+ 644 501
Semi technical	1 258 337	1 159 610	1 123 088	− 135 249
Simple	640 611	958 389	976 359	+ 335 748
Total	3 350 297	4 086 662	4 195 297	+ 845 000

(8) Comparing the inventory done in 1968 to 1982 situation can be concluded as follows:—

—	Increase in Technical irrigation system	644,501 ha
—	Increase in Semi Technical irrigation system	135,249 ha
—	Increase in Simple irrigation system	355,748 ha
	Total	845,000 ha

(9) On Table 5 new irrigation development in First, Second and Third Five Year Development Plan can be seen.

(10) Development of new irrigation system based on inventory done in 1968 and 1982 are listed in Table 4.

(11) Target and realization of irrigation development in III Five Year Development Plan (March 1983 position) can be seen in Table 6 and summarized as follows.

—	New irrigation system development programme	
	* III five year plan target	700,000 ha
	* Realization: up to 1982/1983	375,641 ha
	* Estimated in 1983/1984	72,770 ha
		448,411 ha

or 64 per cent of III five year plan target.

Table 4. Development of New Irrigation Areas and Inventory of years 1968 & 1982 (ha)

No.	Description	Irrigation network				Remarks
		Technical	Semi technical	Simple	Total	
1.	1968	1 451 348	1 258 337	640 611	3 350 297	1
2.	New Irr. Devt. F.Y.D.P. I, II, III/March 1983	509 629	342 806	–	852 435	2
3.	Non Rice Field	–	7 435	–	7 435	3
4.	Net Area of New Irr. Devt.	509 629	335 371	–	845 000	4
5.	Status of 1981/1982:					
	a. Estimation	1 960 978	1 593 708	640 611	4 195 297	5a = 1 + 4
	b. Inventory Sept. 1982	2 095 850	1 123 088	976 359	4 195 297	5b
6.	Changed		–470 620	)		5b – 5a
	a. Upgrading	+134 872		)	0	
	b. Delete			+335 748)		
7.	Total	+644 501	–135 249	+335 748	845 000	7 = 4 + 6

Table 5. Actual Irrigation Development during I, II and III F.Y.D.P. (Until 1981/82)

Programme	F.Y.D.P. I (ha)	F.Y.D.P. II (ha)	F.Y.D.P. III*) (ha)	Total *) (ha)
New Irrigation	191 246	325 942	355 247	852 435
Upgrading and rehabilitation	836 073	527 840	251 429	1 715 342
Tertiary development	–	324 769	839 132	1 163 901

Note: *) until 1981/1982

— Improvement and Upgrading Development Programme

   * III five year plan target   536,000 ha

   * Realization: up to 1982/1983   295,411 ha

   * Estimated in 1983/1984   45,311 ha

                      340,722 ha

or 63 per cent of III five year plan target.

— Tertiary System Development Programme

   * III five year plan target   600,000 ha

   * Realization: up to 1982/1983   1,339,997 ha

   * Estimated in 1983/1984   276,147 ha

                      1,616,144 ha

or 269 per cent of III five year plan target.

7. Irrigation development programme – IV Five Year Development Plan

(1) Priority in IV Five Year Development Plan is focused to the development of new irrigation system and multi purpose irrigation projects.

Based on needs and water resources potential, the multi purpose projects are mostly located in Java, and new irrigation in the outer islands. The new irrigation approach, which should be developed for upland and brackish water fisheries, relies on increased participation of the beneficiaries in investment as well as operation and maintenance.

(2) Irrigation development plan in IV Five Year Development Plan consists of two main activities.

Extensification by means of new irrigation development

Table 6. Target & Implementation III F.Y.D.P. End of March 1983

Program	Target F.Y.D.P. III (ha)	Implementation					Planning 1983/1984 (ha)	Estimation of Implementation until 31-3-84	
		1979/1980	1980/1981	1981/1982	1982/1983	Total		ha	% Terhacap Pelita III
New Irrigation Development	700 000	125 301	106 154	103 792	40 394	375 641	72 770	448 411	64
Upgrading & Rehabilitation	536 000	83 126	90 915	77 388	43 982	295 411	45 311	340 722	63
Tertiary system:	600 000	311 351	461 767	366 277	200 602	1 339 997	276 147	1 616 144	269
a. Irrigation		238 573	351 288	249 271	132 447	971 579	211 782	1 183 361	
b. Swampy area & others		72 778	110 479	117 006	78 155	368 418	64 365	432 783	

Note: Planning 1983/1984

Table 7. Average Cost of O & M

Tahun	Area (ha)	Cost (Rp.)	Average Cost Ha/year (Rp.)
1974/1975	3 657 175	5 851 479 200	1 600
1975/1976	3 724 286	5 786 000 000	1 554
1976/1977	3 249 482	6 273 850 000	1 931
1977/1978	3 771 859	7 920 984 000	2 100
1978/1979	4 346 768	9 967 036 000	2 293
1979/1980	4 474 706	13 267 000 000	2 965
1980/1981	4 541 186	19 771 000 000	4 354
1981/1982	4 577 526	26 009 000 000	5 682
1982/1983	4 506 809	31 235 000 000	6 931
1983/1984	4 888 983	33 275 000 000	6 806

— Intensification by means of irrigation development through:
  o   Upgrading
  o   Rehabilitation
  o   Improvement and replacement
  o   Improvement in operation and maintenance

(3) Irrigation development program in IV Five Year Development Plan can be seen in Table 8 consisting of:

— New irrigation development   656,800 ha

— Upgrading of irrigation by means of:
  o   Construction of reservoir   379,300 ha
  o   Main irrigation network   372,300 ha
  o   Drainage newtork   114,000 ha
  o   Tertiary network   1,858,300 ha

— Rehabilitation of irrigation network   293,600 ha

— Improvement/Replacement
  o   Irrigation structures   6,000 Nos
  o   Canal   2,000 Km
— Improvement in operation and maintenance   4,580,000 ha

(4) Crop yield or production at the end of IV Five Year Development Plan is estimated to a level of 30 million metric ton. (Figures 1 and 2).

8. Irrigation development in the future

Development of a new irrigation system is implemented on land where agriculture has already been practised but no irrigation system exists (rainfed), or opening up new land for agricultural purposes. In this respect there are significant differences between Java island and other islands considering land, soil and water availability for irrigaion.

To have a figure on the difference between Java and other islands is important, especially on the existing systems and its production, in conjunction with their total throughout Indonesia. Out of the total of 7.15 million ha paddy growing areas in Indonesia noted in 1981 (see table 10) Java has the largest-some 3.62 million ha (51 per cent), Sumatera 1.74 million ha (24 per cent) and Kalimantan 0.76 million ha (11 per cent).

Out of 4.5 million ha irrigated area (including swamp) Java has the largest area of 2.64 million ha (59 per cent), Sumatera 0.94 million ha (21 per cent), Sulawesi 0.33 million ha (7.5 per cent) and Kalimantan 0.30 million ha (6.8 per cent). Other islands are less than 4 per cent.

It is obvious that being the largest paddy growing area and the largest irrigated area, Java produced the highest tonnage of rice (63 per cent). Figures for other areas:

Table 8. IV Five Year Development Plan Program for Irrigation Projects

Irrigation Projects	IV Five Year Development Plan Program (Ha)								Cost (10⁶ Rp) (1983)
	New Devt.	Upgrading				Rehabilitation	Improvement & Rehab.	O & M	
		Reservoir	Main syst.	Drainage	Tertiary				
S.I.D. (Planning)									56 000
Special	132 700	30 350	32 830	–	188 500	–	–	–	574 112
Medium	161 700	–	–	–	65 000	–	–	–	330 803
Small	199 000	–	–	–	80 000	–	–	–	168 581
Rehabilitation	8 600	–	181 200	–	325 300	120 300	–	–	586 213
Ex IDA	–	–	–	114 000	364 100	71 400	–	–	324 281
Ex IBRD	111 000	23 950	8 270	–	142 700	–	–	–	240 931
Prosijat	–	30 000	–	–	74 900	–	–	–	88 986
Dit. of River	43 800	295 000	–	–	167 800	101 900	–	–	–
Tertiary	–	–	–	–	300 000	–	–	–	66 000
Village Irrigation Improvement	–	–	150 000	–	150 000	–	–	–	90 000
Improvement & Replacement	–	–	–	–	–	–	6 000 struc. 2 000 km	–	
O & M	–	–	–	–	–	–	–	4 580,000	465 353
Total	656 800	379 300	372 300	114 000	1 858 300	293 600	6 000 struc. 2 000 km	4 580,000	3 071 260*)

Note: Excluding project costs handled by Dit. of River

Sumatera 19 per cent, Sulawesi 8 per cent and Kalimantan 5 per cent.

On the other hand, Java is also the most densely populated island. About 62 per cent of Indonesian population live in Java, 19 per cent in Sumatera, 5 per cent in Kalimantan and 7 per cent in Sulawesi. The population density in Java, Bali, Nusa Tenggara, Sumatera and Sulawesi in persons per square kilometre (psk) is 690 psk, 444 psk, 80 psk, 59 psk and 55 psk respectively.

In agriculture land resources, Java is also the leader among other islands (see table 10), but in terms of proportion of agricultural to total land area, Bali has the highest percentage. If all the potential agriculture lands are developed, Java will be still the most heavily pressured with 1,616 persons per square kilometers of agriculture land (16 persons per ha). Surprisingly Sulawesi with much less population density compared to Sumatera or Kalimantan has more population pressure on agricultural lands. Those indications are very important in the development of agriculture and transmigration and therefore have to be taken into considerations.

Identification of potential for new irrigation area has been conducted by the Directorate General of Water Resources Development (DGWRD). These are shown in table 11. Even though the identification did not cover the whole possible area due to time and budget constraints, it gives very useful tool to generate irrigation plan for future development.

(1) Irrigation development in Java

Java, being the most densely populated in Indonesia's islands, tends to be the concentration of human activities and also human needs. As water is one of the important natural resources for human life, competing demands for available water resources become an increasingly important issue in Java.

Industrial development in Java is progressing rapidly, partly because some industrial inputs are easily and readily available in Java and partly because of marketing and its infrastructures. Communications, labour and raw materials for some industries are more available in Java. Transportation and road net-works have been constructed, which then in turn reduce industrial capital investment. This condition, may increase employment opportunities as long as labor intensive approach is to be adopted.

If industrial activities become more concentrated in Java, this will tend to increase population in Java, thereby worsening problems of over population. As industry in

Table 9. Irrigation Development of IV Five Year Development Plan for Increasing Rice Production

No.	Program/Project	Physical construc. Target Pelita IV (ha)	Without Project					With Project					Increasing of Rice Production	
			area (ha)	C.1	Harvested area (ha)	Yield ton/ha	Production (ton)	Area (ha)	C.1	Harvested area (ha)	Yield ton/ha	Production (ton)	5 Years	1 Year
1	2	3	4	5	6 = 4 × 5	7	8 = 6 × 7	9	10	11 = 9 × 10	12	13	14	15
I.	New Irrigation	656 800	318 600	0.8	254 800	2.04	519 792	351 710	1.4	492 492	2.86	1 408 526	888 734	177 746
1.1	Special Project	132 700	65 700	0.8	52 560	2.04	107 222	71 770	1.4	100 478	2.86	287 367	180 145	36 029
1.2	Medium Small Scale	360 700	145 000	0.8	116 000	2.04	236 640	166 560	1.4	233 184	2.86	666 906	430 906	86 055
1.3	Rehabilitation	8 600	8 600	0.8	6 800	2.04	13 872	8 600	1.4	12 040	2.86	34 434	20 562	4 112
1.4	Ex IBRD	111 000	55 500	0.8	44 400	2.04	90 050	61 576	1.4	85 470	2.86	244 444	153 868	30 774
1.5	Dit. of River	43 800	43 800	0.8	35 040	2.04	71 482	43 800	1.4	61 320	2.86	175 375	103 893	20 778
II.	Upgrading of Irr. System	1 165 600	1 165 600	1.08	1 264 462	2.58	3 259 116	1 165 600	1.36	1 586 700	3.35	3 317 260	2 058 144	411 628
2.1	Special Project	63 180	63 180	0.9	56 862	2.38	135 332	63 180	1.6	101 088	3.4	343 699	208 367	41 673
2.2	Rehabilitation	181 200	181 200	0.8	163 080	2.38	388 130	181 200	1.3	235 560	3.4	800 904	412 774	82 555
2.3	Ex IDA	114 000	114 000	0.2	22 800	1.70	38 760	114 000	1.0	114 000	2.72	310 080	271 320	54 264
2.4	Ex IBRD	32 220	32 220	1.0	32 220	2.38	76 684	32 220	1.6	51 552	3.4	175 277	98 593	19 719
2.5	Prosijat	30 000	30 000	1.2	36 000	2.38	85 686	30 000	1.9	57 000	3.4	193 800	108 120	21 624
2.6	Village	150 000	150 000	1.2	180 000	2.38	428 400	150 000	1.3	195 000	3.4	663 000	234 600	46 920
2.7	Tertiary	300 000	300 000	1.3	390 000	3.06	1 193 400	300 000	1.3	390 000	3.4	1 326 000	132 600	26 520
2.8	Dit. of River	295 000	295 000	1.3	383 500	2.38	912 730	295 000	1.5	442 500	3.4	1 504 500	591 770	118 354
III.	Rehabilitation	293 600	293 600	1	293 600	2.72	798 592	293 600	1.3	381 640	3.4	1 297 712	499 040	99 808
3.1	Rehabilitation	120 300	120 300	1	120 300	2.72	327 216	120 300	1.3	156 390	3.4	531 726	204 510	40 902
3.2	Ex IDA	71 400	71 400	1	71 400	2.72	194 208	71 400	1.3	92 820	3.4	315 588	121 300	24 260
3.3	Dit. of River	101 900	101 900	1	101 900	2.72	277 168	101 900	1.3	132 470	3.4	450 398	173 230	34 646
IV.	Improvement/Replacement													
V.	O & M													
	Total	2 116 000	1 777 800	1.16	1 812 862	2.53	4 577 500	1 810 910	1.36	2 460 872	3.26	8 023 498	3 445 918	689 183

Table 10. Paddy Area, Irrigated Area, Population, and Rice Production in Indonesia (1981)

Region	Paddy area		Irrigated area		Production	Population	
	'000 ha	%	'000 ha	%	%	mill.	%
Java	3 618	50.7	2 645	59.4	62.7	91.3	62.0
Sumatera	1 739	24.3	940	21.1	18.5	28.1	19.0
Kalimantan	762	10.7	301	6.8	5.4	6.8	4.6
Sulawesi	616	8.6	333	7.5	7.8	10.5	7.1
Bali	114	1.6	56	1.3	2.3	2.5	1.7
Nusa Tenggara	266	3.7	163	3.7	3.2	5.6	3.8
Maluku	32	0.4	9	0.2	0.1	1.5	1.0
Irian Jaya	3	–	2	–	–	1.2	0.8
Total	7 150		4 449			147.5	
	*		**				

*Includes,	Irrigated area	= 4,074,400 ha
	Village & rainfed	= 2,619,100 ha
	Tidal swamp	= 374,500 ha
	Inland swamp	= 82,000 ha
**Includes,	Irrigated area	= 4,074,400 ha
	Swampy irrigation	= 374,500 ha

Table 11. Identified Potential Irrigated Agriculture Land

Region	Surface Water Dev. '000 ha			Swampy Dev. (Small) '000 ha	Total '000 ha
	Small Scale	Large Scale	Total		
Java	119	–	119	–	119
Sumatera	1 098	2 275	3 373	1 939	5 312
Kalimantan	114	693	807	946	1 753
Sulawesi	372	325	697	–	697
Bali	12	–	12	–	12
Nusa Tenggara	294	125	419	2	421
Maluku	53	153	206	–	206
Irian Jaya	53	44	97	(?)	97+?
Total	2 115	3 615	5 730	2 887	8 617+?

Java grows rapidly, water use for industry is also very demanding.

Water usage of the highest priority is for life, especially human life. Consequently, first priority on water allocation should be given to drinking water and domestic use. When the standard of living becomes higher, water demand for daily life also increases; partly for ease (garden etc.) and most of all for health.

Water supply projects to purify raw water for domestic use just started a few years ago and therefore water demand for drinking and domestic use is increasing in Java and, in turn, water demands become even more competitive.

Environmental problems became important issues at the beginning of this decade. In towns and cities where people are most concentrated, pollution became high. Water is also needed to reduce degree of pollution by flushing unwanted materials. In water resources planning especially in Java that situation should also be taken into consideration.

With industrial development, demand for housing, and other infra-structures (road, airport etc.) as well as water demand and land demand competition increased in Java. Irrigated land which is the most fertile and productive, is reduced and being used for such development. In compensating for this reductions, development of new irrigation area may not be worthwhile in Java, and instead it is more encouraging outside Java.

Table 11 shows, that beside land demand competition, potential agriculture land to be developed in Java is limited (119,000 ha) compared to other islands (Kalimantan 1.7 million ha and Sumatera 5.3 million ha). Population pressure on agricultural land in Java is also much higher than in other islands. These indicate, if not a warning, that new irrigation development in Java is not promising.

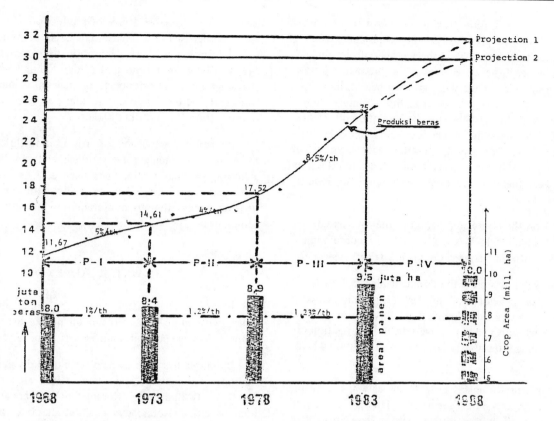

Figure 1. Rice production and crop area I, II, III five year development plan & projection P-IV

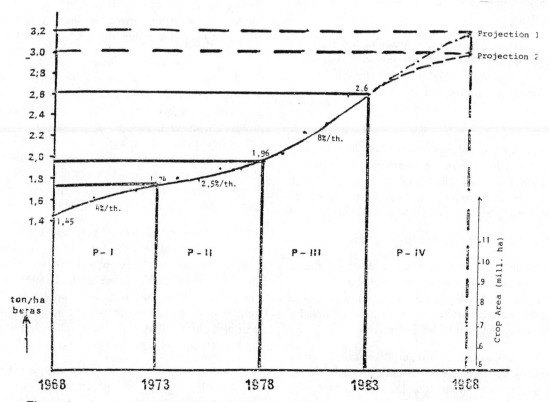

Figure 2. Average rice production/ha FM I, II, III five year development plan & projection P-IV

On the diversification program of export commodities, attention should be given to agricultural products. Among other agricultural products, fishery, especially "tambak" (brackish water fishery), is one of the promising source, considering its high value, short growing period, increasing demand and cashability. Java has the advantage in this matter as its north coastal area is the habitation of brackish fish hatch. As brackish fish needs certain saline concentration for its life environment, fresh water becomes important on reducing the salinity of sea water. Irrigation development in Java therefore is taking into account this requirement as well.

Based on the above considerations the emphasis of irrigation development in Java is not on the new development but dealing with the on-going or existing irrigation systems.

Even water resources development plan in Java is not primarily for development of new irrigation, rather if any water resources development for any purpose (flood control, power etc.) gives positive effects for irrigation (increase cropping intensities), they will be an additional benefit.

The question remains how to allocate the available water in Java to various demands? This is not easy to answer unless all sectors utilizing water have an explicit plan and program. Employing an optimization model will help at least to roughly figure out water allocation, given certain policies, either economic, social or others or tradeoffs among them.

It is important to note that in planning water allocation, existing demands have to be met (considering demand changes) with non agricultural demands having highest priority. The main reason is that agricultural demands are less sensitive to water deficit. Drinking water has the first priority as it is directly life sustaining.

With an increasing water demand in Java, irrigation for agriculture should be analyzed to determine effects of emphasising cultivation of secondary crops which consume less water than rice, or combination of them. Again optimization models could play an important role in that analysis.

(2) Irrigation development in other islands

It is apparent that Indonesia will have to rely on islands outside Java to provide the base of food production areas. Table 11 shows that beside swampy areas, out of identified 5.7 million ha other islands have 98 per cent or 5.6 mill. ha of agricultural land with migration potential.

Possible compensation as a result of reduced irrigated areas in Java is by opening new irrigated area in other islands. In this respect consideration has to be given to the fact that soil in Java is more fertile than most soils in other islands. For the same degree of production, compensating area in other islands will have to be larger than the area lost to urbanization in Java. Irrigation development outside Java will be an important part of developing new areas for transmigration. Development of new areas outside Java will create better conditions so that people area attracted to move from Java to other islands.

Priority for extension of irrigation facilities is given to areas experiencing food shortage and on the basis of achieving regional development balance. The deficit food-producing areas are linked to those with surplus food-producing areas, thereby reinforcing and strengthening their economies.

C. WATER SUPPLY

Indonesia is the fifth most populous country in the world with more than 160 million people living in 3000 islands. Average population density is 77 per sq km.

Indonesia has 27 provinces which are divided into 216 districts (Kabupatens) and these in turn are divided into about 3,300 subdistricts (Kecamatans). There are 54 autonomous cities (Kotamadyas), about 3,300 district towns (Ibu Kota Kecamatan), and about 65,000 villages (Desas).

Indonesia is well endowed with rain fall, ground and surface water resources, but problems of distance, reliability, contamination, excessive demand and conflicting uses preclude simple and rapid development on a wide scale.

Indonesian water resources specialists estimate that house hold and industrial water requirements are about 5 per cent and agricultural needs about 95 per cent of total needs. Much of house hold needs can be supplied from subsurface water and springs, but usually the location and reliability of such sources are not precisely known and their development require exploration, time, and expenses. On balance, from technical and economic standpoints, subsurface and spring sources are preferable.

Many efforts to develop Indonesia's urban and rural areas have been undertaken for the past 16 years through a series of five year development plans or Repelita. The provision of basic services water supply and sanitation for the urban and rural areas were implemented through various development programmes of many government departments/institutions and also through self-helf projects by the communities and the private sector.

During the 3rd 5 year development plan (Repelita III: 1979-1984) the Government embarked upon a "basic need" approach to projects which seek to rapidly provide essential services at low-cost for the cities and towns included in the current and successive Plans. Under the impetus of the United Nations International Drinking Water and Sanitation Decade overall service level targets were set by Government of Indonesia in 1981 for until 1990 as follows: urban and rural water supply to serve 75 per cent and 60 per cent of the total population respectively, and urban and rural sanitation to serve 60 per cent and 40 per cent of the total population respectively. Two major programmes for meeting the targets for urban water supply in the 1980s were the Basic Needs Approach (BNA) programme for cities and larger towns (with populations 20,000 and up), and the Ibu Kota Kecamatan (IKK) programme for kecamatan headquarter towns with population in the 3,000-20,000 range. The development budget allocation including foreign and technical assistance has been increasing. But due to the "balance budget" system adopted by the Government, the increase of development budget for water supply and sanitation should consider other sectoral needs as well.

With regard to the comprehensive master plans for water resources development, it can be reported that only big provinces have such plans. However, such plans are being planned to cover other provinces of Indonesia.

Indonesia have no serious problems such as pipelines approaching the end of their useful life. In contrary, many new projects are being executed, some have been in operation to meet the Decade targets.

The cost recovery of water supply systems are applied to most urban and industrial uses. The tariff structure accomodates low tariffs for the low income groups, applying the volumetric (block) rate. For rural water supply only part of recurrent costs are charged to the users.

In Indonesia, all house connections of water systems are fully metered, except for semi-urban systems; flow-restrictors are used.

The existing law and legislation clearly define ownership to Government for either surface or ground water sources. The Government endeavors through Environmental Law to protect water quality for surface and ground water.

Nevertheless it is felt that additional legislations and guidelines need to be prepared to ensure smooth execution of national water supply and sanitation development plans.

According to the existing laws and regulations, the local governments are responsible for the provision of water supply and sanitation facilities in their respective regions.

The local governments shall plan, execute and supervise water supply and sanitation development projects. After completion of the projects, the system will be operated and maintained by autonomous local water supply and sanitation enterprises. But due to limited local funds, personnel and experience, the National Government is still assisting the water supply and sanitation programs, especially to meet the basic needs in water sanitation for the population.

At national level, there are four ministries (Public Works, Home Affairs, Health and Finance) which coordinate and supervise the development plans, the execution of projects and the operation and maintenance of the facilities. For the National Water Supply and Sanitation Decade Plans, a National Steering Committee was established in 1982 consisting of Directors General of the 4 ministries.

In the water supply and sanitation sectors, there are still shortages of qualified manpower, but this is being solved through the implementation of the Human Resources. Development Plan, in which it was identified that about 17,000 water supply personnel have to be recruited and trained if the Decade plan is to be fully implemented.

At present the bilateral and multilateral aids are used for partly financing the development projects as well as assisting the human resources development.

Public information and participation in the water supply and sanitation sector is an aspect which recently has received much attention in view of the earlier mentioned increase in numbers of customers set as targets for Repelita IV and for the Water Decade. These targets state that by the end of Repelita IV, there will be 3,030,000 house connections, which means an increase of 2,680,000 house connections or customers in the remaining years of the decade.

These targets imply that public information for water enterprises cannot be limited to maintaining established relations with those who are already customers at present, but will have to focus on finding new customers for the water enterprises.

Limited funds and high targets require that the public information and participation programme for the next four years become very effective in reaching the right people and getting the message across to them about the advantages of clean water supply systems. This means that a choice has to be made about the best mixture of media for the public information and participation programme.

Technical co-operation among developing countries (TCDC) also has been encouraged by Indonesia with Bangladesh, Thailand, India, Tanzania etc, among others by receiving trainees or fellowship holders. The activities in this programme include all aspects in water supply and sanitation management (technics, skill improvement, adminsitration and finance, organization etc.).

A mid-decade review was then held by the government revealing the estimated coverage for urban water supply was 40 per cent and for sanitation it was not able to quantify in percentage; while, for rural water supply it was 36 per cent and sanitation 31 per cent. A number of issues particularly constraints and obstacles are hindering the progress in the sector development. In order to reach the Decade's targets by 1990, new approaches should be developed and appropriate measures must be taken. New approaches to be developed should cover:

1. increased attention to sanitation sub-sector;

2. a more balanced input between urban and rural sub-sector;

3. an integrated approach in urban infrastructure development to optimize the use of available resources; to give a greater role to local government in planning and implementation of urban development projects; and to encourage the participation of the private sector;

4. one-river-one-plan approach in the development of water resources in the region to ensure a more orderly development;

5. total package programme in the rural sub-sector in order to attract foreign aids;

6. private investment for the urban sectors;

7. integrated approach to promote greater community participation;

8. reorientation of sector financing from social to economic sector;

Remedial measures recommended in mid-decade review are among others:

1. increase investment in urban and rural water supply and sanitation sectors;

2. facilitate resource mobilization at the local government level, and establish new resources of funding/credit and financing arrangement for the sector development;

3. increase local financial responsibility on cost-recovery and cost of operation and maintenance;

4. greater portion of foreign aids in the financing of local component;

5. increase involvement of local government and community in the sector programme development;

6. extended involvement to other government ministries in the sector programme development;

7. inclusion of communication support component as part of the project activity;

Ministry of Public Works, Directorate of Water Supply
Number of Management & Staff in the Water Supply Sector so far trained

Name of Institutions	1st Five Year Development Plan 1973/1974	2nd Five Year Development Plan 1974/1975-1978/1979	3rd Five Year Development Plan 1979/1980-1983/1984	4th Five Year Development Plan 1984/1985-1985/1986
PDAM/BPAM*				
I. Top Manager				
– Management	–	66	300	242
– Technical Department	–	119	115	312
– Finance/Administration Department	–	173	615	262
II. Middle Manager				
– Technical Section	–	25	72	429
– Finance/Administration Section	–	–	109	247
III. Operator	99	267	775	355
Others	–	–	240	287
Scout/Extention Workers	–	–	770	603
Total	99	650	2,996	2,737

* PDAM: Regional water enterprise

BPAM: Water supply management body

8. strengthening local government institution;

9. further implementation of human resources development;

10. recruit and retain adequate and skilled personnel;

11. greater emphasis for wastewater and water quality surveillance;

12. develop management information system in support of rural and urban water supply and sanitation programmes;

13. better coordination of programme development at central and local level;

14. formulation of government regulation required for better development of water supply and sanitation sectors;

15. further promote bottom-up planning as defined in the government regulation.

Annex 1.

Name of Course.

A. Top Manager

Management

1. Course for Directors of PDAM/Head of BPAM

2. Management Information System Course

Technical Department

1. Course for Technical Director of PDAM/Head of Technical Department

Finance/Administration Department

1. Course for Head of Finance/Administration Department

2. Accounting System Course

3. Budgeting and Expenditures Estimation Course

4. Budget and Finance Report Analysis Course

B. Middle Manager

Technical Section

1. Course for Chief of Production Section

2. Course for Chief of Transmission/Distribution Section

3. Course for Chief of Planning/Supervisory Section

4. Course for Chief of Workshop/Maintenance Section

5. Laboratory Practice Course

Finance/Administration Section

1. Course for Chief of Bookeeping Section

2. Course for Chief of Personnel & Administration Section

C. Operator

1. Head of IKK Installation Unit Course/Operator

2. IKK Construction Supervisor Course

3. Operator Course (Water Treatment)

4. Water leakage survey course (leakage control)

5. Water Works Engineering Course (equipment, mechanics and electricity)

6. Water meter Course (type., model, testing, maintenance and repair)

7. Pipelayer Course

8. Genset & Pumps Course

D. Others

1. Pre-Investment Planning for Community Course

2. Training for Trainers.

3. Training for head of cleaning Department/Project Manager of Community Environmental Sanitation

4. Training for Contractor

5. Community Participation Course

6. Workshop Micro Computer

E. Training for Scout Extention Workers.

D. FLOOD CONTROL

1. Background

Indonesia is an archipelago stretchng about 5,500 km along the equator. This geographical condition gives abundant tropical rainfall to most parts of the country. Annual precipitation of between 2,000 and 3,000 mm is a common figure, and for some regions extreme values up to 7,000 mm have been estimated.

Heavy daily rainfalls occur frequently, generally as a result of tropical thunderstorms. Daily rainfalls exceeding 100 mm is common during rainy seasons, while extreme values of more than 400 mm, with a maximum of 700 mm, have been recorded many times at several parts of the country. The high intensities are generally of short duration and covering relatively small areas, but can be quickly followed up by successive storms, and can therefore result in devastating floods over large areas.

Another natural condition which greatly affects the hydrology of the river-basins is the landscape. The typical landscape of the islands is one of eroded mountain chains with volcanic peaks rising above them up to about 4000 m high in some areas and broad alluvial plains crossed by meandering, sediment laden rivers. The high volcanic mountains are strung along the central spine of the large islands.

Flood is not a new problem for most parts of Indonesia. Traditional houses were built on wooden platforms supported by relatively high pillars and equipped with 2 or 3 boats under the roofs to enable normal daily activities during flood times when the lands were inundated.

2. Brief history

Demands for flood protection in greater scale started to rise in the second half of the last century when population grew rapidly and new agricultural policy was implemented by the colonial government. The size of settlement areas became bigger, life became more complex, and floods were felt to become a real disturbance to daily activities and caused economic losses. Threat to economy was also felt in rural areas where large amount of lands started to be developed as ricefields, sugarcane and other plantation estates. Most of these were located on the flood plains of big rivers.

Protective dikes and barriers were constructed. Some by the Irrigation Service and some by plantation owners and railroad company. Most of these only shifted the damage to another area and did not solve the basic problems of the floods.

More serious works for flood control were established at the beginning of this century. Dams and dikes were built for River Brantas in east Java, followed by the establishment of similar projects at some other places. Two outstanding flood diversion channels are still functioning. The first is the West Jakarta Flood Diversion Channel (1919) and the other is Batang Arau Flood Diversion Channel (1918 — aimed to prevent floods entering the city of Padang).

Although flood problems were felt to be increasing, not much effort had been made to solve them during the first years after independence, because of political unstability. Only a few projects could be completed, although suveys and studies for some other ones had been prepared as well.

When relatively stable political condition could be achieved at the end of sixties, greater plans started to be implemented through Five Year Development Programs. Many flood control projects were established. Considerable results have been achieved so far, but many problems are still awaiting for solution.

3. Policy

At the beginning of the last decade Indonesia was the largest rice importing country in the world. This had been the reason that in the First Five Year Development Program (FYDP) the development of agricultural sector became the dominant component. Flood control projects were also aimed mainly at supporting agriculture. The selection of projects was firstly based on a general policy that efforts should be concentrated on protecting:

— food producing areas with intensive cultivation and dense population.

— agricultural areas producing export commodities.

Success achieved in the First FYDP (1969-1974) was followed by broader efforts in the Second and Third FYDP (1974-1979 and 1979-1984). The general policy remain the same, although some attention had been paid for the preparation of new projects aimed at protecting urban and industrial areas. Surveys and studies for these projects were conducted during that period.

In the present Fourth FYDP (1984-1989) self-sufficiency in rice has been reached, and more attention can be paid to the development of other sectors. Construction of some flood control projects protecting urban areas are presently underway and more studies are being prepared for promoting new ones.

There are four types of flood control projects set up in the FYDPs. They can be described briefly as follows:

1. Emergency projects

This type of project is aimed at providing small scale protection to a certain locality which requires immediate solution. The level of protection is normally low (for 1-5 year return period flood) and the target area is usually also small.

2. Short-term projects

This type of project provides protection to larger areas while the levels of protection are also higher (ranges between 5 and 50 year return period).

3. Volcanic debris control projects

This type of project is similar to the short-term projects, but the flood problem is technically different, because the flood of rivers around volcanoes contains large amount of debris carried from the hillsides.

4. Long-term projects

Regarding the target area and levels of protection, this type of project is also similar to the short-term projects. The difference is that the works included in this project have already been integrated into the overall plan of a river basin development program. Thus the operation of the flood water management has become a part of a comprehensive multi-purpose water management program (e.g. flood storage provided by a multi-purpose reservoir).

4. Outstanding problems

The planning of a flood control project was a heavy task in the past. Success in the future will be more difficult to reach, because of some rising problems. Outstanding ones which can be drawn from recent experiences are as follows:

1. The change of watershed hydrology

Uncontrolled development in upper watersheds will change the river hydrology. Flood frequencies will change and flood control facilities may have to be reviewed accordingly.

2. Sedimentation

Another aspect of watershed degradation is excessive erosion which in turn will cause sedimentation downstream. This will reduce the hydraulic capacity of the river channel and the flood control facilities. If the amount becomes well over the designed figures, then maintenance works will not be sufficient to cope with the problem. River channels may become clogged and reservoirs may be filled up by debris.

3. Waste disposal

At many places people dispose wastes into river channels. This may not create a serious problem in rural areas, but in densely populated developed urban areas it will definitely produce failure of flood control projects. When river channels are choked with rubbish, then the flow capacity will become less.

4. Occupancy of flood plains and high water channels

There are cases when the establishment of houses and other buildings in flood plains which have been planned to serve as a retarding storage basin cannot be prevented. In such cases it is clear that the flood control projects become less effective. High water channel between dikes along a river is meant to become the passage of floods. In large towns, houses are creeping into the river flood plains. This will also make any flood control project less effective.

5. Closing remarks

1. Indonesia is country which is naturally susceptible to flood and has done much effort in controlling floods. Significant projects were started since about 100 years ago, aimed at controlling floods in rapidly developing areas.

2. During the last decade, efforts have been concentrated on protecting agricultural areas, especially aimed at achieving self-sufficiency in staple food production. But at present more attention is being given to urban and industrial areas.

3. Future works will become more difficult due to some rising problems. The outstanding ones are: degradation of upper watersheds (change of hydrology and sedimentation), waste disposal and flood plain, high water channel occupancy.

REFERENCES

1. Directorate of Rivers, Fourth Five Year Development Program, 1984.

2. Ir. Sarbini R. and D. Sasongko, Engineering and Economic Considerations in Planning Flood Control Works in Indonesia, 1978.

3. Directorate General of Water Resources Development, Water Resources Availability and Use in Indonesia, 1983.

4. D. Sasongko, Role of Flood Control Projects in Rural and Urban Development in Indonesia, 1985.

E. HYDROPOWER

I. Energy scene

Demand

1. The relatively high increase of energy demand (annual growth rates averaging 14.9 per cent) during the period of 1975-81 is related to the high growth of GDP of the same period (annual growth rates averaging 8 per cent).

Energy demand in all sectors grew substantially, notably in the industrial sector. Refer to table 1 Energy Consumption by Sector 1974-1985.

Table 1 Energy Consumption by Sector, 1974-1985.

Units: 10⁶ TCE

Sectors	1974	1981	1982	1983	1984	1985
Industry	5.67	15.08	15.65	16.44	17.75	18.51
Transportation	4.88	10.92	10.90	10.77	11.11	11.49
Household	4.40	10.99	10.58	9.77	9.23	8.98
Electricity	0.85	4.59	4.94	6.14	7.37	7.93
Total	15.80	41.58	42.07	43.12	45.46	46.92
GDP Growth		7.9	2.3	4.0		

2. During the slow growth of GDP, 1982-1984 (average of 3.5 per cent) the consumption of primary energy also showed slow growth. Moreover the consumption of kerosene declined (by 12.78 per cent), ADO and FO declined by 2.8 per cent and 2.9 per cent during 1983/1984. Gasoline, fuel oil and IDO remain more or less constant. The consumption of coal and contribution of hydro increased. An improved price structure in 1982 and 1983, to reduce the subsidy of the lower and middle distilates was also considered instrumental in the reduction of kerosene demand.

3. The role of non-commercial energy (mostly used in the rural areas) is still very important to the total energy balance (approximately 56.03 million TCE or 56.05 per cent in 1984), its consumption is mostly related to the low economic capability (beside habits and culture) and to the abundance of non-commercial energy mainly wood and agriculture wastes in the larger islands outside Java.

A higher standard of living in the rural areas, may increase electricity demand substantially which is now pro-

vided by kerosene amounting approximately to 36 per cent of total kerosene consumption in households amounting 2.6 million TCE, but this has to be combined with the possibility of a higher rate of PLN power distribution expansion.

Supply

4. The supply of Energy during the period of high demand was met by increased primary energy production, the addition of processing units (refineries, LNG trains, LPG processing units, hydrocracker etc.), and an increase in the energy conversion sector (power plants).

Table 2 Primary energy production

Units: 10⁶ TCE

	1975	1981	1982	1983	1984	1985
Oil	95.56	152.37	97.83	91.09	93.89	86.42
Gas	7.81	39.49	39.08	42.78	53.48	55.54
Coal	0.21	0.35	0.43	0.44	0.83	1.19
Hydropower	0.3,	0.62	1.37	2.03	2.95	3.17
Geothermal	–	–	0.01	0.07	0.09	0.89

5. As the figures show, Indonesia's Indigenous energy are just starting to be developed mainly for coal, hydro and geothermal and are potential in providing national energy requirements, for the reason they are non-exportable or having a relatively low value in the international market and the possibility of the generation of an economic feed back in the development and utilization of these resources. It is interesting to note that these resources are directly related to development of secondary energy and for coal, also for direct heat and process in the industry.

II. Hydropower

Potential inventory

6. Extensive hydro resource survey has been carried out to develop an overall inventory of potential hydro projects in order that Indonesia's large hydropower potentials could be more systematically developed. A systematic nation-wide resource survey was carried out with funds provided under a World Bank loan and finalized in 1983.

The result of the inventory study shows that a total of 1,275 schemes which were identified will have hydroelectric potential of about 75,000 MW or 401,646 GWH annual energy.

Table 3. Summary of Hydropower Potential

	Installed MW	Capacity (%)	Annual Energy GWH
Existing	1 356	(1.8)	7 062
Under Const./Committed	2 904	(3.9)	11 110
Identified	58 124	(77.5)	321 330
Roughly Estimated	12 592	(16.8)	62 144
Total	74 976	(100)	401 646

Distribution of hydropower potential

7.　Approximately 93 per cent of energy exists in the 4 main islands: Irian Jaya, Sumatera, Kalimantan and Sulawesi. The remaining 5 per cent is in Java and 2 per cent in Bali, Nusa Tenggara and Maluku. Regional distribution of identified schemes is presented in table 4.

8.　Hydropower development is limited by their geographic distribution relative to power demand. The greatest potential, over 25 per cent, lies in Irian Jaya where the demand is less than 1 per cent of total domestic power demand, while Java, which account for 80 per cent of the current demand, has only 5 per cent of the potential.

Table 4. Regional Distribution of Identified Schemes

Islands (1)	No of Schemes (2)	Installed Capacity OPT (MW) (3)	Installed Capacity MAX (MW) (4)	Energy OPT (GWh) (5)	Energy MAX (GWh) (6)	Total Area (km²) (7)	OPT (MW)/ Schemes (8) = (3)/(2)	Unit Potential MW/100 km² (9) = (4)/(7)	Unit Potential GWh/100 km² (10=(6)/(7)
Sumatera	447 (36.8)	10 964 (23.7)	13 959 (24.0)	64 234 (23.3)	75 251 (23.4)	437 606 (30.0)	24.6	3.2	17.2
Java	120 (9.9)	1 644 (3.6)	2 020 (3.5)	9 539 (3.5)	11 238 (3.5)	132 187 (9.1)	13.7	1.5	8.5
Kalimantan	160 (13.2)	9 182 (19.9)	12 450 (21.4)	50 926 (18.5)	62 627 (19.5)	297 631 (20.4)	57.4	4.2	21.1
Sulawesi	105 (8.7)	3 899 (8.4)	6 476 (11.1)	23 583 (8.6)	33 852 (10.5)	123 404 (8.5)	37.1	5.2	27.4
Irian Jaya	205 (17.0)	19 642 (42.5)	22 166 (38.1)	121 652 (44.2)	132 785 (41.3)	303 316 (20.8)	95.8	7.2	43.8
Bali/Nusa Tenggara	120 (9.9)	525 (1.1)	623 (1.0)	3 063 (1.1)	3 285 (1.0)	88 488 (6.1)	4.4	0.7	3.7
Maluku	53 (4.4)	367 (0.8)	430 (0.7)	2 141 (0.8)	2 292 (0.7)	74 505 (5.1)	6.9	0.,	3.1
Total	1 210 (100)	46 223 (100)	58 124 (100)	275 137 (100)	321 330 (100)	1 457 137 (100)	38.3	4.0	22.1

Note: (1) Figures show the areas actually studied. The total areas are 539,460 km² in Kalimantan, 189,216 km² in Sulawesi and 421,981 km² in Irian Jaya

(2) Excluding 65 schemes which are of mutually alternative with others. Total identified 1275 schemes.

(3), (5) Accumulated potential of optimum development at individual sites.

(4), (6) Accumulated potential of max. scaled development at individual sites.

Development type

9. Development types are grouped fundamentally into Reservoir and Run-of-river type. Estimated potential is classified into 32,985 MW (71 per cent) or 177,809 GWH (65 per cent) for the Reservoir type and 13,239 MW (29 per cent) or 97,329 GWH (35 per cent) for the Run-of-river type, on the optimum scale. The distribution of the two groups is shown in table 5.

Distribution of big scale schemes

10. Among the identified schemes are of over 100 MW capacity at the maximum development scale at each site. This total capacity is about 32,946 MW which shares 57 per cent of the total capacity of 1,210 schemes. These big schemes are located in the 4 main islands, especially in Irian Jaya and Kalimantan. The regional distribution of big schemes is shown in table 6.

Economical hydropower potential

11. More than 75 per cent of the potential hydro-power resources in the islands Irian Jaya, Kalimantan, Sulawesi and Sumatera falls in acceptable schemes, based on construction cost per kWh of annual energy production which is less than $US 1.5/kWh.

The undeveloped power in Java is approximately 1,650 MW which represents optimum development size at 120 sites. Out of these, about 60 per cent or 1,000 MW falls in acceptable schemes.

Table 5. Identified Schemes/Potential by Development Type

Islands	Total			Run-of-River			Reservoir		
	No. of Schemes	Inst. Cap. (MW)	Energy (GWh)	No. of Schemes	Inst. Cap. (MW)	Energy (GWh)	No. of Schemes	Inst. Cap. (MW)	Energy (GWh)
Sumatera	447	10 964	64 234	188	2 918	20 836	259	8 046	43 399
	(36.9)	(23.7)	(23.3)	(39.9)	(22.0)	(21.4)	(34.9)	(24.4)	(24.4)
Java	120	1 644	9 539	37	288	1 738	83	1 356	7 801
	(9.9)	(3.6)	(3.5)	(7.9)	(2.2)	(1.8)	(11.2)	(4.1)	(4.4)
Kalimantan	160	9 182	50 926	9	267	1 626	151	8 916	49 300
	(3.2)	(19.9)	(18.5)	(1.9)	(2.0)	(1.7)	(20.4)	(27.0)	(27.7)
Sulawesi	105	3 899	23 583	26	790	6 628	79	3 109	16 955
	(8.7)	(8.4)	(8.6)	(6.0)	(6.0)	(6.8)	(10.7)	(9.5)	(9.5)
Irian Jaya	205	19 642	121 652	130	8 534	64 037	75	11 108	57 615
	(17.0)	(42.5)	(44.2)	(27.7)	(64.5)	(65.8)	(10.1)	(33.7)	(42.4)
Bali/Nusa Tenggara	120	525	3 063	66	258	1 321	54	267	1 743
	(9.9)	(1.1)	(1.1)	(14.1)	(2.0)	(1.4)	(7.3)	(0.8)	(1.0)
Maluku	53	367	2 141	14	184	1 144	39	183	997
	(4.4)	(0.8)	(0.8)	(3.0)	(1.4)	(1.2)	(5.3)	(0.6)	(0.6)
Total	1 210	46 223	275 137	470	13 239	97 329	740	32 985	177 809

Note: Above expressed in terms of potential of optimum sized development at individual sites.

Table 6. Regional Distribution of Big Scale Schemes Identified

Islands	P ⩾ 300 MW		300 MW ⩾ P ⩾ 100 MW		Total	
	No. of Schemes	%	No. of Schemes	%	No. of Schemes	%
Sumatera	0 (0)	0 (0)	25 (24.0)	3 768 (21.8)	25 (20.5)	3 768 (11.4)
Java	0 (0)	0 (0)	3 (2.9)	336 (2.0)	3 (2.5)	336 (1.0)
Kalimantan	8 (44.4)	5 519 (35.2)	18 (17.3)	3 155 (18.3)	26 (21.3)	8 674 (26.3)
Sulawesi	3 (16.7)	1 478 (9.4)	16 (15.4)	2 968 (17.2)	19 (15.6)	4 456 (13.5)
Irian Jaya	7 (38.9)	8 695 (55.4)	42 (40.4)	7 017 (40.7)	49 (40.2)	15 712 (74.7)
Bali/Nusa Tenggara	0 (0)	0 (0)	0 (0)	0 (0)	0 (0)	0 (0)
Maluku	0 (0)	0 (0)	0 (0)	0 (0)	0 (0)	0 (0)
Total	18 (100)	15 692 (100)	104 (100)	17 244 (100)	122 (100)	32 946 (100)

III. Other power sources

Oil

12. Indonesia's total oil reserves are now estimated at about 50 billion barrels. Proven reserves are reported to be from 10 to 15 billion barrels. Present annual production capacity is 575 million barrels (1.6 million barrels/day).

Production for 1982 to 1984 was below that level because of the quota imposed by OPEC. The growth of domestic oil consumption will gradually decrease the absolute net exportable surplus of oil in the future. Studies has indicated that with the present growth of domestic oil consumption Indonesia will be able to supply its own demand well beyond year 2000.

Gas

13. Natural gas reserves are now estimated at 69 trillion cu. feet (tcf) of which more than 85 per cent is non-associated. The Arun field in North Sumatera contains 17 tcf, Badek in Kalimantan 7 tcf, the recently discovered Natuna field in the South China Sea is estimated to contain 35 tcf. Associated gas reserves comprise 10 tcf, majority of which are located in South and Central Sumatera and East Kalimantan.

Domestic consumption at present is just over 80 billion cu.ft./year. As of 1982 Indonesia became the world's largest exporter of LNG and will supply more than 2 billion cu.ft./day (760 billion cu.ft./year).

Coal

14. Total resources are estimated at 23 billion tons of which 18 billion tons are considered lignite. 82 per cent of the resources are located in Sumatera, with 17 per cent in Kalimantan. Smaller resources are known in Sulawesi, West Java, West Irian.

Demonstrated and inferred resources are estimated at 3.5 billion tons and proven reserves are about 1.2 billion tons of which about 700 million tons are located in Kalimantan contract areas. Considering its geological formations, the country's coal resource potential is substantial.

Coal basin studies of the country are part of an on-going project to prepare an inventory of Indonesian coal resources to form the basis of future coal development programs. The investigation of small coal deposits is designed to assist national coal companies develop small mines in Java for local use. The government is interested in developing the country's substantial peat resources in areas where coal is not available and plans to investigate their use in steam power plants and as a fuel for domestic use in steam power plants and to investigate their use (i.e. briquettes). GOI is receiving assistance in the development of peat from Governments of Finland and the Netherlands. Also, GOI, has undertaken a coal transport and utilization study.

Geothermal

15. Surface manifestation of geothermal energy are found on all islands except Kalimantan, but only a few site has been investigated. Potential reserves are estimated at 10,000 MW, distributed as follows: Java 5,500 MW, Sulawesi 1,400 MW, Sumatera 1,100 MW and other islands 2,000 MW.

Substantial drilling will be required to confirm the potential. First large scale generating station (30 MW) was commissioned in 1983. Some 400 MW are planned to be installed by the end of 1983-94 under the fourth and fifth five year plans.

Fuelwood/Biomass

16. Currently there is a program to plant 325,000 hectares of wood annually through the year 2000, of which about 40 per cent would be for fuelwood use. Other activities underway or in the planning stage include an inventory of forest resources, the promotion of private sector involvement in fuelwood production for the use of charcoal briquettes where they are less expensive than kerosene to use, and where fuelwood shortages exist; and the potential for energy use of wood waste (which amounts to about 30 million m^3 annually), especially in sawmills.

Renewable energy development

17. A Study on rural renewable energy development in Kalimantan will assist GOI to formulate and plan a programme for development of renewable energy supply options for meeting the energy needs of selected rural locations. It will also prepare a framework of methodologies and guidelines for formulation and planing of similar programmes for other areas in Indonesia. The project began in March 1984. The supply options considered for the program included mini hydropower, forests, small coal deposits, peat, wood waste and agricultural residues. The study was designed to facilitate the preparation of viable investment projects.

18. The use of other biomass resources, such as rice husk and straw will be addressed in the regional energy

development project in WestJava which is being carried out with assistance from the Netherlands. The study for West Java will develop an energy classification map of the region and indicate priorities for development including fuelwood, biomass and other energy sources.

Demonstration projects

19. Several demonstration projects on the application of photovoltaics have been built in Secang, Central Java (1400 Watt) for clean water pumping, TV and lighting; in Boyolali, Central Java (100 watt) and Majalengka (100 watt), West Java for TV and lighting.

Wind power demonstration projects have also been constructed in Parangteritis, Central Java to produce electricity for TV and lighting.

Small size biogas digesters have been built in several areas using animal waste.

Several local designed gasifier are on test-operations using woods, charcoal or agricultural waste as feedstock to generate electricity and to run diesel engines.

Electricity

20. The programme for diversification of energy has most potential in the electricity sector and has a wide choice of primary energy compared to the transportation sector. The programme towards diversification in the electricity sector was initialized with the commissioning of the geothermal power at Kamojang of 30 MW in 1983, and a smaller plant at the Dieng Plateau and the Suralaya steam coal fired power plant of 400 MW capacity in 1985 for the first phase. Substantial progress has also been achieved in hydropower development. The development and planned programmes towards further utilization of indigenous and renewable energy is shown in tables 7 and 8.

Table 7. Primary Energy of the Electricity Sector.

Units: million TCE

	1974	(%)	1982	1983	1984	(%)
Oil	0.954	80	3.47	3.99	4.06	55.8
Hydro	0.235	20	1.37	2.03	2.95	40.6
Coal	—		—	0.04	0.17	.02
Geothermal	—		—	0.07	0.09	.01
Total	1.189		4.48	6.13	7.27	

Table 8. Generating Capacity by fuel type at the end of Repelita II-III, and plans for Repelita IV

Units: MW

	Repelita II (1979/80)	(%)	Repelita III (1983/84)	(%)	Repelita IV (1988/89)	(%)
Oil	1 937.7	84.7	3 345.4	85.6	5 075.4	55.4
Hydro	350.7	15.3	537.5	13.7	2 012.5	21.9
Coal	–		–		1 830.0	20.0
Geothermal	–		30.0	0.7	250.0	2.7
Total	2 288.4		3 912.9		9 167.9	

21. On the distribution side, the interconnection of the Java electricity grid of 150 kv has been completed. By early 1985 a 500 kv system covering West and Central Java was completed, and will be extended to East Java by 1987. The current generation expansion program of the public electricity corporation (PLN) indicates an increase in capacity to 15,000 MW by 1993/94. The major growth will be achieved by the construction of coal — fired thermal, hydro and geothermal power plants, reducing oil's share of generation from 84 per cent at present to 20 per cent in 1993/94. The latest statistics on captive power generating capacity (1982/83) indicate a total of 3,000 MW or nearly 77 per cent of the public electricity system's capacity; but the growth of these plants on an average annual basis declined substantially from 6 per cent between 1974/75 and 1979/80 to 0.9 per cent in 1980/81 and 0.2 per cent in 1981/82.

22. The rural electrification programme in REPELITA IV will primarily be based on the supply from the existing or planned power grid. Besides, several microhydro (totaling 52 MW) and decentralized diesel power plants (totaling 132 MW) will be constructed to meet the rural needs. It is expected that an additional 7000 villages with around 1.6 million consumers will be electrified through the programmes.

F. WATER QUALITY AND POLLUTION CONTROL

1. Water quality monitoring

1.1. *Scope of water quality monitoring*

The study of water quality is conducted in various ways depending greatly on the requirements for the data and the purpose of the study.

a. Water quality inventory of water resources for the baseline study:

Monitoring is conducted periodically, monthly or every three months for a period of one to two years. The Global Environmental Monitoring System (GEMS) guidelines are used in the sampling and analysis programme.

b. Monitoring of water pollution:

Monitoring of rivers or reservoirs which may be polluted by domestic, industrial or agricultural waste is constantly conducted monthly or every three months. Sampling is done by using the GEMS method and grab system. However, if the study is made in relation to effluent water study, another method is used, namely the composite method, and we are not bound to periodic samples.

The monitoring network as indicated in figure 1 and figure 2 consists of rivers and reservoirs included in the programme, which has been realized during the period of 1979-1983 as a part of five year plan of water quality monitoring.

1.2. *Water quality inventory of natural water*

The aim of the inventory is to develop the water resources for various beneficial uses and to obtain baseline data on locations which are relatively not yet polluted.

During the period of 1979-1983 water quality inventory for baseline study has taken place on 103 rivers, 11 reservoirs and 8 locations of ground water for a total of 203 locations. This monitoring network is at present being extended to other parts of Indonesia.

1.3. *Urban water quality monitoring*

Monitoring of water quality in urban areas assumed to be polluted by domestic and industrial waste water, covers 21 rivers, 1 reservoir and 8 ground water locations on the island of Java and Bali, 1 river in Sumatera and 4 rivers in Kalimantan, for a total of 74 locations.

Figure 1A shows the polluted areas of various rivers, which have been chosen for the monitoring study, i.e. the Ciliwung river, polluted downstream after passing Jakarta city, and the Citarum river where pollution starts at the upstream part due to industrial and domestic waste water from Bandung and surroundings. The Surabaya river which is a branch of the Brantas delta is polluted by industrial and domestic waste water. The level of pollution in those rivers have effected beneficial water uses for drinking water supply and fishery.

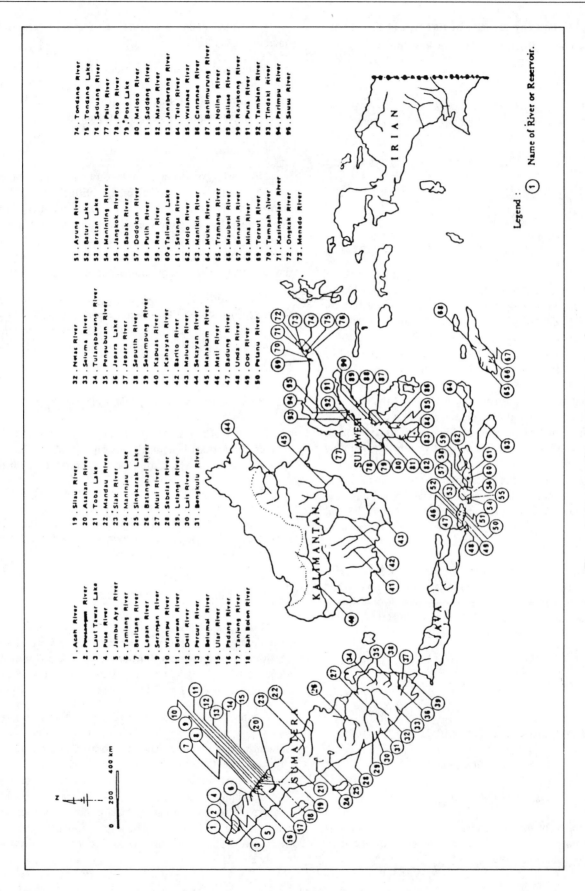

Figure 1. Water quality monitoring network

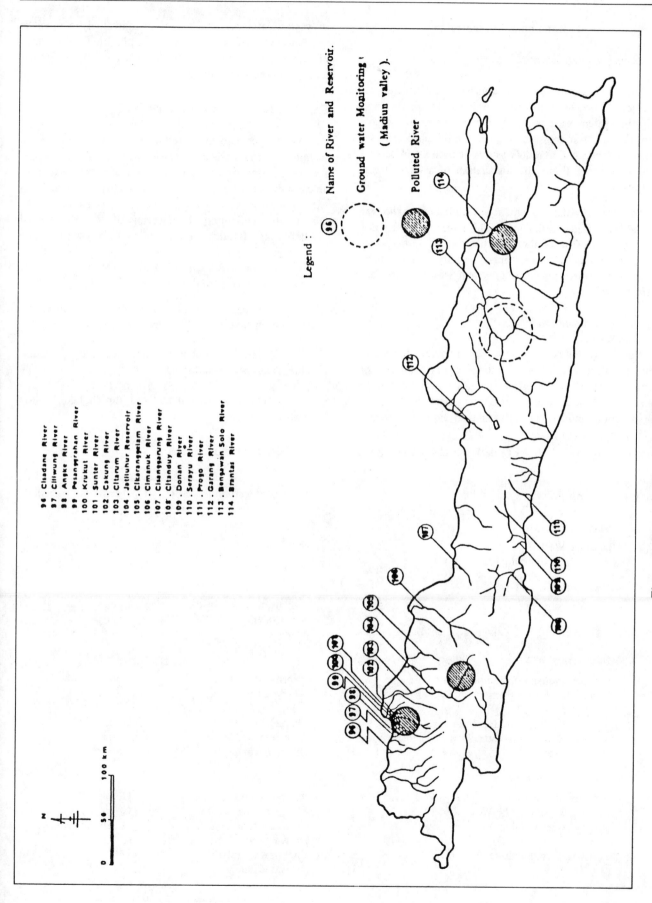

Figure 2. Water quality monitoring network (Java)

2. Water pollution control

2.1. *Domestic waste water*

The purification system for domestic waste in municipal cities has not been properly developed, so for the time being the system used is mostly the conventional method as applied in rural areas, namely the septic tank. The sewerage system for domestic waste is being built in several cities, however without the installation of a waste treatment plant.

The only installation which was built before the war was the Imhofftank in Bandung. This tank is presently not functioning, because of the fact that the incoming pollution load exceeds by far its storage capacity. A pilot plant for domestic waste purification system was built in Tangerang (West Java).

2.2. *Industrial waste water*

Not many industrial plants own a system for waste water purification. Table 1 shows several examples of various types of treatment techniques which have been applied in Indonesia, namely in the real estate in Surabaya and in various industrial plants using an individual system of waste treatment. The system of individual treatment is not yet developed so far that it is applicable for thousands of industries scattered through Indonesia. The use is limited only to big industries.

2.3. *Pilot plant and experimental plant*

As a support to the development of pollution control technique in Indonesia a pilot plant was set up in Tangerang for the purification of domestic waste using the system of an extended aeration activated sludge. This plant which has the capacity to surve 15,000 inhabitants was built by the Directorate of Sanitary Engineering of the Ministry of Public Works. Besides, an experimental plant with a waste water capacity of 1-3 liter/second was built by the Institute of Hydraulic Engineering (DPMA) of the Ministry of Public Works. This experimental plant covers:

a.   Chemical treatment (comprising coagulation and sedimentation) in Cimahi, West Java; already operational.

b.   Chemical treatment and activated sludge in South Bandung; in experimental stage.

c.   Chemical treatment and biofilter in Jakarta; also in experimental stage.

Table 1. Available water pollution control technology in Indonesia

Waste water sources	Treatment technique	Treatment efficiency
Domestic, in urban area		
1. Bandung, West Java. Service area: Central part of the city.	Imhoff tank.	Very low, overload
Industrial estate		
1. Rungkut, Surabaya, East Java.	Oxidation ditch, the load is equivalent to 11,000 people.	Good
Individual industries		
1. Fertilizer industry, Cikampek, West Java. Chromium vi waste from cooling water.	Electrolysis reduction, followed by alkaline sedimentation.	Good
2. Textile industry, Bandung, West Java.	Chemical treatment.	Good
3. Synthetic fibre, Tangerang, West Java.	Activated sludge.	Good
4. Petroleum refineries.	Oil separator.	Good
Pilot plant and experimental plant		
1. Domestic waste water, Tangerang, West Java.	Activated sludge.	Good
2. Industrial area, Cimahi, West Java.	Chemical treatment.	Good
3. Textile industry, Jakarta.	Chemical treatment, Activated biofilter.	Under experiment.
4. Industrial area, Bandung, West Java.	Chemical treatment, Activated sludge.	Under experiment.

V. PROGRESS IN THE IMPLEMENTATION OF THE MAR DEL PLATA ACTION PLAN IN THAILAND*

A. WATER RESOURCES DEVELOPMENT ACTIVITIES IN THAILAND

1. Introduction

Since the United Nations Water Conference, held at Mar del Plata, Agentina in March 1977, Thailand has accelerated various water resources development activities, namely, the improvement of survey, monitoring and evaluation, and data collection; the development of large and small scale water resources including groundwater; as well as the development of on-farm water distribution systems.

In addition, attempts on water supply and sanitation development have been undertaken so as to expand the prosperity to rural areas. Occasionally, hydroelectric power generation has been involved in large-scale project but mini hydropower is another aim to mitigate the energy crisis. Studies have been carried out and protective measures and

ever, Thailand hopes to seek substantial assistance from the developed countries.

2. Irrigation

Water resources development for irrigation has been mainly undertaken by the Royal Irrigation Department. Irrigated area of large-medium scale project, beneficial area of small scale irrigation project, dike and ditch project, and land consolidation project are shown in Table 1.

Pump irrigation projects were constructed by the Royal Irrigation Department and the National Energy Administration. Most of the projects utilize surface water except an area of 6,758 hectares in Sukhothai province where groundwater is utilized. Detailed irrigated areas of the groundwater projects are also shown in Table 1.

Table 1. Accumulated area of irrigation development projects Implemented by the Royal Irrigation Department

Year	Irrigated Area of Large-Medium Scale Project (Hectare)	Beneficial Area of Small Scale Irrigation Project	Dike and Ditch Project (Hectare)	Land consolidation Project (Hectare)		Groundwater Irrigation Project (Hectare)
				Intensive	Extensive	
1981	2 797 214	385 238	1 177 037	69 900	11 246	5 600
1982	2 855 632	464 541	1 177 209	81 870	21 109	5 600
1983	2 918 377	546 602	1 193 817	82 702	33 230.	5 600
1984	3 024 078	634 502	1 215 197	82 702	52 741	6 758
1985	3 089 561	704 521	1 252 820	82 702	63 678	6 758

solutions on environmental effects caused by water resources development have been devised.

Mobilization of internal and external capital resources for improvement and development of the above activities has been sought but little progress has been achieved. How-

3. Hydroelectric development

Medium and large hydroelectric projects

As of September 1986, twelve stations of large and medium scale power projects totalling 2,013 MW with the average annual energy of 5,025 Gwh are in operation. These hydroelectric dams are capable of storing 37,926 MCM. Development during the past four years 1983-1986 comprises four projects, Khao Laem 300 MW, Mae Ngat 9 MW, Sirindhorn Unit 3, 12 MW and Srinagarind Unit 4 reversible pumped turbine 180 MW.

*Country paper prepared for the thirteenth session of the ESCAP Committee on Natural Resources. This paper has been reproduced without formal editing. The views expressed in it are those of the author and do not necessarily reflect those of the United Nations.

**Table 2. Small scale water resources development projects
Department of Land Development**

Project features	No. of Project		Capacity m^3		Beneficial area (Hectares)	
	1984	1985	1984	1985	1984	1985
Small dam	48	26	2 098 300	1 117 500	590	2 788
Pond	78	65	860 888	1 025 818	140	5 217
Weir	23	27	–	–	–	3 150
Swamp Rehabilitation	38	6	703 490	145 000	473	160

Table 3. Construction and maintenance of water resources projects undertaken by Accelerated Rural Development Office

Fiscal Year	Reservoir/Weir		Dredging Swamp/Pond		Pond excavation		Diversion system		Total	
	No. of Project	Cost (x 1 000 Baht)	No. of Project	Cost (x 1 000 Baht)	No. of Project	Cost (x 1 000 Baht)	No. of Project	Cost (x 1 000 Baht)	No. of Project	Cost (x 1 000 Baht)
Beginning- 1976	197	111 381	56	7 253	522	16 358	–	–	775	134 992
1977	65	44 826	53	12 918	110	6 069	–	–	228	63 813
1978	30	32 434	24	6 461	7	411	–	–	61	39 306
1979	15	33 517	28	8 479	20	1 844	1	986	64	44 826
1980	23	48 101	30	17 068	40	4 885	4	1 966	97	72 020
1981	30	82 493	26	13 982	22	5 333	14	7 706	92	109 514
1982	42	140 561	50	28 885	48	12 796	10	7 297	150	189 539
1983	42	115 537	54	34 786	52	15 550	11	10 257	159	176 130
1984	36	134 528	80	35 817	150	37 291	4	7 586	170	233 222
1985	35	157 841	92	53 950	156	52 441	4	1 573	287	265 805
1986	31	140 154	77	45 149	122	40 921	7	19 776	237	246 000
Total	546	1 041 373	570	282 748	1 249	193 899	55	57 147	2 420	1 575 167
Draft Plan 1987	33	112 360	129	67 107	29	8 879	13	23 442	204	121 788

Two projects totalling 252 MW with the average annual energy of 581 Gwh are under construction. These projects, namely Chiew Larn 240 MW and Huai Saphan Hin 12 MW, are expected to be completed in 1987.

List of these projects are shown in Table 4.

Small hydroelectric projects

Small Hydroelectric projects are divided into two groups as follows:

1. First group comprises the projects of which the generating capacity ranges between 6,000-200 KW. To date, eight projects totalling 11,515 KW with the average annual energy of 58.1 Gwh are in operation. Development during the past four years 1983-1986 comprises four projects totalling 4,915 KW with the average annual energy of 23.1 Gwh.

Seven project totalling 13,810 KW with the average annual energy of 73.2 Gwh are under construction. These projects are expected to complete within the year 1987.

List of these projects are shown in Table 5.

Table 4. Medium and large hydroelectric projects

Project name	No. of Units	Installed (MW)	Average energy Gwh	Year of completion
Existing Projects				
1. Bhumibol	7	553.0	1 414.1	May 1964
2. Nam Pung	2	6.0	15.0	October 1964
3. Ubolratana	3	25.0	56.1	March 1966
4. Sirindhorn	3	36.0	59.3	October 1971
5. Chulabhorn	2	40.0	76.4	October 1972
6. Sirikit	3	375.0	1 005.3	June 1974
7. Kang Krachan	1	19.0	77.2	August 1974
8. Srinagarind	4	540.0	1 162.0	February 1980
9. Bang Lang (Pattani)	3	72.0	208.0	June 1981
10. Tha Thung Na	2	38.0	166.6	December 1981
11. Khao Laem	3	300.0	756.0	December 1984
12. Mae Ngat	2	9.0	29.0	September 1985
Total	35	2 013.0	5 025	
Projects under construction				Expected year of completion
1. Chiew Larn	3	240.0	553.7	July 1987
2. Huai Saphan Hin	2	12.0	27.0	1987
Total	5	252.0	580.7	

Table 5. First group of the small hydroelectric projects
(Capacity between 6 000-200 KW)

Project name	Location province	Installed (KW)	Average energy (Gwh)	Completion date
Existing projects				
1. Mae Hong Son	Mae Hong Son	800	6.9	1972
2. Mae Kum Luang	Chiang Mai	3 200	18.4	1982
3. Huai Kum	Chaiyaphum	1 300	3.6	1982
4. Ban Santi	Yala	1 300	6.1	1982
5. Huai Mae phong	Phayao	860	4.7	1984
6. Mae Tian	Chiang Mai	1 930	8.2	1984
7. Mae Chai	Chiang Mai	875	4.6	1984
8. Mae Sariang	Mae Hong Son	1 250	5.6	1985
Total		11 515	58.1	
Projects under construction				Expected year of completion
1. Mae Mao	Chiang Mai	4 330	17.3	1986
2. Mae Tun	Chiang Mai	250	1.8	1986
3. Mae Sa-Nga	Mae Hong Son	5 040	32.6	1987
4. Mae Sap	Chiang Mai	1 360	4.8	1987
5. Mae Hat	Chiang Mai	820	2.8	1987
6. Lam Plok	Trang	1 270	7.8	1987
7. Lam Sin	Phattalung	740	6.1	1984
Total		13 810	73.2	

Table 6. Second group of the small hydroelectric projects
(Capacity less than 200 KW)

Project name	Location Province	Installed capacity KW	Year of completion
Existing projects			
1. Na Bon	Nakorn Sri Thammarat	15	1961
2. Ban Yang	Chiang Mai	124.5	1970
3. Ang Kang	Chiang Mai	10	1978
4. Khun Klang	Chiang Mai	180	1978
5. Doi Pui	Chiang Mai	7	1979
6. Chong Klam	Prachinburi	16	1979
7. Khun Kong	Chiang Mai	12	1980
8. Nam Dang	Chiang Mai	50	1980
9. St. Paul	Chum Porn	15	1980
10. Mae Tia	Chiang Mai	15	1981
11. Pu Muen	Chiang Mai	15	1981
12. Khun Wang	Chiang Mai	20	1982
13. Thung Luang	Chiang Mai	20	1982
14. Bo Keo	Chiang Mai	200	1983
15. Pang Bong	Chiang Mai	12	1983
16. Kam Pong	Chiang Mai	40	1983
17. Mae Chon Luang	Chiang Mai	40	1983
18. Mae Ton Luang	Chiang Mai	35	1984
19. Huai Pui	Chiang Mai	50	1984
20. Tung Lakorn	Chiang Mai	35	1984
21. Mae Hae	Chiang Mai	50	1984
22. Ai Kapoh	Na Ra Thiwat	100	1984
23. Kui Mang	Kanchanaburi	70	1984
24. Pa Pae	Mae Hong Son	10	1985
25. Meo Khun Wang	Chiang Mai	10	1985
26. Huai Moh	Chiang Mai	20	1985
27. Mae Mae	Chiang Mai	12	1985
Total		1 183.5	

Projects under construction			Expected year of completion
1. Huai Nam Khun	Chiang Rai	25	1986
2. Mae Loei	Chiang Mai	12	1986
3. Huai Nam Rin	Chiang Rai	15	1986
4. Mae Sa	Chiang Mai	15	1986
5. Ban Kud Chang	Chiang Mai	40	1986
6. Bang Gae Nai	Chiang Mai	20	1986
7. Khun Lao	Chiang Rai	12	1986
8. Pong Bao	Chiang Mai	15	1986
9. Long Khord	Chiang Mai	120	1987
10. Huai Sat Yai	Prajuab Kirikhun	130	1987
11. Pang An	Chiang Mai	10	1987
Total		414	

4. Domestic water supply

Under the programme for provision of clean water for rural communities, the National Potable Water Project has been established and included in the National Economic Development Plan since 1964. The project objective is to produce both surface and groundwater for consumption in all villages throughout the country. The Department of Mineral Resources (DMR), the Office of Accelerated Rural Development (ARD), the Department of Public Works (DPW), and the Department of Health (DOH) are responsible for development of groundwater in villages where surface water is not available. The National Security Command (NSC) through its Engineering Division joined these four agencies in developing groundwater for the politacally unstable areas near the international borders. Under the work plan of the project, at least 30,000 communities were aimed to have excess to potable groundwater. To achieve this target at least 50,000 water wells, must be drilled.

In keeping with the objectives of the United Nations Drinking Water and Sanitation Decade, the Royal Thai Government has embarked on an ambitious programme of providing clean drinking water for the entire rural population by 1987. The programme is based on Government Agencies teaching the rural population to construct large cement jar to catch rain water and at the same time providing funds on a revolving basis for construction materials. The criteria for minimum drinking water requirement was set at 2 litres per capita per day. According to the latest preliminary survey, the programme has resulted in the construction of 1.3 million 2,000 litre jars and 4.9 million jars of other sizes, which can serve about 70 per cent of the rural population. Therefore, there is still another 30 per cent of the rural population requiring about 1.7 million 2,000 litre jars to be constructed by 1987, in order to reach the goal of the National programme.

The Provincial Waterworks Authority (PWA) was established in 1979 as a state enterprise for urban and rural water supply activities outside Bangkok Metropolitan area. It is understood that larger villages with population above 5,000 are regarded as town and PWA has a mandate to plan and develop piped rural water supply for rural communities at the request of local authorities.

The Metropolitan Waterworks Authority (MWA) is a state enterprise responsible for providing water supply services for Bangkok and nearby cities, namely Nonthaburi and Samutprakarn with total area of 3,082 square kilometres. After the completion of the second project, Stage I – Phase 2 by the year 1986 MWA could increase the total water production to be 2.3 million cubic metres per day by obtaining raw water from surface source.

This amount of supply will be sufficient for serving an equivalent population of 4.5 million people including public services in an area of 450 square kilometres up to the year 1987.

According to MWA's projection, after the year 1987 water shortage will be severe due to increasing of water supply from surface source to compensate ground water phase-out plan. To cope with this situation, MWA presently expand the production and distribution system in accordance with the Third Bangkok Water Supply Improvement Programme (Stage II – Phase I Project). The main objective is to increase the water production capacity from surface source to total daily production of 2.8 million cubic metres to meet sufficiency for water requirements of 5.8 million people covering the service area of 580 square kilometres up to the year 1989.

The raw water to supply MWA's production system is obtained from Chao Phraya River through Klong Prapa raw water canal which is capable to deliver 42 CMS of flow through the length of 29 kilometres.

Presently, a flow of 30 CMS is required to supply the production system up to the year 1987. From the beginning of 1989 required raw water amount will be 36 CMS, and 46 CMS in the year 1991.

The afore-mentioned flow of raw water from surface source will be provided to achieve the Third Bangkok Water Supply Improvement Project target.

Statistics for the sources of water is shown in table 7 to 12.

Table 7. Water wells drilled by the Department of Mineral Resources during 1984-1986

Year	Number of wells	Total depth (ft)	Water quality				Pump installation	
			Fresh	Brackish	Salty	Dry	Hand pump	Motor pump
1984	2 341	324 266	2 183	3	13	142	2 172	14
1985	2 457	335 527	2 303	2	12	140	2 260	45
1986	2 416	336 779	2 291	3	15	107	2 272	22

Table 8. Water wells drilled by the Office of Accelerated Rural Development during 1984-1986

Year	Number of deep wells	Water quality			Dug wells
		Fresh water	Salty water	Dry	
1984	1 253	1 157	39	57	668
1985	1 109	1 109	–	–	586
1986	1 170	1 170	–	–	500

Table 9. Water wells drilled by the Department of Public Works

Year	Number of wells	Water quality	
		Fresh	Salty & Dry
1984	1 088	794	294
1985	1 551	1 189	462
1986	1 500	not available	not available

Table 10. Water wells with handpump installations drilled by the Department of Health during 1977-1986

Number of provinces	Number of amphoe	1977	1978	1979	1980	1981	1982	1983	1984	1985	1986	Total (well)
67	107	190	280	351	710	663	723	889	719	728	5 360	

Table 11. Water sources used by Provincial Waterworks Authority

Source	Urban water supply		Rural piped water supply systems		Total	
	Number	Percentage	Number	Percentage	Number	Percentage
Surface water	167	89.7	367	54.7	534	62.3
Ground water	12	6.5	304	45.3	316	36.8
Surface & Ground water	7	3.8	–	–	7	0.9
Total number of sources	186	100	671	100	857	100

Table 12. Statistics of sources of water supply by Metropolitan Waterworks Authority

Year	Surface water supply	Groundwater supply	Total supply (Million m^3/day)	% from groundwater	Remark
1984	1.659	0.339	1.998	17	
1985	1.877	0.255	2.132	12	
1986	2.071	0.200	2.271	8.8	approximate

B. INFORMATION AND EXPERIENCE ON MEASURES TAKEN SPECIFICALLY IN RESPONSE TO THE MAR DEL PLATA ACTION PLAN AND THE PROBLEMS ENCOUNTERED IN CARRYING OUT THE RECOMMENDATION OF THE UNITED NATIONAS WATER CONFERENCE

5. Assessment of Water Resources

Hydrologic activities are the pre-requisities for water resources development and, in general, they are classified in three categories. Basic hydrologic data collection and processing are those that belong to the first category. The second includes the qualitative and quantitative analysis of data using scientific methods and engineering judgement to assess the water balance of hydrologic cycle. The third category involves the application of the basic data to water resources development and management.

Hydrologic investigations have been carried out by many government agencies according to their needs. They are the Royal Irrigation Department, the National Energy Administration, the Meteorological Department, the Electricity Generating Authority of Thailand, the Land Development Department, the Harbour Department, the Port Authority of Thailand, the Hydrographic Department, the Forestry Department, the Department of Health, and the Industrial Works Department.

Due to the emphasis placed on water resources the government has created many agencies for implementing various programmes in water resources development. As a result, there is a large volume of data collected by these agencies as well as information from field experience. It is therefore, necessary to establish a net work for data/information exchange and to standardize information format for the benefit of all agencies concerned. A National Institute for Hydrology is currently being considered for the purpose of serving as a central organization for research and development and planning and dissemination of information.

6. Water use and efficiency

Over the past two decades irrigation has made a major contribution to Thailand's economy. Over three quarters of the growth in total agricultural output has been due to the expansion of the irrigated area.

However, the outlook for further irrigation development is problematic due to uncertainties in the prospect of rice exports and also due to limited opportunity for expansion of irrigated area at low cost.

To cope with the above problems it is the national policy to devise new strategies related to the agricultural sector by intensifying the use of the existing infrastructure more efficiently. Promotion of crop diversification and export oriented crop is also encouraged.

As a step towards that goal the Royal Irrigation Department has established a working committee to study and evaluate existing projects and to develop a long range plan as well as a clear objective to implement the programme. Pilot projects will be selected to test the improvement/modernization programme. Workshop/seminars in these fields will be held to assist the Royal Irrigation Department in establishing an ambitious programme.

7. Environment, health and pollution control

The concepts of sustainable development and the maximization of resource utilization have long been recognized and this resulted into practice into Thailand's first Environmental Act promulgated in 1975. For instance, consultation with FAO and IBRD experts upon the fish ladder circumstances of Chao Phraya Barrage before 1952 (during 1950-1952); a Science Committee was organized in 1959 to conduct study on the effects of inundation of over 300 km^2 by the Bhumiphol Reservoir which comprises 7 Environmental components namely: Flora, Fauna, Mineral Resources, Public Health, Meteorology, Hydrology and Archaeology.

After the proclamation of Ministerial Regulation in 1981 by the Science and Tech. Ministry RID as an implementing agency for the irrigation/water resource development is entrusted to incorporate a broad spectrum of Environmental/Ecological components to its project study in such projects which have either equal/greater than 12,800 ha of irrigated area or 15 km^2 of inundated area. The said study includes recommendation for monitoring and amelioration programmes.

Regarding the Environmental effects of an irrigation/water resource project, Thailand has a natural diversity which favours development. Those hazardous effects as experienced elsewhere, for example, the prevalence of blood fluke (Bilharzia) and soil degradation to Solonchak/Solonetz conditions, have not been found on Thai soil.

The latest advance in Thailand with regard to the environmental problem is the introduction of the remote sensing as a tool for environmental monitoring. However, a transfer and transformation of high level technology is needed from developed countries into the level needed for local conditions. Thailand Landsat Station is in a state of requiring upgradation in order to function more effectively.

Progress activities of the National Environmental Board concerning the environmental health and environmental standards, particularly with regard to water quality standards since 1983 may be summarized as below:

(i) Effluent:

    (i) (a)   Domestic Effluent Guidelines (Draft Standards):

Set by the Sub-Committee of Domestic Effluent Criteria under the Committee on Water (27 May 1984) and approved by the National Environment Board (31 Jan. 1985) to be issued under the Improvement and Conservation of National Environmental Quality Act.

(ii) Surface Water:

    (ii) (a)   Surface Water Resources Classification and Standards.

         Notification of Ministry of Science, Technology and Energy, 1986.

    (ii) (b)   Chao Phraya River Water Quality Standards.

         Notification of the Office of the National Environment Board, 1986.

    (ii) (c)   Thachin River Water Quality Standards.

         Notification of the Office of the National Environment Board, 1986.

8. Policy, planning and management

National Water Resources Committee had been established to carry out the policy and co-ordinate water resources development plans of the country so as to achieve the target of water resources development according to the national development plan as follows:

— to prevent different socio-economic problems.
— to increase agricultural production.
— to supply basic water demands for the people.
— to prevent shortage of energy within the country for development of populated area and industry.

9. Natural hazards

Flood in Thailand is brought by rainfall associated with the tropical depression rather than by typhoons or cyclones. Flood takes place concentratedly from the middle to the end of the rainy season.

The flood damages recorded in Thailand has not been statistically compiled at the national level. So far, records on flood damages are available separately from the Royal Irrigation Department, the Community Development Department and Bangkok Metropolitan Administration. RID concerns mainly with flood damages to the irrigation projects. BMA has data only for Metropolitan Bangkok, and CDD's data is limited to local districts.

As for the RID, the study on flood damages and mitigation measures are being conducted for a large area in the northeastern part of the country covering the Chi Basin. Also, two programmes of study namely the "water management system and monitoring programme in the Chao Phraya River Basin" and the "Flood forcasting system for the Chao Phraya River Basin" are going to be conducted in the near future.

10. Public information, education, training and research

Many activities related to the field of water resources have been carried out in the last few years. These cover the following topics:

— Study and plan for major river basins in Thailand e.g. Chi River, Bang Nara River, Chantaburi River, Yom River, Songkla Lake, and Sakae Krang River.

— Water quality development project particularly in response to the United Nations Drinking Water and Sanitation Decade.

— Land subsidence in Bangkok metropolitan area with the attempt of phasing out the use of underground water by 1987.

— Flood problem study in major urban cities and Bangkok. Flood forecasting and water management studies for Chao Phraya River will be carried out.

— Study and master plan for domestic water supply at a nation-wide scale. Phasing plan is carried out and partly implemented.

— Use of remote sensing as a tool for effective development and management of natural resources.

— Water resources study for populated area and industry especially in the East Coast areas and around big cities.

C. INFORMATION ON OPPORTUNITIES FOR MUTUAL SUPPORT IN IMPLEMENTING THE MAR DEL PLATA ACTION PLAN

With the growing volume of data distribution, it can be concluded that the application of satellite data has been increasing. This should call for a closer and more realistic regional co-operation in order to reduce cost of data and to produce efficient means for surveying and management of natural resources in the region. Countries covered by a particular LANDSAT receiving station may have to share some of the operating expenses of the station, particularly the access fee. The commercialization of LANDSAT system, while contributing to more efficient operation, also creates several new conditions on the users as well as the ground station operators. In order to ensure available environment for continued long term operation, all parties concerned should join together to work as a family for the common goal.

VI. USSR EXPERIENCE IN THE EXECUTION OF THE MAR DEL PLATA ACTION PLAN ON WATER RESOURCES*

by

Volynov A.**, Vladimirov V.***

Main problems pertaining to the study, use and conservation of water resources throughout the world have been defined at UN Conference on water resources (Mar del Plata, Argentine, 1977).

The Soviet Union actively participated in the preparation and work of the Conference; proposals made by the USSR were reflected in the recommendations called "Action Plan", they are concerned with the following (Ref. 1):

(a) Necessity to develop and improve the system of collecting and processing information covering qualitative and quantitative characteristics of water resources;

(b) Role of planning and forecasting in water management with the aim to ensure co-ordination of programmes of water engineering construction with perspectives of economic and social development in individual regions and countries;

(c) Improvement of the structures of water management;

(d) Significance of all-Union legislature with the help of which different aspects of water resources use and its protection are regulated;

(e) Raising efficiency of water use by reduced consumption per unit of produce owing to the implementation of advanced technology in both industrial and agricultural production;

(f) Necessity of long-term planning of water economy development on a regional basis or at a river basin level.

Solving of food supply programme, development of industry, power engineering, transport and communication means in some countries of ESCAP region are tightly connected with water resources development. In this region about 160 mill.ha is under irrigation constituting some 66 per cent of the world irrigated area with rural population

being 70-85 per cent. According to the data of ESCAP Natural Resources Committee water use should increase by the year 2000 (as compared with 1975) in agriculture — from 1.1 to 4.1 times; in industrial sector — from 1.7 to 2.7 times.

For the region where over 50 per cent of world population lives, realization of "Action Plan" is of urgent concern.

As stated at the 10th Session of the ESCAP Natural Resources Committee (Bangkok, Thailand, 1983) work is underway on "Action Plan" realization in the countries of the ESCAP region (Ref.2).

However, considerable difficulties arise in solving various water-related problems in some countries, therefore exchange of experience on an international scale is of particular importance.

In conformity with recommendations stipulated in the "Action Plan", a number of measures are being implemented in the Soviet Union aimed at solving of national problems and, in accordance with mutual assistance agreements. The USSR co-operates with countries of the region on a bilateral basis, and participates in the work of international organizations.

As regards *water resources evaluation* in the USSR the state integral system of water account and water cadastre is established which provides registration, control, systematization, storage, search and issue of both initial and generalized data (covering river basins, water use sites, administrative-territorial units, national economy sectors, ministries, departments, etc.) concerning resources and quality of ground water and its use. The system has at its disposal modern technical means (computers, communication, remote sensing). The work is inter-departmental: the USSR State Committee on hydrometeorology and environmental control is responsible for general co-ordination.

In conformity with the resolution of the USSR Council of Ministers, the data of state water cadastre should serve as a basis in decision-making associated with planning, forecasting, regulation of the country's water resources use and protection.

As regards *rational use of water* in the USSR a number of legal and organizational measures are envisaged as well

* Country paper prepared for the thirteenth session of the ESCAP Committee on Natural Resources. This paper has been reproduced without formal editing. The views expressed in it are those of the authors and do not necessarily reflect those of the United Nations.

** Deputy Chief, Department of Multipurpose Water Resources Utilization, USSR Ministry of Land Reclamation and Water Management, Moscow.

*** Head of Section, All-Union Designing Association (V/0 "Sojuzvodproekt"), same Ministry.

as activities are planned aimed at attaining higher efficiency of water use and protection of natural water sources against pollution and depletion. In order to furnish analytical information to each state or planning body in the USSR, the state system was introduced for water use account within the framework of statistical information reporting of enterprises (organizations) irrespective of their departmental subordination. Annual reporting covers information on volumes of water withdrawn, used and discharged with their quality indices.

In the USSR various measures are being taken to ensure economical use of water resources. Such measures include elaboration and implementation of advanced and effective patterns of water use and disposal at industrial enterprises and irrigation farming as well. There are limits for water withdrawal from water bodies which should not be violated.

Water withdrawal or waste water disposal is regulated by permissions issued by bodies responsible for the regulation of water use and conservation.

In every permission, water use conditions are specified, namely, annual and seasonal rates of water consumption, possible reduced rates in low water years, conditions of waste water disposal, permissible discharge of pollutants contained in wastewater into water bodies.

In the Soviet Union much attention has been paid to raising the quality and technical level of water supply systems since the UN Conference on water resources as demanded by the international decade of potable water supply and sanitation.

Specific water consumption in cities and rural settlements increased twice as much (about 310 1/day-per urban resident and 45 1/day per rural resident).

Stemming from the first-priority objective of municipal and domestic water supply development "Master Plan for agricultural water supply development for the period to the year 2000" has been elaborated (Ref. 3).

In many regions of the country land reclamation, and in particular, irrigation is indispensible in the intensification of agricultural production.

In the USSR land reclamation serves as a reliable factor contributing to the increase in agricultural produce and alleviating the effects of unfavourable natural-climatic conditions.

For the past 15 years newly irrigated area was devloped in Povolzhyie, Northern Caucasus, the south of Ukraine, in Moldavia.

As of 1984 irrigated area of the USSR made up 19.7 mill. ha. Irrigated land of Uzbekistan yields 96 per cent, of Tadjikistan — 95 per cent, of Turkmenia — about 100 per cent, Kirghizia — 84 per cent, and, Azerbaijan — 76 per cent of total crop production /4/.

Thus, land reclamation of the USSR contributes to the realization of food programme which serves the cause of social and economic development of the country.

In long-term programme of land reclamation adopted in 1984 it is envisaged to make more effective use of existing reclaimed land and to enlarge irrigated area from 30 to 32 mill. ha by the year 2000 (Ref. 3).

On this background of particular importance are problems of guaranteed water supply of irrigated land; great difficulties arise under conditions of water shortage experienced in the southern regions of the country, and specific requirements are set for water in agriculture.

Main trends in attaining higher levels of irrigation systems that ensure economical use of land and water resources are as follows: (Ref. 4, 5.):

— reconstructing existing open systems, equipping them with seepage-proof lining; and devices of water distribution ensuring reduction of water losses;

— implementing subsurface pressure pipelines enabling to attain high efficiency — up to 0.9, and high land use factor — 0.9-0.96;

— employing different methods of irrigation: sprinkling ("Fregat" and "Kuban" sprinkling machines), subsoil and underground irrigation, drip irrigation, mist irrigation;

— wide use of telemechanics and local automation means, creation of automated control systems of irrigation networks.

New types of irrigation machinery are produced commercially, production of pump and power units, automatic devices is also enlarged; in order to facilitate assembly designs of prefabricated items of hydraulic structures for irrigation, networks are unified, new economical kinds of reinforced concrete and nonmetallic pipes have been developed as well as industrially produced flumes for irrigation networks are produced.

Recycling and reuse systems gain scale at the industrial enterprises and power engineering, wasteless systems of technological water supply are being developed and implemented, the latter are considered in the USSR as perspective ones enabling to improve protection of water resources against depletion and pollution.

Implementation of recycling systems of water supply, as well as "dry" technological processes make it possible to considerably reduce consumption of fresh water per unit of produce, to diminish the volume of wastewater. For example, at metallurgical works situated in Donbass — industrial region of the country — 97 per cent of water demands are satisfied with the help of recycling systems, i.e. enterprises' operation mode is approaching to that of wasteless production.

At petroleum processing plants volume of recycling water shares 98 per cent of total water use. Technological units of petroleum processing plants have water-cooling systems replaced by air-cooling ones. For the purposes of wastewater cooling tubular units and air coolers are used.

In order to ensure normal operation of recycling water supply systems much attention is paid to elaboration and implementation of the latest methods, techniques, means and facilities for water treatment, restoration of its quality and stabilization, removal and utilization of pollutants contained in water.

As regards *environmental control* an important role is played by water-related measures.

Annual plans of water resources rational use and conservation stipulate construction of pre-treatment facilities, water treatment and tertiary treatment plants for municipal, industrial and agricultural wastewater; establishment of water conservation zone where a set of measures including technological, sanitary, those of field management, hydraulic construction, reclamative afforestation and the like are taken to prevent pollution and depletion of water reserves; special work is conducted to protect ground water.

"Environmental protection" measures should be integrated in project documents for designs of hydraulic structures and technico-economic substantiation is required.

As regards *policies, planning and management* particular importance is paid to attaining higher efficiency of water-economy programmes in the national and state plans of socio-economic development.

In the field of land reclamation the following programmes have been developed "Scheme of multi-purpose use and protection of the USSR water resources up to the year 2000", and branch-wise "Scheme of development-allocation of land reclamation and water economy of the USSR up to the year 2000" (Ref. 3).

Schemes of multi-purpose use and protection of water resources of main river basins — Dnieper, Kuban, Volga, Syrdarya, Amudarya, Chu are at present at the stage of specification and correction.

Water management and planning is provided with information on the basis of State Water Cadastre.

Automated control systems of water user complexes of the Dnieper and Syrdarya river basins have been designed and put into operation (ACSB-Dnieper and ACSB-Syrdarya) (Ref. 3, 6).

In 1984 owing to measures aimed at the improvement of water economy and irrigation and drainage systems it was managed to reduce the non-used land area, to ensure faultless operation of canals and pumping stations, to increase the number of irrigations on the average from 3.6 to 4.6 times.

Because of rational water use about 1.26 mill. ha of dry land was irrigated as compared with 1.12 mill. ha in 1983.

"Basic Principles of Water Legislature of the Soviet Union and Union Republics" were developed and enforced in 1971. This regulates all legal aspects of water use and protection.

An important measure that stimulates rational patterns of water use is the establishment of water charge for industrial enterprises beginning from 1982.

As regards *detrimental effects of water,* measures are envisaged in the field of flood control on territories prone to inundation.

As a rule, these measures should be considered in a complex while elaborating schemes of multi-purpose use and protection of river basins' resources.

As regards *education, training and research* there are higher and secondary technical schools for training engineers in the field of water economy, hydraulic engineering, land reclamation, hydrogeology, soil science and other disciplines. About 1.7 mill. specialists are employed in the system of the USSR land reclamation and water management.

Research organizations of the country deal with complicated (both theoretical and practical) problems of water economy solving them in accordance with inter-branch and branch-wise programmes and using advanced methods of investigation and technical means — systems analysis, computers, latest devices and equipment.

In higher schools of the USSR, representatives of developing countries are trained, educated and granted scholarships.

A programme for specialists from Asia and the Pacific was conducted under the auspices of higher economics course of the USSR State Planning Committee.

In 1984 Seminar on Effective use of water resources for power engineering development was held in Volgograd.

In 1985 Workshop and Study Tour "Efficiency of capital investments in water economy" was held in Tashkent for specialists of the ESCAP region.

The Soviet Union is ready to host in 1988 Seminar-Workshop "Registration, processing and generalization of information on water resources use" after co-ordinating this question with the ESCAP Natural Resources Division.

As regards *regional co-operation* a number of programmes are conducted in the USSR aiming to solve the problems of rational use and protection of transboundary water bodies.

There are agreements between the USSR and People's Republic of China for the Amour river basin, between the USSR and Mongolia – the Selenga river basin, USSR-Turkey – the Araks, Akhuryan river basins, etc., USSR – Islamic Republic of Iran – the Araks, Gerirud (Tedjen), Airek river basins.

The USSR representative participates as an observer in the Mekong Committee sessions.

A group of Soviet specialists elaborated in 1981 the first stage of the project "Environmental aspects of water economy development in the Mekong river delta" on the instructions of the UN Environmental Programme, thus contributing to the regional investigations of water economy effects over the environment. Accomplishment of proposals presented in the report of this group could help in creation of regional research and training centre to solve various water-related problems typical for delta zones.

As regards *international co-operation* large scope of work is shared by water economy organizations of the USSR in the field of scientific and technological co-operation and rendering technical assistance to socialist and developing countries of ESCAP (Ref. 7, 8).

Soviet specialists prepared proposals concerning reconstruction of existing and construction of newly designed rice systems of Viet Nam with regulation of moisture regime irrespective of climatic conditions with a high level of field management and mechanization thus enabling to obtain gross crop of rice up to 90-100 mill. tons.

Vietnamese specialists were trained in selection of proper irrigation and drainage methods, technology of hydraulic structures construction for natural conditions of Viet Nam. With the USSR technical assistance construction of multipurpose headworks is underway for irrigation, flood regulation and power production; power plant output is about 2 mill. kW.

Based on experience gained in the USSR technical recommendations were developed pertaining to design, construction and operation of rice irrigation systems in Lao People's Democratic Republic.

Within the framework of intergovernmental agreement with India the Soviet water agencies keep contacts in the field of research and technology co-operation covering a wide range of problems: physical modelling and mathematical simulation of hydraulic structures; biological protection of irrigation systems against algae growth; designing of dams; multi-purpose use of surface and ground water, etc.

Technical assistance in the field of hydraulic engineering design is rendered in Afghanistan, Burma, Lao People's Democratic Republic, Mongolia.

Questions of directing the Pyandj river into the old river bed, reconstruction of existing irrigation systems are being solved in Afghanistan, while elaboration of pneumatic water lifts for pastures, of solar photogenerators and wind power plants for water lift is conducted in Mongolia.

REFERENCES

1. United Nations. Report of the United Nations Water Conference, Mar del Plata, Argentina, 1977, New York, 1977.

2. Review of the Implementation of the Mar del Plata Action Plan, Proceedings of the 10th Session of the Committee on Natural Resources, Water Resources Series, No. 59, New York, 1985.

3. N.F. Vasiliev, Land Reclamation personnel on the new stage of fight for increase of Land Fertility. Gidrotechnika i melioratsia, 1985, No. 1.

4. B.G. Shtepa, Technical progress in Land Reclamation, "Kolos", 1983.

5. Land Reclamation and Water Management. Information Review, issue No. 2, Land Reclamation Development in the USSR, 1984.

6. The methods of system analysis in Land Reclamation and Water Management. Edited by B.G. Shtepa, Gidrometeoizdat, L., 1983.

7. USSR for the countries of Asia and Africa: hydraulic engineering. The 1st ICID Regional Conference for Asian and African countries, Tashkent, 1976, M., 1976.

8. V.A. Vladimirov, The Soviet Union helps ESCAP countries in Water Resources studies. "Sovetskaya Panorama", APN Mesenger, No. 85 (2865), 1984.

Part Two :

GROUNDWATER

VII. GROUNDWATER RESOURCES DEVELOPMENT IN THE ESCAP REGION*

INTRODUCTION

1. In view of the urgent need to provide an adequate supply of safe drinking water for the world's population, the United Nations designated the period 1981-1990 as the International Drinking Water Supply and Sanitation Decade.

2. The nature of the water supply problem in the ESCAP region is such that the need to provide safe drinking water is more urgent in rural than in urban areas. This is supported by the fact that out of a reported 1,128 million people without safe drinking water in the developing countries of the ESCAP region, 82 per cent live in rural areas while only 18 per cent are in urban areas.

3. As the rural population in developing countries is scattered over large areas it is not economically feasible to provide rural areas with piped surface-water supply systems. Therefore, ground water plays a very important role in rural water supply in this region, particularly in areas where surface water resources are limited. Besides, it is observed that in many countries and areas — Bangladesh, Guam, India, Japan, and the Republic of Korea, to name just a few — ground water is much cheaper to develop than surface water. In view of the foregoing, the Committee on Natural Resources at its tenth session recommended that the subject of ground-water resources development in the Asian and Pacific region be reviewed at its thirteeth session in 1986.

4. The purpose of this paper is to provide information with regard to the status of ground-water resources development in the ESCAP region, the part played by the United Nations system of organizations in the development of the region's ground-water resources, the problems of ground-water development which are common to some countries in the region, to identify prospects for regional co-operation and to draw specific conclusions and recommendations towards achieving rational development, management and utilization of ground-water resources in the region.

5. While the primary responsibility for meeting the goals of the Decade rests with the Governments of the developing countries, the role of the United Nations and its specialized agencies is to assist the countries in their national efforts towards achieving these goals. The information contained in this paper is expected to provide a basis for the formulation of programmes that will lead to the rational and optimum development of ground-water resources in the region.

6. The secretariat would like to inform the Committee of the co-operation received from the Water Resources Branch, Natural Resources and Energy Division, Department of Technical Co-operation for Development, United Nations Headquarters, in the preparation of this paper by providing country data on ground-water development collected from various government organizations, consultants and specialists.

7. It is hoped that after the consideration of the information provided in this paper, the Committee may wish to make recommendations with regard to further activities to be carried out on the subject of ground-water resources development.

A. GROUND WATER AS AN IMPORTANT SOURCE OF WATER SUPPLY

8. Tapping of ground-water resources for drinking water supply in the region dates back to ancient times and is now widely practised. For example, in the Philippines (1) the use of ground water has been reported since 1521, while in China wells of several hundred metres depth were drilled by using bamboo rods in the sixteenth century.

9. The main reasons for which ground water is a significant source for safe drinking water supply are: it is commonly free of pathogenic organisms as well as of turbidity and colour and therefore can normally be used without any treatment; its temperature and chemical composition are generally constant; its availability is geographically widespread over the entire region and is relatively unaffected by short droughts; and in many arid and semi-arid regions it is the only source of water supply.

10. The complete absence of bacteria and other microorganisms in almost all ground-water resources under normal conditions is due to the fact that the environment of the ground-water reservoir is not conducive to the survival of micro-organisms as it is insulated, lacks oxygen and usually provides some degree of filtration. Hence, it is rare for a newly drilled well in most types of geological units to yield water containing living organisms. Under some circumstances, however, particularly in karstic limestones or in other rocks having large openings or channels, polluted water does have an opportunity to travel considerable distances without destruction of micro-organisms. Even in such cases the movement of organisms into supplies of drinking water can be prevented by proper location of well sites and/or the removal of the sources of pollution.

---

* Originally issued as E/ESCAP/NR.13/6.

11. In many countries ground water has proved to be the most convenient, economical and reliable (being subject to less seasonal fluctuation) source, particularly in rural areas. A recent study has indicated that ground water is one of the main factors which contributed to alleviating the famine that threatened China and India earlier in the century following the rapid growth of population in those countries.

12. The use of ground water is not limited to domestic uses: it is also widely used for agricultural and industrial purposes. For example, almost all the countries in the ESCAP region use ground water for various purposes – domestic, agricultural and industrial. A few island countries, like Fiji, Maldives and Tuvalu, have limited the use of ground water to domestic purposes.

13. Ground-water utilization in various sectors of the economy in selected countries of the ESCAP region is presented in table 1.

14. For the majority of the countries in the region, ground water is a major factor affecting their socio-economic development. In Kiribati, a Pacific island country, ground water is the only source of water supply apart from very restricted practices of rain-water harvesting. In such countries ground water is the key factor in sustaining the lives of their population. In Guam, it is a vital resource for sustaining a viable economy on the island. In Viet Nam, there are many regions in which surface water is not available and ground water is the only source of water supply.

In Australia, ground water is important in augmenting short supplies of surface water. In fact, it is the main source of water for more than half the continent, where reliable surface water supplies are not readily available. In India and Pakistan, ground water is an important source of water supply for irrigation. For instance, India obtains 40 per cent of its irrigation water from ground water. In the Republic of Korea, the water requirements for its industries are satisfied mainly from ground-water resources. In Malaysia, until about 20 years ago surface water was readily available in terms of both quantity and quality. However, a considerable increase in water demand has cuased serious shortages in water supply, and ground-water resources have increasingly assumed an important role for supplementing the surface-water resources. In the Philippines, ground water has been used primarily for domestic water supply. About 28 per cent of the total population are supplied with ground water tapped from wells and springs. Another sector in which ground water is utilized is industry: about 50 per cent of the total industrial water requirement is satisfied by ground water.

In Thailand, the expansion of national economic development programmes, which began in 1955, increased the requirements of water for domestic, agricultural and industrial needs to a level where the water demand could no longer be satisfied by the surface-water resources alone, and ground-water resources had to be resorted to in order to make up the deficit. In New Zealand, the majority of

Table 1. Ground-water utilization (million m³/year) by various sectors of the economy in selected countries of the ESCAP region (tentative figures)

Country or area	Domestic and/or municipal	Irrigation	Industry	Total
1. Australia	1 424	1 297	111	2 832
2. Bangladesh[a]	1 710	5 997	24	7 731
3. Guam	. .	. .	. .	35
4. India	4 600	143 500	1 900	150 000
5. Indonesia	3 640	11	33	3 684
6. Malaysia*	60%	5%	35%	100%
7. Pakistan	. .	40 000	. .	40 000
8. Philippines	2 000	. .	1 000	3 000
9. Thailand	541	202	181	924

Source: Figures are based on country data provided by the Department of Technical Co-operation for Development, United Nations Headquarters, New York, except for Bangladesh.

[a] *National Water Plan Project: Second Interim Report, June 1984,* vol. III, *Groundwater Availability* (Ministry of Irrigation, Water Development and Flood Control, Bangladesh), pp. 2-4.

Note: * Absolute figures not available.

Two dots (. .) indicate that data are not available or are not separately reported.

regions depend entirely on ground water. It is observed that 13 of its 40 large cities and towns currently depend on ground-water resources for water supply.

15. Utilization of ground water in relation to the total water use in selected countries of the region is given in table 2. It will be observed from this table that ground-water utilization constitutes a significant portion of the total water use.

Table 2. Ground-water utilization as a percentage of total water use

Country or area	Percentage
1. Guam	75
2. Iran (Islamic Republic of)	41
3. Japan	16
4. Kiribati	100
5. Philippines	35

Source: Ground water in the Pacific region, Natural Resources/ Water Series No. 12 (United Nations publication, Sales No. E.83.II. A.12), except for the Islamic Republic of Iran, which is based on data from "Water resources profile" (unpublished) prepared by ESCAP.

16. In Japan, the ratios of ground-water use to total water use in various sectors are: industrial use, 41 per cent, domestic use, 28 per cent, irrigation, 6.6 per cent, and air conditioning, 100 per cent.

17. The development of ground-water resources is relatively inexpensive, particularly if it can be tapped at shallow depths. The average approximate cost of ground water, which includes the costs of drilling, well construction, pumps and accessories, fuel/energy, and operation and maintenance, for selected countries of the region is given in table 3.

Table 3. Ground-water extraction cost in selected countries

Country or area	Cost per m^3 at well-head (US dollars)
1. Bangladesh	0.01 (1979)
2. India	0.02 (1973)
3. Japan	0.01-0.04 (1980)
4. Malaysia	0.06-0.09 (1981)
5. Northern Mariana Islands	0.03 (1983)
6. Pakistan	0.01 (1981)
7. Philippines	0.03 (1983)
8. Samoa	0.04 (1983)

Source: Cost figures are based on country data provided by the Department of Technical Co-operation for Development, United Nations Headquarters, New York.

18. According to available information the approximate average costs (including treatment and conveyance costs) of surface-water supply (2) in Bangladesh and India are $US 0.10 (1978) and $US 0.08 (1977) respectively. This suggests that ground water is much cheaper than surface water in these countries. Besides, recent studies indicate that ground water is much cheaper to develop than surface water in countries or areas like Guam, Japan, and the Republic of Korea, although information on comparative cost data is not available.

19. Given the significance that ground water holds for countries of the ESCAP region, the importance of conservation and protection of this natural resource from pollution cannot be overemphasized. As the aquifers are relatively large in size and their turnover is slow, the pollution of ground-water bodies is more critical than that of lakes or rivers. For instance, while the overall residence time for water in lakes is approximately 10 years and for rivers only about 10 days, the average residence time for active (available) ground water is of the order of several hundred years. Thus, when a ground-water body is seriously polluted, its use may have to be discontinued for generations. Besides, cleaning contaminated water is technologically difficult and extremely expensive. Consequently, it is cheaper to take preventive measures than remedial measures.

B. ASSESSMENT OF GROUND-WATER RESOURCES DEVELOPMENT IN THE ASIAN AND PACIFIC REGION

20. Development of ground-water resources in the Asian and Pacific region has occurred since ancient times. However, large-scale development of ground water began only after the Second World War and has been expanding considerably since then. In the Asian part of the Union of Soviet Socialist Republics, which has a considerable geological exploration and drilling capacity, knowledge of ground-water occurrence and potential is quite advanced and even specific problems such as tapping ground water in permafrost have been successfully dealt with.

21. In China, a major thrust in ground-water development was initiated in the 1950s and the country has maintained this momentum until now. Among the areas affected by this major drive are the northern Huang-Huai-Hai plain, the ground-water aquifer of which is tapped primarily for irrigation, the coastal areas of northern and southern China, where deep artesian aquifers are tapped for water supply of cities, towns and industrial areas, the loess areas of the north and the karst areas of the central south.

22. In Bangladesh, India and Pakistan, considerable progress in ground-water development has been achieved involving the drilling of hundreds of thousands of tube-wells

and also the digging of open wells, mainly for irrigation purposes.

23. In Bangladesh (3), the World Bank had financed two deep tube-well projects for 7,000 wells: the first project, financed in 1973, for 3,000 wells had been completed and the second project for 4,000 wells had been approved for co-financing by the Bank, the United Kingdom of Great Britain and Northern Ireland and Australia. The Bank had also financed two shallow tube-well projects: the first for 10,000 wells equipped with diesel pumps and the second for 180,000 tube-wells with hand pumps.

24. Exploration of ground water was initiated in central Burma in about 1980 and, after a pilot development of about 25 wells, the feasibility of further development of ground water in this region was established. Based on the success of this pilot development, the World Bank appraised the first tube-well project in late 1982, and later approved a Bank loan for $US 14 million for the construction of 106 tube-wells for irrigating approximately 7,300 hectares. In Burma (3), as of 1983, there had been no development of ground water for irrigation.

25. In India (3), as of 1983, the Bank had financed three tube-well projects in the State of Uttar Pradesh: the first project, financed in 1962, consisted of 800 wells with traditional design; the second project, financed in 1980, consisted of 500 wells with new improved design concepts; and the third project, financed in 1983, consisted of 2,200 wells with all the design innovations successfully tried out under the second project. The third project involved a Bank loan of $US 101 million. Virtually all Bank-financed ground-water projects have been or are being implemented by national organizations or departments.

26. In Maldives, Singapore and Sri Lanka, ground-water development has faced some difficulties. In some highly populated islands of Maldives, scarce ground-water resources are subjected to exhaustion, sea-water intrusion and pollution. In Singapore, ground-water resources are not significant. In the northern part of Sri Lanka, ground-water development in fractured and karstic low-lying limestones has resulted in sea-water intrusion.

27. In their national efforts towards achieving the goals of the International Drinking Water Supply and Sanitation Decade, several countries, including Bangladesh, Burma, India, Nepal, Pakistan and Viet Nam, are implementing various programmes to supply their rural areas with ground water.

28. In countries such as Malaysia, Bhutan and the Lao People's Democratic Republic, which had not undertaken major ground-water development programmes until recently, plans for large-scale development are now being seriously considered.

29. In the Pacific island countries, such as the Cook Islands, Fiji, Niue, Papua New Guinea, Samoa, Solomon Islands and Tonga, ground water exists in the form of fresh-water lenses, particularly on small islands of less than 100 km² in area and less than 3 km in width. In atolls (4), the fresh-water layer is quite thin and does not generally exceed one metre. Therefore, the exploitable ground-water potential on the atolls is not significant and will not be able to meet the requirements of domestic use. This is particularly true in the case of islands whose width is less than a half mile. In such islands and atolls, most of the domestic water supply is derived from rain-water catchments. Ground water in island countries is developed mostly by means of shallow dug or drilled wells which tap the fresh-water lens in its upper part. In most cases the yields have to be kept low so as to leave the fresh-water lens as undisturbed as possible.

30. The hydrogeological conditions of the Asian and Pacific region vary substantially from place to place. However, in general, the region is endowed with large quantities of ground-water resources. Many areas have vast ground-water reservoirs storing extensive amounts of water and receiving regular annual recharge. According to preliminary findings by a World Bank study (5), large deep underground fresh-water reservoirs exist in Bangladesh, Burma, India and Nepal, particularly in the Ganges, Brahmaputra and Irrawaddy basins, the exploration and development of which are expected to benefit up to five hundred million people living around those basins. A preliminary study also indicated that in Bangladesh fresh artesian aquifers extend to a maximum depth of 5,000 feet below the surface; in the Ganges river plain of India, to a depth of 6,000 feet; in Nepal, to a depth of 5,000 feet; and in Burma, to a depth of 7,000 feet. The same study indicated that, in spite of the great depths at which these aquifers are located, the cost of obtaining water from them could be less than one tenth of the cost of surface water used in irrigation projects for the same areas. The reason given for this is that, as they are artesian aquifers, the water in these deep aquifers is under pressure with the result that if they are tapped by wells, they are expected to supply water indefinitely, often without the use of pumps. In the Philippines, the estimated water requirement for domestic, municipal and industrial uses for the year 2000 is 28 billion m³ per year, while the total net ground-water inflow (or recharge) is 33 billion m³ per year. Therefore, the safe yield of ground water in the country, it appears, will be quite adequate to meet the total water requirements of these sectors until the year 2000. The majority of areas also have underlying aquifers bearing ground water which is of a quality suitable for drinking and other purposes and can be tapped at relatively low depths. A compilation of the estimated ground-water potential and its utilization in selected countries of the region, based on available data, is given in table 4. From

**Table 4. Estimated ground-water potential and ground-water utilization in selected countries
in the region (tentative figures)**

Country or Area	Exploitable potential (Million m³/year)	Utilization (Million m³/year)	Utilization as percentage of potential
1. Australia	37 377	2 832	8%
2. Bangladesh[a]	..	7 731	..
3. Guam	70	35	50%
4. India	..	150 000	..
5. Indonesia	455 520	3 684	1%
6. Malaysia	23 200	..	..
7. Mongolia[b]	6 000	..	..
8. Pakistan	..	40 000	..
9. Philippines	33 000	3 000	9%
10. Republic of Korea	15 000	..	..
11. Thailand	..	924	..
12. USSR (Asian part)	279 000	..	..

Source: Figures are based on country data received from the Department of Technical Co-operation for Development, United Nations Headquarters, except those for Mongolia.

[a] *National Water Plan Project: Second Interim Report, June 1984,* vol. III, *Groundwater Availability* (Ministry of Irrigation, Water Development and Flood, Bangladesh), pp. 2-4.

[b] *Vodnoye Kherzyaistva MHR* (Water Economy of the People's Republic of Mongolia, in Russian), an information booklet (VIZDOK nyomda, Budapest VII, 1983).

Note: Two dots (. .) indicate that data are not available or are not separately reported.

this table, it will be observed that with the exception of Guam, a small island in the Pacific, the remaining countries have so far developed a very small percentage of their exploitable ground-water resources potential for utilization.

31. Assessment of available ground-water potential is generally based on the knowledge of the occurrence of ground water under natural conditions. It requires extensive hydrogeological investigations involving seismic surveys, test drilling and continuous ground-water data collection through observations of springs, wells and boreholes. It is observed that a number of countries have conducted hydrogeological studies and prepared hydrogeological maps. However, the areal coverage of these studies as well as the scope and depth of the investigations vary from country to country. Some of the countries which have not yet carried out appreciable hydrogeological investigations include Kiribati, Maldives and the Lao People's Democratic Republic. In Kiribati, hydrogeological investigations have been restricted to a study of possibilities of ground-water use on the southern islands of the Tarawa atoll and a very limited survey of the fresh-water resources of Butaritari Island. These investigations were mainly concerned with

the observation of water levels in existing wells and taking of water samples to determine ground-water quality. In Maldives, there have been no hydrogeological investigations to provide information on the ground-water potential of its aquifers. In the Lao People's Democratic Republic, there are no records of hydrogeological investigations or of the country's ground-water potential. The list of countries that have carried out hydrogeological investigations and prepared hydrogeological maps is given in annex I.

32. A recent survey by ESCAP on ground-water data observation and collection networks indicated that a considerable number of countries in the region have access to modern techniques in the field of ground-water prospecting and measurement. Annex II provides information concerning the application of these modern methods by various countries in this field. It is observed that 12 countries are using remote sensing techniques, 8 are using isotope techniques and 16 are using geophysical methods for ground-water prospecting and measurement. It should also be mentioned that some countries (Bangladesh, Fiji, India, Thailand and the USSR) have already started carrying out ground-water recharge studies. In Fiji, plans to increase the

ground-water potential by inducing recharge had to be abandoned owing to high concentrations of manganese and iron in the recharge water. Thailand has successfully carried out an experiment on artificial ground-water recharge by disposal of flood waters into infiltration wells. However, artificial ground-water recharge has not yet been carried out on a large scale. The survey also indicated that quite a large number of countries in the region have established ground-water data observation and collection networks for obtaining time-independent data (physiographical, geological, etc.) as well as timedependent data, particularly water levels. The adequacy and reliability of these networks are indicated in annex III.

33. Assessing ground-water availability goes far beyond the stage of data collection. It requires an adequate and reliable ground-water investigation programme that involves the study of the ground-water flow, assessment of the hydrological balance, and of the ground-water budget of the aquifers. Annex IV provides information regarding the adequacy and reliability of the ground-water investigation programmes of some countries of the region as well as the progress achieved in introducing automation (use of computers) in ground-water data processing and dissemination. It is observed that only four countries have adequate ground-water investigation programmes, while seven have programmes of sufficient reliability. It is also observed that 12 countries are using computers for processing and dissemination of ground-water data.

34. In view of the need to meet the immediate and growing water demands, there is a general tendency in many countries of the region to emphasize the need for the provision of additional quantities of water without giving due attention to the conservation and protection of the ground-water resources.

35. One of the effective ways to achieve conservation and protection of ground-water resources in the region is to promote national efforts to formulate and promulgate ground-water legislation as part of the general water legislation. A list of countries that have already enacted national ground-water legislation and the various aspects covered are given in annex V.

36. In Japan, ground-water belongs to landowners, while surface water is controlled by the Government. In 1963, self-governing bodies have been established in the country to exercise control over the drilling of new wells, land development and ground-water extraction.

37. In Thailand, drafting of the Ground-water Act was initiated in 1972 by the Department of Mineral Resources and it became law in 1978. The underlying principle of the Act is government control of ground-water activities. This includes drilling for ground water, its use, and disposal

of waste water into the aquifer through a well. Under the provisions of the Act, no one may utilize ground water from designated "ground-water areas" without an official permit.

38. In Viet Nam, appropriate legislation has been enacted to protect ground water against pollution, particularly by industries. However, it was indicated that at present it has not been possible to prevent occurrences of such pollution.

39. In this connection, it is necessary to stress that efforts should also be made to raise the level of knowledge of the public in general and water users in particular with regard to the nature, behaviour and vulnerability of ground-water resources towards achieving public acceptance of legal and administrative measures which could restrict the freedom of individual water users. Such knowledge is necessary in order to forestall any resistance or outright opposition by the public to the implementation of sound policies for protecting ground water. To this end, public information, education and training programmes that will create greater awareness and understanding of the inherent ground-water problems should be organized.

C. THE ROLE OF THE UNITED NATIONS SYSTEM IN THE DEVELOPMENT OF GROUND-WATER RESOURCES

40. The United Nations and its specialized agencies are actively engaged in the development of ground-water resources in the region. Some of the organizations involved are the Department of Technical Co-operation for Development (Headquarters), Economic and Social Commission for Asia and the Pacific (ESCAP), United Nations Children's Fund (UNICEF), United Nations Development Programme (UNDP), Food and Agriculture Organization of the United Nations (FAO), United Nations Educational, Scientific and Cultural Organization (UNESCO), and World Health Organization (WHO).

41. Based on the available information, the activities of the United Nations system in the field of ground-water resources development in the region are summarized in annex VI.

42. Some of the ESCAP activities in the field of ground-water resources development have included providing technical assistance to developing countries through the Regional Mineral Resources Development Centre (RMRDC) in the form of hydrogeological surveys; and providing advisory services aimed at achieving the accelerated manufacture of hand pumps for rural water supply in the region.

43. These hydrogeological surveys were carried out with the co-operation of the Federal Republic of Germany,

which provided the services of expert hydrogeologists to conduct the survey and field activities. The main purpose of the hydrogeological survey is to explore and identify the ground-water potential of the developing countries in the region with a view to developing these resources. Some of the positive developments that were achieved as a result of this technical assistance are acquisition of some degree of hydrogeological expertise by a large number of countries in the region, particularly with regard to the exploration and exploitation of their ground-water resources, conducting of hydrogeological exploration in most countries, and significant improvement of the general situation regarding availability of information on hydrogeological conditions of the region.

44. In this connection, it should be mentioned that RMRDC has made assistance available upon request to developing countries in the region in the development of their ground-water resources.

45. The ESCAP activity with regard to the accelerated manufacture of hand pumps for rural water supply is aimed at achieving the targets of the International Drinking Water Supply and Sanitation Decade. As hand pumps constitute one of the mainstays in the provision of drinking water from ground-water resources, an urgent need for the accelerated manufacture of hand pumps arises as the developing countries step up their activities in the field of rural water supply that are programmed to achieve their national goals by the end of the Decade. In 1985, the ESCAP secretariat, in co-operation with UNICEF and WHO, fielded interagency advisory missions on the accelerated manufacture of hand pumps to Bangladesh, Burma, Indonesia and Thailand.

46. The secretariat is currently involved in the assessment of groundwater resources related to urban areas, which is the focus of its new Atlas of Urban Geology series. For example, a large portion of the first number in this series, which is devoted to Bangkok, describes the hydrogeology of the Lower Central Plain between Bangkok and the coast. Future studies will focus on other large metropolitan areas of Asia and on some of the small cities of the South Pacific.

D. PROBLEMS OF GROUND-WATER DEVELOPMENT AND PROSPECTS FOR REGIONAL CO-OPERATION

1. Adequacy and reliability of hydrogeological surveys

47. One of the major problems faced by developing countries in the region is the lack of adequate and reliable hydrogeological surveys for the assessment of their ground-water resources. For example, in the Lao People's Democratic Republic there are no hydrogeological records nor

is there any information regarding ground-water potential. In Malaysia, investigations for ground-water development have started only recently and consequently, no comprehensive ground-water resources assessment has yet been made. Investigations carried out so far are primarily geared towards locating ground water in areas with shortage of water supply. Malaysia therefore requires comprehensive hydrogeological surveys to obtain detailed information regarding the hydrogeology of its aquifer systems as well as recharge-discharge relationships, particularly in the hard rock areas. The first hydrogeological reconnaissance in Bhutan, which consisted mainly of morphological studies and analysis of several valleys, was carried out in 1982. These studies were primarily aimed at exploring the possibility of developing ground water to supplement surface water in mountain areas. Maldives has not yet carried out any ground-water investigation except for a local survey on Malé in 1974-1975. In Nepal, the investigation of ground-water resources is generally at the reconnaissance level and covers only limited areas of the country. For example, in the Terai plain a reconnaissance study has been completed but quantitative aspects of ground-water recharge, flow and discharge have not yet been studied. Nepal requires a detailed exploration of its ground-water resources and an assessment of the exploitable potential.

2. Over-exploitation of ground water

48. The knowledge of the ground-water potential available for exploitation is necessary not only to determine the extent to which the total water requirement can be satisfied by ground water but also to ensure that ground water is not extracted in excess of the amount of its replenishment. Problems related to over-exploitation of ground water include declination of ground-water levels, reduction of well outputs, encroachment of sea water along coastlines, subsidence of the land surface and movement of mineralized or polluted waters into the aquifer. Generally, the declination of ground-water levels results in the increased cost of ground water owing to the expenditure involved in deepening the wells and pumping up water from the correspondingly increased depths. In some cases, overexploitation could lower the water table to such depths that the existing wells have to be abandoned.

49. Countries which are facing problems related to excessive withdrawal of ground water in certain locations include Australia, China, India, Japan, Kiribati, Maldives, Republic of Korea, Sri Lanka and Thailand. For example, in Australia (1), a number of basins, such as the Great Artesian Basin, the Burdekin Delta, the Bundaberg area and the North Adelaide Plains, have their ground-water resources developed and extracted to a level reaching or exceeding that which can be sustained by natural recharge. In Thailand increasingly heavy pumpage of ground water in

Bangkok during 1955-1982 caused a decline of 45 to 50 metres in the ground-water levels. The lowering of water levels by these depths had resulted in the abandonment of old wells, increased pumping costs and encroachment of sea water. In order to prevent the situation from getting worse, the Ground-water Act B.E. 2520 was invoked to reduce the pumping rates which resulted in the cessation of declination of water levels, particularly in the central areas of Bangkok. It was also reported that by May 1985, the piezometric level in central Bangkok had risen by about 2.5 metres (6).

50. Another major type of overexploitation problem is the pollution and contamination of ground-water resources as a result of increased economic activities. Drainage waters from irrigated lands, for example, usually contain high concentrations of objectionable minerals. These contaminated waters, which flow off the land through ditches, may seep into the soil and pollute the ground water that is pumped from wells. Countries facing this kind of problem include the Republic of Korea, Thailand and Viet Nam. In the Republic of Korea, the expansion of industry during the last decade and the modernization of agriculture, which involves the increased use of fertilizers and pesticides, have exposed its vulnerable (shallow and permeable) alluvium aquifers to various sources of contamination. In Thailand, until quite recently, shallow ground water was generally free from pollution. However, at present it is observed that ground water has become contaminated in some places where aquifers are directly recharged by polluted rivers or directly reached by irrigation water. Similarly, in Viet Nam, it is observed that in agricultural areas underlain by karstic limestone, fertilizers have reached the karstic water circulation, thus contaminating the ground water.

3. Contamination related to human settlements

51. Contamination of ground water may also be caused by cesspools, septic tanks, leaking sewer systems, and industrial and domestic waste disposal sites. Contamination of this kind is found to be common in the vicinity of large cities and in suburban areas of India and Kiribati. For example, at Semra, India (7), many hand-dug wells were found to contain water with high concentrations of nitrate. This nitrate pollution was found to originate from latrines and animals straying in the vicinity of wells. Similarly, Kiribati has the problem of pollution of ground-water resources near human settlements. According to a recent study by the International Reference Centre (7), nitrate pollution of ground water from on-site sewage disposal systems, particularly in high population density unsewered areas, is becoming a serious problem in other developing countries as well. In New Zealand, the quality of shallow ground water in certain rural areas is observed to be deteriorating as a result of contamination from intensive stocking, factory farming, fertilizer application, irrigation infiltration and septic tanks. In such cases a selective use of aquifers may be advantageous, whereby water from shallow aquifers, normally high in nutrients, is used to water pasture or crops that would benefit from the nutrients while the water from deeper aquifers is used for drinking purposes.

4. Problems related to coastal areas

52. The encroachment or intrusion of salt water is also a serious ground-water problem, particularly in coastal areas. Since a large portion of the region's population is located along the coasts of oceans and salty seas, there are many problems of this kind in the region. Some of the countries which have problems of this nature include Fiji, Guam, Japan, Kiribati, New Zealand, Thailand and Viet Nam. Basically, encroachment occurs when the water levels in a fresh-water aquifer are lowered to a point where salt water can invade beds bearing fresh water. Although the encroachment tends to be a slow process, in an area where pumping is continuous, encroachment tends to become an irreversible process. As ground water is extracted from the wells, the salt water slowly moves through the water-bearing beds in the direction of the wells and, unless corrective measures are taken, the salt water will ultimately begin to contaminate the water in the wells. Such contamination manifests itself in a gradual increase in the salt content of the water being pumped. For example, in Fiji, the majority of boreholes for water supply in Viti Levu are situated near the coast owing to the concentration of population along the coast. This has led to saline intrusion problems at Tagitagi, Singatoka and Korotongo. In Guam, the problem of increased salinity in certain wells is due to the wells located very close to the coastline rather than due to overdraught. In Kiribati, salt-water intrusion into the fresh-water lenses is observed to be the result of over-exploitation, which is becoming a major problem, particularly on the low atoll islands. There is no problem of overdraught in New Zealand; however, salt-water intrusion has taken place in certain regions where abstraction wells have been sited unreasonably close to the interface. In Thailand, the rapid lowering of the water table due to overdraught has caused the shallow aquifers in Bangkok to become contaminated with salt water. In Viet Nam, sea-water intrusion into coastal aquifers is a major problem. For example, in the lower part of its major river basins, as well as in the coastal plains, the average salinity of ground water is approximately 3,000 to 4,000 ppm, while the maximum salinity sometimes reaches as high as 10,000 ppm, thus rendering the ground water unsuitable for drinking.

5. Land subsidence problems

53. In some countries of the region, the withdrawal of large amounts of ground water has caused serious problems of the subsidence of the land surface. Some of the countries facing such problems include China, Japan, and Thailand. In Japan, from 1961 to the present time, the occurrence of land subsidence and/or sea-water intrusion was the result of over-exploitation of ground water brought about by the remarkable growth of industries and the expansion of agricultural production. Land subsidence has occurred in the low-lying land of the plains and basins where the principal cities, Tokyo, Nagoya, Osaka, Yamagata, Kofu, etc., are located (8).

54. In Thailand, over-exploitation of ground water exists in many locations, particularly around Bangkok area. In Bangkok (6), the field evidence of land subsidence has been observed in the form of protrusion of well casings above the ground surface. Estimates based on the protrusion of well casings which were installed about 19 to 26 years ago indicate that the average subsidence rate in the city is approximately 1.8 to 1.9 centimetres per year. A detailed survey of ground levels carried out in Bangkok during the period 1979-1981 indicated that the existing benchmarks are 30 to 80 centimetres below their original elevations recorded 30 to 40 years ago. At present, about half of the city is less than 0.5 metres above the mean sea level (6). As in Bangkok, Shanghai, China experienced a severe subsidence problem between 1921-1965, particularly from 1949 to 1957, during which an increase in ground-water pumpage resulted in a corresponding increase in the rate of subsidence as well as the area affected. The measures taken in China to solve the subsidence problem included: (a) broadening the area from which ground water is extracted; (b) reducing the amount of ground-water extraction; (c) recharging the aquifers artificially wherever possible; and (d) selecting appropriate aquifers for ground-water extraction. These measures were said to be effective and to have achieved positive results.

55. In this connection, it should be noted that where subsidence has occurred, it is not possible to reverse the process by any means whatsoever. In other words, even a complete cessation of pumping and the injection of new water into the ground will not restore the land surface to its original elevation. Hence, it is very important to establish and implement effective ground-water management programmes to forestall land subsidence due to over-pumping.

56. In general, there are two basic approaches to dealing with the problems related to over-exploitation of aquifers: the preventive approach and the remedial approach.

57. The main objective of the preventive approach is to forestall over-exploitation by enacting and enforcing appropriate ground-water legislation. The remedial approach is usefull for cases where the problem of over-exploitation has already taken place and usually requires recharge of the aquifers by artificial means. It should be noted that artificial recharge of aquifers is not always possible, and even if it is, it tends to be a costly process. Another possible measure to solve over-exploitation of ground water is to limit or reduce the supply of ground water and increase that of surface water. In this regard it is necessary to have integrated management of both surface and ground-water resources.

6. Prospects for regional co-operation

58. A serious problem common to most of the developing countries in the region is the shortage of qualified manpower in the field of ground-water resources development at all levels: managerial, supervisory, higher technician, technician and skilled worker. It is also observed that these countries, particularly the Pacific island countries, have difficulties in acquiring the necessary technical know-how as well as in building their professional institutional capabilities.

59. According to a recent survey by ESCAP (9), Afghanistan and Fiji have mentioned requirements for external assistance in most aspects of ground water, including training, fellowship, expertise and equipment. Malaysia's requirements are only for training, fellowships and expert advice. Niue has indicated the need for assistance in preparing topographical, geological and hydrogeological maps, and in conducting hydrogeological and geophysical studies. Its external assistance needs include training within the country, provision of fellowships abroad and provision of equipment. Papua New Guinea has expressed the need for assistance with regard to training, fellowships, expert/consultant services and equipment. The Philippines has indicated its requirement for assistance in the preparation of topographical maps, geological and hydrogeological maps, training, fellowships, expert services and equipment. The assistance required by Sri Lanka and Viet Nam includes hydrogeological and geophysical studies, preparation of geological and hydrogeological maps, and aquifer modelling. Vanuatu needs assistance in conducting hydrogeological and geophysical studies, preparation of hydrogeological maps, and aquifer modelling. It also requires training, fellowships, expert services and equipment.

60. In addition, eight countries or areas (Afghanistan, Hong Kong, Malaysia, Niue, Philippines, Sri Lanka, Tonga and Vanuatu) have indicated that international co-operation in the form of consultancy missions or financing could be

of help in the formulation of new water legislation or revision of the existing ones.

61. Considering the fact that countries in the Asian and Pacific region have different levels of achievement in the development of ground-water resources, the experience of countries which have made considerable progress in this regard may be used for the benefit of other countries with less experience. For instance, India, Pakistan and the USSR have considerable experience in ground-water exploration and development. Through regional co-operation, these countries have a potential to assist others, such as Afghanistan, Bhutan, Fiji, Lao People's Democratic Republic, Nepal, Papua New Guinea, and Vanuatu, in fulfilling their training needs as well as in providing expert/consultant services in ground-water development.

62. The ESCAP secretariat, in discharging its central role of promoting regional co-operation as a follow-up to the Mar del Plata Action Plan on integrated water resources development and management, had given serious consideration to the need for fulfilling training requirements of developing countries in the field of water resources development, including ground-water development, and had initiated and assisted in establishing the Regional Network for Training in Water Resources Development at the recently concluded Intergovernmental Meeting which was held in Bangkok from 27 to 31 May 1986.

63. As regards providing expert/consultant services, technical co-operation among developing countries (TCDC) can play an important role in promoting ground-water resources development in the region. In this connection, the ESCAP secretariat is currently assisting and encouraging the developing countries in utilizing TCDC arrangements through the publication of a register of regional water specialists available for TCDC in 1985 and its supplement in 1986. This register is expected to facilitate the use of the expertise of the region's surface and ground-water specialists to assist developing countries in solving various related and specific problems.

64. Finally, most of the developing countries consider the lack of financial resources to be a very severe constraint in the development of their ground-water resources. In this regard, the establishment and implementation of appropriate pricing policies for the supply of ground water may be helpful as a means of full or partial recovery of fixed and recurrent costs to generate internal financial resources as well as to enhance the ability to secure credits, loans and grants from external sources.

E. CONCLUSIONS AND RECOMMENDATIONS

65. The following conclusions and recommendations may be drawn based on the discussion in the previous sections.

1. Conclusions

(1) Ground water is an important natural resource for the socio-economic development of countries in the region. The enhancement of its development is also a crucial factor in achieving the goals of the International Drinking Water Supply and Sanitation Decade.

(2) Hydrogeological surveys and hydrogeological maps are prerequisites for the effective planning of ground-water development. The lack of these basic data is one of the major constraints which hampers the development of ground-water resources in the region.

(3) Other constraints which hamper the development and rational use of ground-water resources include lack of adequately trained manpower, lack of equipment and lack of financial resources.

(4) For the optimum utilization of ground-water resources, the possibility of conjunctive use of surface and ground-water resources should be considered.

(5) The establishment of ground water legislation is important and necessary to provide a legal basis for the effective management of ground-water resources, including its conservation and protection against contamination.

(6) The success of any legal and administrative measures for conservation and protection of ground-water resources depends to a large extent on the public acceptance of these measures which can be achieved through public education and information dissemination programmes.

2. Recommendations

Recommendations directed at the national level include:

(1) Those countries which have not done so should start taking the necessary steps to carry out the assessment of available ground-water resources in terms of both quantity and quality, on a nation-wide basis rather than on a local basis.

(2) Efforts should be made towards the establishment and/ or expansion of ground-water data observation and collection networks as well as improvement of the existing data compilation, processing and dissemination systems. In this regard, the advantages of automation (use of computers) in ground-water data processing and dissemination should be taken into account.

(3) Planning of ground-water resources development should be carried out within the context of overall water resources development, including surface water, thus permitting a co-ordinated approach to water planning.

(4) Countries which have not yet enacted ground-water legislation should do so as part of the overall national water legislation which should cover various aspects, including water resources management, conservation and protection against pollution.

(5) Efforts should also be made to achieve public acceptance of national water legislation through the organization of public education and information dissemination programmes.

Recommendations directed at the regional and subregional levels include:

(1) In view of the general lack of investigations to assess ground-water potential in the region, international agencies should provide assistance to the developing countries, on request, in their efforts to carry out hydrogeological surveys.

(2) In order to solve the problem of lack of adequately trained manpower in the field of ground-water development, more effort is required in the field of training. In this regard, in addition to what the countries have established at the individual level, there is a need to organize training on a regional basis so that the countries which have the potential can offer such facilities to other countries.

(3) To improve the situation regarding integrated planning, development, use and management of surface and ground-water resources in the region, seminar/study tours should be organized for senior officials of water resources agencies of developing countries.

(4) International organizations should provide assistance to the countries, on request, to improve or draft new national water legislation that takes into account ground-water aspects of water resources.

REFERENCES

1. *Ground Water in the Pacific Region,* Natural Resources/Water Series No. 12 (United Nations publication, Sales No. E.83.II.A.12).

2. *Proceedings of the Expert Group Meeting on Water Pricing,* Water Resources Series No. 55 (United Nations publication, Sales No. E.81.II.F.11), pp. 26-28.

3. "International funding of groundwater development schemes", an informal paper of the World Bank prepared in connection with a conference in London in November 1983.

4. *Water Resources of Small Islands,* Technical Publication Series No. 154 (Commonwealth Science Council) CSC (85) WMR 2.

5. "Big water discovery, South Asia can end poverty," *Overseas Tribune: News of the Indian Subcontinent,* vol. II, No. 22 (Washington D.C., 31 May 1986).

6. ESCAP, *Geology for Urban Planning: Selected Papers on the Asian and Pacific Region,* (ST/ ESCAP/ 394).

7. International Reference Centre for Community Water Supply and Sanitation, a WHO collaborating centre, *Newsletter* No. 160, October/November 1985.

8. "Land subsidence and the environment", *Nature and Resources* (UNESCO) vol. XXI, No. 1 (January-March 1985).

9. "Draft report on the progress in the implementation of the Mar del Plata Action Plan", (ESCAP, 1986).

10. "Issues concerning the financing of water resources development", ACC/ISGW/1985/6, (18 October 1985).

11. *Compendium of Regional Projects for Asia and the Pacific* (Regional Bureau for Asia and the Pacific, UNDP Headquarters, New York, December 1984).

12. "The role of UNESCO in water resources development in South-East Asia", a paper presented at the Workshop on Hydrogeology of the Lower Mekong Basin, Bangkok, 17-20 February 1986.

13. "Hydrogeology and ground-water development of North-eastern Thailand", a paper presented at the Workshop on Hydrogeology of the Lower Mekong Basin, Bangkok, 17-20 February 1986.

14. "Activities of ESCAP/RMRDC in the field of hydrogeology", a paper presented at the Workshop on Hydrogeology of the Lower Mekong Basin, Bangkok, 17-20 February 1986.

15. *Vodnoye Kherzyaistva MHR* (Water Economy of the People's Republic of Mongolia, in Russian), an information booklet (VIZDOK nyomda, Budapest VII, 1983).

16. B.K. Baweja, "Groundwater development in India", *Water Quality Bulletin,* vol. 5, No. 4 (October 1980), pp. 82-83.

Annex I

List of countries that have carried out hydrogeological investigations
and prepared hydrogeological maps

Country/area	Hydrogeological investigations	Hydrogeological maps	Areal coverage of studies and maps
1. Afghanistan	√	√	About 2/3 of the country
2. Australia	√	√	Most parts of the country
3. Bangladesh	√	√	..
4. Bhutan	√	..	..
5. Burma	√	√	..
6. China	√	√	..
7. Cook Islands	√	√	Most parts of the country
8. Fiji	√	√	Most parts of the country
9. Guam	√	..	..
10. Hong Kong	√	..	..
11. India	√	√	85% of the territory
12. Indonesia	√	√	..
13. Malaysia	√	√	..
14. Nepal	√	√	Only a small portion of the country
15. New Zealand	√	..	..
16. Pakistan	√	√	..
17. Papua New Guinea	√	..	..
18. Philippines	√	..	..
19. Republic of Korea	√	√	Only part of the territory
20. Singapore	√	√	..
21. Solomon Islands	√	√	Limited to the capital city Honiara
22. Sri Lanka	√	√	Most part of the territory
23. Thailand	√	√	..
24. Tonga	√	..	..
25. Trust Territory of the Pacific Islands	√	..	..
26. USSR (Asian part)	√	√	Most part of the territory
27. Vanuatu	√	..	..
28. Viet Nam	√	√	Most part of country

Source: Compiled from country data provided by the Department of Technical Co-operation for Development, United Nations Headquarters, New York.

Note: Two dots (. .) indicate that data are not available or are not separately reported.

Annex II

Modern methods used by countries for ground-water prospecting and measurement

Country/area	Remote sensing	Isotope techniques	Geophysical methods
1. Afghanistan	N	Y	Y
2. Australia	Y	Y	Y
3. China	Y	. .	. .
4. Fiji	Y	N	Y
5. Hong Kong	Y	N	N
6. India	Y	Y	Y
7. Indonesia	Y	Y	Y
8. Japan	Y	Y	Y
9. Malaysia	N	N	Y
10. New Zealand	Y	. .	Y
11. Niue	. .	. .	Y
12. Pakistan	Y	. .	Y
13. Papua New Guinea	N	N	N
14. Philippines	Y	Y	Y
15. Republic of Korea	N	N	N
16. Singapore	N	N	Y
17. Sri Lanka	Y	Y	Y
18. Tonga	N	N	Y
19. Trust Territory of the Pacific Islands	N	N	Y
20. Vanuatu	N	N	N
21. Viet Nam	Y	Y	Y

Source: Information provided by countries in the returns to the questionnaire circulated by ESCAP on 1 December 1983.

Note: Y – Yes, N – No.

Two dots (. .) indicate that data are not available or are not separately reported.

Annex III

Adequacy and reliability of ground-water data observation and collection networks in the region

Country/area	Physiographical		Geological		Hydrogeological		Boring description		Well logs		Time-dependent data	
1. Afghanistan	A,	R	A,	R	I,	U	I,	U	I,	U	I,	U
2. Australia	I,	R	I,	R	I,	R	I,	R	I,	R	I,	R
3. Fiji	A,	R	A,	R	I,	U	I,	U	I,	U	I,	U
4. Hong Kong	I,	U	I,	U	I,	U	I,	U	I,	U	I,	U
5. India	A,	R	A,	R	A,	R	I,	R	I,	R	A,	R
6. Indonesia	I,	U	I,	U	I,	U	I,	U	I,	U	I,	U
7. Japan	A,	R	A,	..	..,	..	I,	..	..,	..	I,	R
8. Malaysia	I,	R	I,	R	I,	U	I,	U	I,	U	I,	U
9. New Zealand	A,	..	A,	..	A,	..	A,	R	I,	U	I,	R
10. Niue	..,	..	..,	..	..,	..	..,	..	..,	..	I,	U
11. Pakistan	A,	R	I,	R	I,	R	I,	R	I,	R	I,	R
12. Papua New Guinea	I,	..	I,	..	I,	..	I,	..	I,	..	A,	R
13. Philippines	..,	R	..,	R	..,	R	I,	R	I,	R	I,	R
14. Republic of Korea	A,	R	A,	R	A,	R	A,	R	A,	R	I,	U
15. Singapore	A,	R	A,	R	..,	..	..,	..	..,	..	A,	R
16. Sri Lanka	A,	R	A,	U	I,	U	I,	U	I,	U	I,	U
17. Tonga	A,	R	A,	R	A,	R	A,	R	A,	R	A,	R
18. Trust Territory of the Pacific Islands	I,	R	A,	R	I,	R	A,	R	I,	U	I,	R
19. Vanuatu	A,	R	A,	R	..,	..	I,	U	I,	U	I,	R
20. Viet Nam	I,	..	I,	..	I,	..	I,	..	I,	..	..,	U

Source: Information provided by countries in the returns to the questionnaire circulated by ESCAP on 1 December 1983.

Note: A: Adequate,   R: Reliable,   Time-dependent data: water levels
          I: Inadequate,   U: Unreliable

Two dots (. .) indicate that data are not available or are not separately reported.

Annex IV

Status of ground-water investigation programmes and progress achieved in automation (use of computers) of data processing and dissemination

Country/area	Status of investigation programmes for ground-water resources assessment		Use of computers for ground-water data processing and dissemination
	Adequacy	Reliability	
1. Afghanistan	N	N	N
2. Australia	N	Y	Y
3. Fiji	N	N	Y
4. Guam	N	N	..
5. Hong Kong	Y	Y	Y
6. India	N	N	Y
7. Indonesia	N	N	Y
8. Japan	N	Y	N
9. Malaysia	N	N	N
10. New Zealand	Y	Y	Y
11. Niue	Y	Y	N
12. Pakistan	Y	Y	Y
13. Papua New Guinea	..	..	Y
14. Philippines	N	N	Y
15. Republic of Korea	N	N	Y
16. Sri Lanka	N	N	N
17. Tonga	..	Y	N
18. Trust Territory of the Pacific Islands	N	N	Y
19. Vanuatu	N	N	N
20. Viet Nam	N	..	Y

Source: Information provided by countries in the returns to the questionnaire circulated on 1 December 1983.

Note: Y: Yes, N: No

Two dots (. .) indicate that data are not available or are not separately reported.

Annex V

Aspects considered by existing national ground-water legislations in the region

Country or area	Ownership of ground-water	Right to use ground-water	Protection of ground-water quality
1. Afghanistan	√	√	√
2. Australia	√	√	√
3. Guam	–	–	√
4. Hong Kong	√	√	√
5. India	–	–	√
6. Indonesia	√	√	√
7. Japan	√	√	–
8. Niue	√	–	√
9. Papua New Guinea	√	√	√
10. Philippines	√	√	√
11. Singapore	√	√	√
12. Sri Lanka	–	–	√
13. Tonga	√	√	√
14. Trust Territory of the Pacific Islands	–	–	√

Sources: Groundwater in the Pacific Region, Natural Resources/Water Series No. 12 (United Nations publication, Sales No. E.83.II.A.12). Information provided by countries in the returns to the questionnaire circulated by ESCAP on 1 December 1983.

Note: In addition to the above countries or areas, Mongolia, Thailand and Viet Nam have enacted ground-water laws in order to conserve and protect their ground-water resources; however, the information on the aspects covered by these laws is not available.

Annex VI

List of ground-water resources development projects in the Asian and Pacific region executed and/or financed by the United Nations system

Project title	Year	Beneficiary country	Executing agency	Funding agency
1. Ground-water investigation	1963	Afghanistan	DTCD*	UNDP
2. Ground-water investigation	1971	Afghanistan	DTCD	UNDP
3. Ground-water survey	1974	Bangladesh	DTCD	UNDP
4. Ground-water resources development	1981	Bangladesh	DTCD	UNDP
5. Ground-water surveys, Rajasthan	1965	India	DTCD	UNDP
6. Ground-water in Madras State	1965	India	DTCD	UNDP
7. Ground-water in Madras State Phase II	1968	India	DTCD	UNDP
8. Ground-water studies in Rajasthan and Gujarat	1971	India	DTCD	UNDP
9. Ground-water studies in Ghaggar River Basin	1974	India	DTCD	UNDP
10. Hydrological and artificial recharge Studies	1980	India	DTCD	UNDP
11. Artificial recharge studies Gujarat	1981	India	DTCD	UNDP
12. Ground-water studies in Kasai and Subarnabkka river basins	1984	India	DTCD	UNDP
13. Ground-water investigation in selected areas of Baluchistan	1973	Pakistan	DTCD	UNDP
14. Ground-water development	1980	Countries of Asia and the Pacific	DTCD	UNDP
15. Ground-water development	1974	Sri Lanka	DTCD	UNDP
16. Ground-water data centre	1984	Thailand	DTCD	UNDP
17. Ground-water exploration	1979	Viet Nam	DTCD	UNDP
18. Ground-water survey Phase II	1981	Viet Nam	DTCD	UNDP
19. Support for tube-well command	1981	Bangladesh	FAO	UNDP
20. Ground-water drainage research	1974	India	FAO	UNDP
21. Ground-water reconnaissance	1982	Lao People's Democratic Republic	FAO	UNDP
22. Ground-water development drilling programme	1974	Philippines	FAO	UNDP
23. Pre-feasibility study for coconut irrigation with ground-water	1985	Sri Lanka	FAO	UNDP
24. Assistance to the Irrigation Management Programme Training Activities at the Rural Development Academy in Bogra	1984	Bangladesh	FAO	UNDP
25. Equipment for the Geophysical Wing of the Central Ground-water Board – Phase II water	1983	India	FAO	UNDP
26. Studies for the use of saline water in the command areas of irrigation projects, Haryana	1982	India	FAO	UNDP
27. Ground-water utilization for food crop production	1985	Indonesia	FAO	FAO
28. Irrigation training	1981	Nepal	FAO	UNDP
29. Remote sensing applications for ground-water exploration	1985	Philippines	FAO	FAO
30. Feasibility for second tube-well project	1982	Bangladesh	ADB/IDB*	
31. Roving seminar on ground-water development	1981	Countries of ESCAP region	ESCAP	UNDP
32. Hydrogeological and ground-water development advisory services	1978 continuing	Regional developing countries	ESCAP/RMRDC*	Donor country UNDP
33. Advisory missions on accelerated manufacture of hand pumps for rural water supply	1985	Bangladesh, Burma, Indonesia, Thailand	ESCAP	ESCAP
34. Ground-water irrigation	1962	China	China	World Bank/IDA

Annex VI *(Continued)*

Project title	Year	Beneficiary country	Executing agency	Funding agency
35. Tube-well irrigation	1962	India	India	World Bank/IDA
36. Tube-wells	1973	Bangladesh	Bangladesh	World Bank/IDA
37. Shallow tube-wells	1977	Bangladesh	Bangladesh	World Bank/IDA
38. Bhairawa-Lumbini I	1977	Nepal	Nepal	World Bank/IDA
39. UP tube-wells I	1980	India	India	World Bank/IDA
40. Hand tube-wells	1981	Bangladesh	Bangladesh	World Bank/IDA
41. Deep tube-wells II	1983	Bangladesh	Bangladesh	World Bank/IDA
42. Bhairawa – Lumbini II	1983	Nepal	Nepal	World Bank/IDA
43. UP tube-wells II	1983	India	India	World Bank/IDA
44. Ground-water irrigation I	1983	Burma	Burma	World Bank/IDA
45. Birganj irrigation	1973	Nepal	Nepal	World Bank/IDA
46. Irrigation VIII	1977	Indonesia	Indonesia	World Bank/IDA
47. Narayni zone irrigation	1979	Nepal	Nepal	World Bank/IDA
48. Haryana irrigation I	1979	India	India	World Bank/IDA
49. Irrigation XVII	1982	Indonesia	Indonesia	World Bank/IDA
50. North China plain	1982	China	China	World Bank/IDA
51. Chambal (MP) irrigation II	1983	India	India	World Bank/IDA
52. Haryana irrigation II	1983	India	India	World Bank/IDA

Sources: "Issues concerning the financing of water resources development" (ACC/ISGW/1985/6).

Compendium of Regional Projects for Asia and the Pacific, Regional Bureau for Asia and the Pacific, UNDP Headquarters, New York, December 1984.

"The role of UNESCO in water resources development in South-East Asia," a paper presented at the Workshop on Hydrogeology of the Lower Mekong Basin, Bangkok, 17-20 February 1986.

"Activities of ESCAP/RMRDC in the field of hydrogeology", a paper presented at the Workshop on Hydrogeology of the Lower Mekong Basin, Bangkok, 17-20 February 1986.

"International funding of ground-water development schemes", an informal paper of the World Bank prepared in connection with a conference in London in November 1983.

Note: * DTCD   – the Department of Technical Co-operation for Development, United Nations Headquarters

ADB   – Asian Development Bank

IDB   – Inter-America Development Bank

RMRDC – Regional Mineral Resources Development Centre

IDA   – International Development Association

VIII   GROUNDWATER EXPLORATION AND DEVELOPMENT IN CHINA*

A. ROLE OF GROUNDWATER RESOURCES FOR ECONOMIC AND SOCIAL DEVELOPMENT IN PRC

China has a long history in the utilization of ground-water. Since the foundation of PRC, exploration and development of groundwater resources have been systematically undertaken to meet the ever growing demand for agricultural, industrial and domestic water supply.

In North China there are several great plains including the vast piedmont plain with thick deposits of quaternary sand and gravel forming a good, thick water-bearing strata. The atmospheric precipitation of the Great East Plain is less than 800 mm; the groundwater there receives its main recharge by precipitation through vertical percolation. Towards west, the climate becomes the typical inland dry, and the groundwater in the piedmont plain is mainly recharged by mountain stream infiltration. The total amount of groundwater exploited actually (from water wells and spring water) in North China accounts for 85 per cent of that for the whole country. Most of that amount (more than 80 per cent) is used for irrigation.

In North China Plain, groundwater development provides positive results both for irrigation and for soil reclamation. Groundwater extraction has increased water table fluctuation dramatically and accelerated the vertical water circulation.   Large quantities of groundwater extraction during irrigation period from March to June may cause a conspicuous decline of the water table. The results are, on one hand, that the soil is protected from salinization by declining water table and minimizing groundwater evaporation, and on the other hand, greater space within the groundwater reservoir is provided to receive more rainwater infiltration during the next wet season.

Groundwater plays a very important role in rural water supply. Various types of water collecting structures have been built for different water-bearing formations. Tube wells and large-diameter wells are very popular. Radiating wells (i.e. well with horizontal collectors) are used for extraction of groundwater in loess plateau, Karez – in piedmont plains within arid zone.

---

* Country paper prepared for the thirteenth session of the ESCAP Committee on Natural Resources. This paper has been reproduced without formal editing. The views expressed in it are those of the author and do not necessarily reflect those of the United Nations.

Along with the industrial development and population growth in cities, groundwater becomes more and more important for industrial and municipal water supply. Among 181 big and medium cities in China, 61 cities mainly rely on groundwater for water supply, 40 cities use groundwater and surface water conjunctively.

Hot springs are widespread in China and used for bathing. Starting in the 1960s, many exploration works have been undertaken in urban areas of China (Beijing, Tianjin and Fuzhou).   Geothermal resources in Beijing occur mostly in fissure-karsts in carbonate rocks of Paleo-zoic and Sinian ages at depths of 800-1,500 m (max. 2,400 m) overlain by a series of Mezozoic and Genozoic strata, while in Tianjin they chiefly occur in tertiary sand and gravel aquifers usually at depths of 700-1,000 m. Geothermal water has high temperature (about 50-60°C in Beijing, 80°C in Tianjin) and low mineralization. It has been utilized in different ways, such as in medical treatment, space heating, dyeing, bathing, air conditioning and green-housing.

B. GROUNDWATER RESOURCES EXPLORATION AND EVALUATION

Since 1950s, hydrogeological teams under the Ministry of Geology and Mineral Resources (formerly Ministry of Geology) have been undertaking systematic exploration and mapping.   Small-scale hydrogeological mapping (scale 1/200,000-1/500,000) covered two thirds of the whole country's inland territory. In plain areas (mainly in North China), medium-scale hydrogeological mapping (scale 1/50,000-1/100,000) covered one tenth of the whole country's inland territory.   The results of these explorations have been used for irrigation projection and for solving rural water supply problems.   Thousands of prospecting-production wells have been put into use for farmers and herdsmen. In urban areas more detailed explorations have been conducted (geophysical survey, drilling, and pumping test).

In the late 1970s, the Institute of Hydrogeology and Engineering Geology in co-operation with provincial geological bureaus systematically processed all data collected, and in 1979 published "The Atlas of Hydrogeological Maps of the PRC" which consists of 68 maps (8 nationwide maps, 15 regional maps, 45 provincial and other maps), and is a reflection of the main results of regional hydrogeological investigation in China.

In the early 1970s, regional groundwater resources evaluation was initiated for North China Plain with numerous prospecting and production wells. Both time-independent parameters, and time-dependent parameters of the groundwater system have been carefully studied. Groundwater resources evaluation began to be conducted by means of computer.

During 1981-1985, groundwater resources evaluation for the whole country has been made. The amount of porewater, fissurewater and karstic water are calculated separately.

C. METHODS AND TECHNIQUES USED IN GROUNDWATER PROSPECTING AND DEVELOPMENT

Geophysical methods for groundwater prospecting and development were initiated in the late 1950s. Electrical sondage, electrical resistance profile and electrical logging are the most common methods. In North China Plain, the abovementioned methods are popularly used in groundwater prospecting and development. Each county in part of the plain in Hebei Province has got its own small geophysical group which conducts field survey and compiles maps indicating the direction of ancient river courses, distribution of salty and fresh groundwater and other characteristics. Electrical logging is used for the determination of depth at which screen will be fitted on. Other geophysical methods (seismic prospecting, gravity prospecting) are also used in groundwater exploration, but in less extent.

As an additional measure, isotopic studies have significantly expanded the understanding of groundwater age and recharge, tritium and radiocarbon have been used for identification of groundwater age. Groundwater recharge may be traced through the use of the stable isotopes oxygen-18 and deuterium. For example, such study has been undertaken for Shanghai area.

Application of remote sensing techniques has given some positive results in regional hydrogeological mapping and prospecting for fissure water.

Mathematical model by using computer has been developed for the evaluation of groundwater resources in more than 20 cities, and will have more application in solving groundwater quantity and quality related problems.

Some new drilling techniques have been used for groundwater development (For example, air drilling with down-hole-hammer).

For solving the problem of rural water supply, various types of hand pumps and deep well pumps have been tested and put into use.

D. PROBLEMS RELATED TO GROUNDWATER DEVELOPMENT AND COUNTERMEASURES UNDERTAKEN

There are some hydrogeological problems occuring in intensive groundwater development areas. Over-exploitation of groundwater may cause lowering of water tables, reduction of well outputs, land subsidence, deterioration of groundwater quality. Cone of depression for deep aquifers is enlarging rapidly than that for shallow aquifers. Isotopic study indicates that some deep aquifers are considered to be "fossil" and not replenished. Difference between shallow and deep aquifers behaviour can be illustrated by following example. The Hebei Plain can be divided into two parts: an entirely fresh groundwater area in the west, and fresh groundwater intercalated with saline groundwater area in the east. Within the second area, there is a sequence of shallow fresh groundwater, intermediate saline groundwater, and deep fresh groundwater in the vertical direction. Observation of groundwater level fluctuation indicates that decline of water table for deep fresh water is significant. Cangzhou cone of depression covers an area of 7,000 km^2 with maximum water table depth at about 70 m, while water table for shallow fresh groundwater is more or less stable and is mainly controlled by rainwater infiltration and pumpage.

Land subsidence occurs mainly in large coastal cities with high water consumption, such as Shanghai, Tianjin and Ningpo. For example, in Shanghai the cumulative maximum land subsidence has reached 2.63 m during the period of 1921-1965. Studies indicate that subsided area generally coincides with the extension of the cone of depression. This suggests that land subsidence is chiefly caused by the compaction of unconsolidated layers as a result of intensive extraction of groundwater. Multiple measures have been adopted in Shanghai, including control of groundwater consumption, readjustment of the order of exploitation of individual aquifers, and artificial recharge. As a result, land-subsidence in Shanghai has now been provisionally brought under control.

In China there are also two basic approaches to deal with the problems related to over-exploitation of aquifers: the preventive approach and the remedial approach. Some local groundwater legislations and rules have been enacted. And there have been some positive experiences of artificial recharge of shallow aquifers. For example, Huantai county (area 500 km^2) is located in the northern part of Shandong Province, and is part of the proluvio-alluvial plain with average precipitation of about 600 mm yearly. Because of excessive exploitation of groundwater, the water table is continuously declining. In order to increase groundwater recharge, a series of tests of artificial recharge through ditches and pits were made and remarkable results for artificial recharge were achieved.

E. REGIONAL CO-OPERATION FOR IMPROVING GROUNDWATER DEVELOPMENT

The UNDP-financed project-(Executing Agency-United Nations Department of Technical Co-operation for Development Groundwater Resources Evaluation of the Huang-Huai-Hai Plain (CPR/81/036) was initiated in 1982 and conducted by Institute of Hydrogeology and Engineering Geology under the Ministry of Geology and Mineral Resources. Until now most of the field experiments have been fulfilled in Nangong and Nanpi counties and in the suburb of Shijiazhuang city. Recharge of shallow aquifers and shallow groundwater balance have been carefully studied. Application of computer in groundwater resource evaluation made new progress in this project.

The World Bank Financed Project-North China Plain Agricultural Project covers 11 counties within 4 provinces. In addition to construction of drainage and irrigation works, this project includes components of soil and water resources study. This project will soon come to an end.

Both these projects are contribution of international organizations to groundwater resource exploration and development in China.

In addition, a UNDP study tour on groundwater research and development in China was organized in September 1980. Fifteen participents from foreign countries situated in arid zone from all over the world attended it. Further communication and co-operation between hydrogeologists will be beneficial both to China and to other Asian and Pacific countries.

IX. GROUNDWATER RESOURCES DEVELOPMENT IN THE PHILIPPINES*

INTRODUCTION

Groundwater used by the early natives was obtained from mountain springs and wells dug by hand in the river bank sands. Although the introduction of cased dug wells is not historically recorded, they were already in common use during the 19th century. At present, groundwater is the main source of domestic water supply in most urban and rural areas except Metro Manila and a few other urban communities.

Industrial exploitation of groundwater began with sugar cane plantations. Later, increased demand for rice led to the development of pumpwell irrigation in favorable basins. This was followed by the installation of pumpwell systems in many industries.

Before the Americans arrived, dug wells supplying water for domestic use reached only a few metres below the water table. Water level fluctuated to an average of 3 to over 10 metres. The sides of the wells were lined with blocks of tuff or limestone with lime as bonding material. At present, reinforced concrete culverts or caissons are used. Round wells are from less than 1 to over 2 m in diameter.

The shift to drilled, steel and galvanized iron-cased wells came at the turn of the century. Thereafter, drilling was done using cable tools or percussion rigs. In 1954, the rotary drill was introduced by the Agency for International Development (USAID) through the National Waterworks and Sewerage Authority (NAWASA). For shallow and soft formations, small hand drills of the auger type with accessory jet pumps and the drive and drill shoe are used. Casings are mostly steel, galvanized iron and black iron, although plastic casings are also utilized for small diameter wells.

Groundwater geology investigations started as early as 1915 when W.E. Pratt studied the different artesian wells in the islands. In 1918, L.A. Faustino made an assessment of the groundwater potentials in Manila and suburbs. In the same year, George Heise and Sam Berman conducted tests on the quality of Philippine groundwater. Other early workers include Dr. Antonio Alvir (1930), and Bureau of Mines Director Quirico Abadilla (1931). The systematic assessment of the country's water resources was started by the United States Army engineers and geologists before World War II. The main objective of their study was to determine potential sources of potable water in the country as part of their strategic planning. Further work on groundwater investigations was temporarily stopped during the war but was resumed in 1949 in Los Baños and Calamba, Laguna.

In 1955, the then Bureau of Public Works (BPW) initiated groundwater studies of the six major river basins

---

* Country paper prepared for the thirteenth session of the ESCAP Committee on Natural Resources. This paper has been reproduced without formal editing. The views expressed in it are those of the author and do not necessarily reflect those of the United Nations.

of the country. At the same time, the government embarked on a water supply development programme in the rural areas. Spearheaded by BPW and NAWASA and partly funded by the forerunner of the USAID, the International Cooperation Agency, a lot of deep wells were constructed throughout the country. This was continued, but on a smaller scale by the BPW up to the 1970s. Under this programme, over 100,000 wells were drilled for public domestic supply. However, due to old age and lack of follow-up technical and financial support, majority of these wells are now inoperational and need rehabilitation or replacement.

In the late 1970s, the Ministry of Local Government started the Barangay Water Program (BWP) whose objective is to develop a viable water supply system for rural barangays with population of less than 10,000.

The Local Water Utilities Administration (LWUA) on the other hand, does water resources investigation, construction and development of water supply facilities for communities exceeding 20,000 population. The Rural Water Development Corporation (RWDC), which was established at the start of this decade constructs wells for rural communities of 5,000 to 20,000 population.

Other agencies engaged in groundwater resources investigations are the National Irrigation Administration (NIA), National Water Resources Council (NWRC), Philippines Sugar Commission (PHILSUCOM), Metropolitan Waterworks and Sewerage System (MWSS), and the Bureau of Mines and Geo-Sciences (BMG).

In the early 1960s the Philippine Bureau of Mines (now BMG) started a reconnaissance hydrogeological programme aimed at assessing the country's groundwater resources. The BMG conducts well and spring inventories, geologic mapping, pumping tests and collection of water samples for physical and chemical analyses. Groundwater evaluation includes estimates of annual potential recharge and discharge from the basins and potential available groundwater by the use of existing data and/or the pump testing of wells where feasible.

As of December 1984, about 70 per cent of the country (figure 1) was covered by reconnaissance hydrogeological mapping. The groundwater resources of the remaining 30 per cent however, have been evaluated based on available geologic, hydrologic and well data, without first hand ocular investigation. Scales of hydrogeologic maps produced is usually 1:250,000. A few provinces (Batangas, La Union and Zambales) are covered with 1:50,000 scale maps.

GROUNDWATER DEVELOPMENT

With the active participation of several government agencies in the exploration, development and management of groundwater resources, the country can more or less be assured of an adequate and safe source of water supply to permit full-scale agricultural, commercial and industrial development. However, care must be taken so that these agencies do not compete or conflict with each other in the performance of their functions, investigating and developing the same resources. For this reason, the National Water Resources Council was created to co-ordinate all activities related to water resources studies.

As of 1985, about 33 million or 59 per cent of the total population of the country is served by the public water supply facilities. Metropolitan Manila and adjoining urban areas benefit from the biggest service coverage with about 92 per cent of its total population (7.9 million) being serviced by the Central Distribution System. Of the 14.8 million population of other urban areas, 54 per cent or 8 million inhabitants are serviced by government water supply system. In terms of water service facilities in the rural areas, 24 per cent of the population secure water from wells, 18 per cent from developed springs and 11 per cent from piped systems. These total about 53 per cent, which is more than half of the 33.3 million rural inhabitants. The remaining 47 per cent rely chiefly on the nearest sources of water, such as open wells, rain water cisterns, lakes, rivers and creeks. Water from these sources are of questionable quality such that the incidence of waterborne and water-related diseases is still evident in the country.

To prevent serious negative effects of this situation and upgrade existing water supply facilities in both urban and rural sectors, an inter-agency task force composed of representatives from various water supply agencies formulated in July 1980, an "Integrated Water Supply Program". This resulted in the formulation of the Rural Water Supply and Sanitation Master Plan, 1982-2000, in December 1982; the main objective of which is to provide sufficient water supply and sanitation services to majority of the country's rural households.

Considering the high initial cost of developing surface water as a domestic water supply source, groundwater has been the major source of domestic water needed for the projects constructed under the above-mentioned programmes and likewise for previously constructed water supply projects. Based on this observation, it was estimated that out of the 56 million total population of the Philippines, about 37 per cent or roughly 20.7 million are supplied with groundwater.

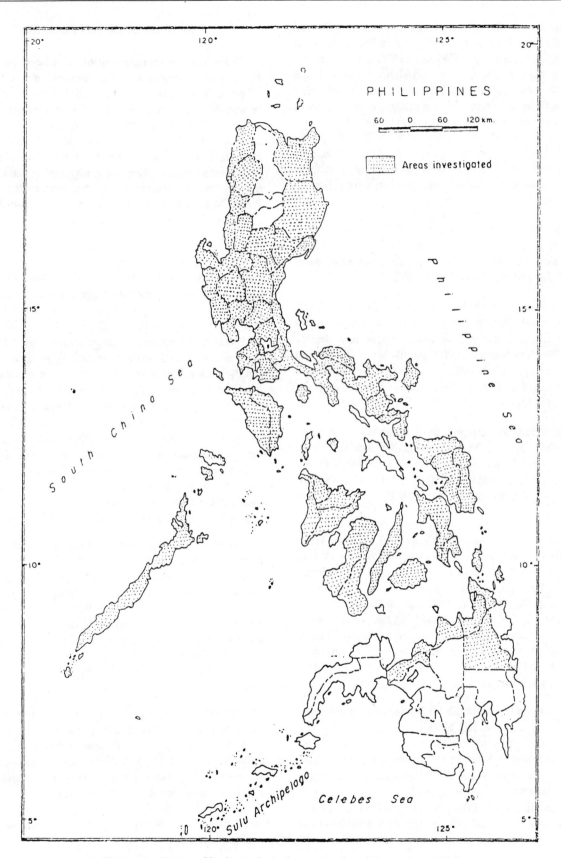

Figure 1. Status of hydrogeological mapping (as of December, 1984)

X. GROUNDWATER DEVELOPMENT IN INDONESIA*

1. INTRODUCTION

The rapid growth of population and industry as well as the desire for a higher standard of living have led to a rapid increase in the amount of water used for domestic, industrial and agricultural purposes. Within this country groundwater has been developed many centuries ago; at the beginning only from dug wells to meet domestic water demand. The deep seated groundwater, however, has only been developed since the middle of the last century in Jakarta after the discovery of a flowing artesian groundwater by successfully drilling at Fort Frederick, a Dutch fortress, in 1843. Since then deep wells have become one of the means to obtain potable water.

Until the commencement of Indonesia's First Five Year Development Plan in 1969, deep groundwater resources had not been extensively developed in most part of the country. At present the rate of groundwater extraction is increasing rapidly, especially due to the large scale of groundwater development for irrigation in rural areas during the dry season, and for the extension of water supplies for many cities. In addition, the growing population and industry in urban areas have also led to the rapid increase of groundwater extraction from private wells in urban areas.

This paper, dealing with groundwater resources, provides information with regard to the status of groundwater development in this country.

2. GROUNDWATER RESOURCE ASSESSMENT

Groundwater resource assessment should be understood as the determination of the sources, extent, dependability, and quality characteristics of groundwater, on which is based an evaluation of the possibilities for their utilization and control. Basically, this assessment comprises two types of measures, i.e. to assess the area of groundwater formation that constitutes the potential groundwater resources of the area, and to determine where or in what aquifer this groundwater is available for development.

Activities in the field of groundwater resource investigation in Indonesia up to the end of the second World

War were conducted strictly in connection with domestic water supply and small scale irrigation purposes. After this period the same activities were still continued. However, intensive groundwater investigation had just been started since 1969, the first year of Indonesia's Five Year Development Plan.

2.1. Assessment of groundwater potential

Assessment of groundwater potential is generally based on the knowledge of groundwater occurrence under natural conditions. It requires extensive hydrogeological investigation to study the configurations of aquifers which are mainly of geological character. It includes hydrogeological mapping, geophysical exploration, test drillings and continuous groundwater data collection.

2.1.1. Hydrogeological mapping

Since 1969, the Ministry of Mines and Energy through the Directorate of Environmental Geology had initiated a programme of systematic hydrogeological mapping, which ultimately will cover the whole of the archipelago. The sheets, scale 1:250,000 cover 1°30' longitude and 1° latitude. The scale 1:250,000 was determined to be the most appropriate for the map, because it copes best with the following aims and boundary conditions:

- clear and exact representation of the hydrogeological data for a fairly large area;

- ability to complete the maps by reasonable means and in relatively short time;

- availability of recent topographic and geological base maps.

The whole series of the systematic hydrogeological maps of Indonesia will comprise more than 150 sheets. Each sheet is to be accompanied by an explanatory note, either printed on the map itself or in a separate leaflet.

Figure 1 shows the status of hydrogeological mapping in August 1986. It can be seen that some 40 per cent of the country has been covered by systematic hydrogeological mapping (60 sheets). Among these, a total number of 19 sheets (6.4 per cent) were published since 1981. Some ten sets of sheet-manuscripts are about to be completed and are planed to be published in the near future.

Beside systematic hydrogeological mapping, the draft of a hydrogeological map at the scale 1:5,000,000 had been prepared in 1981 as the Indonesian contribution to the

* Country paper prepared for the thirteenth session of the ESCAP Committee on Natural Resources. This paper has been reproduced without formal editing. The views expressed in it are those of the author and do not necessarily reflect those of the United Nations.

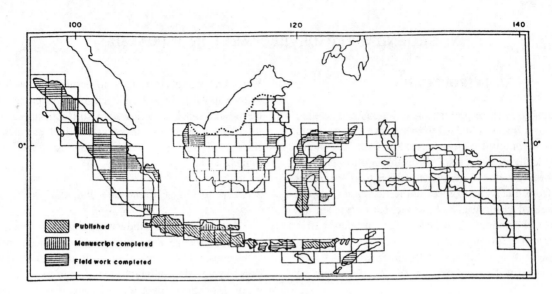

Figure 1. Status of the Hydrogeological Map of Indonesia 1:250,000 in 1986

Commission for Geological Map of the World (CGMW), Sub-Commission for South & East Asia. However, it was recognized that the hydrogeological map at a very small scale 1:5,000,000 is not appropriate to the archipelago country of Indoensia.

In the light of experiences with this mapping project and considering the huge expense both in time and money to cover the whole country in those maps, a small scale national hydrogeological map was prepared and published in 1983. The scale of 1:2,500,000 was considered to be the most suitable because:

— the whole country can be covered in only two sheets, and it provides the first step towards defining the nation's groundwater resources;

— it presents an overall view of the hydrogeological setting which is needed for country-wide planning, and stresses the important role of hydrogeological investigation for the development of this country;

— it provides a basic document for those sparsely inhabited areas of Indonesia in which hydrogeological mapping at a large scale is not relevant at the present time.

The scale of 1:2,500,000 offers a limited scope for cartographic projection of various inter-related data for meaningful documentation of diversified hydrogeological situation in Indonesia. Accordingly, only factors which have relevance to the hydrogeological condition or influences directly to the potential of the groundwater system are depicted on this map.

2.1.2. *Groundwater prospecting methods*

Methods of prospecting for groundwater used in Indonesia was in the beginning the classical scientific hydrogeological methods augmented in recent years by modern geophysical, remote sensing, isotopic and geochemical methods. Detail hydrogeological mapping is normally preceded by examination of aerial photographs, remote sensing and regional geological maps, followed by rapid ground reconnaissance.

Geophysical methods, especially electrical resistivity method, was introduced in 1958 and was applied to groundwater prospecting for the supply of water in the karstic limestone of Gunung Sewu (Yogyakarta). This method was used successfully for the first time to delineate fresh and salt groundwater boundaries in the Island of Madura in 1962. In addition to lithological logging, electrical and gamma ray logging became standard practice later. These methods are routinely used at present to assist field parties in the collection of subsurface geological information.

Seismic refraction method has little relevance to hydrogeology because of the depth, which is too great, and the hidden zone and blind layer problems. The seismic reflection method, however, has great potential for application to groundwater, but faces different problems of making comparatively simple, cheap and portable equipment. This method has been applied to determine the underground river channels or caves occurring in karstic limestone terrains of Gunungkidul and Madura.

Test drillings supported by pumping tests are an essential part of groundwater studies and are conducted routinely during this stage of groundwater potential assessment.

The hydrochemical method is appropriate for groundwater investigations. Of importance is the fact that it is possible to find out the sources of water by graphical interpretation of the data analyzed. The determination of stable isotopes of hydrogen and oxygen in groundwater is particularly valuable in classifying the sources of water in the groundwater system. These isotopes and associated chemical quality parameters have been used in determining the residence time and movement of groundwater in the Jakarta artesian basin.

2.2. Assessment of groundwater resource development

Assessing groundwater availability to be developed requires an adequate and reliable groundwater investigation programme. Once an aquifer has been identified and proved in an area it is necessary to delineate the groundwater system, to determine aquifer constants, to assess the replenishable groundwater resource or safe yield, and eventually to formulate a rough theoretical model of aquifers. This requires integration of the results of pump tests and the recharge study.

Adequate and reliable groundwater investigation, especially for large-scale groundwater developments,

have been initiated in Indonesia since 1971. At that time, under a grant from Great Britain, the British firm of Sir M. MacDonald & Partners performed the groundwater surveys in Yogyakarta area and the limestone terrain of Gunung-kidul for supplementary irrigation water. Several other groundwater development possibilities were also assessed; for example, for the limestone terrains of Madura and Tuban, the Kediri – Nganjuk and Madiun – Solo areas. Furthermore in conjunction with the study of surface water, the possibilities of groundwater development were also assessed in the Lampung, Bali, Lombok and West Timor.

Assessments of groundwater resource developments were also carried out with the purpose of providing sufficient amount of water for city water supplies, such as for the city water supplies of Jakarta, Bandung, Yogyakarta, Semarang etc. Figure 2 shows the location of groundwater development projects carried out in Indonesia.

In executing large scale groundwater development, e.g. for city water supply and irrigation, various stages of groundwater resource planning ranging from reconnaissance to sophisticated optimization-schemes are carried out. In case of large scale groundwater development for irrigation the following stages are conducted:

Stage   I: Reconnaissance, data collection and field visit;

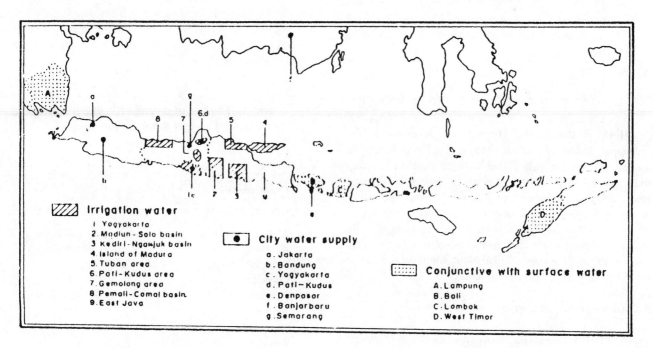

Figure 2.   Map showing locations of groundwater development projects in Indonesia

Stage II: Survey and investigation, i.e. feasibility study of groundwater potential based on detailed exploration;

Stage III: Pilot schemes, i.e. feasibility study of actual field conditions encountered in utilizing groundwater for irrigation;

Stage IV: Full scale development, operating the groundwater system in such a way that certain cost benefit relation attains its maximum value.

The use of groundwater for irrigation by using deep-well pumps is still rather new in Indonesia, because various consideration should be taken into account technically, economically as well as socially. Therefore the development is carried out first in the stage of Pilot Project, before large scale development could be implemented.

The presently used criteria for selecting possible groundwater irrigation schemes for further investigation are:

—   there should be intensive cultivation and dense population in the area;

—   there should be tendency for water shortage which could not be met from surface water;

—   there should be a good response from local farmers and local officials to the need for further careful operation and maintenance;

—   preliminary reconnaissance should have indicated good availability of groundwater potential to be developed.

3. GROUNDWATER RESOURCE DEVELOPMENT

Most of the present groundwater development for municipal, industrial and agricultural supplies in Indonesia are carried out through drilled wells or tube wells. Dug wells generally serve domestic needs, especially in rural areas, although some are also used for irrigation purposes. As the water demand for irrigation increases, construction of drilled wells to deeper aquifers are encouraged. In addition, due to the occurrence of brackish water at shallow depth, wells are also drilled along the coastal areas to supply fresh water to rural communities.

3.1. Groundwater utilization

At present, the utilization of groundwater in Indonesia is increasing rapidly to meet the growing demand of water for domestic, city-water supply, industry and irrigation purposes.

3.1.1. Domestic water supply

In urban and rural areas shallow groundwater has been used to meet the demand for domestic water. For this purpose the shallow dug-well is the most widely used system for groundwater extraction. Driven wells, however, are becoming more and more widespread, particularly — in cities and towns where the public water supply is still inadequate.

The total population of Indonesia is at present about 164 million, about 70 per cent of whom live in rural areas, and the remainder in urban areas. In rural areas the amount of water used for domestic purposes is estimated at 6.89 million m^3/day, assuming a per capita water demand of 60 1/day. About 60 per cent of the domestic water used in rural areas, or about 4.13 million m^3/day, is obtained from groundwater sources, mainly from shallow wells.

In urban areas the amount of water used for domestic purposes is estimated at 7.38 million m^3/day, assuming a per capita water comsumption of 150 1/day. The municipal waterworks supply 3.46 million m^3/day, mainly from spring water and surface water. About 3.92 million m^3/day have to be supplied from other sources, mainly private wells.

In addition to spring water and purification of surface water some city waterworks obtain additional water by means of deep wells- and in some instances, also by shallow wells. The waterwork of Madiun obtains water from a battery of 12 wells tapping water from- aquifers at depth varying between 8.6-17.0 metres. Table 1 shows the rate of groundwater extraction for domestic water supply in some cities in Indonesia.

**Table 1. The rate of groundwater extraction for
domestic water supply in some cities
in Indonesia**

City waterworks	Rate of extraction (1/sec)
Ambon	80
Bandung	535
Banjarbaru	100
Cirebon	500
Denpasar	420
Jember	100
Yogyakarta	280
Kudus	100
Madiun	75
Pare – Pare	100

3.1.2. *Industrial water supply*

In industry, water is used for processing and cooling purposes. With new industries coming in, more water are being used. Due to the nonexistance of adequate public water supply most of the industries built their own water supply systems. Present groundwater abstraction for industries is not known except in a few cases. In Bandung, the industry, primarily the textile factories, consume an estimated amount of 40,000 m³/day of groundwater abstracted from confined aquifers. In addition, a large number of industries built in Jakarta obtain their water supply from private deep wells, currently utilize about 53,000 m³/day. In other cities such as Medan, Padang and Semarang where industries grow rapidly, groundwater utilization is expected to increase considerably.

3.1.3. *Irrigation water supply*

In certain areas of Indonesia, groundwater has been used for many years for agriculture (for secondary crops) during the dry season, for example in the Nganjuk and Madiun areas. By simple means people are able to drill wells up to ten metres deep penetrating the shallow flowing artesian aquifers. In the Madiun basin more than 1,000 driven wells had been constructed producing more than 0.38 million m³/day of flowing artesian water.

The Groundwater Development Project of the Directorate of Irrigation II had initiated in Java a number of groundwater projects since 1970. The pilot scheme of this groundwater development was carried out in the limestone terrains of Gunungkidul and Madura, as wells as in the artesian basins of Kediri – Nganjuk and Madiun-Ponorogo. In some area the development of groundwater is also carried out in conjunction with surface water, such as in Bali, Lombok and West Timor. Figures in table 2 show the rate

Table 2. Rate of groundwater extraction for irrigation in 1986 by the Groundwater Development Project

Projected area	No. of wells	Irrigated area (Ha)	Rate of extraction (10^3 m³/day)
D.I. Yogyakarta	55	1 298	34
Madiun	61	4 465	55
Kediri – Nganjuk	136	6 100	82
Madura	51	1 785	26
Other part of East Java	26	920	20
Bali	4	100	2.5
Lombok	5	151	3
Total	338	14 819	222.5

of groundwater extraction for irrigation in some pilot schemes of the Groundwater Development Project.

3.2. *Problems of groundwater development*

The increasing water demand and the growing importance of groundwater as a source of supply will bring about the rapid development of groundwater; the rate of groundwater extraction will therefore increase rapidly. The growing population and industry in urban areas such as Medan, Jakarta, Bandung, Semarang and Denpasar have also led to rapid increase of groundwater extraction from private wells.

The principle problems arising from overdraw of groundwater – are excessive depression of its level. In coastal plain, excessive pumping of groundwater may cause sea water encroachment. These undesirable effects of groundwater exploitation have been noticed in some parts of the coastal plain of Medan Belawan (North Sumatra) and in the northern coast of Java.

3.2.1. *Lowering of piezometric surface*

Rapid lowering of water levels have been noticed in the northern part of the Metropolitan city of Jakarta, the cities of Bandung, Semarang and Medan.

In 1900 the pressure head of the deep groundwater system in northern and central Jakarta was at 5 to 15 metres above sea level and wells were generally flowing. The piezometric surface in these areas dropped continuously by 0.1-0.2 metres/year until the early 1970. In 1980 in the main part of northern and central Jakarta piezometric levels of confined aquifer system were generally below sea level and had reached 10-20 metres in areas where the industrial development was intensified (Figure 3).

The total extraction of shallow and deep confined groundwater from about 2,500 drilled wells is currently about 1.5 m³/sec. In response to this overexploitation, water levels in the confined system have dropped by 1-7 m/year during the last tree years and are locally at 20-30 metres below sea levels.

Despite the heavy drawdown of head levels in the coastal plain, sea water encroachment is still low, due to the low permeability of the lower aquifer system. However, brackish groundwater of the shallow aquifer systems (less than 100 m depth) has encroached as far as 5-7 km inland. Land surface lowering became evident in central Jakarta after 1977.

Within the Bandung basin about 51,950 m³/day of water for industries is obtained from private drilled wells, tapping confined groundwater. Extensive development of

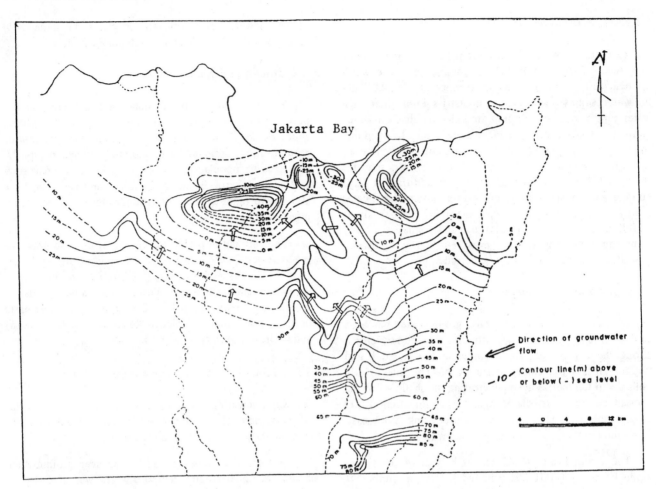

Figure 3. Piezometric contour lines of the second confined aquifer system of Jakarta (40-150 m) in December 1982

the confined aquifer for the water supply of Bandung city started at the end of 1981 when the newly established well field was put in operation. At present the well field produces about 45,600 m³/day consisting of 19 production wells tapping largely from the confined aquifers at depth of 45-160 metres.

The effects of groundwater extraction are most serious in the vicinities of the well field of the city water works. Measurements taken in June 1983 indicate that the water level of the confined groundwater had dropped 12-28 metres from its original level prior to pumping, in May 1981. In the period 1983-1985 the water levels show further lowering of 2-7 metres in the eastern wells and 9-15 metres in the western wells. The present dynamic water levels vary from 20 to 30 metres below the ground surface.

3.2.2. *Salt water intrusion*

Saline water intrusion is a general problem where wells are located too close to the coastline. Along the coastal plains of Indonesia saline or brackish water-bearing layers are often found above as well as below the fresh water aquifers. The fresh groundwater becomes one of the most important sources for this plain which is mostly densely populated. The groundwater is utilized largely for industrial and domestic purposes.

Heavy pumping of groundwater may cause sea water encroachment. Contamination of saline water may also take place around the poorly constructed wells. These undesirable effects of groundwater exploitation have been noticed in some parts of the northern coastal plain of Java.

A considerable potential of groundwater development for irrigation occurs along the coast in the limestone terrains of Tuban and Madura. The intrusion of sea water, however, is likely to be a major constraint on the development of this groundwater. Heavy pumping may invite salt water encroachment and drilling inland will increase considerably the construction and operation costs.

3.2.3. *Contamination related to human settlement*

Beside the natural effects of hydrogeological environment, human activities also have significant effects on groundwater quality. Man's use and reuse of water for domestic, industrial or agricultural purposes result in the discharge of liquid or solid wastes into the geologic environment. This, in turn, affects and degrades both surface and groundwater quality, which is constantly changing because of the continual replenishment of the aquifers by new or recycled water.

In Indonesia deterioration of groundwater quality is caused by several sources deriving from liquid or solid wastes produced under domestic, industrial or agricultural environments. Many of these sources of pollution endanger the quality of groundwater resources, especially if one considers the geographical and geological situation of many coastal plains in respect to their near-shore position, their dense population and intense agricultural use as well as the growing industrialization in the surrounding of the major cities.

The most widely distributed potential source of groundwater pollution in Indonesia both in rural and urban areas are domestic septic tanks where public sewer systems are not available. Typical agricultural sources of groundwater pollution derives from irrigation return flow, animal wastes, fertilizers and pesticides as a single cause or as a combination of all causes. The contamination may be extremely high if several factors together contribute to the degradation of groundwater, e.g. groundwater table near landsurface with low gradient and low groundwater velocity, the area is irrigated using fertilizers and pesticides. The combination of some of these factors is probably the main reason for excessive salt content of shallow groundwater of the irrigated coastal plain or basin areas in Indonesia.

A preliminary study on water quality of shallow groundwater in the urbanized and industrialized areas of Jakarta give an example of water pollution indication in this area. Most of the shallow groundwater from dugwells has a high bacterial content. In addition, the constituents of detergent, organic material and nitrogen compounds become higher in areas of densely populated and in some industrial centres.

3.2.4. *Land subsidence possibility*

It is known that groundwater resources development and the resulting piezometric level decline may cause land subsidence. Excessive reduction of artesian pressure in thick alluvium like in Jakarta, may induce compaction of aquifer and adjacent silt and clay layers, and finally cause lowering of ground surface or land subsidence.

Although there have been some apparent changes in the environmental conditions at some places in the central part of Jakarta, yet it is not clear that they are due to land subsidence. This case has long been the subject of discussion without conducting any effective investigation.

An evaluation of geology and groundwater hydrology of the Jakarta area, elevation survey discrepancies, and the results of deep-subsurface investigation indicate that Jakarta has characteristics of an area subject to probably undergoing compression subsidence. Additionally a near surface settlement due to urban development may occur in the coastal alluvium.

3.2.5. *Problems in operation and maintenance of tube well irrigation schemes*

In Indonesia the construction of tubewell irrigation schemes including the construction of tubewells, canalizations and pumpsets are provided by the Government. In line with the Government policy, the operation and maintenance of the tubewells and other equipments should be taken over later on by the Water Users' Associations or Farmers' Associations.

The organized development of tubewell for irrigation is still much in its infancy in Indonesia. Tubewell pumps and engines are relatively sophisticated items of machinery which cannot be repaired at village level. Skilled mechanics and extensive workshop facilities for their proper maintenance are therefore needed which are not available at the village level. In addition, operation of deep well-pumps require supporting facilities such as fuel and spare parts for pump replacements which are sometimes beyond the farmer's capacities.

4. GROUNDWATER LEGISLATION

Before the promulgation of the Law on Water Resources Development in 1974, most of the legislation in force governing water resources in Indonesia dated back to the time of the Dutch Administration. The Dutch Administration legislation is outdated, for today's situation is much different than before. Today, the administration of groundwater resources is conducted by the Indonesian Government through the Ministry of Mines and Energy.

To implement the 1982 government regulation of water resources management, and to ensure the organizing of groundwater development nationally, a ministerial regulation on groundwater management was issued by the Minister of Mines and Energy in 1983. Guideline on the implementation of this groundwater management was issued by the Director General of Directorate General of Geology and Mineral Resources on 18 March 1985.

As defined in paragraph (2) article 5 of the Law No. 11 of 1984 on water resources development and Article 6 of the Government Act No. 22 of 1982 on water resources management, the administration of underground water resources and of hot springs, since these are mineral and geothermal resources, is under the competence of the Minister who is responsible for mines. To abstract groundwater for certain purpose is, however, subject to licensing. Licenses are issued by the Governor after having obtained technical recommendations from the Minister who is responsible for mines. Furthermore, controls of groundwater related to health is under the competence of Ministry of Health (Regulation of Minister of Health No. 528/Men-Kes/Per/XII/1982).

Based upon Article 3 paragraph (2) of the Regulation of Minister of Mines and Energy No. 03/P/M/Pertamben/83 on groundwater management, the Minister's authority and responsibility for the implementation of groundwater management is carried out by the Director General of Geology and Mineral Resources. This authority and these responsibilities, as stated in Article 2 of this Ministerial Regulation includes:

a. Co-ordinating all activities of groundwater inventories in which interests of public, department and other related institutions are considered;

b. Arranging groundwater utilization and development;

c. Controlling and supervising groundwater abstraction in relation to the licensing of groundwater abstraction and groundwater conservation;

d. Managing and processing groundwater data that can be used as basic information data;

e. Managing and issuing licenses to water-well drilling companies.

To ensure the organizing of groundwater development nationally guidelines on the implementation of groundwater management was decreed by the Director General of Geology and Mineral Resources. This decree regulates the responsibility and institutional arrangement of groundwater development, the licensing of groundwater abstraction and drilling firm as well as the control and supervision that should be carried out thereafter.

SELECTED REFERENCES

1. Directorate of Environmental Geology (1983). *Groundwater utilization in Indonesia.* Report prepared for the Economic and Social Commission for Asia and the Pacific at its tenth session, Bangkok 25-31 October 1983.

2. _____ (1986) Legislation and institutional arrangement of groundwater development in Indonesia.

3. A. Djaeni (1983). *The quality of Groundwater in Indonesia.* Report prepared for the Unesco regional workshop on water quality in large urban areas of Southeast Asia, Manila 5-10 December 1983.

4. Santo Purnomo Hadiwiyoto (1984). *Prospek pengembangan airtanah* (Prospect on groundwater development). Paper prepared for Seminar on Hydrology, Faculty of Geography, University of Gajahmada, Yogyakarta 14-15 December 1984.

XI. INTEGRATED GROUND AND SURFACE WATER MANAGEMENT IN ARID ZONES*

by

Altshul A.H.**   Ussenko V.S.**
Pluznikov V.N.**   Cherepansky M.M.**

Due to its natural properties, the groundwater is a most reliable source of the domestic/potable water supply because it is better protected from pollution, features stable temperature, contains but few organic impurities. Due to these properties, the utilization of groundwater is constantly increasing with each passing year.

Groundwater is considered a valuable commercial mineral whose utilization is regulated by special legislative and standard documents as well as by the system of administrative control. In contrast to other commercial minerals (i.e. solids, mineral oil and gas), the groundwater features a number of peculiarities which should be taken into account when estimating the prospects of its utilization in the national economy including the irrigation purposes.

One of the most significant peculiarities of the groundwater is its constant regeneration ability. In absolute majority of cases, during water intake's operation not only the consumption but the additional forming of usable storage and resources of groundwater take place. Its forming takes place due to changing boundary conditions in the groundwater flow line and, as a result, of increasing the groundwater supply in the area of its distribution. The additional source of water supply increase is, in this case, the surface water which is hydraulically interconnected with the groundwater, and in some cases the groundwater adjoining the acquifier being used, as well as decrease in evaporation from the water table acquifier when its level drops down. In course of different water economy activities (i.e. immediate runoff regulation by water storages, development of irrigated agriculture, etc.) newly created groundwater storages under favourable hydrogeological conditions may be reliable source of a wide water supply and land irrigation. Natural water regeneration principle provides for increasing the usage of groundwater.

Due to interrelations between all natural water resources, their transformation and regulation abilities, it is necessary, when planning groundwater utilization, to take into account the possibility of artificial water replenishment.

By assigning the priority to using groundwater for the needs of domestic/potable water supply, it is necessary to account for its resource replenishing ability and possibility of switching over to its utilization for other purposes. Thus, currently available excessive water resources may be used for irrigation purposes, whereas in perspective, when the domestic/potable water demands increase, the assimilated capacities for groundwater extraction may be gradually switched over to satisfying these demands.

The groundwater is most favourable source for satisfying the consumers with high demands for reliability (availability) of a water supply system, since the groundwater due to its persistence is characterized by negligible changes over a period of time. The choice of calculated supply (or the guaranteed volume of water consumption) when trying to satisfy the demands from the groundwater depends not only on the runoff variations, but also on the extent to which the groundwater supplies have been investigated, since it is almost always possible to increase the groundwater forced intake in critical situations.

Forced increasing of the groundwater intake means a short-time water pumping at an yield which is greater than its average annual replenishment rate, with subsequent compensation for the water intake consequences (naturally or artificially) during the periods of low water demands.

Integrated ground and surface water management may be an important activity in a more intensive groundwater intake for irrigation purposes. The practice of a separate evaluation of their resources does not provide for using local water resources more efficiently which causes the necessity to substantiate costly and sometimes premature transfers of the surface runoff. The analysis of the runoff deficit in some river basins carried out when compiling the schemes of integrated management of water resources has shown that this deficit is observed during some months in a year and even not every year. Therefore, under favourable hydrogeological conditions it is feasible to use groundwater in these periods by means of active pumping with subsequent replenishment during years or periods with high water.

---

* Paper prepared for the thirteenth session of the ESCAP Committee on Natural Resources. This paper has been reproduced without formal editing. The views expressed in it are those of the authors and do not necessarily reflect those of the United Nations.

** Cental Research Institute for the Integrated Use of Water Resources, Minsk, USSR.

When putting into economic use the groundwater interrelated with the surface runoff, there appear two inseparable problems which must be solved when performing the water economy and technical and economic calculations on substantiating the parameters and modes for the integrated ground and surface water management. The first problem relates to the necessity of evaluating the changes (reduction) in river runoff caused by the groundwater intake (this is the problem of accounting for surface and groundwater interrelations when planning the water economy balances). The other problem relates to the necessity of choosing such groundwater intake modes which would, in the optimal sense, ensure the complex development of the territorial water resources on condition that the ecological requirements for nature protection are observed (this is the problem of optimal control of integrated water resources).

The groundwater as an irrigation source may be classified as follows (3):

— *Basic source* in case of independent irrigation. This is the case when in the investigated basin there are excessive storages of groundwater of the required quality. There may exist an alternative in choosing the source: groundwater or surface water. The problem should be solved on the basis of the technical and economic reasoning. When the groundwater is used independently, its intake mode corresponds to that of water usage by agricultural crops;

— *Supplemental source,* when the groundwater is used for increasing water supply in the irrigation area and replenishing the irrigation system in the vegetative period, during certain seasons and in the years with low water when there exists water deficit in the surface source. This is the case of the integrated use of the surface and groundwater when the water intake mode of the latter corresponds to the water deficit mode in the basic irrigation source;

— *Seasonal source,* when the groundwater is used during certain seasons;

— *Periodic source,* when the groundwater is used for irrigation in certain years with low water. This is the case of a common water deficit in the basin and the necessity of providing maximum possible irrigation areas;

— *Temporary spring,* when the groundwater is subsequently switched over to serve another purpose (i.e. for water supply) or when the groundwater is temporarily used for irrigation though its use has initially been planned for other purposes.

As to the duration of the groundwater source utilization which affects the methods of calculating water intakes and the irrigation system, three cases may be considered:

— using the source for indefinitely long time (termless utilization);

— prolonged (but limited in time) groundwater utilization (for a planned period);

— short-term seasonal groundwater utilization during its forced intake in certain seasons or in the years with low water (with complete or partial restoration of the initial hydrogeological conditions in the area of water intake during subsequent seasons or years).

The possibilities of groundwater utilization for irrigation purposes should be confirmed by way of a specialized hydrogeological regional survey aimed at selecting the prospective groundwater deposits. The groundwater deposits should be considered as part of total regional water resources.

The prospects of using the groundwater deposits for irrigation purposes and its recommended withdrawal volume should be determined by the legislative provisions on the priority of the groundwater utilization mainly for the domestic/potable water supplies and in the desert zones for pasture watering as well. Thus, the prospective deposit volume should be evaluated by subtracting the future needs in it for the domestic/potable water supplies from the total volume of regional reserves. The water demands for the above purposes are determined on the basis of current design works by taking into account the future organization of public services for a longterm period with a certain "safety margin".

In case the demands for the domestic/potable water supplies as well as for pastures' watering for a given area are equal to or exceed 75 per cent of the potential operational fresh groundwater storages, their deposits should be assigned the catergory of non-prospective for irrigation and should be reserved for the domestic/potable purposes. However, under such conditions and by accounting only for replenishable potential operational groundwater storages not excluded is the possibility of their temporary utilization for irrigation purposes in the period untill the exclusive usage of the reserved storages for water supply.

Only those fresh groundwater deposits may be considered prospective, where water supply and pasture irrigation demands are less than 75 per cent of the prospective underground storage of water. The main attention in the design and research activities should be paid to discovering the possibilities for using the very replenishable part of the prospective operational storages for irrigation purposes.

In case of their suitability for irrigation purposes, the operating storages of the groundwater deposits which do not correspond to the norms of the domestic/potable water supply as well as those with mineralization as high as 5 g/l should be totally used for these purposes. The 5 g/l upper limit of the groundwater mineralization allows its use for irrigation purposes. The groundwaters with 1, 1-3 and 3-5 g/l mineralization level are considered separately. The groundwater with mineralization over 5 g/l may be used for irrigation after diluting it with fresh water.

In deciding new water intakes, and when there exist several alternatives, the priority should be assigned to the groundwater wells with yield of 20 l/day and more. When reconstructing those irrigation systems where the groundwater use may be integrated with a vertical drainage (irrespective of the well yield), the groundwater is preferably used.

A groundwater storage may be considered prospective for irrigation if during its utilization it ensures a forced discharge and in case the natural or artificial supply sources contribute to regenerating the drawdown storage.

The time intervals and annual duration of a forced utilization of a groundwater storage as well as the time (duration) of using the equipment for artificial regeneration of their storage should all be calculated on the basis of hydrodynamic models of storages as well as technical and economic calculations for the groundwater storages.

The biggest prospective for irrigation groundwater storages is related to quaternary sediments found in intermount depression and sheves, debris cones, river valleys and in irrigation regions. Their storages are basically formed due to river and irrigation water losses and minus that part which is wasted in evaporation from the groundwater level. Hence, the intensive groundwater intakes in the amounts comparable to their regenerated operational storage results in redistribution of water balance components and, consequently, in reducing waterway yields due to recapturing transient (return) groundwater. It is recommended to arrange groundwater intakes so that their utilization should not increase losses from water passages (irrigation channels).

Intrastratum water extraction from the platform-type artesian basins as well as that of groundwater in arid regions practically does not reduce surface runoff. It facilitates general increase of water resources for irrigation.

Under conditions of considerable transformations of river basins in the interests of the national economy, important links are established between separate components of water resources as well as between centralized and distributed water consumption objects within vast territories. If it were the initial stage of the water economy development, it would have been possible to let these links reveal themselves spontaneously. Under present conditions the process of forming the water economy systems should be controlled consciously and be based on the analysis and thorough evaluation of emerging and planned dependencies between the resource sources and water consumption objects.

Of all the set of problems whose evaluation and development are necessary in the near future, a particular attention in this paper is paid to evaluation and control aspects of integrated ground and surface water management.

The evaluation aspect is put forward by the pressing need of evaluating as accurately as possible the groundwater resources in the water economy balance of the territory by taking into account their hydraulic relations with the rivers.

The authors for quite a considerable time have been evaluating the influence of groundwater use onto the river yields under different climatic conditions. The results of recent years' research are summarized in a monograph (2). It gives a systematic presentation of analytic methods for evaluating the river yields reduction during groundwater intakes' operation, as well as the methods of electro-analogue, numeric and realtime simulation and practical case studies. These methods are mainly employed for evaluating the influence of a large centralized water intakes on the yield under different hydrogeological conditions. Presently, under consideration is the task of evaluating the influence of using multiple single wells (or groups of them), say, agricultural, which are dispersed over the territory.

On the whole, it may be concluded that for the current state of knowledge the problems of evaluating the river yield reduction with the help of physical and mathematical simulation methods are fairly well developed to be practically feasible. Lately, such information is prepared prior to designing groundwater intakes.

The control aspect of the integrated surface and groundwater management makes it principally possible to determine such parameters and operating modes of the intakes (river and groundwater) as well as for enriching available water resources which for the fixed community of water consumers allow to minimize the resources allocated for meeting their water demands and to increase reliability (actual calculated water supply) of the water management system or else to increase the volume of water resources used.

Based on generalized methods and practice known from hydrological and water economy measures taken for satisfying water demands, we have developed sets of simulation models and programme packages for calculating integrated surface and groundwater management, which will enable solving the tasks set under the following diversity of initial conditions:

(a) by a required water intake mode from the sources – constant; conditionally constant (by calculated water supply needs); alternating (stochastic);

(b) by the degree of mastering river runoff – natural (domestic); seasonal and over-year regulation;

(c) by ways of hydrological information input – recorded discharge hydrograph; calendar rows of hydrometric observations; hydrological rows obtained by statistical test methods;

(d) by nature of hydraulic links between groundwater used and the river: i.e. complete, incomplete, no links.

As a result of the calculations using the simulation models, there may be obtained the volumes and modes of excessive and insufficient water resources in the system, the requirements for groundwater intake and its artificial regeneration. The algorithm calculation is applied for primary use of surface water, whose current resources in the water intake line are determined in accounting for all interventions into the water regime up the river flow as well as the needs for reserving in this line or transfering down the flow a complex water flow meeting the interests of other water consumers. In case of diminishing-due to seasonal and year-by-year fluctuations, – of river runoff resources below the established level, groundwater storages come under forced use. Due to this, the river runoff may be more fully used (at fixed parameters of its use), since idle water removing is reduced, and a deeper water storage usage in years with low water is permitted as compared to autonomous use of both water resources. The feasibility of adopted decisions is checked by fulfilling the set calculated operating volume of the water economy system. Determined among these decisions at the design stage are the optimal (by minimum criteria)

calculated resources spent on meeting the demands of the water consumers which are members of the system.

As a result of system operation simulation by water economy rows, complete characteristics of volumes, depths and water deficit frequencies may be obtained.

The problems discussed in this paper have been approbated on the rivers of Central Asia within the USSR territory.

An important theoretical problem solved with the aim of increasing the reliability of calculations or integrated surface and groundwater management is the evaluation of groundwater intake influence on the runoff in a non-stationary (forced and discrete) mode. It is necessary to take into account the mechanism of groundwater forming under natural and affected by their use conditions (in particular, evaluating the effects of watertable acquifer evaporation on its drainage and smoothing year-by-year groundwater runoff fluctuations in the zones of regional depressions, etc.). Finally, it is supposed to develop a theory of year-after-year regulation of subsurface runoff in water bearing deposits in the framework of general methodology of controlling the development and functioning of complex water economy systems.

REFERENCES

1. Mirzaev S.Sh., Valiev X.I. (1977). Groundwater reconnaissance and evaluation for irrigation. Fan, Tashkent.

2. Forecasting of groundwater usage impact on hydrogeological conditions (1985). Nauka i Technika, Minsk.

3. Guidelines for Compiling Water Use Budgets, (1974), New-York.

Part Three :

ENVIRONMENTAL ISSUES

XII. ENVIRONMENTAL ISSUES OF WATER RESOURCES DEVELOPMENT IN THE ESCAP REGION*

INTRODUCTION

1. Throughout the ESCAP region, the constructions of water resources development projects such as dams, reservoirs, irrigation systems, embankments, water intakes and canals are being fostered in order to harness water for the benefit of the people. Numerous projects, both large and small, are intended to meet steadily growing demands for domestic and industrial water supply, food and energy. The beneficial effects of such projects also concern transportation, recreation and mitigation of damage caused by floods.

2. Water resources projects are often considered as playing a vital role in ensuring future economic and social development in many countries of the region, some of which have extensive experience and good traditions of sound water resources exploitation. It is estimated that at least 50 per cent more agricultural land has to be irrigated to satisfy the need for food products; the hydropower potential of about 1,000,000 MW, as yet exploited only slightly, has to be developed sufficiently to meet the region's electricity needs; safe drinking water has to be supplied to more than 1 billion people suffering from inadequate supplies of potable water in the developing countries of the region.[1] Thus, it is quite clear that the accelerated development and extensive utilization of water resources are inevitable in the future.

3. With the expansion of water resources development activities in the region, more attention is being paid to the impact of these projects on the environment because all water resources projects produce, in one way or another, environmental changes, some beneficial and some not. In the past, decisions on such projects were dictated by technical and economic factors, but nowadays environmental considerations are also playing an increasing role in the process of making decisions and formulating policies on water resources development activities.

4. Over the past years the Commission, through its legislative committees, has given increasing attention to the problem of the integrated relationship between environment and development, In particular, the Committee on Natural Resources at its tenth session recommended that environmental issues of water resources development be discussed at its thirteenth session. The present paper is intended to facilitate the discussion on the subject by showing the scope of the water resources development activities in the region, bringing to the attention of the countries some of the major environmental impacts of these projects and identifying ways to avoid or reduce the adverse effects.

I. ENVIRONMENTAL IMPLICATIONS OF WATER RESOURCES PROJECTS

A. Dams and reservoirs

5. Multi-purpose hydro-schemes embracing dams and reservoirs contribute significantly to the economic development of many countries of the region. Hydropower installations account for approximately one quarter of the total electricity generation capacity in the ESCAP region. If all the economically exploitable hydropower potential were harnessed, most of the region's present and future electricity needs could be satisfied.

6. Since the 1950s, the rate of construction of dams and associated reservoirs, designed mainly for generating electricity, supplying water for irrigation, domestic and industrial needs, and for flood control in the region, has been very impressive. In 1950, there were 1,717 dams over 15 m height in service in the ESCAP region, of which 394 were located in the developing countries. In 1982, as many as 23,210 dams were listed, including 20,623 in the developing countries (see table 1). Eighty per cent of these dams are in China, where, starting from 8 dams in 1950, 18,587 dams have been constructed in 32 years. That is 11.3 times more than the rest of the developing countries of the region during the same period. In fact, most of the dams in China are less than 30 m in height and they are practically all embankment dams. India and the Republic of Korea have also been building dams and reservoirs intensively. In 1982, there were 1,085 dams in India and 628 in the Republic of Korea. As for the industrialized countries of the region, 2,142 dams of various types constructed in Japan by 1982 accounted for 83 per cent of the total. The pace of dam construction is expected to increase in the region. There are several grandiose projects, such as the Three Gorges hydroelectric project on the Chiang Jiang River in China and the Dihang hydro-project on the Brahmaputra River in India, which, if constructed, will have the world's biggest electricity generation capacity, of 13,000 MW and 20,000 MW respectively. They will also be beneficial in controlling floods and developing navigation.

---

* Originally issued as E/ESCAP/NR. 13/11.

[1] *UNEP Asia-Pacific Annual Report 1983*, p. 6.

Table 1. Number of dams over 15 m in the ESCAP countries, by period of completion

Country or area	Number of dams			
	Until 1950	1951-1977	1978-1982	Total
Afghanistan	–	2	–	2
Australia	122	198	54	374
Bangladesh	–	1	–	1
Bhutan	–	–	–	–
Brunei Darussalam	–	1	–	1
Burma	1	1	–	2
China	8	16 492	2 095	18 595
Fiji	–	–	2	2
Hong Kong	13	24	–	37
India	202	797	86	1 085
Indonesia	14	12	7	33
Iran (Islamic Republic of)	–	17	4	21
Japan	1 173	833	136	2 142
Lao People's Democratic Republic	–	1	–	1
Malaysia	1	10	1	12
Maldives	–	–	–	–
Mongolia	–	–	–	–
Nepal	–	–	1	1
New Zealand	28	38	6	72
Papua New Guinea	–	3	–	3
Pakistan	3	30	5	38
Philippines	1	5	3	9
Republic of Korea	116	443	69	628
Samoa	–	–	–	–
Singapore	–	2	1	3
Sri Lanka	23	41	5	69
Taiwan (a province of the People's Republic of China)	12	23	2	37
Thailand	–	22	19	41
Viet Nam	–	1	–	1
Total	1 717	18 997	2 496	23 210

Source: International Committee on Large Dams, *World Register of Dams,* (1984).

7. The environmental effects of dams and reservoirs are felt far beyond the sites of the projects because such large engineering structures change to a large extent the overall hydrological regimes of the rivers on which they are constructed. The nature, importance and magnitude of impacts will vary considerably from one reservoir to another owing to the influence of a number of variables: size, shape, and depth of reservoir; inflow and outflow rates; range of fluctuations in water level; climate and weather; geology and geomorphology; and soils in the watershed, along the reservoir shores, and in affected downstream areas; tectonic characteristics of the reservoir site; vegetative cover in the reservoir site; distance of the reservoir from the sea; riverine flora and fauna which may be affected by the impoundment; importance and value of resources and features to be flooded; and type and extent of human and animal diseases associated with the aquatic system. Some of the major impacts typical for countries of the region are described below.

1. Sedimentation

8. Although erosion and sedimentation processes are part of the natural evolution of landscape, they can be accelerated by man's activities. Thus, dams and reservoirs may disturb the natural process of erosion, transport and deposition of bed load and suspended material. Sediments are deposited upstream from the dam owing to the reduction of flow velocity in the reservoir, while erosion and degradation of the river channel may occur downstream from the project site.

9. Depletion of storage capacity is the most significant upstream effect of reservoir sedimentation. The silt that accumulates behind a dam may cause considerable ecological and engineering problem and abolish the reservoir's ability to perform its intended functions, such as water supply, flood control, hydropower generation, navigation and recreation. The range in rates of reservoir sedimentation is very large. In temperate climatic regions, the sedimentation of a reservoir is usually a slow process. But in tropical, subtropical and arid areas, which form a large part of the ESCAP region, sedimentation rates can be very high. Many reservoirs in the region have had their usable capacity completely obliterated by sediments after only a few years of operation. It has been reported that in China, 178 reservoirs in the Huggang District of Hubei Province lose 6 million m^3 of storage capacity each year owing to silting. Many small reservoirs had to be abandoned after just two or three years of operation and some larger hydroelectric stations had to be taken partially out of operation. The survey of 33 large- and medium-sized reservoirs in the Chiang Jiang river basin revealed that 16 are already more than half filled with silt, and the average useful life will not exceed 13 years.[2]

---

[2] Vaclav Smil, *The Bad Earth: Environmental Degradation in China* (Armonk, New York, M.E. Sharpe, Inc., 1984).

10. In India, the expected siltation rate of the Nizamsagar reservoir in Andra Pradesh was set as 5,163,000 m³ a year. However, the actual rate has reached 13.8 million m³ a year. The reservoir is estimated to have lost 60 per cent of its storage capacity. As can be seen from table 2, other reservoirs in India have suffered high siltation rates as well. In fact, only a few of the reservoirs now operating in India have escaped excessive siltation problems and many have experienced siltation rates well above those predicted. In the Islamic Republic of Iran, the reservoir created by the Sefid Rud Dam, one of the largest in the country, with a design life expectancy of 100 years, has already half filled with sediment since its completion in 1962. The reason is that the actual sediment rate almost tripled the design figure which was apparently based on insufficient data.[3]

Table 2. Annual rates of siltation in selected reservoirs in India

(Thousands of cubic metres)

Reservoir	Assumed rate	Observed rate	Ratio of observed to assumed siltation
Bhakra	24 144	33 903	1.39
Maithon	5 696	7 792	1.37
Mavurakshi	698	3 065	4.39
Nizamsagar	5 163	13 841	2.68
Panchet	7 314	11 492	1.57
Tungabhadra	12 069	16 710	1.38

Source: Report of the Reservoir Sedimentation Committee, Ministry of Irrigation, India, June 1982.

11. Clearly, the rate at which a reservoir silts up depends on the amount of sediments carried by the river which feeds it, and that, in turn, depends on the rate of soil erosion in the river's catchment area. The rate of soil erosion increases dramatically in areas with excessive deforestation rates since, for example, high-intensity rains can quickly wash away the soils of the tropics. Highly erodible soils, like loess, in arid and semi-arid zones with inappropriate cultivation practices and inadequate vegetation cover, are also prone to intensive soil erosion.

12. The other important factors affecting the deposition of sediments in reservoirs are:

(a) Water discharge conditions in main and tributary rivers, including seasonal and short-time variations;

(b) Volume and geometrical shape of the reservoir and morphological characteristics of main and tributary rivers;

(c) Water quality (salinity, temperature, etc.) and the possibility of flocculation of suspended material;

(d) Hydrodynamic conditions within the reservoir, including wind-induced and density currents, stratification, turbulence, etc;

(e) Reservoir operation regime.[4]

13. On the other hand, as a result of siltation in the reservoir, clear water flowing downstream causes channel degradation and bank erosion. The deposition of silt in the reservoir also results in some loss of natural nutrients downstream and thus may decrease the productivity of the flood plains downstream of the dam. Another effect of reservoir sedimentation is possible erosion of the river delta.

14. Since reservoir sedimentation influences all parts of a river basin and leads to several adverse effects, a detailed study of alterations in erosion and sedimentation processes has to be carried out on any proposed dam project.

2. *Inundation*

15. The creation of reservoirs often leads to the inundation of large areas of land. In many cases the flooded area contains thousands of hectares of valuable agricultural land. In India, for example, more than 40,000 ha of farmland were submerged by the Srisailam hydroelectric scheme; that land had provided a livelihood for about 100,000 local villagers. In Sri Lanka about 3,000 ha of land cultivated with various crops will have been flooded owing to the construction of the Victoria dam.[5]

16. The flooding of a reservoir without clearing the area beforehand is a common practice. The inundated land is often covered with forest having not only commercial value but also great ecological importance, particularly in tropical and subtropical zones. Thus, in Malaysia, the Temenggor dam project has resulted in flooding of valuable forest area, threatening the survival of 100 species of mammals and 300 species of birds.[6] In India, one of the main considerations taken into account in shelving the proposed dam project was the threat to the tropical forest in

---

[3] *Civil Engineering* (American Society of Civil Engineers) March 1983, p. 51.

[4] Ake Sundborg, "Sedimentation problems in river basins" *Nature and Resources,* (UNESCO), vol. XIX, No. 2, 1983, p. 16.

[5] E. Goldsmith and N. Hildyard, *The Social and Environmental Effects of Large Dams,* volume one, *Overview* (Wadebridge Ecological Centre, Camelford, Cornwall, United Kingdom, 1984), p. 49.

[6] *Ibid.,* p. 55.

the Silent Valley and its unique wildlife. Several more water resources development projects have been abandoned in the region in view of possible adverse effects on the environment. In Malaysia, for instance, the Tembeling hydropower project has been cancelled[7] on the grounds that, if it had been implemented, 130 km^2 of tropical rain forest, which serve as the habitat for a number of rare species, would have been inundated.

17. Damming a river rapidly alters its water quality. After the closure of a dam and creation of a reservoir, biological productivity in the reservoir rises as inundated vegetation and soil release nutrients into the water. Abundant nutrients cause excessive weed and algae growth which may lead to deoxygenation of the water, hinder fishing, harbour disease vector organisms and increase evaporation losses. In Australia, Bangladesh, China, India, Indonesia, Pakistan, the Philippines, Thailand and some other countries of the region, the greatest problems are caused mainly by free-floating species such as water hyacinth, which is considered the world's greatest nuisance weed. However, in time the weed may become a resource rather than a nuisance owing to its rapid growth and ability to remove pollutants from water. It is thought that water hyacinth may provide a cheap treatment for sewage and industrial waste, as well as a source of methane, alcohol, fertilizer and cattle food.

18. Some of the most important and serious problems of dam construction are connected with evacuation and resettlement of the people whose homeland is flooded by the waters of man-made reservoirs. Approximate data on the number of persons resettled owing to creation of several selected water reservoirs in the region are given in table 3. Moreover, there are some large projects the construction of which will trigger the veritable exodus of hundreds of thousands of affected dwellers. In China, the gigantic Three Gorges multi-purpose scheme is estimated to displace 1.4 million people; in the Philippines, the construction of 40 proposed new large dams could affect more than 1.5 million.[8]

3. Seismic effects

19. In some cases large dams and reservoirs have been found to have triggered earthquakes. The actual mechanism whereby reservoirs induce seismic movements is not yet well known. It is assumed that the weight of impounded water imposes new stresses on the earth's crust which, in turn, may generate seismic activity owing to the existence of layers having varying compressibility. Such

Table 3. Resettlement of people owing to the construction of selected dams and reservoirs in the ESCAP region

Name of project and date of completion	Country	Number of people relocated
Bhakra, 1963	India	36 000
Damodar (4 projects, 1959)	India	93 000
Gandhi Sagar	India	52 000
Lam Pao	Thailand	30 000
11 projects 1963-1971	Thailand	130 000
Nam Ngum, 1971	Lao People's Democratic Republic	3 000
Nam Pong, 1963	Thailand	25 000-30 000
Nanela, 1967	Pakistan	90 000
Pa Mong (projected)	Thailand/Lao People's Democratic Republic	310 000-480 000
Tarbela, 1974	Pakistan	86 000
Upper Pampanga, 1973	Philippines	14 000

Source: A.K. Biswas, "Impacts of hydroelectric development on the environment", Energy Policy, December 1982, p. 349.

seismic activities have been recorded for a number of dams and associated reservoirs in the ESCAP region. For example, major earthquakes presumably induced by reservoir creation occurred at Hsinfengkiang in China in 1962 (magnitude 6.1 on the Richter scale) and at Koyna in India in 1967 (6.5 on the Richter scale).[9] The delegation of India at the 13-th session of the ESCAP Committee on Natural Resources stated that there was no conclusive evidence that the earthquake was a result of the Koyna reservoir filling. In both cases the dams themselves were damaged. Moreover, the Koyna earthquake, with its epicentre being either in the vicinity of the dam or directly under the reservoir, resulted in 177 deaths, 2,300 injured persons and destruction of more than 80 per cent of the houses in the village of Koynanagar.[10] This region has long been known as a non-seismic area but experienced a series of tremors after the filling of the Koyna reservoir which was started in 1962. Other dams and reservoirs in the countries of the region suspected of triggering off minor earthquakes are Benmore in New Zealand (1966), Kurobe in Japan (1961),

---

[7] Water Power and Dam Construction (United Kingdom), vol. 35, No. 5 (May 1983), p. 5.

[8] Goldsmith and Hildyard, op. cit., pp. 15-16.

[9] Ibid., p. 107.

[10] Chopra Ravi, "The social and environmental impact of big dams", Social Action, vol. 33, No. 2, p. 180.

[11] Goldsmith and Hildyard, op. cit., p. 114.

Talbingo in Australia (1972)[11] and Danjiangkan in China,[12] where more than 100 minor earthquakes have been experienced.

20. Dams can be designed to resist collapse during earthquakes, and sites where large dams and reservoirs are to be constructed have to be investigated thoroughly for potential earthquake hazards. The need for caution is especially great in areas that are known to be seismically active.

4. *Microclimate changes*

21. Local changes in the microclimate, favourable or not, are caused by man-made water reservoirs. The area affected depends mainly on a climatic zone, local meteorological conditions and dimensions of the reservoir, and extends, as a rule, over the territory adjacent to the water body. The major microclimatic effect is increased atmospheric moisture.[13] In tropical and arid zones, evaporation from the water surface is very high. If there is no wind, the large evaporated water mass remaining over the reservoir cools off during the night, thus creating fog banks on the reservoir perimeter and causing changes in air temperature.

22. It has been observed that the microclimate becomes less continental in the vicinity of reservoirs located in temperate or semi-arid zones. In China, for example, meteorological studies carried out near the Danjiangkan reservoir have revealed a moderating effect of the reservoir on the climate. The mean summer temperature around the reservoir has decreased by about 1°C and the average winter temperature has increased by about the same amount.[14]

B. Irrigation

23. Irrigation plays a crucial role in promoting agricultural development in the ESCAP region, where 60 per cent of the world's irrigated land is found. Since the early 1960s, the total irrigated area in the region has increased by 36.7 per cent, from 94.1 million to 128.6 million ha in 1983 (table 4), and it covers 28 per cent of the arable land in the region.

24. FAO predicts that up to the year 2000, irrigated areas in developing countries could expand at the rate of 1.7 per cent a year, three quarters of the expansion taking place

in Asia.[15] More than 84 million ha, or 66 per cent of the total irrigated area of the region, are located in China and India. Japan, Pakistan and the Republic of Korea, where irrigated lands account for more than 50 per cent of the arable land are the most advanced countries in the development of irrigation, while in Australia, Malaysia, Mongolia, Nepal and the Pacific island countries, land under irrigation occupies less than 10 per cent of the arable land.

25. The introduction of irrigation leads to significant ecological changes. There is no doubt that an irrigation project has a favourable effect on the microclimate after the area is irrigated: relative humidity is increased, evaporation rates are lower, and in certain cases temperatures are also modified favourably. However, many irrigation schemes in the region have resulted in degradation of cropland and water quality, and in the spread of water-related diseases. Since the impact of irrigation on the environment tends to be cumulative, the results can best be seen in those regions where irrigation has been practised intensively for a relatively long time. Therefore, the illustrative examples have been drawn from the countries of the region with traditional irrigated agriculture. But, it should be recognized that the same practices may have a much more rapid and severe effect when introduced into the fragile and delicately balanced ecosystems of some of the developing countries of the region.

1. *Waterlogging and salinization*

26. In India, the Islamic Republic of Iran, Pakistan and some other countries of the region, irrigated agriculture accounts for more than 90 per cent of total fresh-water use. However, it is estimated that only about 40 per cent of water taken into major distribution networks reaches the fields, and even there losses from faulty irrigation practices are high, further reducing the efficiency of water use and leading to degradation of valuable cropland. Irrigation water is typically brought to crops through unlined canals and ditches that allow vast quantities of water to percolate. Flood irrigation methods widely practised in the region also contribute to the infiltration of water. Where drainage is inadequate, the ground-water level gradually rises, eventually entering the crop's root zone and waterlogging the soil. In arid and semi-arid zones, waterlogging may be accompanied by salinization as water near the soil surface evaporates and leaves behind a damaging residue of salt. But even before often saline ground water reaches the surface, it starts affecting crop yields by interfering with the capacity of plants to take up moisture and oxygen. Thus, in Shaanxi Province in China (where the impact of waterlogging on wheat and cotton production has been carefully

[12] A. Biswas, "Environment and sustainable water development" in *Water for Human Consumption, Man and his Environment*, 1982, p. 384.

[13] Interim Committee for Co-ordination of Investigations of the Lower Mekong Basin, *Environmental Impact Assessment: Guidelines for Application to Tropical River Basin Development* (1982), p. 37.

[14] Biswas, *loc. cit.,* p. 383.

[15] Food and Agriculture Organization of the United Nations, *Agriculture: Toward 2000* (Rome, 1981), p. 65.

Table 4. Cultivated land and irrigated area in the ESCAP region
(Thousands of hectares)

Country or area	Cultivated land, 1983	Irrigated area			Irrigated area
		1961-1965	1969-1971	1983	Cultivated land (Percentage)
Afghanistan	8 054	2 208	2 340	2 660	33.0
Australia	46 572	1 115	1 474	1 750	3.7
Bangladesh	9 136	501	1 054	1 848	20.2
Bhutan	98	–	–	–	–
Brunei Darussalam	7	–	–	1	14.2
Burma	10 077	681	849	1 011	10.0
China	100 894	35 200[a]	42 000	45 144	44.7
Democratic People's Republic of Korea	2 290	500	500	1 060	46.3
Fiji	236	–	1	1	0.4
India	168 350	25 523	30 183	39 500	23.4
Indonesia	20 310	4 100	4 371	5 418	26.7
Iran (Islamic Republic of)	13 700	4 800	5 184	4 000	29.2
Japan	4 806	3 176	3 312	3 240	67.4
Lao People's Democratic Republic	890	13	18	118	13.2
Malaysia	4 340	333	338	334	7.7
Mongolia	1 313	–	10	38	2.9
Nepal	2 332	77	116	230	9.8
New Zealand	466	82	109	230	49.3
Papua New Guinea	374	–	–	–	–
Pakistan	20 490	11 139	12 904	14 720	71.8
Philippines	11 250	896	1 150	1 400	12.4
Republic of Korea	2 167	682	993	1 190	54.9
Samoa	122	–	–	–	–
Sri Lanka	2 186	361	436	538	24.6
Thailand	19 370	1 729	1 965	3 472	17.9
Viet Nam	7 585	992	980	1 730	22.8
Total:	457 415	94 106	109 872	128 633	28.1

Source: FAO Production Yearbook, various issues.

[a] ESCAP estimation.

A dash (–) indicates that the amount is negligible.

recorded) it was found that normal yields could still be obtained when the ground-water level was from 2 to 3 metres below the soil surface. When it rose higher, cotton and wheat yields fell drastically (see table 5).

Table 5. The impact of waterlogging on crop yields, Shaanxi Province, China

Ground-water depth	Harvest as a portion of normal yield	
	Wheat	Cotton
(metres)	(percentage)	
2-3	100	100
1-2	50	65
0.5-1	20	50
0.5 and higher	0	10-20

Source: Bruce Stokes, *Bread and Water: Growing Tomorrow's Food* (Worldwatch Institute, Washington D.C.).

27. The distribution of saline lands in the region is presented in table 6. The problem of waterlogging and salinization is particularly urgent, as the processes are continuing at a rapid pace, in China, India, the Islamic Republic of Iran and Pakistan.

Table 6. Distribution of natural saline lands in the ESCAP region

(1 000 ha)

Country	Area	Country	Area
Afghanistan	3 101	Iran (Islamic Republic of)	27 085
Australia	357 340	Malaysia	3 040
Bangladesh	3 017	Mongolia	4 070
Burma	634	Pakistan	10 456
China	36 658	Sri Lanka	200
India	23 796	Thailand	1 456
Indonesia	13 213	Viet Nam	983

Source: Based on *World Soil Map*, V.A. Kovda, USSR, cited in E. Goldsmith and N. Hildyard, *The Social and Environmental Effects of Large Dams* (Wadebridge Ecological Centre, Camelford, Cornwall, United Kingdom, 1984), appendix two.

28. In the Indus Valley in Pakistan, there is one of the largest irrigation systems in the world. With the fast extension of irrigation there, started about 40 years ago, ground-water levels have risen from an average depth of 25 m up to near the soil surface.[16] In the country as a whole, more than 10 million ha out of 14.7 million under irrigation are now estimated to suffer from salinity and waterlogging. Of that land, 2 million ha are classified as severely affected by salinity, 4 million as suffering patchy salinity, and 4 million as being poorly drained. Overall, 23 per cent of the country's land is affected in varying degrees by salinization or waterlogging, that figure reaching 80 per cent in the Punjab.[17] According to some estimates, 40,500 ha of irrigated land are degraded annually owing to waterlogging and salinization. Over the past seven years, Pakistan has spent $US 31 million on its On-Farm Water Project with the aim of reducing the seeping of water from the 63,100 km canal network and thus preventing waterlogging. In addition, nearly 200,000 tube-wells have been installed to exploit ground water and lower the water table. Nevertheless, Pakistan is to spend about $US 317 million during the 1985/86 financial year to continue to combat salinization and to improve its irrigation systems.[18]

29. In India, the area of land affected by waterlogging and salinization is estimated at 10.5 million ha, constituting almost a quarter of 39.5 million ha under irrigation.

30. Owing to soil salinization and waterlogging, large areas of irrigated land in the region have been abandoned, thus contributing to the spread of desertification, the expansion of which is estimated at one million ha per annum in Asia.[19] Taking into account the fact that a large part of the arable land is already under cultivation in the countries of the region, those countries can hardly afford to lose valuable agricultural lands because of the adverse implications of irrigation while their efforts are directed at increasing food production.

2. *Spread of water-borne diseases*

31. In tropical and subtropical areas, the introduction of perennial irrigation schemes appears to enhance the favourable conditions for the incidence and spread of water-related diseases, such as malaria and schistosomiasis. Relatively few studies have been undertaken to compare the distribution and intensity of these diseases in areas

---

[16] *World Environment Handbook*, p. 255.

[17] Goldsmith and Hildyard, *op. cit.*, p. 140.

[18] *World Water* (United Kingdom), October 1985, p. 13.

[19] ESCAP, "State of the environment in Asia and the Pacific" vol. two, 1985, p. 20.

before and after irrigation development, but those that have been carried out point to surface irrigation practices as a significant factor in the increase in the prevalence of malaria, schistosomiasis and other water-borne diseases.[20]

32. In spite of the efforts of the World Health Organization, malaria remains one of the most widespread and lethal diseases, and affects about 80 million persons in the region.[21] Malaria is endemic in many countries of the region. For example, in 1980 alone, about 71 million cases were reported in the region: 4.0 million in South Asia, 3 million in East Asia and 0.1 million in Papua New Guinea. China and India accounted for 85 per cent of the cases in the region.[22]

33. It is estimated that more than 200 million people residing in rural areas are infected with schistosomiasis and that between 500 and 600 million persons are exposed to infection.[23] Approximately 50 per cent of the people suffering from this disease are found in Asia.[24] Schistosomiasis is endemic in China, Indonesia, the Lao People's Democratic Republic, Malaysia, the Philippines and Thailand.[25] In China, the number of infected persons is currently estimated to be 1 million, in comparison with 10 million in 1955 when the national programme of the control of schistosomiasis started. In the central and southern parts of the Philippines, about 4 million persons are exposed to the risk of infection in 141 municipalities in 22 provinces.[26]

3. Degradation of water quality

34. Degradation of both ground- and surface-water quality owing to irrigation development has become a serious problem in some areas of the region. Ground water, in the process of its percolation through soil, leaches out soluble salts and thus generally contains more dissolved salts than surface water. However, the natural process of leaching can be intensified in areas under irrigation, as soluble salts are concentrated in the upper soil layer and around plant roots. Various pollutants, such as nitrogen compounds and pesticides, which are used widely in irrigated agriculture, may also be washed out by filtrating

water into ground water. Owing to the growing use of fertilizers, nitrate contamination is increasing rapidly in areas under perennial irrigation.

35. Salty water from irrigation systems is generally returned to the nearest river, inevitably increasing the river's salt content. For downstream agriculture, it poses the problem of irrigation with increasingly saline water. Thus, in Pakistan the waters of the lower Indus River are polluted by salty irrigation return flow from irrigation systems in the upper part of the basin.

36. In some river basins with highly developed irrigation, much of the river's water is extracted even before it reaches downstream areas. As a result, the flow of the river is reduced to the extent that it can no longer prevent the intrusion of sea water into the delta or its early reaches. In Bangladesh, for this reason sea water intrudes up 100 km upstream in the Ganges River distributaries, thus creating problems for drinking water supply and agriculture.

37. The potential effects of irrigation and proposed remedies for their alleviation are summarized in table 7. It may be noted that there are a number of measures which can be taken to prevent the extensive environmental damage that might have been caused by irrigation. Even waterlogging and salinization are not inevitable consequences of irrigation development and can be alleviated by sound design and construction of irrigation and drainage systems and efficient water management, especially by reduction of seepage losses from irrigation networks and by better farm water management. To achieve this, the delivery of correct amounts of irrigation water must be based upon research on local soil conditions, crop needs and climatic factors. It also requires accurate methods of flow measurement, the willingness of the farmers to abide by the recommendations, and routine water measurements, and an efficient supervisory organization. Adequate drainage systems have to be included in the irrigation schemes to control ground-water levels wherever possible. The quality of the water used for irrigation should also be monitored. Some of the brackish water sources may be used on the condition that adequate dilution is achieved by mixing with fresh water. If such measures, as well as others, are taken, the development of irrigation can bring essential economic benefits with minimal harmful effects to the environment.

C. Ground-water exploitation

38. Ground water is used extensively in some parts of the region for drinking water supply as this source is usually of high quality and in most cases not contaminated, and is free of mud and sediment. With the increased availability of pumping equipment, ground water is also becoming the preferred source of supply for irrigation, especially in the

---

[20] Draft guidelines on the environmental impacts of irrigation in arid and semi-arid regions (UNEP/WG 31/3), p. 12.

[21] ESCAP, "State of the environment . . .", p. 266.

[22] ESCAP, "State of the environment . . .", p. 267.

[23] WHO, Technical Report Series 728, "The control of schistosomiasis", p. 20.

[24] ESCAP, "State of the environment . . .", p. 266.

[25] WHO, Technical Report Series 728, p. 20.

[26] Ibid., pp. 79-80.

Table 7. Impacts of irrigation development

Causal activity	Possible impact	Possible remedies
Surface irrigation	1. Waterlogging 2. Soil salinization 3. Increase of diseases 4. Degradation of water quality	1. Increased irrigation efficiency 2. Construction of drainage systems 3. Disease control measures 4. Control of irrigation water quality
Sewage irrigation	1. Contamination of food crops 2. Direct contamination of humans 3. Dispersion in air 4. Contamination of grazing animals	1. Regulatory control 2. Tertiary treatment and sterilization of sewage
Use of fertilizers	1. Pollution of ground water, especially with nitrates 2. Pollution of surface flow	1. Controlled use of fertilizers 2. Increased irrigation efficiency
Use of pesticides	1. Pollution of surface flow 2. Destruction of fish	1. Limited use of pesticides 2. Co-ordination with schedule of irrigation
Irrigation with high silt load	1. Clogging of canals 2. Raising of level of fields 3. Harmful sediment deposits on fields and crops	1. Avoiding use of flow with high silt load 2. Soil conservation measures on upstream watershed
High velocity surface flow	1. Erosion of earth canals 2. Furrow erosion 3. Surface erosion	1. Proper design of canals 2. Proper design of furrows 3. Land levelling 4. Correctly built and maintained terraces
Intensive sprinkling on sloping land	1. Soil erosion	1. Correctly designed and operated system

Source: Adapted from UNEP "Draft guidelines on the environmental impacts of irrigation in arid and semi-arid regions", 1979.

alluvial plains where ground water is nearer the surface. Unlike most major irrigation projects which rely on surface water as a source of supply, taking many years to plan, construct and bring to full fruition, projects supplied with ground water are usually relatively small and have a very short development period; sometimes a tube-well can be installed within a few days and at relatively small cost. In the northern provinces of China, for example, nearly one million wells have been sunk since the middle of the 1950s. During the 1960s and 1970s, 1.6 million tube-wells were installed in India resulting in increase in the land irrigated by ground water from 29 per cent in the early 1950s to 40 per cent in the mid-1970s.[27]

1. Depletion of ground water

39. Ground-water reserves are recharged by the natural infiltration of surface water. However, ground water is often pumped at rates that exceed replenishment, result-ing in the depletion of the resource, the lowering of ground-water levels or decreased pressure in the aquifers. Excessive ground-water exploitation and subsequent lowering of ground-water tables appear to be increasingly common in the region. Thus, in Thailand, in the Bangkok metropolitan area, it has been estimated that in 1982 1.3 million m³/day were pumped from public and private wells, while studies undertaken by various experts have recommended that the safe yield in the area should be around 600,000 m³/day, taking into account reasonable aquifer recharge.[28] This extremely high rate of extraction exceeding the recommended safe yield by more than twice has caused a rapid decline in the ground-water level of about 2.5 m per annum. In the North China Plain, where irrigated crop farming is impossible without ground-water, and major cities in this zone, including Beijing, are critically dependent on ground-water pumping for basic domestic and industrial supply, ground-water overdrafts have led to rapid ground-water level drops amounting to 4.4 m a year in the Baimiao district of Tianjin Province. Near Changzhou, in Jiangsu

---

[27] Goldsmith and Hildyard, *op. cit.,* p. 12.

[28] *World Water* (United Kingdom), July 1985, p. 16.

Province, the drop has been almost 50 m in three decades.[29] In Tamil Nadu State in southern India, water tables fell by 25-30 m over the 1970s owing to overpumping of ground water for irrigation.[30] Large parts of Bangladesh also suffer from overpumping and subsequent decline in the water table by as much as one metre per year. In many cases, ground water cannot be further pumped by the widely used No. 6 hand pump, designed to lift water from depths reaching 7 m and utilized throughout the country in 65,000 villages.

2. *Land subsidence*

40. The ground-water withdrawals accompanied by the decline of its level often cause land subsidence or land surface settling. Subsidence rates can range from 1 cm to 50 cm per 10 m drop in ground-water level, depending on the thickness and compressibility of the water-bearing formations. Surface sinking owing to ground-water withdrawals has been observed in several parts of the region. Impressive cases of land subsidence have been reported in China. In Shanghai city, a cumulative amount of subsidence equal to 2.63 m was recorded over the period from 1921 to 1965.[31] As a result of this phenomenon, the city suffered great damage as water overflowed the Chiang Jiang river banks flooding the depression, and industrial, commercial and social development were severely affected.[32] However, because the city is not critically dependent on ground-water supplies, extraction rates were lowered and since 1963 the aquifers have been replenished with 17 million m³ of surface water a year, and the problem is now basically under control.[33] However, in the cities in the North China Plain relying heavily on ground-water supplies, the subsidence rate has been increasing. In the eastern subrubs of Beijing, it averages 20-30 cm a year. In Tianjin, the surface sinking has amounted to 2.15 m since 1950.[34]

41. In Bangkok, owing to the large-scale extraction of ground water from unconsolidated deposits of sand, gravel and clay for industrial and domestic needs, the ground-water level has dropped more than 50 m since the mid-1950s. The resulting 50-60 cm of subsidence over a 20-25 year period has aggravated the city's flooding problems, and a rapidly increasing rate of subsidence approaching 14 cm per year has been experienced in the eastern and southern areas. According to a recent study, Bangkok, where the land surface is only from 0.5 m to 1.5 m above sea level, will be below sea level by the year 2000 if ground-water extraction continues at the rate of approximately 1.3 million m³/day.[35]

42. In Japan, 59 districts of a total area of 9,520 km², accounting for 12 per cent of the habitable land of the country, have been identified as affected by land subsidence; most of them are located in industrial regions on the coast. The principal cause of subsidence in almost all districts is the excessive withdrawal of ground water for industrial purposes, domestic uses and irrigation. Among the sinking areas are Niigata, Chiba, Osaka and Tokyo; the maximum subsidence of 4.57 m was observed in the period 1920-1975 in the north-eastern section of Tokyo.[36] However, after a number of restrictions had been imposed on ground-water extraction, the water levels recovered and the subsidence rate first decreased and then stopped.

3. *Salt-water intrusion*

43. In coastal areas, excessive exploitation of ground water inevitably leads to salinization of coastal fresh-water aquifers owing to intrusion of salt water from the sea. Salt-water intrusion threatens to contaminate the drinking water supplies of many coastal cities and towns in the region. The situation is especially severe in those areas where ground-water tables have been lowered far below sea level, and induced salt-water intrusion has caused deterioration of the water quality. Thus, the shallow aquifers, which once supplied fresh water to consumers, have become contaminated with salt water in Manila and Jakarta, where the ground-water levels have declined to as much as 150 m and 30 m below sea level respectively.[37] Intrusion of salt water is also a major problem impeding municipal water supply development in Bangkok.

44. Intrusion of sea water, with considerable detrimental effects on soil and vegetation, has been reported in the coastal zones of Australia, Bangladesh, China, India, Thailand, Viet Nam and the South Pacific islands, where excessive extraction of ground water is widely practised. In small islands and atolls of the Pacific, the inhabitants of which depend to a large extent on ground water for their domestic supplies, ground-water reserves and fresh-water

---

[29] Smil, *op. cit.,* p. 94.

[30] Sandra Postel, *Water: Rethinking Management in an Age of Scarcity,* Worldwatch Paper 62, December 1984, p. 23.

[31] Laura Carbognin, "Land subsidence: a worldwide environmental hazard", UNESCO, *Nature and Resources,* vol. XXI, No. 1, 1985, p. 9.

[32] ESCAP, *Geology for Urban Planning: Selected Papers on the Asian and Pacific Region* (ST/ESCAP/394), p. 26.

[33] Smil, *op. cit.,* p. 94.

[34] Laura Carbognin, *loc. cit.,* p. 9.

[35] ESCAP, *Geology for Urban Planning . . .,* p. 8.

[36] Laura Carbognin, *loc. cit.,* p. 7.

[37] ESCAP, *Geology for Urban Planning . . .,* pp. 14 and 24.

lenses floating on sea water are highly vulnerable to salt-water intrusion, owing to the low surface elevation and small size of the islands and atolls.[38]

45. A number of measures can be taken to avoid the adverse implications of ground-water exploitation. First of all, to prevent depletion of ground-water reserves, safe yields of aquifers have to be determined and should not be exceeded. In order to decrease and stop subsidence, demand for ground water may be reduced by using alternative sources and, in some cases, ground-water extraction has to be fully stopped and replaced with other sources of water. Artificial replenishment of ground-water reserves by the infiltration of surface water can be successfully applied if the quality of water injected is satisfactory.

D. Flood control works

46. Floods represent a serious problem in many river basins throughout the region, particularly in the areas affected by typhoons. Flood plains occupy up to 20 per cent of the territory in several countries of the region. The percentage is much higher in Bangladesh, where about two thirds of the territory lies in the flood plains of the Ganges and Brahmaputra rivers. In the ESCAP countries, the cost of damage caused by floods was estimated at more than $US 5 billion in 1981 and has been steadily increasing in most of the countries affected by floods. In India, for example, the annual average damage cost has increased from less than $US 200 million during the first half of the 1960s to $US 1,000 million for the second half of the 1970s.[39] Meanwhile the total area subject to flooding has doubled, from 20 million ha in 1971 to 40 million ha in 1981.[40] In China, 10.6 million ha were affected by floods during 1984. The loss of agricultural products in an area of 5.3 million ha of farmland damaged by floods is estimated to have exceeded 30 per cent in comparison with the average production of normal years.[41]

47. To mitigate floods or their effects and thereby reduce the damage, engineering works, often referred to as structural measures, are traditionally and widely used in the countries prone to this natural disaster. Structural measures

include construction of dams, reservoirs, levees and flood-walls, channel modifications and floodways. Dams and reservoirs are constructed upstream of the area they are intended to protect. The environmental impacts of such projects have already been described in section A of this paper.

48. One of the main methods used for controlling floods is the construction of levees along the river in order to confine flood waters to the part of the flood plain where its passage causes little or no damage. The total length of the levees in 10 selected countries of the region exceeds 200,000 km (see table 8).

Table 8. Length of flood-control levees in selected ESCAP countries (1984)

Country	Length of levees km	Country	Length of levees km
Bangladesh	4 963[a]	Malaysia	437
China	170 000	New Zealand	3 000
India	11 868[a]	Pakistan	4 150[b]
Japan	9 682	Philippines	572
Republic of Korea	17 640	Thailand	445

Source: Based on information provided to the ESCAP secretariat by the countries of the region.

[a] For 1980.

[b] For 1981.

49. Levees occupy relatively small areas on flood plains, but can produce catastrophic results if they are breached or overtopped. The problems of drainage congestion can also be created behind the embankments. This impact has been observed in India, where the levees were constructed along some sections of the Brahmaputra and Kosi rivers.[42] To avoid this problem, it is recommended that drainage outlets be provided so that drainage of valleys is not impeded. The environmental impacts of levee construction might include alteration of the riverside benthic fauna and flora, which perhaps causes changes in the trophic chain; fish stocks could also be affected by the elimination of spawning grounds.

50. Improving flow conditions by channel modifications may enable flood water to be passed at a lower level than

[38] ESCAP, *Proceedings of the Meeting on Water Resources Development in the South Pacific* (Suva, March 1983), Water Resources Series No. 57 (United Nations publication, Sales No. E.84.II.F.7), p. 5.

[39] ESCAP, *Water Resources Journal,* June 1983 (E/ESCAP/SER. C/137), pp. 1-2.

[40] Darryl, D'Morte, *Temples or Tombs* (New Delhi, 1985), p. 14.

[41] ESCAP, *Water Resources Journal,* June 1985 (E/ESCAP/SER. C/145), p. 42.

[42] R.P. Malhotra and R.L. Qazi, "Impact of environment by irrigation/multipurpose projects" in *Indo-Soviet Workshop on Evaluation and Modelling of Impacts on Environment of Water Resources Projects, New Delhi, September 1985* (New Delhi, Central Board of Irrigation and Power, 1985), p. I-92.

would occur naturally. In general, modification of natural stream channels by clearing, dredging and straightening is more appropriate to small streams, but may also result in minor improvements in the passage of flood flows in large watercourses. The environmental effects of flood-control channel modifications can be quite severe in some cases. Although these effects vary considerably, those observed include water quality degradation and loss of terrestrial and aquatic habitat. Probably the most considerable effects are caused by dredging activities. Dredging a waterway, of course, destroys local benthic life; and in an estuary, increasing the depth can induce penetration of salt water further upstream.

E. Interbasin water transfer

51. In some countries of the region, interbasin water transfer is becoming an attractive option in redistributing the available water resources in conformity with the demand for water. Mass water transfer over long distances from a water-surplus region to a water-deficient area to promote the agricultural and industrial development of that area could be achieved by diverting the course of water or by constructing a large canal.

52. Australia, India, Japan, Malaysia and Pakistan have constructed some projects varying in scope to divert water from one basin to another. In addition, India, the Islamic Republic of Iran, Nepal and Thailand are seriously considering the feasibility of other such projects, and China has recently taken a decision to start diverting annually 15 km^3 of water from the Chiang Jiang River to the North China Plain. Some of these projects envisage water diversions which would occur solely within the country. Others may concern the interests of the co-basin countries.

53. Mass water transfer schemes undoubtedly have not only important economic effects but also significant environmental consequences, which need to be carefully analysed and assessed. The environmental impacts of a large-scale water-transfer scheme could best be evaluated in three groups separately for (a) the exporting basin, (b) the route of conveyance, and (c) the importing basin.[43] For each group it is recommended to consider the impacts on:

Physical system

Water quantity: level; discharge; velocity; ground water; losses.

Water quality: sediments; nutrients; turbidity; salinity and alkalinity; temperature effects; toxic chamicals.

Land implications: erosion; sedimentation; salinity; alkalinity; waterlogging; changes in land-use patterns; changes in mineral and nutrient contents of soil; earthquake inducement; other hydro-geological factors.

Atmosphere: temperature; evapotranspiration; changes in microclimate and macroclimate;

Biological system

Aquatic: benthos; zooplankton; phytoplankton; fish and aquatic vertebrates; plants; disease vectors.

Land-based: animals; vegetation; loss of habitat; enhancement of hibitat.[44]

54. The impacts to be anticipated in the exporting basins include changes in the flow, sediment load and channel configuration resulting from decreased discharge of the river. The decrease in discharge also has important implications for salinity conditions and the ecology in the estuary. These potential impacts depend mainly on the regime of diversion from the river. Concerning the impacts of conveyance on ground- and surface-water systems along the route, the systems are to be carefully selected considering the possibility of seepage from transfer canals. In areas of delivery, the possibility of increasing salinity in agricultural areas receiving the additional irrigation water is to be assessed first. In addition, throughout the transfer scheme under consideration, the effects on water quality, health and climate are to be looked into as well.

II. PROSPECTS FOR CO-OPERATION

55. There is a need for intensified regional co-operation in the field of environmental management in water resources development. Some countries have accumulated essential experience and knowledge in environmentally-sound development of their water resources. This experience and knowledge could be very useful for those countries starting to plan and carry out large water resources development programmes, in helping them to avoid repeating the mistakes made by the other countries in the past. Further regional co-operation should be aimed at the exchange of information and experience on identification of the potential implications of water resources development projects, application of methods and techniques for their evaluation, and legal and institutional aspects of incorporating environ-

[43] Charles Greer, "The Texas Water System: Implications for Environmental Assessment in Planning for Interbasin Water Transfers," in *Long-distance Water Transfer* (Dublin, Tycooly International Publishing Limited, 1983), p. 83.

[44] G. Golubev and A. Biswas, *"Large-scale Water Transfers: Emerging Environmental and Social Experiences"* (Dublin, Tycooly International Publishing Ltd., 1983), p. 4.

mental considerations into water resources development planning.

56. In particular, collaboration in elaboration and application of appropriate methods and procedures, adapted to local conditions, for studying and assessing the environmental implications of water-related development activities could be very fruitful, as interest in this subject has recently become widespread in the region. The assessment of environmental impacts is considered as a means of developing essential information for planning and decision-making in order to assure that a proposed development project is compatible with the environment. The developed countries of the region have created some mechanisms for predicting the impacts of new development projects on the environment. Thus, Japan has instituted administrative procedures for the environmental impact assessment of certain major public projects, including large-scale water development projects, and guidelines for the assessment of such projects have been issued by its Environmental Protection Agency and governmental organizations concerned. Australia and New Zealand conduct environmental impact assessment for major water resources development projects which may have possible significant effects on the environment.

57. A number of the developing countries of the region have also introduced procedures for environmental impact assessment with a view to ensuring that environmental factors are taken into account in the Government's decision-making. The Philippines, for instance, introduced the environmental impact statement system and set up a specific governmental agency, the National Environmental Protection Council, by Presidential Decree N 1151 of 6 June 1977.[45] In the Islamic Republic of Iran, section 7 of the Environmental Protection and Enhancement Act 1974 authorizes the Department of Environment to require environmental impact statements. The Republic of Korea introduced the Environmental Preservation Law in 1977, which requires, in certain cases, preparation of environmental impact statements. In India all major water resources development projects have to be approved by the Department of the Environment before starting their implementation. Indonesia, Malaysia, Pakistan and Thailand have governmental acts which contain provisions for production of information on environmental impact for selected projects. Environmental impact assessment is conducted on an *ad hoc* basis in Bangladesh, the Cook Islands, India, Indonesia, Pakistan, Singapore, Sri Lanka, and some other countries of the region.[46]

58. However, in practice, developing countries are sometimes reluctant to request preparation of environmental impact assessment because of the belief that it may cause unacceptable delays in implementation of a development project, and the cost of the assessment may be too high. In addition, it is thought that some of the existing methods requiring highly specialized expertise are too sophisticated to be carried out in developing countries, where lack of background data and qualified specialists is common. In view of this, some developing countries have tried to develop simplified methods of environmental impact assessment suitable for their conditions. Thus, India and Thailand have developed guidelines for environmental assessment of development projects, which could be adapted, with necessary modifications, by other countries of the region to the assessment of their development projects.[47] In addition, the Interim Committee for Co-ordination of Investigations of the Lower Mekong Basin has elaborated guidelines for conducting environmental impact assessment for the development programmes of tropical river basins.[48] This set of guidelines is intended to provide a discussion of the importance of and procedures for conducting environmental impact assessment of large river development plans, and therefore could be useful to planners, engineers and developers of tropical river basins located in the region.

59. Furthermore, it is essential to promote regional co-operation in education, training and research related to environmental aspects of water resources development in order to strengthen the ability of the countries concerned to identify the potentially adverse impact of water resources development projects on the environment, effectively take them into account and minimize any eventual damage. In this connection, the possibilities presented by the recently established regional network for training in water resources development should be fully utilized in the field of environmental protection in water development activities.

III. CONCLUSIONS AND RECOMMENDATIONS

60. There is a growing awareness in the countries of the region that economic development based on intensive use of natural resources, including water resources, should take place without deterioration of the environment. It is also widely recognized that the environmental considerations should not retard the sustained rate of economic growth, since many of the negative consequences of water resources development projects can be avoided or

[45] *Environmental Impact Assessment Handbook* (Manila, 1983), p. 2.

[46] Brian D. Clark, Ronald Bisset and Peter Wathern, *Environmental Impact Assessment: A Bibliography with Abstracts* (New York, R.R. Bowker Co., 1980), p. 473.

[47] ESCAP "State of the environment . . .", p. 425.

[48] Interim Committee for Co-ordination of Investigations of the Lower Mekong Basin, *op. cit.*

substantially alleviated if they are clearly identified and taken into consideration at the conception stage of the project. Therefore, the elaboration of a balanced approach to water resources development and environmental protection is very important.

61. In this connection, it is recommended that the developing countries of the region should:

(1) Adopt appropriate measures for the integration of environmental management into water resources development programmes;

(2) Study, consider and evaluate thoroughly the potential environmental implications of water resources development projects by using various methods of environmental impact assessment applicable to their conditions;

(3) Incorporate environmental features into the design, construction, operation or maintenance of particular water resources development projects in order to reduce or eliminate undesirable consequences, and to enhance environmental quality;

(4) Formulate long-term policies that reflect changing water demand patterns consistent with efficient use of water and better appreciation of the environmental effects.

It is recommended that the following action be taken at the regional level:

(1) Relevant information on the impact of water resources development projects, methods of their evaluation, and the organizational, administrative and legal aspects of environmental management in water resources development should be compiled and disseminated among the countries of the region as widely as possible.

(2) National environmental management efforts towards the protection, development and utilization of water resources should be co-ordinated and supported.

(3) Co-operation on a TCDC basis among interested developing countries in the development and application of the most appropriate methods and techniques of environmental impact assessment of water resources development projects should be promoted.

(4) Consideration should be given to the organization of a regional workshop on management of the environmental impact of water resources development projects for the purpose of exchanging national experience in this field, with a view to achieving environmentally sound development of water resources in the region.

(5) The education and training efforts of developing countries should be supported in order to enhance their ability to assess the status of water resources, and to formulate and carry out water resources development strategies compatible with the need to protect and improve the environment for the benefit of all.

XIII. APPLICATION OF ENVIRONMENTAL IMPACT ASSESSMENT TO WATER RESOURCES DEVELOPMENT PROJECTS*

INTRODUCTION

1. Water resources development is one of the most significant activities in the developing countries of the Asian and Pacific region. It is, however, recognized that water resources development, besides having many beneficial effects, may also have adverse environmental impacts, either directly or indirectly, on a short- or long-term basis.

2. Throughout the region, there is also growing recognition that incorporation of environmental considerations into the planning stage of such development projects could avoid costly delays and economic misinvestment. The nature and types of such environmental impacts are discussed in some detail in another document entitled "Environmental issues of water resources development in the ESCAP region" (E/ESCAP/NR.13/11) prepared for the thirteenth session of the Committee on Natural Resources.

The purpose of the present paper is to briefly review the concept and methodologies of environmental impact assessment as a planning tool for integration of environmental considerations into water resources development projects. Considering the common problem of practical application of environmental impact assessment, the paper also endeavours to review the criteria for selection of projects requiring environmental impact assessment in the field of water resources development.

A. The concept of environmental impact assessment

3. The process of environmental impact assessment has been developed to overcome the limitations of incorporating environmental considerations in the traditional economic and technical evaluation of projects. It is intended not only to be used to identify impacts which will result from development projects, but also to be employed as an environmental management planning tool which can fill many roles

---

* Originally issued as E/ESCAP/NR.13/13.

in project planning, the primary role being to facilitate the efficient utilization of natural resources and to make development efforts sustainable in the long run. The process is forward-looking, seeking to predict the status of the environment with and without the development alternatives. It includes identification, measurement, analysis, interpretation and transfer of technical knowledge and judge-

ment. It keeps the people affected by the project informed of the implications of the project on their life patterns and can also contribute to better co-ordination and co-operation among the various agencies involved in the project.

4. The sequential action of conducting environmental impact assessment is presented in figure 1.

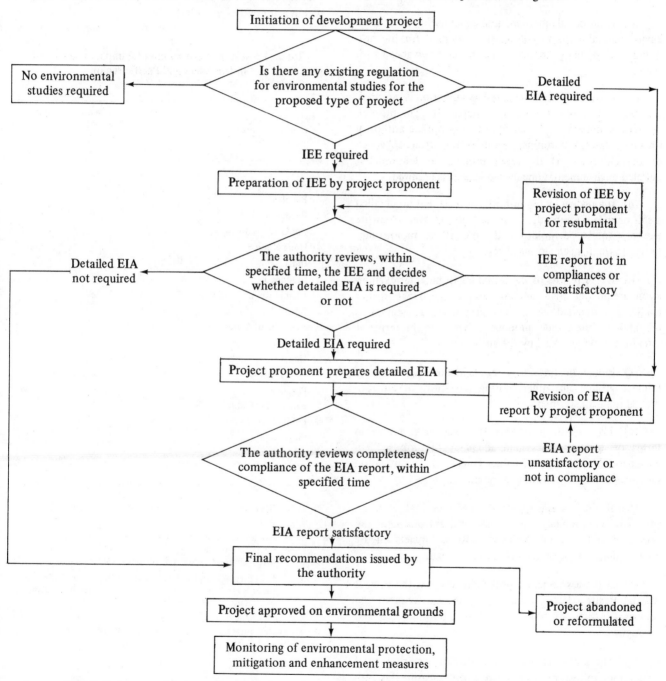

Source: ESCAP, *Environmental Impact Assessment: Guidelines for Planners and Decision Makers* (Bangkok, 1985) (ST/ESCAP/351).

Notes: EIA = environmental impact assessment;

IEE = initial environmental examination

Figure 1. Sequential action of EIA

5. The sequential action of conducting environmental impact assessment may be briefly described as follows:

(a) The project proponent examines whether any environmental study is required for the type of projects being proposed and if so, whether a detailed assessment is required straight away or a preliminary evaluation called initial environmental examination will suffice.

(b) If no initial environmental examination or detailed environmental impact assessment is required for the proposed project, the proponent is permitted to go ahead with the project.

(c) If an initial environmental examination is required, the project proponent is asked to prepare it. The purpose of that examination is to enable the appropriate authority (in many cases, Environment Ministry/Department/Agency of the Government) to screen projects to determine if detailed environmental impact assessment is required.

(d) If a review by the authority reveals that no detailed assessment is warranted, the project is approved from the environmental viewpoint, with prescribed monitoring/mitigation/enhancement measures.

(e) If the results of the initial environmental examination are inconclusive and indicate the need for further analysis, a detailed environmental impact assessment is prepared by the project proponent, based on the terms of reference to be provided by the authority.

(f) Public hearings may be held to take views of interest groups and others during the study of environmental impact assessment.

(g) The authority reviews the assessment report in terms of appropriateness and adequacy of proposed environmental protection, enhancement and mitigation measures and the monitoring programme.

(h) If the assessment report indicates that with appropriate environmental protection and enhancement the project would have no significant adverse impacts on the environment, its implementation can proceed.

(i) If the assessment report indicates that the project has significant deleterious impacts on the environment, the project is either abandoned or grossly reformulated and redesigned.

(j) The authority should monitor the environmental protection, mitigation and enhancement measures as provided for in the assessment report, during the construction as well as the operational phase of the project. Environmental impact assessments should be scheduled so that they also include the provision for review and comments from the various concerned agencies. Public hearings, although not common in developing countries, are considered to be an important component.

6. The incorporation of environmental impact assessment into the institutional and legislative framework of the countries is emerging in most countries of the Asian and Pacific region. The current status of this assessment in the region is presented in table 1.

Table 1. Status of environmental impact assessment in the Asian and Pacific region

Country or area	Status of environmental impact assessment		
	1	2	3
Australia	x		
Bangladesh			x
Burma			x
China		x	
Hong Kong			x
India			x
Indonesia	x		
Islamic Republic of Iran		x	
Japan			x
Republic of Korea	x		
Malaysia		x	
Nepal			x
New Zealand		x	
Pakistan		x	
Papua New Guinea	x		
Philippines	x		
Singapore			
Sri Lanka		x	
Thailand		x	

1 = Specific laws/regulations on environmental impact assessment.

2 = No specific laws/regulations, but having general legislation on environmental protection which empowers a government agency to require it for particular projects.

3 = No formal requirement, but informal procedures to incorporate environmental considerations into planning of specific types of projects.

Source: ESCAP, *State of the environment in Asia and the Pacific* (based on survey carried out by ESCAP in 1977 and subsequently updated).

7. Experience in environmental impact assessment of water resources development projects in some countries of the region has revealed that although there are many constraints for application of assessment to such projects,

Table 2. EIA costs and time in Thailand

Name of Project	Type of Report	Project cost (million baht)	EIA cost (million baht)	EIA cost as percentage of total project cost	Time spent (months)	Total Equivalent Man/month
Pattani Multipurpose Project	EIA	2 737.10	3.063	0.11	10	137.7
Quae Noi Multipurpose Project (Khao Laem)	EIA	9 110.0	0.7	0.01	6	107.5
Chiew Larn Multipurpose Project	EIA	7 035.10	3.7	0.05	12	82.38
Upper Quae Yai Multipurpose Project	EIA	10 953.0	4.5	0.04	12	64.95
Nam San, Nam Man, Nam Loei Multi-purpose Project	EIA	7 612.0	5.37	0.07	12	150.6
Kud Multipurpose Project	EIA	8 092.0	5.027	0.06	11	132.0
Lang Suan Multipurpose Project	EIA	6 248.0	2.4	0.04	9	75

Source: Electricity Generating Authority of Thailand.

especially in developing countries, much effort has been made to overcome them. It has also been found that the cost and time of environmental impact assessment preparation in most instances are insignificant compared with what is needed to complete the project. For example, a recent study in Thailand shows that assessment costs and time may be rather small compared with the overall project costs and planning time (table 2).

8.   It should be worth while to compile similar information from other countries in the region and to share them with other developing countries which are now introducing the environmental impact assessment system.

B. The selection of projects requiring environmental impact assessment

9.   It is desirable to identify the kinds of activities which are likely to cause significant environmental consequences, so as to make assessment more efficient and to avoid wastage of efforts, time and resources. This screening process for identifying projects requiring such assessment has been developed in various ways. In some countries of the region, no guidelines exist to determine whether assessment is required; a decision depends upon the judgement of experts on a case-by-case basis. Even in this case, some implicit criteria exist to assist a judgement. An example drawing on the experience of the Philippines is presented below; in other countries, various screening procedures have been developed and differing requirements have resulted in considerable disparities as to a number of such assessments undertaken in individual countries:

General criteria for the preparation of environmental impact assessment documents in the Philippines

(a)   Changes in land-use patterns;

(b)   Changes in energy supply/demand;

(c)   Increased development in floodplains;

(d)   Discharge of substantial toxic materials or chemicals;

(e)   Significant changes in ambient air/water quality;

(f)   Destruction of important natural, ecologically significant, historical or cultural resources;

(g)   Destruction of fish/wildlife habitats, especially, pertaining to rare and/or endangered species;

(h)   Substantial displacement of people/community structure;

(i)   Significant changes in surface/ground-water quantity;

(j)   Potential threats to health, safety or property;

(k)   Exceeding the natural, physical, biological or spatial carrying capacity of an area (e.g. community, ecosystem, municipality or city).

Source: National Environmental Protection Council of the Philippines, *Environmental Impact Assessment Handbook (1983).*

10.   There are several methods available to assist the screening process, including: (a) positive lists and negative lists, (b) project thresholds, (c) environmental sensitivity criteria, and (d) initial environmental examinations.

(a)   *Positive lists and negative lists*

11.   Positive lists are those of projects requiring environmental impact assessment, while negative lists are those not

requiring it. Lists are one of the simplest approaches to screening. They offer an easy-to-use system which is readily understood by all concerned. Positive lists may be compiled by a review of existing development activities, identifying those giving rise to significant environmental damage. Some indication of the environmental importance of categories of projects may also be gained by examining the existing licensing requirements. The problem is to gain the acceptance of all parties on the entry of individual project types on particular lists.

12. This approach varies from simple designation of the project types, such as construction of major dams, to detailed designation. As an example of detailed designations, Malaysia has lists of exempted and non-exempted projects, some of which are shown below:

Lists of exempted and not-exempted projects for environmental impact assessment in Malaysia

Drainage and irrigation

Not exempted

(1) Man-made lakes and artificial enlargement of lakes

(2) Drainage of wet-land wild-life habitats or of virgin forest

(3) Ground-water development for industrial, agricultural or urban supply

(4) Irrigation from rivers

(5) Coastal reclamation

Exempted

Drainage improvement and irrigation of existing agricultural land Water supply.

Not exempted

(1) Run of the river water supply

(2) Supply from ground water

(3) Dams, impounding reservoirs and catchments

(4) Surface pipelines (excluding small crossings)

Exempted

(1) Urban reticulation

(2) Service reservoirs

(3) Local pumping stations

(4) Water treatment plants (except large capacity plants)

Note: A project listed as exempted need not be subjected to preliminary assessment if:

> (a) It is not to be implemented in an environmentally sensitive area.
> (b) It conforms to all environment-related regulations.
> (c) All existing environmental guidelines and codes of practice will be observed.

Source: Department of Environment of Malaysia. "The environmental impact assessment handbook, procedure and guidelines", second draft (1979).

13. Although this approach is convenient and very easy to use, the preparation of lists involves one disadvantage. Individual projects of the same general type may have considerable variations in size, process and layout, which may give rise to varying environmental consequences. Thus, it is considered that this method is inadequate unless it is used in combination with other methods.

(b) *Project threshold approach*

14. The project threshold approach depends upon the establishment of thresholds for key features of the project or its environment. If a threshold is exceeded, an environmental impact assessment will be required. Such thresholds can range from environmental factors to project factors. Project size and cost are frequently employed as thresholds. With regard to dams and reservoirs, storage volume and storage surface area are generally used. Thresholds for such projects in Thailand are given below:

Dam and reservoir
storage volume: more than $100,000,000$ m^3 or
storage surface area: more than 15 km^2
Irrigation
irrigation area: more than $12,800$ ha

Source: Notification of types and sizes of projects or activities requiring assessment reports and measures for the prevention of and remedy for the adverse effects on the environmental quality issued by the Minister of Science, Technology and Energy of Thailand.

15. Reliance upon one threshold may give rise to a number of incorrect decisions. It is, therefore, required to evaluate a series of different thresholds together. However, care should be taken to prevent establishing a large number, making the evaluation work cumbersome and time-consuming. It should also be noted that thresholds may need frequent revisions, particularly in the light of experience gained and inflation, when financial criteria are applied.

(c) *Environmental sensitivity criteria*

16. Since the environmental consequences of a project are functions of both the project and the receiving environment, sensitivity of the environment provides another means for screening. Environmental sensitivity may be determined in two distinct, but complementary ways. One approach is to determine the importance of individual components of the area: in this approach, the characteristics of the environment are given emphasis. The other approach is to determine the carrying capacity of the area in relation to the degree or intensity of interference or

disturbance. This approach implies a predetermined series of values and requires considerable amounts of information concerning the environment.

17. The use of environmental sensitivity criteria in a screening exercise has the advantage of being simple and easy to use, however, if it were applied alone, it would have the disadvantage of ignoring project characteristics. It is, therefore, important to balance project criteria with these criteria. An example of the list of environmental sensitivity criteria in application in the Philippines is presented below:

Environmental sensitivity criteria for environmental impact assessment in the Philippines

(1)   All areas described by law as national parks, watershed reservoirs, wildlife preserves and sanctuaries;

(2)   Areas set aside as aesthetic potential tourist spots;

(3)   Areas which constitute the habitat for any endangered or threatened species of indigenous Philippine wildlife (flora and fauna);

(4)   Areas of unique historic, archaeological or scientific interest;

(5)   Areas which are traditionally occupied by cultural communities or tribes;

(6)   Areas frequently visited and/or hard-hit by natural calamities (geologic hazards, floods, typhoons, volcanic activity, etc.);

(7)   Areas with critical slopes;

(8)   Areas classified as prime agricultural land;

(9)   Recharge areas of aquifers;

(10) Water bodies characterized by one or any combination of the following conditions:

    (a)   Tapped for domestic purposes;
    (b)   Within the controlled and/or protected areas declared by appropriate authorities;
    (c)   Which support wildlife and fishery activities.

(11) Mangrove areas characterized by one or any combination of the following conditions:

    (a)   With primary pristine and dense young growth;
    (b)   Adjoining mouth of major river systems;
    (c)   Near or adjacent to traditional productive fry or fishing grounds;
    (d)   Which act as natural buffers against shore erosion, strong winds and storm floods;
    (e)   On which people are dependent for their livelihood.

(12) Coral reef characterized by one or any combination of the following conditions:

    (a)   With 50 per cent and above live coral line cover;
    (b)   Spawning and nursery grounds for fish;
    (c)   Which act as natural breakwater of coastlines.

Source: Proclamation No. 2146 of the Philippines, proclaming certain areas and types of projects as environmentally critical and within the scope of the environmental impact statement system established under Presidential Decree No. 1586.

(d) Initial environmental examination

18. Initial environmental examination is a preliminary examination for determining whether the project is likely to involve significant environmental effects. It assesses the potential environmental effects of a proposed project within a very limited budget, and it is based upon information which is readily available. If the results of the examination indicate that a detailed environmental impact assessment is not required, the experts involved prescribe the necessary environmental management measures including mitigation, enhancement and monitoring activities. Initial environmental examination requires deeper analysis than other screening methods and consequently more time and resources. It ought to be applied to those projects in which considerable uncertainty exists as to the need for environmental impact assessment. The advantage of this approach is that it will result in improvements in project design for those not subject to assessment.

19. Obviously, each of the methods described above has its advantages and disadvantages; consequently a combination of the methods should be sought to overcome the individual weaknesses of each. Such combination should be designed taking into account the assessment procedure in an individual country; in other words, an appropriate screening process should be developed within the purview of the total assessment system in each country. As an example of the total screening process, it may be noted that in Malaysia, positive and negative lists, environmental sensitivity criteria, and initial environmental examination (preliminary assessment) are all used for screening activities. An examination is first made of the positive and negative lists in order to identify those projects requiring assessment.

Projects on these lists are screened to ensure that they are not situated in an environmentally-sensitive area; If they are, then an initial environmental examination is required. Those projects not on either of the lists are subjected to further screening, comprising the following six main areas of investigation:

    (a) Siting of the project;

    (b) Demand for resources;

    (c) Waste production;

    (d) Labour requirements;

    (e) Infrastructure needs;

    (f) Regulations, guidelines and code of practice.

Within each area, the answers to a detailed series of questions indicate the need for environmental impact assessment.

20. Furthermore, it should be realized that the assessment should not be applied only to individual projects but also to comprehensive development policies, plans or programmes. In the absence of a mechanism for examination of projects in aggregate, the impacts of the projects might be found individually acceptable, although their cumulative effects would not. The only way to avoid this problem seems to be to apply assessment regionally to comprehensive development policies, plans or programmes.

C. Methodologies for environmental impact assessment on water resources development projects

21. A number of environmental impact assessment methodologies have been developed for identifying, predicting and evaluating the environmental impacts of development projects. Some of the typical methodologies are: (a) checklists, (b) matrices, (c) networks, (d) overlay mapping, (e) adaptive environmental assessment and others. In this section, major advantages and disadvantages of these methodologies will be reviewed.

(a) Check-lists

22. Check-lists are lists of environmental parameters or impact indicators. There are four categories in use: (a) the simple check-list is a list of parameters with no guidelines on how environmental parameters are to be measured and interpreted; (b) the descriptive check-list includes an identification of environmental parameters and guidelines on how data should be measured; (c) the scaling check-list gives, in addition to the information given in a descriptive check-list, the subjective scaling of these parameters; and (d) the scaling-weighting check-list, which is similar to the scaling check-list, but also provides information on the subjective evaluation of each parameter with respect to all the other parameters.

23. All of these check-lists are adequate for identification of impacts. Simple, descriptive check-lists merely identify the potential impacts without applying any sort of rating on their relative magnitude. Scaling and scaling-weighting check-lists are better for decision makers because they provide measurement and evaluation methods. However, these values are partly based on subjectivity and represent the value judgement of the experts, which may be different from those of other sections of the society or even among different groups of experts.

24. Check-lists are one of the most basic methodologies used in impact assessments. They have been adopted in many countries of the region, such as in India, the Philippines and Thailand. As completion of a general, all-inclusive list for every type of project is likely to be a very large and cumbersome procedure, specific check-lists have been developed for certain types of projects. An example of the general check-list for water resources development projects is presented in table 3.

(b) Matrices

25. The matrix method basically incorporates a list of project activities with a list of environmental characteristics or impact indicators. The combination of such lists as horizontal and vertical axes will allow identification of a cause-effect relationship between the activities and impacts. Column headings generally list the project activities, while the row headings show the environmental characteristics of the affected system. Entries in the resulting matrix cells may simply show that an interaction takes place (the simple interaction matrix) or they may be qualitative or quantitative estimates of the interactions (quantified and/or graded matrices). For quantitative estimates, weighting criteria can be applied to determine the significance or magnitude of impacts. The cause-effect relationship of project activities and the environmental parameters for with and without project conditions, with and without management and so on, can be displayed depending on the construction of the matrix.

26. The matrix method was initially developed by Leopold and others of the United States Geological Survey. The Leopold matrix has served as the basis of many matrices which have since been developed. In the Leopold matrix, the following three operations are required in each cell:

    (a) If an impact is possible, place a diagonal slash across the cell;

Table 3. Check-list for water resources development projects

Project component	A/B	Physical resources								Ecological resources				Human use values													Quality-of-life values						
		Surface-water hydrology	Surface-water quality	Ground-water hydrology	Ground-water quality	Soils	Geology/seismology	Erosion/sedimentation	Climate	Fisheries	Aquatic biology	Terrestrial wildlife	Forests	Agriculture/irrigation (if applicable)	Aquaculture	Water supply	Navigation	Recreation	Power (if applicable)	Flood control	Dedicated area uses	Industry	Agro-industry	Mineral development	Highways / railways	Land use	Socio-economic	Resettlement	Cultural/historical	Aesthetic	Archaeological	Public health	Nutrition
Dam and reservoir	A	3	2	2	1	-	-	3	1	((3))	((3))	(3)	2	2	(3)	(3)	(2)	(2)	(3)	(3)	3	-	-	(2)	((2))	3	(3)	3	1	((3))	1	((2))	(3)
	B	3	-	3	-	2	3	-	1	-	((3))	((3))	-	(3)	-	(3)	-	-	(3)	-	-	-	-	1	1	-	(3)	3	-	-	-	1	-
Irrigation system	A	1	3	2	-	3	-	2	-	(3)	(3)	1	-	(3)	(3)	(3)	-	(1)	-	-	-	(2)	(2)	-	1	3	(3)	-	-	-	-	(2)	(3)
	B	2	3	3	1	3	3	3	1	-	3	-	-	-	-	(3)	-	-	-	-	-	-	-	-	1	-	-	-	-	-	-	-	-
Hydroelectric power and transmission	A	-	-	-	-	-	2	1	1	-	-	1	3	1	-	-	-	-	3	-	1	3	3	-	-	3	(3)	-	-	2	-	-	-
	B	1	-	1	1	2	2	1	-	-	1	1	3	-	-	-	-	-	-	-	1	-	2	1	-	-	-	-	-	-	-	-	-

Source: National Environment Board of Thailand, Guidelines for Preparation of Environmental Impact Evaluations (1979).

Notes: (a) (A) means significant impact of project on environmental resources, whereas (B) means impact of the environment on the project.

(b) Numerical value of 3 means probable major impact, 2 means intermediate, and 1 means significant but relatively minor.

(c) Numbers in parentheses indicate effects are mostly enhancement of environment. Numbers in double parentheses represent combination of adverse and beneficial effects. Numbers without parentheses represent either adverse or beneficial effects.

(b) On the upper side of the slash, place a number from 1 to 10 indicating the magnitude of possible impact (1 is the least, 10 is the highest).

(c) On the lower side of the slash, place a number from 1 to 10 indicating the importance of potential impact, that is, the weighting of the degree of significance of impact.

27. An illustration of the application of the Leopold matrix to the Quae Yai Dam Project in Thailand is presented in table 4. This example reveals that the impact of the project on the environment of Quae Yai would be most significant on the health of the people. Other adverse impacts would be on downstream water quality, archaeological artifacts and tourism, in that order, Leopold matrix analysis can also be conveniently applied to evaluation of the merits of various alternative sites for the project, by comparing the "overall impact index" (assessed 679 for the site given in the example).

28. Matrices are strong in identifying impacts; they can present interactive effects and some of the dynamic characteristics of impacts. They are also highly visual and effective for conveying these impacts to a lay audience. On the other hand, matrices fail to make explicit the network of intermediary relationships which exist in a complex system, and they sometimes become too cumbersome.

Table 4. Application of the Leopold matrix to the Quae Yai Dam project in Thailand

Environmental components	Proposed action	Migration of labour	Dam construction	Transmission line	Reservoir filling	Heavy metal discharge	Growth of aquatic weed	Relocation of inhabitants	Overall impact index
Health		5/8	4/6		5/8	4/7	6/6		168
Spawning of fish			3/4		3/6	3/7	5/5		76
Archaeological artifacts		4/6			8/8				88
Tourism				7/6	7/6				84
Downstream water pollution			7/7		7/8	2/4			113
Social and economic aspects								8/7	56
Forestry			4/2						8
Fishery			2/5			2/5			20
Navigation					6/5				30
Aquatic plants					6/6				36
								Total =	679

Note: The numbers of the upper sides of the slashes indicate the magnitude of possible impacts (1 is the least, 10 is the highest), while the numbers of the lower sides indicate the "weight" of possible impacts.

29. The matrix method is employed quite extensively for environmental impact assessment. In the Asian and Pacific region, the applications of this method can be found, for example, in the environmental impact statements of the Pa Mong Dam/Reservoir project, the Pattani multi-purpose water resource development project in Thailand, and so on.

(c) *Networks*

30. The network method is an attempt to realize a series of impacts triggered by a project action. This method starts with the preparation of a list of project actions and then generates cause-condition-effect networks (chains of events). Types of impacts which would initially occur are identified for each project action. The next step is to select each impact and identify those which may be induced as a result. This process is repeated until all possible impacts have been identified. Sketching this in network form results in what is commonly referred to as "an impact tree". An example of this approach is presented in figure 2.

31. One advantage of this approach is that it allows the user to identify impacts by selecting and tracing out the events as they might be expected to occur. It identifies both short- and long-term effects as well as direct and indirect impacts. On the other hand, a major problem of this method is achieving the degree of detail necessary for informed decision-making. If the environmental condition changes are described in detail and all possible interrelationships are included, the resulting networks could be too extensive and complex. Another problem is that only adverse environmental effects are usually considered in the network format.

32. This approach may be suitable for single-project assessment but not for large-scale, regional projects for which the display may sometimes become so extensive that it will be of little practical value, particularly when several alternatives are being considered. This method has been applied to many environmental impact assessments, for example, to that of the Nong-Pla Reservoir project in Thailand.

(d) *Overlay mapping*

33. This method uses a set of transparent maps of a project area's environmental characteristics (physical, social, ecological and aesthetic). The study area is subdivided into geographical units, topographic features, or differing land uses. Within each unit, information is collected on a

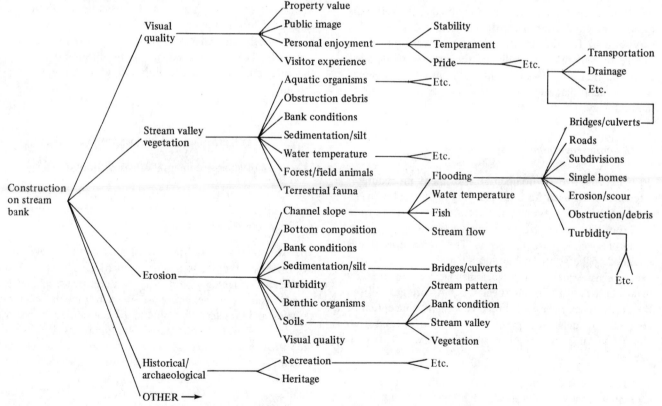

Source: United States Department of Defense, Corps of Engineers, *Environmental Considerations: Proposed Policies and Procedures* (1977).

Notes: (a) The line in this illustration is to be read as "has some effect on".

(b) It is emphasized that the cause-effect chain presented here should be viewed as only a small part of a large overall impact tree.

Figure 2. Impact tree for a hypothetical bank stabilization project

variety of parameters subdivided among such categories as climate, geology, physiography, hydrology, soils, vegetation and wildlife habitats. Within each category, those parameters which are most relevant to particular problems are considered. All maps are superimposed to produce a composite of all parameters. With this series of overlays, land-use suitability, engineering feasibility and compatibility of alternative projects are evaluated visually to obtain the best combination. Overlay techniques using computer mapping have been well developed.

34. One of the most distinct advantages of this method is its visual presentation through maps. It provides a very effective, visual mode of synthesizing and conveying alternatives to a lay audience. It is also effective in selecting alternatives and identifying land-use conflicts or trade-offs, in their spacial dimensions. One of the disadvantages is that it is highly subjective, relying almost entirely on the assessor to identify, evaluate, and judge compatible and incompatible land uses. It also suffers from a tendency to oversimplification. It does not specify cause-effect relationships nor does it separate direct from indirect impacts. Finally, it needs a considerable amount of information; thus, it tends to be expensive and time-consuming.

35. In practice, this approach is rarely used as the sole basis of environmental assessment. It is said that this method is very helpful for the assessment team in performing the matrix or network, especially in the process of detailed environmental impact assessment. It is also used frequently as a data management system and as an assessment methodology.

(e) *Adaptive environmental assessment*

36. The adaptive environmental assessment procedure is intended to be used for both planning and actual management of the area or resources. Central to the procedure are workshops and extensive communication among a selective group of specialists and managers. The entire procedure is intended to be very flexible and adaptable to the varying needs of assessment. A project manager sets up a study team consisting of various specialists. A core group from the study team runs workshops, constructs conceptual or computer models, and produces analytical output from alternative runs, while other specialists are called in as needed.

37. This approach includes data and facilities for handling ecosystem trends and dynamics, enabling particular projects or plans to be assessed in the context of continual change and higher-order interactions. There is also a greater likelihood that environmental aspects will be dealt with directly in the context of planning formulation and decision-making, by implementing model development prior to the

finalization of proposals, and involving decision makers in the process of operating the model. On the other hand, the method depends heavily on a small group of experts, and has no provision for public input. This method may be time-consuming and expensive. The adaptive environmental assessment model serves less as an assessment of individual projects and more as a tool to integrate impact analysis into large-scale plan 'formation and execution. This approach has been used in this region for the Nam Pong environmental management project by the Interim Committee for Co-ordination of Investigations of the Lower Mekong Basin.

(f) *Others*

38. The environmental evaluation system is one of the scaling-weighting check-lists, developed for water resources development projects by Battelle Columbus Laboratories in the United States. It is initially based on a hierarchical check-list of attributes or parameters, each to be represented by a numerical value. In order to sum environmental values with appropriate emphasis, each attribute is assigned a weight. The appropriate distribution of weights among all parameters is determined by a team of experts, using a modified Delphi method to quantify subjective judgements. The environmental values on a particular attribute are calculated by multiplying the environmental quality index by its weight and all values for each alternative are then summed. Total project impact is the difference between the total quality under the with and without project conditions.

Project impact =

   [sum of all environmental values with project]

   − [sum of all environmental values without project]

39. As an example, the application of this method to the Pattani multipurpose water resource development project in Thailand is shown in table 5.

40. Although the applications of this method have not been many, the environment evaluation system has a number of advantages: it is very comprehensive in that it provides an extensive check-list of environmental characteristics and impacts that should be considered in water resources projects; both spatial and temporal aspects of identified impacts are accounted for in the weighting system; it is highly replicable because the direction for identification and evaluation of impacts is explicit; and finally, all evaluations are made by a multidisciplinary team. However, it also has some important disadvantages: a considerable amount of information tends to be lost by the aggregation of all values into an overall index; it ignores economic impacts and only partially deals with social impacts.

Table 5. Application of the environmental evaluation system to the Pattani multi-purpose water resource development project in Thailand

Components		Value in environmental quality without project	Value in environmental quality with project	Net change of value in environmental quality
Ecological	Terrestrial	883	693	−190
	Aquatic	484.3	721.6	237.3
	Subtotal	1 367.3	1 414.6	47.3
Physico-chemical	Land	518.5	368.3	−150.2
	Surface water	535.9	351.9	−194.0
	Ground water	530.8	270.6	−260.2
	Atmosphere	405.6	355.3	−50.3
	Subtotal	1 990.8	1 336.1	−654.7
Human interest	Health	247.6	779	531.4
	Socio-economic	806.0	1 586.2	780.2
	Aesthetic and cultural	660.5	618.2	−42.3
	Subtotal	1 714.1	2 983.4	1 269.3
	Total	5 072.2	5 734.1	661.9

Note: Beneficial or adverse impact of the project is shown by the net change of value in environmental quality.

41. The water resources assessment methodology was developed by the United States Army Corps of Engineers. Like the environment evaluation system, it may be described as a scaling-weighting check-list, but there the comparison ends because the water resources assessment methodology does not aggregate the various scores on each environmental parameter.

42. As already indicated, each of the methods is considered subjective to some degree and none of them is good for every application. A project manager facing the selection of the methods appropriate to a particular situation should, therefore, review available methods and, if possible, examine previous assessments of the same type of projects where one or the other method has actually been employed. The actual selection of the methods will depend on the level at which the assessment is pitched. A method which is strong in predicting long-term trends might be appropriate to assessing comprehensive national resources development plans, while another method with a well-developed facility for quantifying impacts and analysing trade-offs might be appropriate for assessing an individual project.

43. The following considerations might be useful for the selection of the methods:

(a) Various types of development projects have different methodological requirements because they affect different components of the environment;

(b) The size and type of the project, environmental setting of the area, and availability of pertinent data, are important factors for the selection of methods;

(c) A comparison of different alternatives or identification of mitigation measures will determine the resulting impacts;

(d) In the actual case there may be various constraints from limited resources, time, available data and others, which should be taken into account in selecting a methodology.

D. Conclusions and recommendations

44. It has been recognized by most countries of the Asian and Pacific region that integration of environmental considerations into water resources development projects is essential. For this purpose, various kinds of environmental impact assessment methodologies have been developed in many countries of the region, and a number of experiences have been accumulated on such assessment of water resources development projects. From the review and analysis of these experiences, one can draw the following conclusions and recommendations:

For national action

(1) The establishment of environmental impact assessment procedures, either legislative or administrative, is

necessary for integration of environmental considerations into water resources development projects. Furthermore, an institutional mechanism of co-ordination and co-operation between concerned agencies in carrying out such assessment should be established.

(2) The assessment should be conducted as early as possible in the planning stage, in order to integrate the results into project planning and design and to avoid any possible economic set-back or ecological disaster at a later stage.

(3) Environmental impact assessment should be applied not only to individual projects but also to comprehensive development plans or programmes.

(4) Training courses, workshops and seminars should be organized to make decision makers and planners familiar with conceptual, procedural and technical aspects of environmental impact assessment. Technical aspects, especially should be emphasized as the selection of appropriate methodologies is essential for successful assessment.

For regional action

(1) Exchange of information and experience should be promoted among various countries in the region through case studies, seminars and study tours. Compilation and analysis of information on actual cost and time involved in completing the environmental impact assessment, as compared with the cost and time involved in project implementation, should be undertaken.

(2) Guidelines, manuals or training materials should be developed to disseminate the concept, procedures and methodologies of environmental impact assessment on water.

(3) A subregional co-ordination mechanism should be developed, when a national project is likely to have effects on the environments of neighbouring countries.

(4) A regional seminar/workshop should be organized to discuss various problems of the application of environmental impact assessment to water resources development projects.

45. The Committee may wish to review the methodologies and criteria for selection of projects requiring environmental impact assessment as presented in this document and offer its views and comments, as appropriate. It may also consider adopting recommendations for national and regional actions as presented above with appropriate modifications as may be suggested during the meeting.

SELECTED REFERENCES

1. Committee for Co-ordination of Investigation of the Lower Mekong Basin, "Environmental impact assessment – Guidelines for application for tropical river basin development" (Bangkok, 1982).

2. Department of Environment of Malaysia, "The environmental impact assessment handbook: procedure and guidelines", second draft (1979).

3. ESCAP, *Environmental Impact Assessment: Guidelines for Planners and Decision Makers*, (Bangkok, 1985) (ST/ESCAP/351).

4. ESCAP, "State of the environment in Asia and the Pacific" (1985).

5. Kim, Young-HWA, "Developing stepwise environmental impact assessment guidelines for the multipurpose dam projects" (Asian Institute of Technology, Bangkok, 1984).

6. B.N. Lohani and N. Halim, *Recommended Methodologies for Rapid Environmental Impact Assessment in Developing Countries: Experiences Derived from Case Studies in Thailand* (1983).

7. H.F. Ludwig, "Guidelines for preparing environmental impact assessment for water resources projects in developing countries", Draft report submitted to PEEM (Geneva, 1984).

8. National Environment Board of Thailand, *Guidelines for Preparation of Environmental Impact Evaluation* (Bangkok, 1979).

9. National Environmental Protection Council of the Philippines, *Environmental Impact Assessment Handbook*, (1983).

10. Paul Tomilinson, "The use of methods in screening and scoping", in *Perspectives on Environmental Impact Assessment*, eds. Brian D. Clark and others (Aberdeen, 1984), pp. 163-193.

11. Kiravanich Pakit and Silithan Boriboon, "Identification of water pollution impacts," in *Environmental Management for Developing Countries* (Asian Institute of Technology, Bangkok, 1983), pp. 95-109.

12. United States Department of Defence, Corps of Engineers, *Environmental Considerations: Proposed Policies and Procedures* (1977).

XIV. ENVIRONMENTAL ISSUES OF WATER RESOURCES DEVELOPMENT IN INDONESIA*

1. INTRODUCTION

Water resources development requires a conscious effort to manage and utilize resources for the purpose of improving the quality of lives of the people. However, development which aims at improving living standard and welfare of the people always causes changes in one or more of the biological, physical, chemical, and socio-cultural components of the environment.

There are two main impacts of development to the environment, these are positive and negative impacts. The negative impact should, therefore, be mitigated by some actions in order to conserve resources. In addition, the demand for water is increasing as a result of increase of the population and the increase of their needs. On the other hand water resources are not unlimited either in it's quality or quantity.

Considering the guideline of the state policy that development aims are not only bringing prosperity or spiritual contentment but also achieving a balance between the two, the utilization of natural resources must be in equilibrium with the harmony and balance of the living environment. The institution concerned should carry out an impact analysis on every development project which will have negative impact. The impact analysis can be done before implementation, during construction and after project is completed or in operational phases.

2. PRESENT RESOURCES AND ENVIRONMENTAL CONDITION

Indonesia comprises more than 13,000 islands, covering land area of about 1,919,443 sq.km. Such condition evidently shows its diversity in resource distribution which in turn influences the distribution of population. Java, which has the most fertile land, depreciated drastically due to pressure of its dense population. Roughly 22.8 per cent of its land is forest land at various conditions.

As is common in the wet tropical area, rainfall is heavy and comes in relatively short periods. Protective

---

* Country paper prepared for the thirteenth session of the ESCAP Committee on Natural Resources. This paper has been reproduced without formal editing. The views expressed in it are those of the author and do not necessarily reflect those of the United Nations.

forest cover is vitally important in order to reduce the effects of destructive rainfall. Roughly 74 per cent of the land area is covered by forest. A total of 23 million ha, however, is identified as shrub or unproductive forest, whereas 20 million ha is identified as critical land.

An attempt has been made to identify critical land more closely, resulting in 36 river basin development management projects having priority and to be treated carefully. Within those river basin development management projects a total of about 10.4 million ha is classified as critical land spreading up in 79 river basins. Of the above figure, 4.9 million ha is very urgent and should get properly treated. In regard to limited capability and budget allocation, super priority is given to 22 river basins where 1.6 million ha of critical land will be handled.

Since 1978 assessment has been done to the erosion intensity of several river basins in Java and some basins in Sumatera. In 1980 further deliberations has been done on the problems of erosion and sedimentation in Indonesia, with special regard to four river basins, which are representatives of all river basins in Java, i.e. Cimanuk, Citanduy, Bengawan Solo and Brantas.

Based on that study it was reported that the erosion rate for river basins in Java is ranging from 0.1 to 23 mm/year, while outside of Java it is ranging 0.03 to 0.87 mm/year.

The measurement on sediment concentration between 1959 and 1976 indicated that the maximum concentration for river basins in Java is ranging from 1,500 to 20,000 mg/l, while outside of Java it is ranging 150 to 10,000 mg/l.

Within the fourth five year development plan it is planned to develop the following:

— extensification of food crop areas	2 million ha
— extensification of plantation	1.7 million ha
— intensification programme	3.9 million ha
— water resources development/irrigation	1.5 million ha
— transmigration programme	1.5 million ha
— rehabilitation, greening movement and reforestation	1.3 million ha

The above activities need co-ordination programme, monitoring of land use and environment conservation.

3. ENVIRONMENTALLY ORIENTED WATER RESOURCES DEVELOPMENT

Water resources development has its supporting activities, especially in agricultural sector, where self-sufficiency in staple food has been achieved recently. However, the impact of the development cannot be avoided. One of the major impacts from many development actions is evidenced by changes in water quality both in the vicinity and down stream of the project areas. On the contrary, environment condition in the upstream could also influence the project structure below and may have general impacts on the structure, due to degradation of environmental condition as related to hydrologic cycles, changes in the suspended and dissolved material contents in the water. Such condition causes increasing problems in operation and maintenance, decreasing life time of the structure and increasing rehabilitation cost.

3.1. *Policies for protection of the environment*

Prior to the implementation of a water resources development project, planners and decision makers should consider an integrated studies of technical, economic, and environmental factors. Government of Indonesia has paid attention concerning protection of the environment through law and regulation dealing with environment. Some of these regulations are as follows:—

— The Act of the Republic of Indonesia No 11 of 1974 concerning water resources development.

— The Act of the Republic of Indonesia No 4 of 1982 concerning basic provisions for the management of the living environment.

— Government Regulation of the Republic of Indonesia No 29 of 1986 concerning environmental impact analysis which became effective on January 1987.

The President of Indonesia, in his speech on the Environment Day, 5 June 1982 gave his message on the environment oriented development. Among other things he said were:

(a) The principle of environment is interconnection and interdepency between one sector to another, one country to another and one generation to other generation hence, co-operation in high spirit of solidarity across sectoral, regional, and national and between generations should be developed.

(b) Ability to match the need and the capability of natural resources should be explored. Increasing the need of human life should be controlled in order to use the resources wisely.

(c) To increase human resources in order to develop without giving negative impact to the environment. Industrialization in the near future should be able to develop techniques in reducing industrial waste and saving the natural resources. The failures of the developed countries in the past in maintaining the environment should be avoided.

(d) To develop self-conciousness about environment within the society and then it will develop into personal self conciuosness.

(e) To develop community organizations (non-governmental organizations) to push societal participation to attain the environmental management.

3.2. *Guidelines for planning studies*

At planning stage, all aspects should be assessed closely either technical, economical, socio-cultural aspect and the impact of development to the environment. The latest comprises biological, non biological (physical and chemical) and socio-cultural aspects. Due to variety of the consultants' ability and background (cultural, education and experiences) whitin the DGWRD formal guidelines for study has been established. These guidelines, however, are still subject to improvement, to accommodate the environmental aspects properly.

4. IMPACT ANALYSIS

Although government regulation concerning impact assessment have just been signed recently, the impact analysis has already been carried out for some years especially in the problem areas. The format of standard analysis and procedures, varies. The executing consultants are also limited in number, commonly Universities (Centre of Environment Studies), and foreign consultants. It is relatively new field of study and still developing, follows the current techniques and requirements. The example of impact analysis are as follows:

(a) Ecological survey of Delta Upang swampland development (South Sumatera) in co-operation with Bogor Agricultural Institute, 1975.

(b) Ecological study of Delta Sabak-Berbak and Delta Dendang — Tanjung, Jambi (Sumatera) in co-operation with Affiliation Research and Industry Institute, Bandung Technological Institute, 1976.

(c) Bali Irrigation Environmental Impact Analysis in co-operation with ELC and ADC, 1980.

(d) Pondok and Sangiran (East Java) Irrigation Environmental Impact Analysis.

(e) Upper Jatiluhur (West Java) project in co-operation with Nippon Koei, 1981.

(f) Wonorejo (East Java) Proposed dam and Irrigation Environmental Impact Analysis 1981.

(g) Widas (East Java) Dam and Irrigation Project Monitoring of the Environmental Impact, 1981.

(h) Jatigede Dam (West Java) Environmental Impact Analysis in co-operation with Ecological Institute; Pajajaran University, 1982.

(i) Palasari Dam (Bali) Quarry Impact Analysis in co-operation with Centre of Environmental Studies, University of Udayana, 1983.

(j) Environmental Impact Analysis of the Kedung Ombo Dam, Ecological Institute, UNPAD, 1984.

(k) Environmental Impact Analysis of the Sermo Reservoir in co-operation with Population & Environment and University of Gajah Mada, 1985.

(l) Environmental Impact Analysis of the Cihurip Irrigation Project, Centre of Water Resources Development Research and Development 1985.

(m) Segoro Anakan (Central Java) Environmental Monitoring and Optimal Use Planning Project, 1985.

In order to increase the ability of the Public Works staffs on the Environment Impact Analysis, a course has been held regularly in University of Indonesia, Centre of Human Resources and Environment Studies.

REFERENCES

1. Annonymous, 1986. Environment Oriented Development, Ministry of Public Works.

2. _____, 1986. Forestry Development Plan (draft — unpublished).

3. D.G.W.R.D., 1985. Guidelines for Water Resources Development Project.

4. Notodihardjo M. and Badrudin Mahbub, 1981. Erosion and Sedimentation in Indonesia — an overview, The South East Asian Regional Symposium on Problems of Soil Erosion and Sedimentation, Asian Institute of Technology, Bangkok, Thailand.

XV. PROBLEMS OF RIVER WATER QUALITY CONTROL UNDER CONDITIONS OF INTENSIVE IRRIGATION DEVELOPMENT IN ARID ZONES*

by

Razakov P.M.**

SUMMARY

Population growth of the globe, especially in the developing countries, raises the problem of their food supply. Land irrigation, the share of which comprises about 80 per cent of the total water consumption, should play the leading role in providing the population with food products and in economic independence of the developing countries by increased output of grain. Irrigated land area in the world has reached 310 mill.ha, i.e., it increased 3 times in comparison with 1950.

About 500 mill. tons of mineral fertilizers and nearly 3 mill. tons of various chemicals are applied annually to soils, and up to 30 per cent of this amount is washed out into streams or detained in the atmosphere. The growth of irrigation is accompanied by irretrievable water consumption, the increase of drainage water flow from irrigated fields, the deficiency and impairment of river water quality. Under these conditions for multipurpose water resources use of river basins, for requirements on water quality of different branches of economy – drinking water supply, agriculture, industry, there should be established an ecological limit for water withdrawal from rivers, introduction of optimum irrigation and drainage regimes with advanced irrigation and drainage systems, current monitoring and forecasting of river water quality changes, effective control and management of water resources in river basins. These problems are under consideration in this article for the conditions of the arid zone in Central Asia.

INTRODUCTION

Intensive development of irrigation and saline land improvement, development of desert and semidesert areas in Central Asia became an important factor for economic growth of all republics in this region. These changes are visually demonstrated when developing semidesert lands of the Golodnaya, Dzhizak and Karshi Steppes, where large irrigation and water management multipurpose projects were established and, building industrial base, infrastructure which made it possible to create highly efficient up-to-date irrigation systems equipped with advanced types of drainage. The greater portion of cotton, rice, fruits and grapes in the country is produced on these lands.

In accordance with the National Plan of development during 1986-1990 and for the period up to 2000 the irrigated land area in the USSR will reach 23-25 mill.ha by 1990. Central Asia – the region of ancient traditional irrigation, is situated in extremely arid zone. The history of land irrigation dating back thousands of years is marked by the continuous struggle of farmers against soil salinization. Newly irrigated lands have an advanced system, while a considerable part of old irrigated lands is still on a rather low technical level. Due to water resources deficiency in the region, further development of irrigation is possible by way of introducing water-saving technology, scientific and technical progress in land reclamation and water management. Intensification and extension of agricultural production became a powerful factor influencing the environment. The impact of this could be observed in changes in soils, vegetation, the animal kingdom, hydrological and hydrogeological conditions of the territories, water quality in rivers, lakes, reservoirs, especially their hydrochemical regime, and water salinity.

Characteristics of natural conditions and water situation in river basins of central Asia

The largest in the world multipurpose water reservoir projects are constructed in Central Asia: Toktogul, Nurek etc., pump irrigation canals such as Amudarya-Bukhara canal, Dzhizak and Karshi canals with total height of water lift of 150 m and discharge up to 200 m³/sec, the unique canals – Yuzhnyi Golodno-Stepsky canal, Ferghana canal, Amudarya-Bukhara canal, Karakum canal (discharge at head – 600 m³/sec, total length – over 1,200 km) etc.

The territory of Central Asia is notable for high sum of effective temperatures (2,800°-5,400°C per year), high amount of solar radiation, considerable energy potential,

---

* Paper prepared for the thirteenth session of the ESCAP Committee on Natural Resources. This paper has been reproduced without formal editing. The views expressed in it are those of the author and do not necessarily reflect those of the United Nations.

** Central Asian Research Institute of Irrigation (SANIIRI), Tashkent, USSR.

great number of cloudless days. Natural and climatic conditions here allow to grow the most heat-loving crops and obtain up to 3 crop yields per year in a number of regions. This fact makes it possible to produce up to 95 per cent of raw cotton, about 40 per cent of rice, 25 per cent of melons, 32 per cent of fruits and grapes out of total output in the country. Owing to high rates of new land development in the region the irrigated land area has doubled and reached 7.2 mill.ha, and agricultural output increased 4 times. The newly irrigated lands have advanced irrigation and drainage systems with high efficiency up to 0.78-0.82 in the Golodnaya Steppe, Dzhizak, Karshi Steppes etc., while the efficiency of old systems comprises 0.5-0.6 (I). However, only about 30 per cent of all irrigated lands have new systems. Within the near future it is planned to carry out the reconstruction of irrigation systems in order to complete it by 2000.

Use of saline water for irrigation, water quality requirement and forecasting of river water salinity

Water resources deficit and increase of their salinity necessitate wide use of slightly saline water for irrigation.

Within the last years the number of scientific publications on the use of saline water for irrigation and its impact on crop yields have considerably increased. A discrepancy in recommendations made by the scientists was revealed there in. This is indicative of inadequate studies of physical and chemical processes in soil during irrigation by saline water, the influence of initial type of soil and groundwater salinization, phase of plant development, irrigation technology, etc. The recommendations of scientists and designers on the use of water with salinity up to 1.5 g/l for irrigation and in certain cases up to 2 g/l and more are intended mainly for coarse and medium soils with short irrigations, or with available advanced systems of drainage and leaching regime of irrigation.

A classification of suitability of saline drainage water for irrigation has been developed with regard for drainage conditions of the territory, soil texture, Cl/SO_4 ratio, total dissolved solids and chlorine content. According to this classification the water of Class II could be used for irrigation of majority of crops and soil types, but with adequate drainage conditions; water of Class III — for coarse soils under the condition of annual leachings and with regard for salt tolerance of crops; water of Class IV is of limited usage.

According to data presented by V.A. Kovda (3) the dilution of one volume of water with salt content of 2 g/l required 2-3 volumes of fresh water, for 5 g/l — it required 6-8 volumes. The situation with dilution of drainage water is aggravated when river water turns to be saline. The use of saline water results in the increase of osmotic pressure of soil solution and reduction of nutrient consumption by plants. There are a lot of classifications and various criteria for evaluation of irrigation water quality. Very often the use is made of I.I. Antipov-Karataev classification, evaluating the danger of soil alkalinization and revealing the relationship between sodium concentration in water and absorbed natrium in the soil.

In the United States of America wide use is made of the Gapon formula for evaluation of alkalinization by natrium-adsorbtion relationship. I. Sabolch and K. Darab evaluated the danger of alkalinization for the conditions in Hungary depending on the content of magnesium in irrigation water. On the whole, when using saline water it is necessary to control salt accumulation in the soil solution.

Due to soil salinization on a part of lands of old irrigation with shallow occurence of groundwater, up to 30-50 t/ha of salts is washed out to drainage flow with leaching and irrigation water. Under optimum irrigation and drainage regime washing out of salts could be reduced to 10-12 t/ha (I).

Irrigation-induced desertification or secondary salinization could be increased with extension of irrigation on large areas in the arid zone without utilization of advanced types of drainage. Large leaching rates used for maintaining negative salt balance on lands with shallow drainage result in wasteful use of river water, removal of useful micronutrients together with toxic salts, humus, pesticides, calcium — the source of fertility in the region, etc., impairment of physical properties, soil texture. At the same time a new problem arises concerning the distribution of large amounts of salts removed from irrigated fields. Part of them is discharged with drainage water into rivers and the other one is diverted into special water-salt receivers, depressions, located on the boundaries of irrigated lands. Discharge of drainage water into the rivers increases the irrigation capacity of rivers, however, on the other side, the quality of river water deteriorates and its salinity increases. Return water from irrigated land area located in the upper reaches of rivers owing to gypsometering position of the territory is discharged into rivers due to absence of possibility to accumulate it beyond the boundaries of river basins. This is pertinent to the Tajik SSR and the Surkhansherbad valley in the upper reaches of the Amudarya River, the Kirghiz SSR, the Ferghana valley in the Uzbek Soviet Socialist Republic. On the whole, the salinity of water there due to slight salinization of soils does not exceed 2-3 g/l. Considerable increase of river water salinity is observed in the middle course of rivers, where salt concentration in the runoff from agricultural irrigated lands has reached 3-8 g/l.

Studies of hydrochemical regime of rivers, forecasting of the river water salinity due to natural and anthropogenic changes in the basins are of great importance for designing and planning of water economy development in the region, secondary use of saline water for irrigation, etc. When forecasting river water salinity most often the use is made of water budget and basin methods, different variations of statistical analysis of the river flow series.

The first method seems to be the simplest one. Water and salt budget is estimated for different sites with regard for water withdrawal for irrigation, rates of development and quality of river water, irrigation and drainage waters discharge into river, their salinity. This method requires reliable information on the above mentioned components, and implementation of the forecasts on soil conditions for all water economy regions of the basin, including the forecast of salinity and volume of return water. This task is rather complicated and labour-consuming, as the planned growth of irrigated lands is overlapped by zonal capacities of the basin, by forecasted organizational, technical and operational problems, and by the condition of irrigation systems, etc.

A combined statistical and budget method was developed for water salinity forecasting, which was used for the Amudarya River (4). Statistical analysis of flow function by this method was carried out with regard for the irrigation tendency in the basin, as well as salt runoff and salt concentration in water along sites of the Amudarya with the use of decomposition into Fourier series.

Obtained results of the forecast are corrected by budget method with regard for all water withdrawals for irrigation and discharges of drainage water back into the river. New water management changes (new sources of water withdrawal and water discharge) during the forecasted period of 5-6 years are taken into consideration by introducing special correction.

Influence of agricultural chemicals used in irrigation farming, on river water quality

In the zone of intensive irrigation in Central Asia use is made of 300-400 kg/ha of mineral fertilizers, various means of plant protection, such as pesticides, herbicides, defoliants etc. Only 35-40 per cent of applied nitrogen and 15-20 per cent of phosphorus is assimilated by plants, the rest is transformed into forms which are assimilated by the plants with difficulty, migrate with water underground, into drainage network and rivers. Without special water conservation measures about 25 per cent of nitrogen and 5 per cent of phosphorus is removed into main drains from total amount applied on irrigated fields. According to the

data of the VNIIVO (All-Union Research Institute for Water Resources Conservation) removal of pesticides from non-irrigated lands averages 1 per cent, and 4 per cent from irrigated lands out of total applied amount, and in certain cases the removal may reach 15-20 per cent (5). In accordance with the SANIIRI data the removal of different pesticides makes up 0.2-0.3 per cent (6). Within the nearest 20-30 years the pesticides alongside with integrated methods would play an important role in plant protection against pests, diseases and weeds. Thus, the amount of applied fertilizers in the world has increased three times within the last 15 years, chemicals — 2.5 times and such rates would be continued till the year 2000.

Pollution of river water with industrial and agricultural wastewater exceeding standard concentrations results in damage to population health using this water for drinking purposes, fishery and agriculture and other branches of the national economy (7, 8, 9). The total damage involves ecological, social and other losses. Irrigation development projects should plan water conservation measures to prevent damage caused by wastewater discharges to water consumers of downstream areas. With regard for these factors it is economically more expedient to treat wastewater before it is discharged into rivers. Water economy development regardless of the impacts on the environment causes a lot of secondary, underestimated effects (damages), the sum of which could equal or exceed the benefit of the development itself (10).

As a rule, large rivers have no administrative or political boundaries, therefore the use of water resources or discharge of polluted wastewater into the rivers have international or interstate effect and infringes upon the interests of all water users of the basin. The problem of water distribution and quality control of the rivers in Central Asia flowing on the territory of 3-4 Union Republics puts forward the plan of co-ordinated actions of water users for the whole basin, regulation of water withdrawals and water discharges to maintain the critical water levels in the lower river reaches. Thus, according to the data presented by S.A. Polivanov (11) the increase of water salinity in the lower reaches of the Syrdarya River over 1.5 g/l after 1990 would make up 360 mill. roubles for the agriculture (with drinking water supply from underground sources) due to the increase of water prices up to 0.11 rouble/m^3. In connection with the above-stated, the problem of systematic control of river water quality and development of large-scale water conservation measures becomes very important.

At the SANIIRI the studies are carried out within several years on the behaviour of chlororganic pesticides in water, bottom deposits, hydrobionts, higher aquatic plants both in large main drains and in lagoons — water and salt receivers. The capability of chlororganic pesticides to accumulate in biological objects, results in the fact, that inspite of their small amount in the water their content in all objects of aquatic ecological system is several times higher. Fish is most sensitive to water pollution by pesticides, and in a number of organizations of the United States and the USSR it is used as biological indicators of water pollution (12, 13). Accumulation of chlororganic pesticides grows with the increase of the size and age of organisms by one order and higher. The results of studies revealed essential reduction of chlororganic pesticides during passage of drainage water through lakes or water reservoirs. To a great extent it depends on the water body configuration, its overgrowing with different plants, the extent of flow, etc.

Laboratory and field studies show that higher aquatic plants promote cumulation of chlororganic pesticides, their detoxification, acceleration of wastewater treatment and removal of organic pollutants from them. An important role in this process belongs to rich microflora developed in the medium of microphytes. However, these processes should be under control.

With regard for water resources deficit and increase of their salinity, different measures are being developed for stage-by-stage cutting-off of large main drains and their diversion from the rivers depending on water quality in them, namely salinity, with subsequent discharge of this water into natural depressions and lakes beyond the limits of irrigated areas. On the conveyance stretches of main drains saline water could be used for growing fodder crops, etc., salt-resistant crops on sandy areas with deep occurrence of groundwater. Such tests were conducted by various organizations with utilization of saline water of the Caspian Sea (14) and drainage water (15). A number of main drains with comparatively low mean annual salinity should have double control: during winter-spring period when water after leachings of irrigated lands is diverted into depressions, and drainage flow of the vegetation period with salinity of 2-3 g/l is discharged into the river. Prior to the discharge into river, biological treatment should be provided to remove biogenic substances, pesticides, suspended solids etc., which would result in augmentation of water resources under conditions of their deficiency. All water discharged from irrigated lands situated in the upper river reaches should be also treated to remove agrochemicals.

CONCLUSION

Intensive development of irrigation made it possible during comparatively short time to increase irrigated areas more than twice, and agricultural output — up to 4 times. However, with the approach of exhaustion of water resources of the main rivers in Central Asia — the Syrdarya and Amudarya a number of negative sides of this problem

emerged in the water economy of the region. These ecological changes are most vividly exhibited in the lower reaches of the rivers and in their deltaic parts. On the basis of forecasts on river water salinity, evaluation of the amount of agricultural chemicals entering the rivers with drainage water, a number of water conservation measures are suggested to maintain critical levels of salinity — 1.5 g/l in the lower reaches of the Syrdarya River, and up to 1 g/l in the lower reaches of the Amudarya River. These measures consist in stage-by-stage differentiated cutting-off of the main drains with high water salinity and their diversion beyond the limits of the irrigation zone to sandy areas under fodder crops. It is suggested to treat slightly saline drainage water to remove pesticides, biogenic elements on the conveyance stretches of the main drains and lakes up to their discharge into the rivers.

REFERENCES

1. Dukhovny V.A. — Water management complex in the irrigation zone//Moscow.-"Kolos".-1984.-p. 255 (in Russian).

2. Usmanov V.U. — Evaluation of suitability of saline water for crop irrigation. From the book: Use of saline water in agriculture//Ashkhabad.-"Ylym".-1984.-p. 32-36.

3. Kovda V.A. — Use of saline water.-Papers of Soyuzvodproekt//Moscow.-1980.-Issue 53.-p. 5-12.

4. Razakov R.M., Raziev I.B., Vilenchik V.B. — On a method of forecasting water salinity of the Amudarya River//"Izvestya Akademii Nauk Uz. SSR".-1985.-No. 6.-p. 6-11.

5. Bredikhina E.I., Moskovkin V.M., Uyrkov V.V. — Evaluation of pesticide removal with surface and drainage flow//"Gidrotehnika i melioratsiya".-1979.-No. 2.-p. 5-9.

6. Orlova A.P., Dounia-Barkovskaya O.S. — Forecasting of chemical removal from irrigated area//Papers of the SANIIRI.-1981.-Issue 165.-p. 12-16.

7. Bukorez A.I., Rubenchik B.L., Slepyan E.I. et al.-Ecology and cancer//Kiev: "Naukova dumka".-1985.-p. 256.

8. Saffiotti V. — Review of pesticides carcinogenesis data and regulatory approaches. In: Carcinogenic risk-strategies for intervention//Lyon.-1979.-p. 151-166 (IARC Sci.Publ.No. 25).

9. Nature conservation and application of chemicals in agriculture and forestry (Edited by Slepyan E.I.)//Leningrad.-"Nauka".-1985.-p. 145.

10. Asit K. Biswas. – Environment and sustainable water dev.//IV-th World Congress on Water Res. – Argentina.-1982.-p. 375-392.

11. Polinov S.A. – Ecological evaluation of water resources//"Khlopkovodstvo".-1985.-No. 3.-p.33-37.

12. Biomonitoring: emerging tool for control of toxicants in water//Environment Midwest.-1979.-p. 4-6.

13. Theoretical problems of biotesting (Edited by Temitchenko M.N. Volgograd.-1983.-p. 181).

14. Bekov E.M., Nasroullaev S.M., Gazieva T.M. – Some results of agricultural crop irrigation by the water of the Caspian Sea. From the book: Use of saline water in agriculture//Ashkhabad.-1984.-p. 161-165.

15. Pushkareva Z.P., Orlova A.P. – Reclamation of light desert soils for irrigated farming with the use·of saline water. From the book: Natural conditions and resources of the USSR deserts, their rational use//Ashkhabad.-1984.-p. 312-314.

Part Four :

SMALL DAMS AND MINI-HYDRO

XVI. Potential for small dams and mini-hydropower generation in the least developed
countries and developing island countries of ESCAP region

167

XVI. POTENTIAL FOR SMALL DAMS AND MINI-HYDROPOWER GENERATION IN THE LEAST DEVELOPED COUNTRIES AND DEVELOPING ISLAND COUNTRIES OF ESCAP REGION*

INTRODUCTION

1. In most of the least developed countries and small Pacific island countries of the ESCAP region national power grids serve only the capital and a few major towns. The development of rural areas is severely hindered by the lack of power supplies. Extending the power grid for scattered populations is usually prohibitively expensive. Even villagers are often unable to pay the usual tariff. However, hilly or mountainous areas in most of the least developed and small island countries generally have access to an important potential power supply, water power. With the recent development of new types of turbines and other equipment and the technologies of utilization of local labour and materials, mini-hydropower has become a more achievable and valuable low-cost source of energy which can accelerate the development of remote areas by creating employment through small industries as well as providing electric power for domestic use. However, the economy of mini-hydro development is largely site specific.

2. In the ESCAP region, Afghanistan, Bangladesh, Bhutan, the Lao People's Democratic Republic, Maldives, Nepal, Samoa and Vanuatu are considered least developed countries. All of these, with the exception of Maldives, have hydropower potential and are included in this study. In addition, two Pacific island countries, Fiji and Solomon Islands, have been included. The other smaller Pacific island countries do not have favourable topography and appreciable surface waters for consideration in hydropower development.

3. Section I presents the installed electric power generating capacity and annual generation in 1984 in each of these nine countries. It reflects the low level of electric power supply and also the need for electric power development. Section II describes the estimated technical hydro potential and the identified mini-hydro potential in each of these nine countries.

4. Section III presents case studies on the development of mini-hydropower in China, India and the Philippines, including their achievements and development strategies. These countries were selected for inclusion in this study since China and India have the longest history in the development of mini-hydropower schemes, while the Philippines has started an ambitious programme recently. The experience gained in the development of mini-hydropower

---

* Originally issued as E/ESCAP/NR.13/1.

in these countries would be beneficial to others making endeavours in this field.

5. Section IV briefly reviews the new technology in mini-hydropower development and the measures taken in some countries in the region in order to make mini-hydro projects economical and increasingly justifiable.

6. Section V presents three alternative types of electric power generation and their generating costs for an isolated rural community or a small electric power system. It also describes the main factors which determine the economy of mini-hydro projects. For economic comparison with the three alternative types of electric power, the cost per kWh of mini-hydro generation is estimated based on an estimated capital cost and plant factor.

I. ELECTRIC POWER SUPPLY AND NEED FOR MINI-HYDROPOWER DEVELOPMENT

7. As shown in table 1, as of 1982 the installed generating capacity of the power system of *Afghanistan* and the self-generating industries was 433.6 MW, consisting of 265.3 MW hydro, 52.3 MW thermal, 58.0 MW diesel and 58.0 MW gas turbines. During 1982/83, 760 million kWh of electricity (or 54 kWh per capita) were generated. More than 80 per cent of electricity was consumed in the capital city, Kabul, only about 6 per cent of the total population having access to electricity. The highest transmission voltage was 110 kV in 1982. However, a 220 kV transmission line from the Union of Soviet Socialist Republics to Kabul was under construction, which would connect the Balkh, Ghori — Parwan and Kabul regions.

8. In *Bangladesh,* the principal domestic energy resources are large deposits of natural gas and hydro potential in the south-eastern part of the country. All petroleum and coal requirements must be met by imports. As of 1984, the total installed capacity of the power system of the country, including self-generating industries, was 1,121 MW, consisting of 130 MW hydro, 590.5 MW steam, 314.5 MW gas turbines and 86 MW diesel (table 1). In 1984, the total power generated by the public electric utility and self-generating industries was 5,402.8 million kWh (or 52 kWh per capita). The total number of connections served in 1980/81 was 568,309. It is roughly estimated that only about 5 per cent of the population had access to electricity. The Rural Electrification Board established in 1977 is

Table 1. Installed electric power generating capacity and annual generation in least developed and selected Pacific island countries

Country	Area (Km²)	Population 1984 (1 000)	Installed electricity generating capacity in 1984[a] MW					Annual generation in 1984 (10⁶ kWh)	Per capita generation (kWh)	Estimated percentage of population served
			Hydro	Steam	Diesel	Gas turbines and Geothermal	Total			
I. Least developed countries										
Afghanistan	652 090	17 670	265.3	52.3	58	58	433.6[b]	760.1[b]	65.6	6
Bangladesh	143 998	96 730	130	590.5	86	314.5	1 121	5 402.8	51.8	5
Bhutan	47 000	1 390	3.5	–	15.6	–	19.1	22.6	16.3	...
Lao People's Democratic Republic	236 800	4 320	153.75	–	25	–	178.75[c]	1 250[c]	289[h]	4
Maldives	298	170	–	–	3.5	–	3.5	8.6	50.6	...
Nepal	140 797	16 110	113	–	25	–	138[b]	228.5[b]	14.8	5
II. Selected Pacific island countries										
Fiji	18 272	690	80	20	88.8	–	188.8	306.8	444.6	40
Samoa	2 935	160	4.63	2.5	11.64	–	18.77	33.8	211.3	...
Solomon Islands	28 446	270	–	–	8.0[f]	–	8.0[f]	18.5[f]	68.5	...
Tonga	699	100	–	–	6.55[e]	–	6.55[e]	11.25[e]	112.5	35
Vanuatu	14 763	130	–	–	6.37	–	6.37	17.3	133.1	...
III. Selected developing countries										
China	9 596 961	1 051 550	25 599.7	54 242.8	267.4	7.0	80 116.9	376 991	358.5	...
India	3 287 590	746 740	13 058.0	25 750.0[g]	–	–	38 808.0[b]	131 000[b]	175.4	...
Philippines	300 000	53 350	1 677.1	2 404.7	874.3	1 086.8[d]	6 042.9	21 557	404.1	52

[a] *Source:* United Nations, "Electric power in Asia and the Pacific, 1983 and 1984" (manuscript).

[b] As of 1982.

[c] As of 1983. A total of 805 x 10⁶ kWh was exported to Thailand from July 1984 to June 1985.

[d] Including 192.8 MW of new and renewable sources of energy power plants.

[e] As of 1982/83.

[f] As of 1982, excluding capacity of self-generating industries.

[g] Including nuclear 860 MW.

[h] Per capita consumption was only 30 kWh in 1984.

Note: Three dots (. . .) indicate that data are not available.

A dash (–) indicates that the amount is nil or negligible.

responsible for supervision and control of rural electricity distribution.

9. The current power system of *Bhutan* comprises a number of load centres all fed by isolated stations or imported power substations. As of 1984, the total electric power generating installed capacity, including that of self-generating industries, was 19.1 MW, comprising 3.5 MW hydro and 15.6 MW diesel (table 1). Total generation in 1984 was 22.6 million kWh (or 16.3 kWh per capita). For public supplies, in addition to power generation by the Department of Power, electricity was imported from the West Bengal State Electricity Board and the Assam State Electricity Board of India. The Chukha hydroelectric power

XVI. Potential for small dams and mini-hydropower generation in the least developed
countries and developing island countries of ESCAP region

169

project, with four units of 84 MW each, was scheduled to be completed in 1985. With the completion of this project, there will be adequate power supply in the lower and upper western regions of Bhutan.

10. The *Lao People's Democratic Republic,* is located in the middle reach of the lower Mekong basin. It is generally a hilly and mountainous country; however, Vientiane, the capital, is located in the Vientiane Plain. The total electric power installed capacity as of 1983 was 178.75 MW, of which 153.75 MW (86 per cent) was hydro and 25 MW (14 per cent) was diesel based (table 1). The main hydro-electric power plant, the Nam Ngum project, with a total installed capacity of 110 MW in 1983, supplies the city of Vientiane and the surrounding areas. In 1984, its installed capacity was expanded to 150 MW. During the period from July 1984 to June 1985, the power plant generated a total electricity of 945 million kWh, of which 140 million kWh was consumed in Vientiane. Some 755 million kWh surplus power was exported to Thailand, which in turn re-exported 18 million kWh to southern parts of the Lao People's Democratic Republic. Other hydro plants and diesel generators are small in capacity, supplying only local rural demands. The total consumption of electricity in 1984 is recorded at 130 million kWh or 30 kWh per capita. In 1984, the number of total customers was 29,902. It is estimated that only 4 per cent of the population had access to electricity.

11. *Nepal* is situated on the southern slopes of the Himalayas. More than 80 per cent of the country is comprised of hills and mountains. As of 1982, Nepal's installed generating capacity was 138 MW, of which 113 MW (82 per cent) was hydro, and 25 MW diesel based (table 1). The electric power supply grid exists only in the central part of the country. In the eastern region, in 1982 the demand was about 5 MW, of which 3.4 MW was met by diesel generating stations and the balance imported from India. In the far western region, the demand was entirely met by imports from India. In 1982, the total electricity generation in the country was 228.5 million kWh (or 14.8 kWh per capita). This compares with 358 kWh in India, and 52 kWh in Bangladesh, as shown in table 1. It is estimated that only about 5 per cent of the population has access to electricity.

12. The *Fiji* Electricity Authority is the major supplier of electricity to the public in Viti Levu, Vanua Levu and Ovalau islands. As of 1984, more than 90 per cent of the installed capacity was in Viti Levu. Until the commissioning of Monasavu hydro station on Viti Levu in 1983, all generation was by diesel power plants. In 1984, 290.8 million kWh, or 99 per cent of the country's total generation, was generated by the 80 MW Monasavu hydro station. The major existing diesel generating plants were kept as standby facilities. In addition to the public power supply which reached about 38 per cent of all Fijian households, electricity was also generated privately by the Fiji Sugar Corporation and Emperor Gold Mines, as well by a number of remote resorts and villages.

13. The public power supply system of *Samoa* consists of a fairly extensive grid network covering the heavily populated western portion of Upolu and a smaller power system at Saleloloaga in southern Savaii. Public electricity on Upolu (97 per cent of total generating capacity) is generated from two sources, imported diesel fuel and indigenous hydro in a ratio of 2.5: 1 in 1984. The four existing hydro plants of Upolu are the run-of-river type and have a minimal pondage capacity (average one to two hours). The total generating capability varies widely from 4.5 MW in the wet season down to only 1.0 MW in the dry season. The Sauniatu hydro project (3.5 MW) was scheduled to be commissioned in 1985. In addition to the public power supply system, generating plants installed by the self-generating industry (mainly Samoa Forest Product Ltd.) had a capacity of 2.5 MW, utilizing wood as the energy source.

14. *Solomon Islands* comprises a scattered archipelago of mountainous islands and low-lying coral atolls stretching across approximately 1,400 km. In 1982, the Electricity Authority supplied electricity only to seven towns: Honiara, Auki, Gizon, Kira Kira, Santa Cruz, Munda and Buata. The total 8 MW capacity was from diesel engines. The capital city of Honiara has two stations with a total capacity of 7 MW. The remaining 1 MW supplies the other six towns. There were a number of private generating stations owned by timber companies and churches.

15. The electric supply system of *Vanuatu* is totally diesel-based (table 1) and consists of: (a) an urban power system around Port Vila on Efate Island; (b) a second urban system for Luganville on Santo Island; and (c) three small rural systems, two on Malekula and one on Tanna. The diesel plant on Efate Island serving Port Vila has a total capacity of 4.97 MW (or 79 per cent). Total generation in 1984 was 17.3 million kWh, or 133 kWh per capita.

II. MINI-HYDROPOWER POTENTIAL IN LEAST DEVELOPED AND DEVELOPING PACIFIC ISLAND COUNTRIES

16. In *Afghanistan,* the total hydropower potential was estimated to be 5,000 MW (11) excluding that of international rivers. As of 1982, only 265.3 MW, or 5 per cent of the potential, was exploited. Information on the potential of mini-hydro development was not available.

17. In *Bangladesh,* in spite of the very large river systems, hydropower potential resources were rather modest, because of the flat terrain. Its technical hydropower potential was estimated at 8,500 million kWh, of which 800 million kWh had already been exploited by 1982 (1). The Mini-hydro Committee was formed in February 1981. The Committee identified 12 mini-hydro sites with a total installed capacity of 1,275 kW for detailed investigation.

18. Because of the topography and numerous snow-fed rivers and streams, *Bhutan* had enormous potential for hydropower generation. The preliminary estimate for total potential was about 20,000 MW at 30 per cent of load factor (18). Although six mini-hydro schemes had been constructed, only limited exploitation (3.5 MW) had taken place. In the absence of urban centres and because of the spread of villages, economic exploitation of other mini-hydro projects did not appear viable except for those regions especially selected for accelerated development.

19. The *Lao People's Democratic Republic* was endowed with large hydro potential. The secretariat of the Interim Mekong Committee had identified 53 tributary hydro projects with a total installed capacity of 12,683 MW (9). As of 1984, hydropower with a total installed capacity of 154 MW, or 1.2 per cent of the potential, had been developed. There were two existing mini-hydropower plants. The Lower Se Done station with an installed capacity of 2,550 kW was completed in 1970, and supplied electricity to Pakse. The Nam Dong station, with an installed capacity of 1,250 kW, supplying electric power to Luang Prabang and surrounding villages, was completed in 1971. To meet the localized electric power demand, 10 mini-hydropower projects with an installed capacity ranging from 900 kW to 16,000 kW were identified by the secretariat of the Interim Mekong Committee in 1980. Three projects, Nam Khan, Nam Ngiou and Nam Pa, were selected for detailed study. The Nam Khan project, with a proposed installed capacity of 4,600 kW, could generate sufficient electric power to meet the demand of Luang Prabang for the next decade. The Nam Ngiou project, with an installed capacity of 2,700 kW, would supply cheap power to neighbouring Xieng Khouang and Pone Savanh towns. Field investigations on the hydrology, topography, geology and power market of those two projects were completed in May 1985 (8).

20. *Nepal* was endowed with a large potential of hydropower. The theoretical potential and economic hydropower potential were estimated at 83,000 MW and 27,000 MW respectively. Up to 1982, only 113 MW, or 0.4 per cent, of the economic potential had been developed. With a view to enhancing the development of small hydropower in the remote and backward hilly areas in the northern part of the country, the Small Hydel Development Board was set up in 1975 under the Ministry of Water Resources. The Board was responsible for planning, construction and operation and maintenance of small hydroelectric plants with capacity below 5,000 kW. For several centuries, the villages had been using the streams for generating mechanical power used in agricultural processing. There were about 25,000 water wheels in operation in 1983. But with the construction of a few more efficient small hydroelectric plants in the last three decades, the local people became quite keen to develop hydropower for electricity generation. Up to 1980, the Board had made preliminary investigations at 150 sites. It had a programme of 47 projects ranging in size from 45-1,000 kW for construction during the sixth plan period (1980-1985). Based on the available information (3) (10), as of 1984 there were 12 mini-hydro projects with a total installed capacity of 2,221 kW in operation and 17 projects with a total installed capacity of 5,004 kW under construction. There were another 16 projects with a total capacity of 1,786 kW under investigation. The construction cost per kW installed ranged from $US 1,212 to $US 3,981 for projects completed during the period 1981-1984. For the projects under construction in 1984, the construction cost ranged from $US 3,321 to $US 4,700 per kW.

21. In *Fiji* more than 20 mini-hydro sites had been investigated with technical assistance from China, India, Japan and New Zealand (2). The schemes investigated in detail by the Indian and New Zealand teams ranged in output from 50 kW to 1,000 kW to supply electricity to the villages on small islands. About 90 per cent of the population lived on the two main islands of Viti Levu and Vanua Levu. On Viti Levu, the electricity supply from the 80 MW Monasavu hydro plant would eventually become available to most villages through extensions of the network. On Vanua Levu, the public electricity supply system was gradually expanding with the co-generation of electricity of the Sugar Corporation mills fuelled by bagasse. About 10 per cent of the population living on small islands needed electrification under the Government-subsidized rural electrification programme. An Australian consulting firm had been contracted by the Fiji Electricity Authority to examine and make cost analyses of potential hydro sites. The Energy Department hydro schemes included a 12-hp hydro-powered sawmill in an isolated village on Kadavu, a 5 kW electrification project at Nasoqo, a remote village of Viti Levu, and a 5 kW electrification project at Wairiki on Taveuni (18).

22. In *Samoa,* four hydro projects with installed capacity ranging from 400-3,500 kW were completed from 1981 to 1984 on Upolu Island. The Government policy was to reduce diesel fuel consumption by existing diesel power plants as much as possible. There were a number of potential hydro sites on Upolu Island, i.e. Malololelei (2,000 kW),

Afiamalu pumped-storage (5,000 kW) and Afulilo-Fagaloa (10,000 kW). The permeability and deep weathering of much of the volcanic land forms of Samoa resulted in considerable seepage losses of surface waters. Determination of the extent of these losses was a major difficulty in the planning of hydropower projects. The feasibility study of a wood-fuelled power plant using a mixture of old coconut stems, husks and chipped wood waste from a sawmill with a capacity of 6,000 kW had been undertaken. It was expected to provide firm power in the dry season when hydro plant outputs were low.

23. In *Solomon Islands,* many mini-hydro sites had been considered for implementation. The Lungga hydro project to supply electricity to Honiara had been studied in detail. A three-stage development with an ultimate installed capacity of 21 MW was included in the national development plan of 1980-1984. Malaita Island had good potential for mini-hydro power schemes and reconnaissance had been undertaken on the Malu'u, Kwaitoa and Manakwai rivers. In Santa Ysabel Island, an interim design had been completed for a mini-hydropower scheme on the Jejevo River to supply electricity to the provincial capital Buala. At Atoifi, an existing 50 kW hydropower plant had provided electricity to a mission hospital since 1974. Construction of a 30 kW mini-hydro scheme on the Manakwai River on Malaita Island was nearing completion in 1983. The lack of technical manpower and financial resources was identified as the two main constraints for the mini-hydro development programme. Another major problem was the long distance from the capital to some islands.

24. In *Vanuatu,* a number of studies had been undertaken for identifying some potential hydro sites. A project site on the Teouma River (Efate Island), approximately 14 km from Port Vila, was proposed with a capacity of 2.1 MW and another project site on Sarakata River (Santo Island) near Luganville was proposed with a capacity of 1.84 MW. The permeability of the underlying volcanic formations and the frequency of Karstic formations contributed to making reservoir construction prohibitively expensive in most project areas.

III. CASE STUDIES

A. China

1. *Progress and prospects*

25. Up to the end of 1983, there were 76,000 mini-hydropower plants with a total installed capacity of 8,500 MW, and annual generation of 20,000 GWh (table 2). One third of the counties relied mainly on mini-hydro for their electricity supply. Of that total amount, 2,670 MW was interconnected to the national power grid, representing 31 per cent of the total mini-hydro capacity (13). The link with the national power grid helped mini-hydro plants to operate more efficiently and more economically. The exploitable potential of mini-hydro was estimated at about 70,000 MW, with an annual generation of 200-250 billion kWh (16).

2. *Institutional structure for planning and programming*

26. If the river was located within one province but involved more than one prefecture, the planning of the water resources development was carried out by the provincial bureau of water conservation. After approval of the development plan, the detailed design of the project was undertaken by the county if the unit capacity was less than 500 kW. The county-level hydropower agency was usually the responsible office dealing with the design, construction, operation and maintenance of mini-hydro plants. Many counties had a total installed capacity of 10-20 MW and distribution lines of several hundred kilometres in length.

27. In planning a mini-hydro station, the main concerns were geological exploration, hydrological investigation, selection of types of structures and layout, survey of power market, and estimation of construction cost. The feasibility study of a plant with a capacity greater than 500 kW had to be approved by the provincial department of water conservation. The design document of a plant with a unit capacity less than 500 kW had to be approved by the department which was responsible for water conservation at the prefectural or county-level.

28. A mini-hydro unit with a capacity less than 500 kW was usually manufactured by a local factory. In order to simplify the procedures of supply and to speed up the construction schedules, equipment had to be supplied by the manufacturer in complete sets. More than 100 factories with a total production capacity of 1,000 MW of mini-hydro machinery per year had been established.

3. *Operation and maintenance*

29. After the station was built and a small power grid set up, the management of supply, operation, personnel and financial resources was carried out by the local organization that built the station. State regulations stipulated that profits from mini-hydro plants should not be handed over to the public financial accounts. Instead, they should be used for mini-hydro development after all operating expenses and loan repayments had been paid. When the local grid was linked with the state grid, the ownership rights and management were not handed over to higher authority and the financial affairs and operating of the local grid remained unchanged.

Table 2. Hydropower potential and mini-hydropower potential of least developed and selected Pacific island countries

Country	Area (Km²)	Technical hydropower potential (MW)	Economic hydropower potential (MW)	Existing hydropower generating capacity (MW)	Existing mini-hydro generating capacity (MW)	Cost of completed mini-hydropower — Per kW installed ($US)	Identified mini-hydro project sites — Number	Identified mini-hydro project sites — MW
I. Least developed countries								
Afghanistan	652 090	5 000	...	265	–	–	–	–
Bangladesh	143 998	1 188	...	130	–	–	12	1.275
Bhutan	47 000	20 000[g]	...	3.5	3.5	–	–	–
Lao People's Democratic Republic	236 800	12 683[e]	...	153.8	3.8	...	10	45.7
Maldives	298	–	–	–	–	–	–	–
Nepal	140 797	...	27 000	113	2.72[d]	1 200-4 000	16	1.8
II. Selected Pacific island countries								
Fiji	18 272	301	...	80	...	...	20	...
Samoa	2 935	...	...	4.63	4.63	...	3	17.0
Solomon Islands	28 446	...	...	–	–	–	2	21.0
Tonga	699	–	–	–	–	–	–	–
Vanuatu	14 763	...	...	–	–	–	2	3.94
III. Selected developing countries								
China	9 596 961	378 000	...	25 600	8 500[a]	400-1 000[f]	...	70 000[a]
India	3 287 590	...	89 000	13 058	236.5[b]	1 250-2 500	...	5 000-10 000
Philippines	300 000	8 000	...	1 677	25-30[c]	1 300-2 400	100	120

[a] Small-scale hydropower with unit capacity below 6,000 kW or plant capacity below 12,000 kW. As of 1983.

[b] As of 1980, 82 mini-hydro stations, up to a unit size of 5,000 kW.

[c] As of 1982.

[d] As of 1984.

[e] Excluding the potential hydropower of the Mekong mainstream projects.

[f] 800-2 000 ¥RMB per kW: Source: (14)

[g] Source: (18), assuming 30 per cent load factor.

4. *Economic considerations*

30. The construction cost of mini-hydro plants varied widely owing to different topographic and hydrologic conditions. Generally speaking, a minimum cost of 600-800 yuan RMB (1 $US = 3.2 yuan RMB in 1985) per kW installed could be expected under very favourable conditions. The maximum cost could be ¥RMB 2,000 per kW. About ¥RMB 1,000 to ¥RMB 1,400 per kW was the average cost. The above figures were low compared with the costs of the large- and medium-sized hydropower stations currently under construction in China, ¥RMB 1,600 per kW.

31. It was very difficult to compare those cost figures in China with those of other countries, because the price system for labour and commodities was different. The special economic features of mini-hydro plants in China were: (a) short construction period and quick results; (b) full utilization of local labour and materials; and (c) local manufacturing of the machinery and equipment.

B. India

1. *Progress and prospects*

32. Mini-hydro development in India consisted of two categories: category I, small isolated hydropower projects in the hills, mainly the Himalayas, where small perennial streams were available; and category II, small installations in the plains which utilized larger discharges and low heads along irrigation canals and small dams. As of 1980, 82 mini-hydro stations, up to a unit capacity of 5 MW, were in operation with a total installed capacity of 236.5 MW. That included 68 mini-hydro stations, up to a unit capacity of 2 MW with a total installed capacity of 50 MW. In 1980, there were 37 mini-hydro stations with a total installed capacity of 211.5 MW under construction. A preliminary survey indicated the potentials of category I and category II to be of the order of 3 and 2 million kW respectively (1). (table 2)

2. *Institutional structure for planning and programming*

33. The overall planning was the responsibility of a central organization called the Central Electricity Authority. The actual execution of mini-hydro projects rested with the State authorities. The organizational structure for planning, investigation and execution varied from State to State, but generally speaking it was done by either the Government agencies or the State electricity boards which were semi-government organizations. After the commissioning of the units, the operation and maintenance of the power stations was entrusted to the State electricity boards. Supply of electric power to remote rural areas was being accorded a very high priority in India.

34. Considerable work had been done to assess the potential for minihydro schemes, and the hydropower potential assessment for plant capacity from 3 MW to 10 MW had already been done. For installations below 3 MW, further work was under way to assess its potential. It was found that desk studies were not sufficient, as it was observed from on-site visits that in many cases, even though the catchment area seemed big enough for a mini-hydro project, the stream was completely dry during some periods. It was decided that stream-flow gauging over a reasonable period was necessary before any investment decision was taken.

35. In site selection for isolated mini-hydro projects, two major factors taken into consideration were: (a) nearness of the load centre, to avoid, as far as possible, high voltage transmission lines; and (b) the potential load demand, which might include home lighting, small-scale industries, irrigation and water supply pumping.

36. As of 1980, the largest of the mini-hydro units manufactured locally had a capacity of 1,000 kW or so. Units

of 1,500-2,500 kW capacity were also being manufactured in the country.

3. *Operation and maintenance*

37. Because of the remoteness of most of those isolated mini-hydro stations, it was usually difficult to get trained personnel to operate and maintain them. Consequently, the trend was to design and manufacture units which were simple to run and maintain. Training of local young people was also essential.

4. *Economic consideration*

38. The conventional hydropower stations of large installed capacity had a capital cost ranging from Rs 3,000 to Rs 7,000 per kW at 1980 prices (Rs 7.93 = $US 1). The upper limit of the cost of the mini-hydro schemes considered economically feasible varied from Rs 8,000 to Rs 15,000 per kW. Other factors, such as urgent need as well as availability of resources of a particular State, also played an important part in the choice of scheme. The cost of the schemes recently completed or under construction generally ranged from Rs 10,000 to Rs 20,000 per kW.

C. The Philippines

1. *Progress and prospects*

39. As of 1981, three mini-hydro plants with a total installed capacity of 500 kW were in operation. A programme to install 300 MW of total capacity at about 240 power plants was envisaged for completion before 1987. Some 100 potential sites with a total capacity of 120 MW had been identified. There were two primary objectives of that programme: (a) substituting for diesel-fuel-based electricity generation, and (b) stabilizing and reducing, if possible, the price of electricity for the rural population.

2. *Institutional structure for planning and programming*

40. The National Electrification Administration had developed a nation-wide system of electricity distribution co-operatives. Over 100 co-operatives provided decentralized management centres in all provinces. They made field investigations, collected data, oversaw design consultants and construction contractors. They owned and operated the power plants.

41. Experienced engineering firms existed in the Philippines; however, they had limited experience specifically on mini-hydro plants. Under Asian Development Bank funding, an expatriate consulting firm would provide, for a limited period, a design review function which would allow

the local firms to expand their mini-hydro expertise. The local construction industry was fully competent in the construction of mini-hydro projects.

42. By the end of 1981, three power plants with an aggregate capacity of 500 kW were designed and manufactured with technology available domestically. In 1982-1983, another 10-12 MW of capacity was planned to be installed using a mixture of domestic and imported designs and with local manufacture except for some electrical components.

3. *Operation and maintenance*

43. At the end of 1981, electric power grids covered almost every town on the eight major islands (over 90 per cent of the population). As far as the mini-hydro plants were concerned, each co-operative was owned by its members. There was a board of directors elected on a district basis and a general manager appointed by the board. The co-operatives investigated, constructed, operated and maintained the mini-hydro plants.

4. *Economic considerations*

44. For planning purposes the criterion of $US 1,000 at the 1982 price level was used for its civil works (1). High-head system equipment might cost from $US 350 to $US 500 per kW for units above the capacity of 500 kW. At the other end of the scale, the cost of a small unit of low-head could exceed $US 1,400 per kW. A criterion for the development of a mini-hydro site was that the generation costs should be equal to or less than those of the grid in the area, which was about 6 United States cents per kWh.

IV. BRIEF REVIEW OF MINI-HYDRO TECHNOLOGY AND MEASURES OF REDUCING CONSTRUCTION COST

45. During the last two decades considerable impetus has been given to mini-hydro development, resulting in world-wide acceptance of its economic feasibility. Mini-hydro technology is a mature technology and is widely available in many developing countries. The cost of hydropower is highly site specific and the present technological improvements are directed towards the reduction of cost which can be effected by adopting standardized turbines and generator sets, simple civil engineering and utilization of local materials and manpower.

46. There are many modified and innovative designs of turbines exclusively for mini-hydro generation. In the process of developing turbines, certain innovative design changes have been brought about, such as the Turgo turbines

in the impulse category and the tube, bulb and rim turbines in the reaction category. All these types have high operating efficiency. A third category, which is the cross-flow turbine, has medium efficiency, but is of a much simpler and cheaper design and is essentially suitable for micro- and mini-hydro plants. For selecting the best type of turbine, many factors have to be taken into consideration, such as operating head, the variation of flow, cost of civil engineering works, efficiency and cost of turbines, operation and maintenance costs.

47. One of the significant advances that has been made in recent years is the adoption of electronic load control. Formerly, complex mechanical water flow governors were used to control the turbine speed and thereby the voltage and frequency of the electric output. Their mechanical complexity and unreliability contributed greatly to the cost of mini-hydro projects. Now electronic load controllers are available as the most reliable method of controlling the output of mini-hydro plants.

48. Penstock design and construction are a substantial part of the cost of a mini-hydro project. Wood-stove pipes, steel-lined or pre-stressed concrete pipes have been successfully used instead of steel pipes with economical results.

49. Local manufacture is usually a way of saving both foreign exchange and local expenses. This is possible because most civil works and conventional small turbines have a high labour component. In China, the turbines are manufactured and civil engineering works are undertaken by the communities who will own and operate the mini-hydropower plant. The generators and transformers are usually manufactured in regional factories. The know-how is brought in by members of other communities having experience in the same activity. As shown in table 2, the per kW construction cost of completed mini-hydropower plants in China is much lower than that in other countries. One of the main reasons is the wide use of local labour, materials and technology.

50. A country equipped with casting and forging facilities as well as relatively sophisticated metal-fabricating equipment should be able to acquire a much wider range of mini-hydro technological capabilities. While conceiving a mini-hydro development programme, it is essential to keep in mind the overall foreseeable development of the industrial infrastructure of the country.

51. While turbines are difficult to standardize, the generators, transformers and associated regulating equipment can be restricted to a limited number of standard sizes. For simplification, in all cases, the equipment should be closely associated with the national bureau of standards. A reduction in the total number and complexity of the parts will lead to reductions in the cost of manufacture, and easier as well as cheaper maintenance.

XVI. Potential for small dams and mini-hydropower generation in the least developed
countries and developing island countries of ESCAP region

175

V. ALTERNATIVE SOURCES OF ELECTRIC POWER GENERATION AND ECONOMY OF MINI-HYDROPOWER

A. Diesel generation

52. At present the diesel power plant is the most popular type of electric power generation in small towns, factories and other enterprises. The capital cost of a diesel station is comparatively low. The starting and shutting-down of a generating unit is rather simple and requires only a small number of operators. However, all the least developed countries of the region and the Pacific island countries import diesel generation units and fuel from abroad, and the price of diesel has gone up very rapidly since the two crises of oil in 1973 and 1980, although a fall has been experienced recently. In order to save foreign currency, these countries are making efforts in seeking other economic means of electric power generation to meet the increasing demand or to replace the inefficient obsolete diesel power plants.

53. The construction cost of a diesel power plant varies with unit size and location. Assuming capital cost of $US 700 per kW for a 1-2 MW unit, a 7 per cent interest rate, a useful life of 20 years, annual operation and maintenance costs, excluding fuel, of 5 per cent of capital cost, and a plant factor of 50 per cent, the fixed cost per kWh generation is estimated at 2.3 United States cents per kWh. The international market price of diesel fuel has varied greatly in recent years. Assuming the price of diesel oil at plant $US 35 per barrel and fuel efficiency at 0.3 kg per kWh, the fuel cost is roughly estimated at 7.6 cents per kWh. Total cost per kWh of diesel generation is therefore estimated to be of the order of 9.9 cents. If the price of diesel oil were $US 15 per barrel, the fuel cost and total generation cost per kWh would become 3.2 cents and 5.5 cents respectively.

B. Wood-fired power generation

54. Power generation utilizing wood-fired steam is a proven technology that is already in commercial operation in the Philippines. The Government of Samoa has made a detailed study on the wood-fired power plant project. The project is for a 2 x 2.5 MW plant with capital cost of $US 10 million, or $US 2,000 per kW installed (5). The biomass fuel is expected to be based on senile coconut stems arising from a coconut replanting scheme. Assuming a sustainable yield of 20 cu m per hectare per year, 0.885 tons per cu m and ultimate annual generation of 30 million kWh, a dedicated energy plantation to support a 5 MW plant could require up to 5,000 hectares of land.

55. Assuming capital cost of $US 2,000 per kW, 7 per cent interest rate, useful life 30 years, annual operation and maintenance costs, excluding fuel, of 5 per cent of capital cost, and plant factor 50 per cent, the fixed cost per kWh generated is estimated at 6.0 United States cents. Based on fuelwood requirements of 3 kg greenwood per kWh generated and $US 15 per ton of greenwood at power plant, the fuel cost is estimated at 4.5 cents per kWh. The total cost per kWh generated is estimated to be of the order of 10.5 cents.

C. Solar photovoltaics

56. Solar photovoltaics is a small electricity generating device, which is favourable for individual house lighting. The quality and convenience of light are higher than those of the benzene/kerosene light system. In India, under the national solar photovoltaics energy demonstration programme, total production as of May 1984 was 22 kW. Up to May 1984, nearly 20 remote villages had been supplied with street lights through these systems and more than 130 solar pumps had been installed under the demonstration programme (18). In Fiji, three villages were electrified with solar photovoltaic units in 1982/83. Each village received about 20 units with a capacity of 35 watts each. The unit cost including installation, is $US 584. However, the unit controller ($US 60) and battery ($US 90) has a useful life of 4 and 3 years respectively (20). Assuming the useful life of the unit is 10 years and the interest rate 7 per cent, the annual cost is estimated at $US 135.1. If the unit provides light 4 hours a day and 365 days a year, the cost per kWh is estimated to be of the order of 260 United States cents.

D. Economy of mini-hydro power

57. In the case of mini-hydro power generation, the cost per kWh mainly depends on two factors: capital cost per kilowatt of firm power and plant factor of the power plant. As shown in table 2, the construction costs per kilowatt installed vary widely. Its range is $US 400 to $US 1,000 in China, $US 1,250 to $US 2,500 in India, $US 1,300 to $US 2,400 in the Philippines and $US 1,200 to $US 4,000 in Nepal. It depends to a great extent on the magnitude of hydraulic head and discharge, generating unit size, complexity and size of civil works, availability of technology and trained manpower for using local materials and manufacturing turbines, generators and other equipment. Generally speaking, with the same technology, the mini-hydro plants of higher heads and larger sizes, cost less per kW installed.

58. The second main factor, the plant factor, depends on the availability of a flow-regulating facility, such as reservoir or pondage, and the characteristics of the power market. A large reservoir will enhance the firm power output in

the dry season significantly, and improve the plant factor. If the customers use electricity mainly for domestic lighting, the load factor (or plant factor for an isolated plant) of the small system may be as low as 20 per cent. If the customers consist of agricultural processing industries, manufacturing industries, irrigation pumping and domestic lighting, the load factor can be as high as 50 per cent. Another way to improve the plant factor is to interconnect the isolated plant with a large regional power grid. A larger grid with diversified customers usually has a higher load factor. The outputs of the secondary power in the wet season can also be absorbed by the larger power grid by the interconnection. However, the cost of the required additional transmission lines must be considered.

59. Assuming a capital cost $US 1,000 per kW installed, interest rate of 7 per cent, a useful life of 30 years, annual operation and maintenance expenses of 1 per cent of capital cost, and an annual plant factor of 50 per cent, the cost per kWh generated is estimated at 2.07 United States cents. If the plant factor is changed to 20 per cent, the unit cost becomes 5.17 cents per kWh. If the capital cost is increased to $US 2,000 per kW, the unit cost becomes 10.34 cents per kWh, with a plant factor of 20 per cent.

VI. CONCLUSIONS AND RECOMMENDATIONS

60. From the preceding sections, the following conclusions and recommendations may be made.

(1) In all of the least developed countries and Pacific island countries included in this study, the public electric power grids mainly supply electricity only to the capital and a few major towns. In the least developed countries, only 4 to 6 per cent of the population have access to electricity (table 1). In order to promote agricultural industries, increase employment opportunities and improve living standards in rural areas, there is a great need to develop electric power resources.

(2) Many least developed countries, such as Afghanistan, Bhutan, Lao People's Democratic Republic and Nepal, are endowed with vast potentials of mini-hydro power resources, which can be economically exploited, while many Pacific island countries, such as Fiji, Samoa, Solomon Islands and Vanuatu, have identified a number of mini-hydro sites which are capable of generating substantial amounts of electricity.

(3) In planning a mini-hydro scheme, considerable efforts are required in geological exploration, hydrological investigation, selection of types of machinery, equipment, structures and layout, survey of power market, estimation of construction cost and related economic and financial

studies of alternative sources of electric energy. Each site has its own specific character. A great effort must be made to reduce the investment cost; otherwise many sites can never be feasible from the point of view of either national economy or the financial capability of local customers. Availability of technology, trained manpower and facilities for investigation and construction of structures utilizing local materials and labour, and in manufacturing of turbines and other equipment, play important roles in the reduction of capital costs of mini-hydro projects.

(4) The economy of a mini-hydro scheme is closely related to its scale, the prospective plant factor, and the operation of the plant. The local requirements of electric power and the possibility of interconnection with the regional power grid should be carefully considered during the planning stage.

(5) With a capital cost of $US 2,000 per kW and a plant factor of 50 per cent or higher, the mini-hydro project would become economically justifiable as compared with the diesel power plant, wood-fired power generation and solar photovoltaics.

(6) Local governments of the least developed countries and the Governments of the developing Pacific island countries lack trained manpower, adequate financial resources and industrial support for the planning and construction of mini-hydro schemes to meet their electrification needs. Assistance from central Government and/or foreign countries in training of personnel, technology transfer and financial support are indispensable.

(7) It is recommended that countries:

(a) Pay increased attention to the institutional and training needs of the local governments for the proper planning and implementation of mini-hydro development projects;

(b) Carry out training courses and research programmes on the new technology to reduce the capital costs of mini-hydro projects;

(c) Formulate policies for supplying electric power to rural and remote areas in the context of national energy development plans.

61. The Committee might wish to recommend more adequate financial support to the concerned international organizations and the ESCAP/UNIDO/UNDP Asia-Pacific Regional Network for Small Hydropower in their efforts to carry out the following:

(a) Study the socio-economic benefit of rural electrification and advisory missions on planning and management of rural electrification;

XVI. Potential for small dams and mini-hydropower generation in the least developed
countries and developing island countries of ESCAP region

177

(b) Strengthen the necessary assistance on request to the least developed countries and the Pacific island countries in the investigation and development of mini-hydro potential;

(c) Promote development and research on the manufacturing of equipment for mini-hydropower plants in the ESCAP member countries;

(d) Disseminate relevant information and experience concerning economic development of mini-hydro potential in developing countries of the region.

REFERENCES

1. ESCAP, *Small Hydropower Development, Renewable Sources of Energy*, vol. IV (1982).

2. Asian Institute of Technology, *Small Hydropower for Asian Rural Development,* edited by Colin R. Elliott (1983).

3. *Nepal: Issues and Options in the Energy Sector,* UNDP/World Bank Report No. 4474-NEP (August 1983).

4. *Bangladesh: Issues and Options in the Energy Sector,* UNDP/World Bank Report No. 3873-BD (October 1982).

5. *Western Samoa: Issues and Options in the Energy Sector,* UNDP/World Bank, Report No. 5497-WSO (June 1985).

6. ESCAP, *Water As a Factor in Energy Resources Development,* Water Resources Series No. 60 (1985).

7. *Economic Survey, Fiscal Year 1984/85,* (Government of Nepal, 1985).

8. Interim Mekong Committee, *Annual Report,* 1985.

9. Interim Mekong Committee, *Inventory of Promising Tributary Projects in the Lower Mekong Basin,* vol, II Laos, WRD/MKG/INF/L. 408 (Rev. 1), (December 1970).

10. *Newsletter of the Asia Pacific Regional Network for Small Hydro Power* No. 4 (1985), Hangzhou Regional Centre for Small Hydro Power, ISSN 0256-3118.

11. ESCAP, *Electric Power in Asia and the Pacific, 1981 and 1982* (1984).

12. ESCAP, *Proceedings of the Meeting on Water Resources Development in the South Pacific,* Water Resources Series No. 57 (1983).

13. Deng Bingli, "Small hydro in China: progress and prospects", *Water Power and Dam Construction* (February 1985).

14. Cheng Xuemin, "Small hydro: lessons from experience", *Water World* (December 1985).

15. Ministry of Water Resources, *Chinese Experiences in Mini-hydropower Generation,* (United Nations Industrial Development Organization, 1985).

16. Bai Lin, "The role of small hydro in rural electrification", *Water Power and Dam Construction* (February 1985).

17. Solomon Islands, *National Development Plan, 1980-1984,* vols. I and III (April 1980).

18. ESCAP, *Regional New and Renewable Sources of Energy, Development Programme for Asia and the Pacific* (1985).

19. *Vanuatu: Issues and Options in the Energy Sector,* UNDP/World Bank Report No. 5577-VA (June 1985).

20. Herbert A. Wade, "Solar photovoltaic lighting applications in Fiji", *ESCAP Energy News,* vol. 2, No. 1 (August 1984).

Part Five :

ESCAP COMMITTEE ON NATURAL RESOURCES
THIRTEENTH SESSION, 14-20 OCTOBER 1986

XVII. REPORT OF THE ESCAP COMMITTEE ON NATURAL RESOURCES ON ITS THIRTEENTH SESSION, 14-20 OCTOBER 1986*

A. SUMMARY OF CONCLUSIONS AND RECOMMENDATIONS**

The significant conclusions and recommendations of the Committee are listed below.

The Committee:

1. Commended the secretariat for the two documents prepared in the context to review the overall progress made in the implementation of the Mar del Plata Action Plan by the member countries of the region (paragraph 12).

2. Noted the regional review in the documents on the current status of the implementation of the plan in 22 countries and areas of the region which had responded to ESCAP's questionnaire and the additional information provided by the representatives from 10 countries during the session and recognized that despite considerable constraints significant overall progress had been achieved in implementing the Plan (paragraph 13 and 14).

3. Noted the steps taken by the countries in the region in achieving the goals of the International Drinking Water Supply and Sanitation Decade. It also noted ESCAP's efforts in promoting TCDC in water related activities and urged the secretariat to continue these efforts (paragraph 16).

4. Endorsed, in general, the recommendations contained in the two secretariat documents (paragraph 17).

5. Noting that implementation of the Mar del Plata Action Plan requires support measures both at national, regional and international levels, encouraged the least developed and developing countries to mobilize resources from within and urged the donor countries and international or United Nations agencies to assist them by bilateral and/or multilateral arrangements in financing water resources development projects. It further noted that regional and international perspectives of water resources development should also be considered (paragraph 19).

6. Commended the secretariat for the preparation of the two background documents which dealt with environmental issues of water resources development in the region (paragraph 21).

---

* Formerly issued as E/ESCAP/539.

** This summary does not form part of the report adopted by the Committee.

7. Recognized the importance of integrating environmental considerations into water resources development projects and the necessity of environmental management in this sector (paragraph 22).

8. Noted the major environmental problems usually encountered in the development of water resources in the region and stressed the importance of monitoring, studying and assessing of environmental implications of water resources development projects and desirability of public participation in environmental assessment of such projects (paragraph 24).

9. Recognized that environmental impact assessment (EIA) was one of the most effective means to integrate environmental considerations into water resources development projects and pointed out that information and experiences on EIA application should be widely disseminated among the countries of the region (paragraphs 26 and 28).

10. Generally endorsed the recommendations as included in the two background documents and expressed its view that the secretariat should encourage and support the exchange of information and experiences regarding environmental management in water resources development particularly through organizing pertinent workshops/seminars (paragraph 29).

11. Endorsed the contents, particularly the conclusions and recommendations of the background document on development of ground water resources, and commended the secretariat for preparing a useful and comprehensive document which provided a sound basis for ground water development policy in the region (paragraph 30).

12. Noted that in accordance with the decision of the forty-second session of ESCAP, the report on problems and prospects of the development of shared water resources in the region had not been prepared by the secretariat and consequently not presented for discussion (paragraph 38).

13. Taking into account the preponderance of views of the member countries, decided that the secretariat prepares a general report on shared water resources development in various regions of the world. The report shall also include case studies of successful implementation of shared water resources development. This report based on the study should be included in the work programme and be presented at the fourteenth Committee session. In preparing such a report careful consideration should be given to the objections raised by one delegation and the report would not cover bilateral problems (paragraph 40).

14. Noted the strong objection raised by one delegation. Also noted that every country had the right to associate itself or not with every United Nations activity, but if the member countries who are interested in particular activities for their socioeconomic development they should not be barred from such activities (paragraph 41).

15. Commended the progress achieved by the secretariat in the implementation of the work programme in the water resources sector (paragraph 42).

16. Expressed its appreciation on the report on the potential for small dams and mini-hydropower generation in the least developed countries and developing island countries and generally endorsed the recommendations therein (paragraph 43).

17. Considered two reports related to energy resources programme: one containing a description of activities undertaken since the last Committee session, the other containing an overview of the contribution of new and renewable sources of energy to the regional energy supply (paragraph 49).

18. In commenting on the reports, commended the efforts of the secretariat and specifically the Regional Network on Biomass, Solar and Wind Energy in completing the second focal points meeting (paragraph 53).

19. Endorsed the two reports (paragraph 55).

20. Commended the substantial progress achieved by the secretariat in the implementation of the work programme in mineral sector including the training activities in various areas of mineral resources exploration and development. Expressed satisfaction with the activities undertaken in the appraisal of geology and distribution of mineral and hydrocarbon resources in the region, compilation of geological and thematic maps, and preparation of technical publications on special topics (paragraph 57).

21. Recognized the need for coastal countries to obtain better knowledge of the marine resources placed under coastal countries' jurisdiction by the United Nations Convention on the Law of the Sea so as to promote effective planning, development and management of these resources. Endorsed the secretariat's programme on Marine Resources and expressed its support for the proposed studies and related missions (paragraph 63).

22. Supported and endorsed all the activities of the regional remote sensing programme and commended the programme for its performance (paragraph 67).

23. Endorsed the TCDC activities under the project and recommended that such activities should be expanded during the next phase (paragraph 69).

24. Noted the progress on the work of the Interagency Task Force on Water for Asia and the Pacific (paragraph 69).

25. Noted that a new programme element 2.5 Non-conventional water development had been introduced in the draft programme of work and priorities 1988-1989 of the water resources programme (paragraph 79).

26. Generally endorsed the draft programme of work, 1988-1989, and in particular supported the activity on the regional network for training in water resources development. Assigned high priority to programme elements 2.1, 2.2 and 2.4 (paragraphs 80 and 83).

27. Endorsed the changes suggested in the work programme of the energy resources programme for 1986-1987 (paragraph 85).

28. Generally endorsed the 1988-1989 draft programme of work and priorities of the energy resources programme while noting the reservation expressed by one delegation in taking up the programme element 3.4 (ii) concerning a technical study: Study on resources options for electric power generation in the 1990s (paragraph 86).

29. Made suggestions that (a) the lowest priority given on the element 2.2 should be lifted, (b) the project description sheets under 2.2 and 2.3, the activities concerning the solar photovoltaic project conceived under the Tokyo Programme of Action, in particular, the second phase of the project "the Regional Co-operation in Research, Development and Demonstration of Solar Photovoltaic Power System for Rural Areas" should be implemented under programme element 2.2 and the possible availability of financial contribution should be indicated in the project description sheet (paragraph 87).

30. Did not propose any changes in the programme of work and priorities of the mineral resources programme for 1986-1987 and endorsed the draft programme of work and priorities for 1988-1989 (paragraph 91).

31. Suggested, as regard the programme element 1.2 on technical support to regional and subregional projects, that the secretariat co-operate within the East Asia Resources Assessment Programme that is currently being formulated and implemented under the combined auspices of CCOP, the Circum-Pacific Map Project (CPMP) and the International Union of Geologic Sciences (IUGS) (paragraph 93).

32. Manifested its continuing support to the Regional Mineral Resources Development Centre (RMRDC) (paragraph 97).

33. Endorsed the programme of work and priorities of the marine resources programme for 1986-1987 and

the draft programme of work and priorities, 1988-1989 (paragraph 100).

34. Expressed its appreciation that collaboration had been established with the Office of the Special Representative of the Secretary General for the Law of the Sea and that close co-operation had been maintained with CCOP and CCOP/SOPAC, and furthermore, was hopeful that the co-operation would be continued even after the two intergovernmental bodies had become fully independent (paragraph 101).

35. Did not propose any additional changes in the programme of work and priorities of the cartography and remote sensing programme for 1986-1987 other than those contained in the document and endorsed the draft programme of work and priorities for 1988-1989 (paragraph 105).

36. Noted that most of the activities indicated in the programme changes and those under the draft programme of work and priorities for 1988-1989 will be implemented by the ESCAP Regional Remote Sensing Programme which is funded by UNDP (paragraph 106).

37. Also pointed out that training activities on cartography and remote sensing should be implemented within the existing facilities or in co-operation with established mechanisms in the region (paragraph 107).

38. Expressed concern that there is no cartographic project under the draft programme of work and priorities for 1988-1989 (paragraph 108).

39. Endorsed, after modifications, the provisional agenda for the fourteenth session of the Committee on Natural Resources (paragraph 114).

40. Endorsed the provisional agenda for the sixteenth session of the Committee on Natural Resources (paragraph 115).

B. REPORT OF THE SESSION

I. Organization of the session

1. The Comittee on Natural Resources held its thirteenth session at Bangkok, from 14 to 20 October 1986.

Attendance

2. The session was attended by the following member countries of ESCAP: Australia, Bangladesh, China, Democratic Kampuchea, France, India, Indonesia, Japan, Lao People's Democratic Republic, Malaysia, Netherlands, Pakistan, Philippines, Republic of Korea, Thailand, USSR,

United Kingdom, United States, and Viet Nam. Representatives of Finland, the Federal Republic of Germany and Turkey also attended in accordance with paragraph 9 of the terms of reference of ESCAP.

3. The following United Nations bodies and specialized agencies were represented: United Nations Department of Technical Co-operation for Development (UNDTCD), United Nations Development Programme (UNDP), United Nations Environment Programme (UNEP), Food and Agriculture Organization of the United Nations (FAO), World Bank, and United Nations Industrial Development Organization (UNIDO). Observers from the International Commission on Irrigation and Drainage (ICID) and the Asian Institute of Technology (AIT) were also present.

Opening of the session

4. The Executive Secretary of ESCAP opened the session.

5. In his opening statement, the Executive Secretary said it was essential that all natural resources available in the region be developed fully and used optimally in order to raise the living standards of the region's huge population.

6. Refering to the principal subject of the session which was water, he noted that while the resource was apparently abundant, it was becoming increasingly scarce in terms of availability, distribution and quality. Some Asian countries suffered from acute shortages of water while many battled against periodic flooding. He stressed the extreme importance of concerted efforts in the proper planning and development of the region's water resources, to ensure their wisest use for the benefit of all people and with consideration to possible environmental impacts.

7. Refering to issues to be considered by the Committee, the Executive Secretary noted that the region was endowed with vast ground-water resources. He requested the Committee to provide guidance to the secretariat in assisting countries with the development of those resources, as well as on follow-up actions relating to environmental issues in developing water resources and to the implementation of the Mar del Plata Plan of Action.

8. He noted that a good number of member countries had built up considerable expertise in developing their national water resources. However, there was potential for further collective efforts at the subregional and regional levels, with the agreement of members concerned, as stipulated in the Commission's terms of reference. Beside support activities, there was considerable scope for technical co-operation among the region's developing countries. The technical know-how of some countries could significantly boost the efforts of others less well endowed. He expressed ESCAP's readiness to take up a greater catalytic

role in this field, if members so desire and provided that financial support for the secretariat's activities in water resources development and management was increased.

Election of officers

9. The Committee elected H.E. Mr. Benjamin T. Leong (Philippines) as Chairman; and Mr. Boonyok Vadhana-phuti (Thailand) and Mr. Hiroomi Sakai (Japan) as Vice-Chairmen. It also elected Mr. Sarbini Ronodibroto (Indonesia) as Rapporteur-cum-Chairman of the Drafting Committee.

Adoption of the agenda

10. The Committee considered the agenda as presented in documents E/ESCAP/NR.13/L.1 and E/ESCAP/NR.13/L.2. One delegation stated that item 7 should not be in the agenda of the Committee as the Commission at its forty-second session had decided that the secretariat need not prepare the report envisaged under item 7. Another delegation stated that since the Commission in its forty-second session had expected that the thirteenth session of the Committee would be in a position to consider the matter it was pertinent in all appropriateness to retain the agenda item 7 as presented in the ESCAP documents.

11. The Committee adopted the following agenda:

    1. Opening of the session.

    2. Election of officers.

    3. Adoption of the agenda.

    4. Progress in the implementation of the Mar del Plata Action Plan.

    5. Environmental issues of water resources development in the ESCAP region.

    6. Development of ground-water resources.

    7. Report on problems and prospects of the development of shared water resources in the region.

    8. Activities of ESCAP in regard to natural resources:

        (a) Water resources;

        (b) Energy resources;

        (c) Mineral resources;

        (d) Marine resources;

        (e) Cartography and remote sensing.

    9. Activities of other international bodies in the appraisal, development and management of water resources.

10. Consideration of the draft programme of work and priorities, 1988-1989; and programme changes in the programme of work, 1986-1987:

    (a) Water resources;

    (b) Energy resources;

    (c) Mineral resources;

    (d) Marine resources;

    (e) Cartography and remote sensing.

11. Consideration of the agenda and arrangements for subsequent sessions of the Committee.

12. Other matters.

13. Adoption of the report.

II. Progress in the implementation of the Mar del Plata Action Plan
(Agenda item 4)

12. The Committee considered documents E/ESCAP/NR.13/4, E/ESCAP/NR.13/5 and E/ESCAP/NR.13/5/Corr.1 prepared by the ESCAP secretariat and noted the information provided therein. It commended the secretariat for these documents prepared in the context to review the overall progress made in the implementation of the Mar del Plata Action Plan by the member countries of the region. In pursuance of the Economic and Social Council resolution 1981/80 of 24 July 1981, the Secretary-General, in consultation with the concerned organizations of the United Nations system, formulated a questionnaire, "Progress in the implementation of the Mar del Plata Action Plan: present status of and prospects for water resources development at the national level," as a means of gathering the necessary information from Member States for evaluation. This activity was undertaken as part of a global review.

13. The Committee noted the regional review on the current status of the implementation of the Plan in 22 countries and areas of the region, which responded to the questionnaire, covering nine main areas: (i) policy, planning, legislation and institutional arrangements; (ii) shared water resources development; (iii) assessment of water resources; (iv) flood loss management; (v) International Drinking Water Supply and Sanitation Decade; (vi) water resources development and use for agriculture; (vii) education, training and public participation; (viii) research and development; and (ix) technical co-operation among developing countries in water resources development.

14. The Committee noted with interest the additional information provided by the representatives from 10 countries in their respective statements and country papers

concerning the topics covered by the Mar del Plata Action Plan and recognized that despite considerable constraints significant overall progress had been achieved in implementing the Plan.

15. Some of the problems highlighted by a number of countries were: experienced or anticipated problems with major structures approaching the end of their useful lives requiring considerable public investments for rehabilitation or replacement; inadequacy of networks for collecting water resources data; their processing, storage, retrieval and dissemination; lack of water resources assessment especially ground-water; flood hazard; deterioration of lands due to water logging and salinization; lack of trained manpower and equipment; and inadequate financial resources.

16. The Committee noted the steps taken by the countries in the region in achieving the goals of the International Drinking Water Supply and Sanitation Decade. It also noted ESCAP's efforts in promoting TCDC in water related activities and urged the secretariat to continue these efforts.

17. The Committee endorsed, in general, the recommendations contained in secretariat documents, summarized as:

(a) The countries which do not have a central mechanism for co-ordinating the competing uses of water may consider establishing one to ensure integrated and optimum development of water resources.

(b) The countries which have not formulated a national master water plan, or which need their existing plan to be updated, may consider giving serious consideration to this matter.

(c) The countries which need amendments to, or enactment of adequate water legislation may consider initiating steps to frame and enforce such an instrument.

(d) Pricing structures need to be revised towards recovering fixed and recurrent costs. Efforts should be made to reduce government subsidy and to generate funds for efficient maintenance and operation of the projects. Conservation incentives should be introduced.

(e) Development of human resources is an area which should be given high priority consideration. Greater efforts are required in the field of training at all levels. In addition to what the countries have established at the national level, regional co-operation would be useful in overcoming deficiencies in training needs. Countries which have the capacities could accept trainees from other member States.

(f) The need for fellowship assistance for training abroad, for expatriate expertise, and for the supply of project equipment has been expressed by most of the countries, therefore avenues should be explored to meet such needs.

(g) It was further urged that the countries concerned increase their efforts in: extending data collection networks; introducing computers for data processing and management; adopting investigation programme for water resources assessment; improving structural and non-structural arrangements for mitigating flood losses and drainage problems.

18. Some of the delegations in particular noted the need for promoting research and introduction of advanced technology, improved planning, development and management; and protecting the scarce water resources for equitable distribution. Some delegations noted that limiting and eliminating the arms race under the conditions of peace and security and partial diversion of funds therefrom could be a source of additional funds for development of natural resources in the ESCAP region. Some delegations, however, regretted that matter had been introduced as it was outside the mandate of the Committee and was irrelevant in the context of the subject under discussion.

19. The Committee noted that implementation of the Mar del Plata Action Plan, which encompasses a large spectrum of activities at national, regional and international levels, requires support measures both at national and international levels. Least developed and developing countries are encouraged to mobilize resources from within. The donor countries and international or United Nations agencies are also urged to assist them by bilateral and/or multilateral arrangements in financing water resources development projects, supporting the efforts for national self-reliance. It was further noted that regional and international perspective of water resources development should also be considered.

20. The secretariat noted that completed questionnaire received after the finalization of the documents would be incorporated in subsequent review.

III. Environmental issues of water resources development in the ESCAP region
(Agenda item 5)

21. The Committee considered documents E/ESCAP/NR. 13/11 and E/ESCAP/NR.13/13 which dealt with environmental issues of water resources development in the region and commended the secretariat for the preparation of these background papers.

22. The Committee recognized the importance of integrating environmental considerations into water resources development projects and the necessity for environmental management in this sector.

23. Several delegations, in their statements and country papers, highlighted the environmental problems associated with water resources development, and presented brief accounts of administrative and technical measures adopted towards achieving rational utilization and protection of water resources. One delegation provided some information and data pertaining to his country to replace corresponding information contained in the secretariat paper E/ESCAP/NR.13/11.

24. The Committee noted that major environmental problems usually encountered in the development of water resources in the region included resettlement of population, inundation of valuable lands, erosion, degradation of river channels, siltation. of reservoirs, earthquake inducement, changes in microclimate, spread of water-related diseases, degradation of water quality, depletion and contamination of aquifers, land subsidence, intrusion of saline water leading to degradation of agricultural lands and depletion of flora, fauna and fishery resources. It stressed the importance of monitoring, studying and assessing of environmental implications of water resources development projects and desirability of public participation in environmental assessment of such projects.

25. The Committee considered that potential adverse effects of such projects could be avoided or alleviated if they were clearly identified, and environmental considerations were integrated into all phases of water resources development: planning, construction and operation.

26. The Committee recognized that environmental impact assessment (EIA) was one of the most effective means to integrate environmental considerations into water resources development projects. It further noted that several countries had been using various EIA procedures and methods.

27. The Committee noted that several methods were available for screening of projects requiring EIA. Taking into account common problems and experiences in application of EIA, the Committee considered that it would be useful to utilize the available methods for identifying projects which would require EIA.

28. The Committee noted that there were a number of methodologies for application of EIA each of which had its advantages and disadvantages. Consequently, in applying EIA to water resources development projects, a combination of methods may be sought, taking into account environmental information base and local conditions. In this context, it was pointed out that information and experiences on EIA application should be widely disseminated among the countries of the region.

29. The Committee generally endorsed the recommendations as included in the documents presented under agenda

item 5, and expressed its view that the secretariat should encourage and support the exchange of information and experiences regarding environmental management in water resources development particularly through organizing pertinent workshops/seminars. A view was expressed that a regional study on various aspects of environmental implications of large-scale water resources development projects should be carried out.

IV. Development of ground water resources
(Agenda item 6)

30. The Committee considered document E/ESCAP/NR. 13/6 prepared by the secretariat and endorsed its contents, particularly its conclusions and recommendations.

31. The Committee commended the secretariat for preparing a useful and comprehensive document which provided a sound basis for ground water development policy in the region.

32. Following the general endorsement of the conclusions and recommendations in the document, one delegation suggested the inclusion of one paragraph, urging countries to recognize their obligation to inform, consult and negotiate with other concerned countries in the planning and development of their shared transnational hydrogeologically connected ground water resources and proceed in a spirit of mutual trust and co-operation in all their activities affecting the common resources. Another delegation indicated that this matter concerned all countries of the world and was engaging the attention of several international bodies and should not therefore, be included, particularly, in view of complexity of determining hydrogeological continuity of aquifers.

33. The United States delegation suggested that the aspect of contamination related to human settlements should be given adequate emphasis in view of the increasing industrialization of countries in the region. It was also pointed out that according to the United States experience widespread distribution of low levels of pollution, particularly those of some organic compounds, were more deleterious and moving faster through the ground than anticipated. Therefore, it suggested that such experiences be highlighted by the secretariat for the benefit of the countries in the region, and for this purpose, it offered to provide the secretariat with a selected list of United States publications on such hazards.

34. The USSR delegation, in endorsing the ESCAP document, emphasized the importance of the conjunctive use of surface and ground water resources and provided information on the experiences on integrated ground and surface water management in arid zones of the USSR.

35. The Committee noted with interest additional and updated information provided by a number of delegations regarding the status of ground-water resources development in their respective countries. The representatives of member countries in their statements informed the Committee of the aquifer conditions in their countries, stressed the importance of undertaking hydrogeological investigations and preparation of hydrogeological maps, presented brief accounts of the problems they had experienced related to ground-water development, and emphasized the conjunctive use of surface and ground-water resources.

36. As regards technical co-operation among developing countries in the field of ground water resources development, the People's Republic of China announced the hosting of the Twenty-first Congress of the International Association of Hydrogeologists at Guilin, China, in October 1988. India also announced that its Central Ground Water Board is currently providing training facilities to professionals and sub-professionals of various countries in the region through various international agencies as well as bilateral assistance programmes.

37. The Committee noted with interest the activities of the World Bank in ground-water development (particularly with regard to the new information pertaining to deep artesian aquifers) and the assistance provided to the countries in the region in this field.

V. Report on problems and prospects of the development of shared water resources in the region
(Agenda item 7)

38. The Committee noted that in accordance with the decision of the forty-second session of ESCAP (para. 497 document E/ESCAP/536) the report on problems and prospects of the development of shared water resources in the region had not been prepared by the secretariat and consequently not presented for discussion under item 7.

39. One delegation proposed that the Committee give the secretariat a mandate to prepare and submit at the next session a report on the problems and the prospects of developing shared water resources in the region. The same delegation also suggested that this report should be technical and general in nature elaborating on the multilateral benefits of shared water resources development and need not contain bilateral problems. Another delegation, referring to the decision taken in the forty-second session of the Commission that the secretariat need not prepare the report envisaged under agenda item 7, objected to this proposal. In the discussion that took place many delegations participated.

40. The Committee, taking into account preponderance of views of the member countries decided that the secretariat prepare a general report on shared water resources development in various regions of the world. The report shall also include case studies of successful implementation of shared water resources development. This report based on the study should be included in the work programme and be presented at the fourteenth Committee session. In preparing such a report careful consideration should be given to the objections raised by one delegation and the report would not cover bilateral problems.

41. The Committee noted the strong objection raised by one delegation. The Committee also noted that every country had the right to associate itself or not with every United Nations activity, but if the member countries who are interested in particular activities for their socio-economic development they should not be barred from such activities.

VI. Activities of ESCAP in regard to natural resources
(Agenda item 8)

A. *Water resources*

42. The Committee had before it document E/ESCAP/NR.13/7 containing a summary of the activities of the secretariat in water resources development undertaken since the last Committee session, and commended the progress achieved by the secretariat in the implementation of the work programme in this sector.

43. The Committee expressed its appreciation on the report on the potential for small dams and mini-hydropower generation in the least developed countries and developing island countries contained in document E/ESCAP/NR.13/1, and generally endorsed the recommendations therein.

44. Some delegations provided the Committee with up-to-date information and data in mini-hydropower development in their countries.

45. The representative of China expressed the readiness of his country to share their expertise on mini-hydropower development with the least developed and developing island countries of the region.

46. The USSR delegation expressed the continued co-operation with ESCAP in the activities of water resources sector. It pointed out that rational use of natural resources, with the public sector playing a decisive role in this process, is of utmost importance, among others, for securing sovereignty of developing countries over their natural resources. The same delegation indicated that an important

prerequisite for this purpose is the establishment of the system of international economic security, and further proposed to discuss co-operation in the field of water resources at the next Commission session in the context of its proposed integrated programme for the expansion of trade, economic, scientific and technological co-operation in Asia and the Pacific. Some delegations expressed explicit reservation on the formulation on the use of the terms "establishment of the system of International Economic Security" and "Integrated Programme". Some delegations expressed reservations regarding the relevance of the subject to this discussion of the Natural Resources Sector.

47. The representative of Japan expressed support for ESCAP activities in the field of water resources. He also indicated that two projects: (a) improvement of systems of compilation of damage caused by typhoon and floods, and (b) improvement of disaster prevention systems based on risk analysis of natural disasters related to typhoons and heavy rainfall, financed by the Government of Japan would not only provide benefits to the Typhoon Committee members, but also to the countries of the Panel of Tropical Cyclones.

48. One delegation requested assistance in developing run-of-the-river hydropower systems, and also called upon the secretariat to prepare a compendium of major and medium rivers of the region. The same delegation also proposed that while the potentials of small dams and mini-hydropower generation in the least developed countries are looked into, the prospects and potentials of hydropower generation through large dams must not also be lost sight of.

B. Energy resources

49. In the field of energy, the Committee had before it documents E/ESCAP/NR.13/8 and E/ESCAP/NR.13/14. While the former contained a description of activities undertaken since the last Committee session, the latter contained an overview of the contribution of new and renewable sources of energy to the regional energy supply.

50. The activities included twenty-nine missions, ten meetings, seminars and workshops, five training courses and eleven reports and publications produced during the year. In addition, in order to fulfil its role as a co-ordinating hub of energy activities in the region the secretariat was invited to contribute to twelve meetings, seminars and workshops organized by various other organizations.

51. In the new and renewable energies field the Committee's attention was called to the revised priority project package recommended by the recent second focal points and consultative meetings. It was indicated that some of these projects have been suggested for inclusion into the 1989-1991 phase of the UNDP funded intercountry programmes for REDP and PEDP.

52. Some of the secretariat activities, as well as the workshops, seminars and training courses organized, had benefited from the financial support of UNDP, the Government of Australia, Japan, France, the Netherlands, the Council of European Communities, as well as from the contribution of host facilities and/or consultants from the Republic of Korea, the Philippines, India, Thailand, Indonesia, Viet Nam, France, China and the United States of America among others. For such support the secretariat expressed gratitude and appreciation.

53. In commenting on the reports, the efforts of the secretariat and specifically the Regional Network on Biomass, Solar and Wind Energy in completing the second focal points meeting were commended. The need to finalize arrangements for the training course in Pakistan at an early date under the photovoltaic technology for development programme was emphasized. In this connection, it was welcome that the first training course in Indonesia would be conducted early 1987.

54. In commenting on organizational arrangements, a suggestion was made that the REDP, PEDP and BSW Network projects would operate in the concerted manner under the purview of the Natural Resources Division. The Committee felt that this matter should be further considered at its next session. The Committee also felt that no new institutional support mechanism should be pursued in this respect.

55. The Committee endorsed the reports.

C. Mineral resources

56. The Committee had before it document E/ESCAP/NR.13/16 containing a summary of the activities of the secretariat in mineral resources development undertaken since the last Committee's session.

57. The Committee commended the substantial progress achieved by the secretariat in the implementation of the work programme in mineral sector including the training activities in various areas of mineral resources exploration and development. It expressed satisfaction with the activities undertaken in the appraisal of geology and distribution of mineral and hydrocarbon resources in the region, compilation of geological and thematic maps, and preparation of technical publications on special topics.

58. The Committee noted with appreciation that China was ready to consider holding, in China, a training project on equipment and techniques for small-scale mining

and exploratory tunnelling as follow-up of the recommendations made at the "Workshop on Drilling, Sampling and Borehole Logging" held at Wuxi, China, in November 1985, subject to further consultations. It was also requested that the proceedings of this workshop be published.

59. One delegation noted with appreciation a number of technical advisory missions on different aspects of mineral resources exploration and development undertaken by the Regional Mineral Resources Development Centre last year.

60. In this context, the Vietnamese delegation informed the Committee that a "Conference on Geology of Indochina" will be held in Ho Chi Minh City in early December 1986 and, that a Workshop on "Geochemical Exploration Methods in Tropical Rainforest Environment" jointly organized by ESCAP/RMRDC and the General Department of Geology of Viet Nam will precede this Conference. It welcomed the participation from ESCAP secretariat and member countries. The delegation of Democratic Kampuchea strongly protested against the use of word "Indochina" because this would mislead the Committee and would lead the Committee to endorse the policy of an "Indochina federation". China objected to the use of the word "Indo-China" in this context and supported the position of the Democratic Kampuchea. The USSR delegate on the other hand noted that the term "Indo-China federation" was not used during the Committee deliberations on the item. Some delegations objected to the mention, in this report, of this so-called "conference" which has nothing to do with ESCAP.

61. The Committee expressed its appreciation to UNDP, France, Japan and the Netherlands for their support in funding these activities. Moreover, it gratefully acknowledged the technical assistance provided by experts of the Federal Republic of Germany, France, Japan, Poland, the United States of America and the USSR at its workshops, seminars, and training courses.

D. *Marine resources*

62. The Committee had before it document E/ESCAP/NR.13/17 which set out highlights on issues relevant to ESCAP member and associate member states concerning implementation of the United Nations Convention on the Law of the Sea and document E/ESCAP/NR.13/18 that summarized recent developments at the Preparatory Commission for the International Sea-bed Authority and for the International Tribunal for the Law of the Sea.

63. The Committee recognized the need for coastal countries to obtain better knowledge of the marine resources placed under coastal countries jurisdiction by the United Nations Convention on the Law of the Sea so as to promote effective planning development and management of those

resources. In this context it endorsed the secretariat's programme on Marine Resources. The Committee expressed its support for the proposed studies and related missions on the legal economic and technical implications of the Convention at the national and regional levels which will enable the systematic assessment of specific needs of the countries.

64. With reference to document E/ESCAP/NR.13/18 which had been presented for information of the Committee, one delegation requested the secretariat to revise and update the document to reflect fully the process and outcome at the Preparatory Commission in 1985 and 1986 to avoid misunderstandings.

65. Appreciation was expressed to the Government of France for financially supporting the missions on the Law of the Sea and to UNDP for continuing support of the regional projects assisting CCOP and CCOP/SOPAC.

E. *Cartography and remote sensing*

66. The Committee considered the activities in regard to cartography and remote sensing as presented in document E/ESCAP/NR.13/9, covering the report of the regional remote sensing programme during 1985/1986. It is noted that the activities in the document were being carried out under the special UNDP funded regional project RAS/81/034.

67. It supported and endorsed all the activities of the regional remote sensing programme and commended the programme for its performance.

68. The Committee appreciated UNDP's continued support of the project for a second phase from 1987 to 1991.

69. It was noted that there are strong remote sensing activities within the region, and the Committee endorsed the TCDC activities under the project and recommended that such activities should be expanded during the next phase of the project using existing facilities in the region and emphasized continuing support for symposiums, workshops and training.

VII. Activities of international bodies in the appraisal, development and management of water resources
(Agenda item 9)

70. The Committee noted the progress reported in the document E/ESCAP/NR.13/12 on the work of the Inter-agency Task Force on Water for Asia and the Pacific (ITFW). The Task Force promoted co-operation and collaboration among the participating bodies in support of regional programmes and projects for investigation, development and management of water.

71. The representative of the Food and Agriculture Organization of the United Nations (FAO) informed the Committee that FAO had been operating since 1983 a regional project covering five regional developing countries for improving land productivity with proper land and water management. FAO had also been active in promoting use of renewable energy for irrigation and water lifting, and in information exchange and training programme on water use and water management.

72. The representative of the United Nations Environment Programme (UNEP) informed the Committee of UNEP's establishment of a global data base with headquarters in Geneva. He also referred to UNEP's regional seas programmes in South Asia and the East Asia regions. UNEP planned to bring out an Annual Review of Lakes and Rivers in the Asia Pacific region, collaborated with UNESCO in a project on integration of environmental aspects into water resources training programmes, supported ESCAP's proposal to organize a regional workshop on managing environmental impacts of water resources development projects and was willing to collaborate with ESCAP in this regard. UNEP co-operated with ESCAP in organizing national workshops on environmental impact assessment (EIA) for decision makers, and with South Asia Co-operative Environment Programme (SACEP) in a regional workshop on EIA in SACEP countries. UNEP had also prepared a State of the Art report on rivers in the Asia Pacific region.

73. The United Nations Department of Technical Co-operation for Development (UNDTCD) provided technical assistance to water resources programmes in the ESCAP region, and implemented water resources projects in this region. Presently it had water resources projects in India, Bangladesh and Thailand. UNDTCD was currently assisting Thailand in establishing a Groundwater Data Centre. UNDTCD also recently prepared a paper on "choice of low cost drilling technology".

74. UNDP had provided financial support to projects in many areas of the natural resources sector both at national and regional levels. The regional projects executed by ESCAP included the Regional Energy Development Programme, the Pacific Energy Development Programme, Strengthening of the ESCAP Regional Mineral Resources Development Centre, Technical Support for Regional Offshore Prospecting in East Asia, Investigation of Mineral Potential of the South Pacific, Technical Assistance to the Southeast Asia Tin Research and Development Centre and the Regional Remote Sensing Programme. The UNDP representative also informed the Committee that the Third Meeting of Aid Co-ordinators had endorsed the UNDP Intercountry Programme for the next five years (1987-1991). Within this Programme, UNDP expects to provide programme support to ESCAP-executed projects in the area of natural resources and energy at the level of $ 15 million, subject to final approval by UNDP Governing Council in early 1987.

75. The World Bank representative informed the Committee of the Bank's involvement in the water resources sector, especially in the assessment of ground-water resources including exploration of deep artesian aquifers in South Asia. He also informed the Committee of the recent initiative undertaken and currently being undertaken by the World Bank for development of multinational hydropower projects. Finally, he reported to the Committee the increasing attention being made by the World Bank in promoting afforestation activities. In this connection, he referred to the Five-year Action Programme for Tropical Forest inaugurated in 1985 jointly by USAID, UNDP, World Resources Council and the World Bank.

76. The Committee took note with interest the appreciation of several member governments for receiving both financial and technical benefits from various international organizations and United Nations agencies and also from donor countries on bilateral and multilateral basis in their efforts to develop natural resources in their countries.

77. The Malaysian delegation gave a brief account of Malaysia's activities in water resources in collaboration with the International Hydrological Programme (IHP) organized by UNESCO. He stated that a total of 21 national agencies are involved in these collaborative activities and a total of 55 projects are being undertaken.

VIII. Consideration of the Draft programme of work and priorities, 1988-1989; and programme changes in the programme of work, 1986-1987
(Agenda item 10)

A. *Water resources*

78. The Committee reviewed the draft programme of work and priorities, 1988-1989, and the programme changes in the programme of work, 1986-1987 on water resources, as set out in documents E/ESCAP/NR.13/21 and E/ESCAP/NR.13/21/Corr.1. The Committee noted that no changes were proposed for the 1986-1987 work programme in these documents.

79. The Committee noted that programme element 2.1(i)(c), Assessment of experience in application of solar and wind energy in water resources development and prospects for application in the region, has been set up as a separate programme element 2.5, Non-conventional water development. It further noted that this rearrangement did not

affect the overall content and resource requirements presented in the draft programme of work contained in document E/ESCAP/NR.13/21.

80. The Committee generally endorsed the draft programme of work, 1988-1989 and in particular supported the activity on the regional network for training in water resources development. Some delegations informed the Committee about their present training activities and capabilities in water resources development. Malaysia reconfirmed the nomination of its National Training Centre for Water Management as a participating institute in the Regional Network for Training in Water Resources Development. Viet Nam expressed its interest in participating in the Regional Network and nominated Institute of Water Resources, Ministry of Water Resources, as a participating institute in the Regional Network.

81. The representative of the USSR confirmed its readiness to host, in co-operation with ESCAP, a workshop on the role of water use statistics in long-term planning for water resources development and to provide assistance in the formulation of guidelines for preparation of national master water plans.

82. One representative inquired about the present status of the seminar on safety evaluation of existing dams to be held in 1987. Another representative called the attention of the financing agencies and donor countries to the need for extrabudgetary funds to fully implement the proposed work programme of the secretariat in the field of water resources.

83. One representative sought clarification on priority assignment to the programme elements of the work programme 1988-1989, and this was provided by the secretariat. The Committee assigned high priority to programme elements 2.1, 2.2 and 2.4.

B. *Energy resources*

84. The Committee considered documents E/ESCAP/NR. 13/3 and E/ESCAP/NR.13/10. While the former contained the 1986-1987 work programme and changes adopted by the Commission at its forty-second session in 1986, the latter was the 1988-1989 draft programme of work and priorities.

85. The Committee endorsed the changes suggested in the work programme for 1986-1987 as reflected in the document E/ESCAP/NR.13/3.

86. The Committee generally endorsed the 1988-1989 draft programme of work and priorities as contained in the document E/ESCAP/NR.13/10 while noting the reservation expressed by one delegate in taking up the programme element 3.4(ii) concerning a technical study: Study on resource options for electric power generation in the 1990s.

87. The Committee, however, made suggestions that (a) the lowest priority given on the element 2.2 should be lifted (b) the project description sheets under 2.2 and 2.3, the activities concerning the solar photovoltaic project conceived under the Tokyo Programme of Action, in particular, the second phase of the project "the Regional Co-operation in Research, Development and Demonstration of Solar Photovoltaic Power System for Rural Areas" should be implemented under programme element 2.2 and the possible availability of financial contribution should be indicated in the project description sheet.

88. The Committee noted with appreciation the statement made by the representative of Japan that his Government would consider the possibility of extension of its financial support to institutional cost of the BSW Network till the middle of 1988, with the understanding that the substantive programme be continued further within the existing regular budget resources.

C. *Mineral resources*

89. The Committee reviewed document E/ESCAP/NR. 13/20 on the draft programme of work and priorities for 1988-1989 and programme changes in the programme of work for 1986-1987.

90. The Committee did not propose any changes in the programme of work and priorities for 1986-1987 and endorsed the draft programme of work and priorities for 1988-1989.

91. In endorsing the draft programme for 1988-1989 some delegations strongly supported the programme element 1.4 containing activities on analysis of the impact of global structural changes on the mineral industry in the region.

92. The delegation of Malaysia suggested that ESCAP makes available expertise to evaluate countries' needs for, or organize workshops or seminars on mineral data base systems. The results of studies on projected demands and trends of minerals in the short and long term would be more beneficial from a proper mineral data base in that remedial mineral development plans and policies could be readily formulated in advance.

93. As regard the programme element 1.2 on technical support to regional and subregional projects, the Committee suggested that the secretariat co-operate within the East Asia Resources Assessment Programme that is currently being formulated and implemented under the combined auspices of CCOP, the Circum-Pacific Map Project (CPMP) and the International Union of Geologic Sciences (IUGS).

94. In respect to the programme element 1.5 on geology and urban development, the delegation of China expressed its support for the activities and indicated that it would co-operate to the extent possible.

95. It urged that the planning of the activities by the secretariat in the area of geology for urban planning, specifically the Expert Working Group Meeting on Urban Geology of Coastal Areas be accelerated so that the activity could be carried out before the end of 1987.

96. The Committee noted with appreciation that China was ready to consider hosting a workshop on equipment and techniques for small-scale mining and exploratory tunnelling in 1988/1989 under the programme element 1.3, if the availability of travel funds could be ascertained by ESCAP secretariat.

97. The Committee manifested its continuing support to the Regional Mineral Resources Development Centre (RMRDC). It noted with appreciation the offer of Viet Nam to make a cash contribution to the Centre. The Indonesian delegation announced that it would continue to contribute $US 15,000 annually to the Centre and urged the other member countries to follow this example. The delegation of the Republic of Korea announced a cash contribution of $US 7,500 to the Centre.

98. Several delegations indicated that should the Centre be closed at the end of 1986 for lack of financial support then some of the activities presently carried out by the Centre be organized and implemented by the Natural Resources Division in the future.

99. The delegation of France indicated that in this event it would be prepared to consider continuing support to these activities.

D. *Marine resources*

100. The Committee noted with interest that the Programme on Marine Resources had been allocated two regular budget professional posts and that the proposed activities under this programme were complementary to the work undertaken by CCOP and CCOP/SOPAC in that they were focused on the legal, economic and policy implications of the United Nations Convention on the Law of the Sea. It therefore endorsed the programme of work and priorities, 1986-1987 and the draft programme of work and priorities, 1988-1989.

101. The Committee expressed its appreciation that collaboration had been established with the Office of the Special Representative of the Secretary General for the Law of the Sea and that close co-operation had been maintained with CCOP and CCOP/SOPAC. The Committee further-

more, was hopeful that that co-operation would be continued even after the two intergovernmental bodies had become fully independent.

102. As regard the draft programme of work and priorities, 1988-1989, one delegation proposed that the programme element output 1.2 (i) be modified to read as follows: "Reports to the Committee on Natural Resources on the specific needs of the interested developing countries of the region in marine resources development and that programme element output 1.4 (iii) (b) be modified as follows: "A study on strengthening national capabilities of interested developing countries of the region in marine resources development".

103. Another delegation requested that programme element 1.3 as set out in the draft programme of work and priorities, 1988-1989, retain the same wording as set out in programme element 1.2 in the programme of work and priorities, 1986-1987.

E. *Cartography and remote sensing*

104. The Committee reviewed document E/ESCAP/ NR.13/15 containing the programme changes in the work programme for 1986-1987 and the draft programme of work and priorities for 1988-1989.

105. The Committee did not propose any additional changes in the programme of work and priorities for 1986-1987 other than those contained in the document and endorsed the draft programme of work and priorities for 1988-1989.

106. The Committee noted that most of the activities indicated in the programme changes and those under the draft programme of work and priorities for 1988-1989 will be implemented by the ESCAP Regional Remote Sensing Programme which is funded by UNDP.

107. The Committee also pointed out that training activities on cartography and remote sensing should be implemented within the existing facilities or in co-operation with established mechanisms in the region.

108. The Committee expressed concern that there is no cartographic project under the draft programme of work and priorities for 1988-1989. In this regard, the Committee welcomed the offer of the United States delegation of a set of eight base maps at a scale 1:2,000,000 being compiled by the United States Geological Survey for the East Asia Resources Assessment Programme.

109. The Committee noted with appreciation the offer of the USSR to host in 1988 a seminar on application of remote sensing data for mapping and metallogenic analysis of geologic environments affected by plate tectonics.

IX. Consideration of the agenda and arrangements for subsequent sessions of the committee
(Agenda item 11)

A. *Fourteenth session*

110. The Committee reviewed the draft provisional agenda for the fourteenth session, document E/ESCAP/NR.13/2.

111. The Committee noted that although in previous fora the issues: (a) Institutional arrangements (item 5 (a)); and (b) Energy trade (item 5 (b)) were considered important, because of changes in priorities those were now considered less important. Therefore it recommended deletion of those sub-items from the agenda.

112. The Committee recommended that the other two elements under item 5 be amended as follows: (a) Prospects for production and utilization of coal, natural gas and electricity; (b) Human resources development. The Committee further recommended that these two issues be considered by the preparatory expert advisory meeting for the Committee.

113. The Committee also proposed deletion of agenda item 6 (a): Networking arrangements under the new and renewable sources of energy subject areas.

114. The Committee endorsed the following modified agenda for its fourteenth session:

1. Opening of the session.

2. Election of officers.

3. Adoption of the agenda.

4. Current energy situation and demand management achievements:

   (a) Regional energy scene;

   (b) Regional energy economy patterns, including demand management, price and non-price policies and energy conservation measures.

5. Energy issues:

   (a) Prospects for production and utilization of coal, natural gas and electricity;

   (b) Human resources development.

6. Strategies required in the accelerated development of new and renewable sources of energy:

   (a) Contributions of new and renewable sources of energy to the regional energy supply;

   (b) Co-operative research, development and demonstration achievements and future plans.

7. Activities of ESCAP in regard to natural resources:

   (a) Energy resources (other than those activities referred to above under energy and other programmes);

   (b) Water resources;

   (c) Mineral resources;

   (d) Marine resources;

   (e) Cartography and remote sensing.

8. Activities of other international bodies in the appraisal, development and management of energy resources.

9. Consideration of the programme of work and priorities, 1988-1989; and programme changes in the programme of work, 1986-1987:

   (a) Energy resources;

   (b) Water resources;

   (c) Mineral resources;

   (d) Marine resources;

   (e) Cartography and remote sensing.

10. Consideration of the agenda and arrangements for subsequent sessions of the Committee.

11. Other matters.

12. Adoption of the report.

B. *Sixteenth session*

115. The Committee endorsed the provisional agenda for the sixteenth session as follows:

1. Opening of the session.

2. Election of officers.

3. Adoption of the agenda.

4. Review of the implementation of the Mar del Plata Action Plan.

5. Preparation of national master water plans: issues and guidelines.

6. Problems caused by natural water related disasters, and long-term effective measures for mitigation of damage.

7. Water quality monitoring systems in the ESCAP region.

8. Activities of ESCAP in regard to natural resources:

   (a) Water resources (other than those activities referred to above);

   (b) Energy resources;

   (c) Mineral resources;

   (d) Marine resources;

   (e) Cartography and remote sensing.

9. Activities of other international bodies in the appraisal, development and management of water resources.

10. Changes in the programme of work and priorities, 1990-1991 concerning the appraisal, development and management of natural resources:

   (a) Water resources;

   (b) Energy resources;

   (c) Mineral resources;

   (d) Marine resources;

   (e) Cartography and remote sensing.

11. Consideration of the agenda and arrangements for subsequent sessions of the Committee.

12. Other matters.

13. Adoption of the report.

X. Other matters
(Agenda item 12)

116. The United States delegation informed the Committee that the twenty-eighth International Geological Congress would be held in Washington, D.C. in 1989.

XI. Adoption of the report
(Agenda item 13)

117. The Committee adopted the report on its thirteenth session on 20 October 1986.

XVIII. LIST OF DOCUMENTS PRESENTED TO THE THIRTEENTH SESSION OF THE COMMITTEE ON NATURAL RESOURCES

5.B.1. LIST OF ESCAP SECRETARIAT DOCUMENTS

Symbol number	Title	Agenda item
E/ESCAP/NR.13/L.1 E/ESCAP/NR.13/L.1/Corr.1	PROVISIONAL AGENDA	3
E/ESCAP/NR.13/L.2 E/ESCAP/NR.13/L.2/Corr.1	ANNOTATED PROVISIONAL AGENDA	3
E/ESCAP/NR.13/1	THE POTENTIAL FOR SMALL DAMS AND MINI-HYDROPOWER GENERATION IN THE LEAST DEVELOPED COUNTRIES AND DEVELOPING ISLAND COUNTRIES	8 (a)
E/ESCAP/NR.13/2	PROVISIONAL AGENDA FOR THE FOURTEENTH SESSION	11
E/ESCAP/NR.13/3	PROGRAMME OF WORK AND PRIORITIES FOR ENERGY, 1986-1987 AND PROPOSED PROGRAMME CHANGES	10 (b)
E/ESCAP/NR.13/4	SUMMARY OF GOVERNMENT RESPONSES	4
E/ESCAP/NR.13/5 E/ESCAP/NR.13/5/Corr.1	REVIEW OF PROGRESS	4
E/ESCAP/NR.13/6	DEVELOPMENT OF GROUND-WATER RESOURCES	6
E/ESCAP/NR.13/7	ACTIVITIES OF ESCAP IN REGARD TO NATURAL RESOURCES: WATER RESOURCES	8 (a)
E/ESCAP/NR.13/8	ACTIVITIES OF ESCAP IN REGARD TO NATURAL RESOURCES: ENERGY RESOURCES	8 (b)
E/ESCAP/NR.13/9	REPORT OF THE REGIONAL REMOTE SENSING PROGRAMME	8 (e)
E/ESCAP/NR.13/10	DRAFT PROGRAMME OF WORK AND PRIORITIES, 1988-1989 – ENERGY RESOURCES	10 (b)
E/ESCAP/NR.13/11	ENVIRONMENTAL ISSUES OF WATER RESOURCES DEVELOPMENT IN THE ESCAP REGION	5

Symbol number	Title	Agenda item
E/ESCAP/NR.13/12	REPORT ON THE ACTIVITIES OF THE INTER-AGENCY TASK FORCE ON WATER FOR ASIA AND THE PACIFIC	9
E/ESCAP/NR.13/13	APPLICATION OF ENVIRONMENTAL IMPACT ASSESSMENT TO WATER RESOURCES DEVELOP-MENT PROJECTS	5
E/ESCAP/NR.13/14	ASSESSMENT OF THE CONTRIBUTION OF NEW AND RENEWABLE SOURCES OF ENERGY TO REGIONAL ENERGY SUPPLY	8 (b)
E/ESCAP/NR.13/15	CARTOGRAPHY AND REMOTE SENSING – CONSIDERATION OF THE DRAFT PROGRAMME OF WORK AND PRIORITIES, 1988-1989; AND PROGRAMME CHANGES IN THE PROGRAMME OF WORK, 1986-1987	10 (e)
E/ESCAP/NR.13/16	MINERAL RESOURCES – ACTIVITIES OF ESCAP IN REGARD TO NATURAL RESOURCES	8 (c)
E/ESCAP/NR.13/17	MARINE RESOURCES – ACTIVITIES OF ESCAP IN REGARD TO NATURAL RESOURCES	8 (d)
E/ESCAP/NR.13/18 E/ESCAP/NR.13/18/Corr.1	DEVELOPMENTS AT THE PREPARATORY COMMISSION FOR THE INTERNATIONAL SEA-BED AUTHORITY AND FOR THE INTER-NATIONAL TRIBUNAL FOR THE LAW OF THE SEA	8 (d)
E/ESCAP/NR.13/19	MARINE RESOURCES – CONSIDERATION OF THE DRAFT PROGRAMME OF WORK AND PRIORITIES 1988-1989; AND PROGRAMME CHANGES IN THE PROGRAMME OF WORK, 1986-1987	10 (d)
E/ESCAP/NR.13/20	MINERAL RESOURCES – CONSIDERATION OF THE DRAFT PROGRAMME OF WORK AND PRIORITIES, 1988-1989; AND PROGRAMME CHANGES IN THE PROGRAMME OF WORK, 1986-1987	10 (c)
E/ESCAP/NR.13/21 E/ESCAP/NR.13/21/Corr.1	CONSIDERATION OF THE DRAFT PROGRAMME OF WORK AND PRIORITIES, 1988-1989; AND PROGRAMME CHANGES IN THE PROGRAMME OF WORK, 1986-1987: WATER RESOURCES	10 (a)
E/ESCAP/NR.13/22	DRAFT PROVISIONAL AGENDA FOR THE SIXTEENTH SESSION (1989)	11

5.B.2. DOCUMENTS PRESENTED BY OTHER ORGANIZATIONS AND COUNTRIES

THE ACTIVITIES OF THE WORLD METEOROLOGICAL ORGANIZATION (WMO) IN THE ASSESSMENT, DE-
VELOPMENT AND MANAGEMENT OF WATER RESOURCES

WATER FOR DEVELOPMENT
WATER RESOURCES   – THE ROLE OF WMO
WATER RESOURCES   – ASSESSMENT AND MONITORING

CO-OPERATION IN WATER RESOURCES DEVELOPMENT IN SOUTH ASIA WITH PARTICULAR REFERENCE
TO THE GANGES-BRAHMAPUTRA BASINS AND THE DEEP ARTESIAN AQUIFERS OF THE AREA

DEVELOPMENT OF GROUNDWATER RESOURCES IN THE PHILIPPINES

COUNTRY REPORT IN RELATION TO "PROGRESS IN THE IMPLEMENTATION OF THE MAR DEL PLATA
ACTION PLAN" IN THE PHILIPPINES

PROGRESS IN THE IMPLEMENTATION OF THE MAR DEL PLATA ACTION PLAN IN THAILAND

USSR EXPERIENCE IN EXECUTION OF "ACTION PLAN" ADOPTED AT UN CONFERENCE ON WATER RE-
SOURCES (MAR DEL PLATA, ARGENTINA, 1977)
PROBLEMS OF RIVER WATER QUALITY CONTROL UNDER CONDITIONS OF INTENSIVE IRRIGATION
DEVELOPMENT IN ARID ZONE
THE PROBLEM OF INTEGRATED GROUND AND SURFACE WATER MANAGEMENT IN ARID ZONES

WATER RESOURCES DEVELOPMENT IN CHINA
GROUNDWATER EXPLORATION AND DEVELOPMENT IN CHINA

THE THAILAND GROUNDWATER DATA CENTRE – AN OUTLINE
(UNDP-UNTCD-DMR PROJECT THA/83-004)

ICID'S ACTIVITIES IN THE FIELD OF WATER RESOURCES DEVELOPMENT AND MANAGEMENT

COUNTRY PAPERS BY INDONESIA:–

- CARTOGRAPHY AND REMOTE SENSING
- ENVIRONMENTAL ISSUES
- WATER QUALITY & POLLUTION CONTROL
- HYDROPOWER
- FLOOD CONTROL
- WATER SUPPLY
- GROUNDWATER DEVELOPMENT
- LOWLAND DEVELOPMENT
- WATER RESOURCES DEVELOPMENT IN INDONESIA
- IRRIGATION

XIX. LIST OF PARTICIPANTS AT THE THIRTEENTH SESSION OF THE COMMITTEE ON NATURAL RESOURCES

MEMBERS

AUSTRALIA

Representative: Mr. T.B. Roberts, Assistant Secretary, Water Policy and Intergovernmental Organizations Branch, Department of Resources and Energy, Canberra

Alternate: Dr. Peter Howarth, Deputy Permanent Representative of Australia to ESCAP, Australian Embassy, Bangkok

BANGLADESH

Representative: Mr. Mohammed Ali, Secretary, Ministry of Irrigation, Water Development and Flood Control, Government of Bangladesh, Dhaka

Alternates: Mr. A.W. Chowdhuri, Economic Counsellor and Alternate Permanent Representative of Bangladesh to ESCAP, Embassy of the People's Republic of Bangladesh, Bangkok

Mr. Tauhidul Anwar Khan, Director, Bangladesh Water Development Board, Dhaka

CHINA

Representatives: Mr. Ji Chuanmao, Senior Hydrogeologist, Department of Hydrogeology and Engineering Geology, Ministry of Geology and Mineral Resources, Beijing

Mr. Zhong Shukong, Counsellor and Deputy Permanent Representative of the People's Republic of China to ESCAP, Embassy of the People's Republic of China, Bangkok

Alternates: Mr. Jiang Minxi, Deputy Chief, International Co-operation Division, Bureau of Foreign Affairs, Ministry of Geology and Mineral Resources, Beijing

Ms. Zou Youlan, Deputy Chief, International Co-operation Division, Department of Foreign Affairs, Ministry of Water Resources and Electric Power, Beijing

Mr. Ye Xun, Senior Engineer, Office of Water Resources, Ministry of Water Resources and Electric Power, Beijing

DEMOCRATIC KAMPUCHEA

Representative: H.E. Mr. Pech Bun Ret, Ambassador Extraordinary and Plenipotentiary and Permanent Representative of Democratic Kampuchea to ESCAP, Bangkok

Alternates: Mr. Kheang Khaon, Minister-Counsellor, Deputy Permanent Representative of Democratic Kampuchea to ESCAP, Bangkok

Madame So Se, Minister-Counsellor, Deputy Permanent Representative of Democratic Kampuchea to ESCAP, Bangkok

Madame Chhe You Kheang, Counsellor, Assistant to the Permanent Representative of Democratic Kampuchea to ESCAP, Bangkok

FRANCE

Representative: Mr. Jean-Julien Bidaut, Counsellor and Permanent Representative of France to ESCAP, Embassy of France, Bangkok

INDIA

Representative: Mr. N.K. Sarma, Member (WP), Central Water Commission, and ex-officio Additional Secretary, Ministry of Water Resources, New Delhi

Alternate: Mr. B.S. Basrurkar, Assistant Permanent Representative of India to ESCAP, Embassy of India, Bangkok

INDONESIA

Representative: Mr. Sarbini Ronodibroto, Director of Planning and Programming, Directorate

General of Water Resources Development, Ministry of Public Works, Jakarta

Alternates: Mr. H. Muh. Amron, Expert Staff to the Head of Directorate of Irrigation Programming, Directorate General of Water Resources Development, Ministry of Public Works, Jakarta

Mr. Soekardi, Head, Sub Directorate of Hydrogeology, Directorate of the Environmental Geology, Ministry of Mining and Energy, Bandung

Ms. Sri Redzeki, Chief of Section at the Directorate of Water Supply, Directorate General of Housing, Building and Urban Planning, Ministry of Public Works, Jakarta

Mr. Rachmat Ranudiwijaya, Second Secretary and Assistant Permanent Representative of Indonesia to ESCAP, Embassy of the Republic of Indonesia, Bangkok

JAPAN

Representative: Mr. Yoshiyuki Yamaguchi, Senior Officer for River Development Co-ordination, Development Division, River Bureau, Ministry of Constructions, Tokyo

Deputy Representative: Mr. Hiroomi Sakai, First Secretary and Deputy Permanent Representative of Japan to ESCAP, Embassy of Japan, Bangkok

Alternates: Mr. Akira Nishino, Deputy Director, Regional Planning Division, Planning Department, Agricultural Structure Improvement Bureau, Ministry of Agriculture, Forestry and Fisheries, Tokyo

Mr. Masato Kakami, First Secretary and Deputy Permanent Representative of Japan to ESCAP, Embassy of Japan, Bangkok

Miss Keiko Ito, Assistant to the Permanent Representative of Japan to ESCAP, Embassy of Japan, Bangkok

LAO PEOPLE'S DEMOCRATIC REPUBLIC

Representative: Mr. Darakone Pathammavong, Second Secretary and Alternate Permanent Representative of the Lao People's Democratic Republic to ESCAP, Embassy of the Lao People's Democratic Republic, Bangkok

Alternate: Mr. Bounhang Sengchandavong, Third Secretary, Embassy of the Lao People's Democratic Republic, Bangkok

MALAYSIA

Representative: Mr. Fateh Chand, Deputy Director-General, Geological Survey of Malaysia, Kuala Lumpur

Alternate: Mr. Tham Weng Sek, Director, Department of Mines, Ipoh, Perak

NETHERLANDS

Representative: Mr. Hugo van der Goes van Naters, Counsellor and Permanent Representative of the Netherlands to ESCAP, The Royal Netherlands Embassy, Bangkok

PAKISTAN

Representative: Mr. Javid Zafar, Commercial Counsellor and Alternate Permanent Representative of Pakistan to ESCAP, Embassy of Islamic Republic of Pakistan, Bangkok

PHILIPPINES

Representative: H.E. Mr. Benjamin T. Leong, Assistant Minister for Planning and Project Management, Ministry of Natural Resources, Manila

Alternates: Atty. Eligio Estella, Assistant Director, Bureau of Lands, Manila

Mr. Lope R. Villenas, Chief, Planning and Evaluation Division, National Water Resources Council, Manila

REPUBLIC OF KOREA

Representative: Mr. Jong-Hwan Kim, Director, Economic Geology Division, Korea Institute of Energy and Resources, Seoul

Alternate: Mr. Hong-Jae Im, Second Secretary and Assistant Deputy Permanent Representative of the Republic of Korea to ESCAP, Embassy of the Republic of Korea, Bangkok

THAILAND

Representative: Mr. Leck Jindasanguan, Deputy Director-General for Operation and Maintenance, Royal Irrigation Department, Bangkok

Alternates: Mr. Boonyok Vadhanaphuti, Director, Division of Project Planning, Royal Irrigation Department, Bangkok

Mr. Nukool Thongtawee, Director, Operation and Maintenance Division, Royal Irrigation Department, Bangkok

Mr. Niyom Niyamanusorn, Deputy Director-General, Public Works Department, Bangkok

Mr. Vudtinunt Silamut, Water Quality Control Division, The Metropolitan Water Works Authority, Bangkok

Mr. Praphorn Charuchandr, Senior Sanitary Specialist, Department of Health, Bangkok

Dr. Apichart Anukulamphai, Secretary, Committee for Co-ordination and Acceleration of Water Resources Development, Bangkok

Mr. Suwit Watthanachan, Director, Ground Water Division, Department of Mineral Resources, Bangkok

Mrs. Vachi Ramarong, Expert, Department of Mineral Resources, Bangkok

Mr. Prina Leepattanapan, Director of Field Operations Division, The Office of Accelerated Rural Development, Bangkok

Mr. Vraluck Chatarupavanich, Director, Energy Investigation Division, The National Energy Administration, Bangkok

Mr. Sunthad Somchevita, Director, Environmental Policy and Planning Division, Office of the National Environment Board, Bangkok

Mr. Surajitta Chaisiri, Agronomist Level 7, Soil and Water Conservation Division, Land Development Department, Bangkok

Mr. Kasivat Paruggamanont, First Secretary, International Organizations Department, Ministry of Foreign Affairs, Bangkok

Mr. Anek Chandarawongse, Acting Expert on Water Resources Development, Water Resources Development Committee, National Economic and Social Development Board (NESDB), Bangkok

Mr. Paibul Ruangsiri, Engineer 7, The National Research Council of Thailand, Bangkok

Mr. Chatpong Chucharoen, Director of Corporate Planning Department, The Provincial Water Works Authority, Bangkok

Mr. Wuthi Poonudon, Assistant Director, Hydro Power Engineering Department, Electricity Generating Authority of Thailand, Bangkok

Observers: Mr. Prasert Milintangul, Chief, Research and Applied Hydrology Section, Hydrology Division, Royal Irrigation Department, Bangkok

Mr. Snguan Jamprawit, Chief, Ground Water Investigation Section, Geotechnical Division, Royal Irrigation Department, Bangkok

Mr. Sirirat Temiyanond, Chief, Data and Information Section, Programme Co-ordination and Budget Division, Royal Irrigation Department, Bangkok

Mr. Yossarin Bhimsakka, Plan and Policy Analyst Level 6, Division of Rural Water Supply, Department of Health, Bangkok

Mr. Nopadon Mantajit, Chief, Policy and Planning Analysis, Department of Mineral Resources, Bangkok

Mr. Dome Sittivate, Civil Engineer Level 5, Engineering Division, Land Development Department, Bangkok

Mr. Vichit Thongcharoen, Chief of Groundwater, The Office of Accelerated Rural Development, Bangkok

Mr. Wittaya Polprapai, Rural Development Planner, Office of the Committee for Coordination and Acceleration, Water Resources Department, Bangkok

Mr. Niyom Maprajong, Engineer 6, The National Energy Administration, Bangkok

Mr. Thanade Dawasuwan, Civil Engineer 7, Public Works Department, Bangkok

Mr. Kasem Juntrasuta, Clerk Level 4, Foreign Agricultural Relation Division, Ministry of Agriculture and Cooperatives, Bangkok

Mr. Chowarit Salitula, Second Secretary, International Organizations Department, Ministry of Foreign Affairs, Bangkok

Mr. Pornchai Taranatham, Chief, Water Quality Section, Environmental Quality Standard Division, Office of the National Environment Board, Bangkok

Mr. Chaisak Srisuwanakarn, Chief, Biological and Bio-chemistry analysis Section, Water Quality Control Division, The Metropolitan Water Works Authority, Bangkok

Mr. Kriengkrai Ragadanuraks, Research Project Analyst 6, Research Project and Co-ordination Division, The National Research Council of Thailand, Bangkok

Mr. Sarawoot Chayovan, Head of Water Resources Development Project, The Provincial Water Works Authority, Bangkok

Mr. Payak Ratnarathorn, Chief, Water Resources Planning and Development Division, Electricity Generating Authority of Thailand, Bangkok

UNION OF SOVIET SOCIALIST REPUBLICS

Representative: Mr. B.S. Nabrodov, Director of the Department, Ministry of Land Reclamation and Water Management, Moscow

Alternates: Mr. B. Nikolayev, Counsellor and Deputy Permanent Representative of the USSR to ESCAP, Embassy of USSR, Bangkok

Mr. V. Fedortchenko, First Secretary, Embassy of USSR, Bangkok

Mr. A.L. Sukhov, Third Secretary, Department of International Economic Relations, Ministry of Foreign Affairs, Moscow

Mr. V. Nebenzia, Attache and Assistant Permanent Representative of the USSR to ESCAP, Embassy of USSR, Bangkok

UNITED KINGDOM OF GREAT BRITAIN AND NORTHERN IRELAND

Representative: Dr. Clive R. Jones, Regional Geologist for Asia and Latin America, British Geological Survey, Nottingham

Alternates: Mr. Peter Cormack, Counsellor and UK Permanent Representative to ESCAP, British Embassy, Bangkok

Mr. J.S.L. Wood, Second Secretary and UK Deputy Permanent Representative to ESCAP, British Embassy, Bangkok

UNITED STATES OF AMERICA

Representative: Mr. Maurice J. Terman, Chief, Asian and Pacific Geology Office of International Geology, U.S. Geological Service, Virginia

Alternates: Mr. David E.T. Jensen, First Secretary and Alternate Permanent Representative of the United States of America to ESCAP, Embassy of the United States of America, Bangkok

Ms. M. Corinne Kearfott, Second Secretary and Deputy Permanent Representative of the United States of America to ESCAP, Embassy of the United States of America, Bangkok

VIET NAM

Representative: Mr. Pham Quoc Tuong, Deputy Director General, Department of Geology, Hanoi

Alternate: Mr. Le Van Minh, Third Secretary and Deputy Permanent Representative of the Socialist Republic of Viet Nam to ESCAP, Embassy of the Socialist Republic of Viet Nam, Bangkok

OTHER STATES*

FINLAND

Representative: Mr. Raimo Anttola, Counsellor (Development Co-operation), Embassy of Finland, Bangkok

GERMANY, FEDERAL REPUBLIC OF

Representative: Mr. Roland Lohkamp, Counsellor and Permanent Observer of the Federal Republic of Germany to ESCAP, Embassy of the Federal Republic of Germany, Bangkok

TURKEY

Representative: H.E. Mr. Reha Aytaman, Ambassador, Embassy of the Republic of Turkey, Bangkok

UNITED NATIONS SECRETARIAT

Department of Technical Co-operation for Development (UNDTCD) — Dr. Dan Gill, CTA and Senior Hydrogeologist, Project THA/83/004, Ground Water Data Centre in Thailand, c/o UNDP, Bangkok

UNITED NATIONS BODIES

United Nations Development Programme (UNDP)

Mr. Y.Y. Kim, Regional Representative, UNDP, Bangkok

Mr. David M. Thorup, Deputy Regional Representative, UNDP, Bangkok

Mr. A. Selvanathan, Deputy Regional Representative, UNDP, Bangkok

Mr. J. De Graaff, Assistant Regional Representative, UNDP, Bangkok

Ms. Sirisupa Soonsiri, Programme Officer, UNDP, Bangkok

Ms. Netnarumon Sirimonthon, Programme Officer, UNDP, Bangkok

United Nations Environment Programme (UNEP)

Mr. Nay Htun, Director and Regional Representative, UNEP Regional Office for Asia and the Pacific, UNEP, Bangkok

Mr. R.D. Deshpande, Environmental Affairs Officer, UNEP Regional Office for Asia and the Pacific, UNEP, Bangkok

SPECIALIZED AGENCIES

Food and Agriculture Organization of the United Nations (FAO) — Mr. K.H. Gorey, Chief Technical Adviser, Project BGD 83013, c/o UNDP, Dhaka

World Bank — Mr. A.H. Shibusawa, Special Adviser to the Vice President, South Asia Region, World Bank, Washington

United Nations Industrial Development Organization (UNIDO)

Mr. A.S.H.K. Sadique, Regional Adviser on Industrial Development, ESCAP/UNIDO Division of Industry, Human Settlements and Technology, ESCAP, Bangkok

Mr. Sunil Mahajan, Associate Expert, ESCAP/UNIDO Division of Industry, Human Settlements and Technology, ESCAP, Bangkok

NON-GOVERNMENTAL ORGANIZATION

Category II

International Commission on Irrigation and Drainage (ICID) — Mr. Sawet Yasaravana, Civil Engineer Grade 8, Design Division, Royal Irrigation Department, Bangkok

OTHER ORGANIZATION

Asian Institute of Technology (AIT) — Dr. Tawatchai Tingsanchali, Chairman of Water Resources Division, AIT, Bangkok

---

* Member of the United Nations, participating in a consultative capacity under paragraph 9 of the terms of reference of the Commission.